The Missing Will
&
A Dubious Codicil

The Missing Will
&
A Dubious Codicil

A Double Autobiography

MICHAEL WHARTON

The Hogarth Press
LONDON

Published in 1992 by
The Hogarth Press
20 Vauxhall Bridge Road
London SW1V 2SA

The Missing Will first published by
Chatto & Windus Ltd 1984
First Hogarth Press edition offset
from the original edition 1984

A Dubious Codicil first published by
Chatto & Windus Ltd 1991

Parts of *The Missing Will* were first published
in the *Daily Telegraph* and the *Sunday Telegraph*,
with whose kind permission they are reproduced.

A CIP catalogue record for this book is
available from the British Library.

ISBN 0 7012 0981 X

Cover design and illustration by Jeff Fisher

Printed and bound in Great Britain by
Mackays of Chatham PLC, Chatham, Kent

The Missing Will

TO NICHOLAS

RIDENDUM . . . IUBES RENOVARE DOLOREM

Contents

I

The Deformative Years

My earliest memories of Wharton are of a time when I did not know that any other place existed: the great house, where, in its different styles, the whole history of English domestic architecture could be traced; the terraced gardens; the smooth green lawns; the long avenues of ancient elm, beech and oak leading the eye to the bridge and the double lake; the deer-park; the 'wilderness', meticulously planned by 'Mad Wharton' in the eighteenth century to suggest, at least to his own infatuated eye, all that he liked best among the landscapes of England, ranging in their different styles from the fens of Lincolnshire to the crags of Cumberland; and beyond these vast domains, in the hazy distance, whatever a child's mind might fancy of possible outer worlds.

More intimately known – at least to these flashes of uncertain memory – are the great kitchen gardens with their walls of old red brick (said by an amateur 'antiquarian' uncle to date back to the time of the large Roman villa which sixteen hundred years before had occupied one small corner of the present house). These gardens, tended by an army of gardeners, produced the finest peaches, nectarines and pears in England, to say nothing of the once celebrated Wharton Apple, with its subtle flavour, sharp and sweet, which seemed to include all possible fructose tastes in one.

There was the Long Gallery in which, by some oversight of nursemaid or governess, I once strayed, to be found (so I was told later) dazzled and overwhelmed by the innumerable pictures in which could be traced the whole history of European art since Byzantine times; then taken back, half fainting with precocious ecstasy, to the nursery wing.

There was the nursery wing itself, larger than many a sizeable gentleman's house, where I played with my bricks and little engines or listened to stories of ogres, dragons and peasants (or 'people', as the only nanny I remember at all vividly, Nanny Forbes from Elgin, used to call them, striving, as was her duty, to inculcate in me at an early age a consciousness of their complete difference from such beings as myself).

I remember too, the small four-poster bed in which I slept, five hundred years old, the gift of King Edward IV to my Yorkist ancestor, with its elaborately carved oaken frame, its sumptuous coat-of-arms with sixty-four quarterings at the head, its canopy and curtains of convoluted velvet, disposing me to a habit of vivid dreaming which I have never lost. Even at the age of four, I am told, I used to long for bedtime and the dreams it would bring, dreams in which supernatural splendours, exceeding only by a little the magnificence of my real surroundings, mingled with intimations of other worlds in which Nanny Grant's 'people' would sometimes disconcertingly appear, old, ugly, bent, misshapen, stretching out arthritic hands as though begging for release from mean streets where rain of inferior quality fell forever.

Have I no early memories of – let us call them the 'personages', since nothing less will do – of my own family? They are vague compared with my memories of the great park and all that it contained. I remember my father, a huge, distant, rumbling figure; my mother, scented, elegant, her voice a melodious chime which seemed to mingle with the sound of the French clocks which struck the quarters in the long, sleepy, summer afternoons (by a household rule they never struck in winter). I glimpsed her once drawing on long gloves for some dinner party, perhaps, when fifty guests would be at table in the stupendous dining-room with its phantasmagoria of crystal and silver. I remember that glimpse because to my surprise a single tear fell from her left eye.

How was I to know that the piece of paper she held in her hand

– distastefully crumpled, dirty and out of place even to my child's eye – was a 'telegram' just arrived from the War Office to announce the death of my elder brother the Viscount in action on the Western Front? I imagine, wrongly perhaps, that the dinner party went on. Grief would come later, and would be apparent only to a few.

It may seem odd to say this. But far more vivid in my memory than father, mother, brother, sister or even Nanny Findlay is an experience I had when I was five, perhaps, one autumn afternoon. There was a part of the gardens where I had been told never to go. It was the Maze, said to be the largest and most complicated in England. According to my 'antiquarian' uncle it had originally been laid out by druids to delude and confuse the Roman legions advancing through Britain to enforce, among other things, the abolition of the druidic order.

Into this sinister and complex diagram of tall beech hedges, trimmed by special gardeners who could be relied on not to 'talk', I innocently ventured. The leaves were already turning brown and gold. The twists and turns of the path seemed, and perhaps were, endless. Perhaps, as Nanny Ritchie had hinted, the Maze had no centre and no way out. Soon I was lost, and a feeling came over me, enormous, indescribable, in which, in their different styles, could be traced all the traditions of English Gothic horror, romantic anguish and hopeless day-dreaming, passing rapidly away, galloping like cloudy horses into a darkening sky and leaving behind only the one question: Who am I?

Who, indeed? I was born on 19 April 1913, not at Wharton, but at a small, respectable house in a respectable road in a respectable part of Shipley in the West Riding, a mill town which was to become part of 'Greater Bradford'. I remember nothing of our neighbours. There was something which made us different from them. I and my brother and sister, the one ten years, the other seven years older than myself, were the fruit of a double exogamy.

My father, Paul Sigismund Nathan, was a younger son of Bernhard Nathan and Henrietta Seemann, of Magdeburg in Germany. They had emigrated to England in the 1860s to become part of the influential foreign element, mostly German, which did a great deal to advance the Bradford wool trade. My grandfather was half Jewish, half German; my grandmother also had Jewish blood, in what proportion I cannot say, because nobody ever told me and I have never found out. But neither of them was a practising Jew (nor, I believe, was either of their own parents). My grandfather was said, soon after they settled in Bradford, to have driven the visiting rabbi with imprecations from his door; my grandmother was positively anti-semitic, I believe: at any rate she was so anxious to disavow any Jewish antecedents that she made sure that none of her children, three sons and two daughters, married people with Jewish blood.

They lived in a large, gloomy house with a gloomy, shrubbery-infested garden, called Oaklea, a magnate's house, a few miles away from us by tramline, in Manningham, then a superior part of Bradford where such people as the Rothensteins and Eurichs lived and Delius was born. They had several servants and a German governess from Upper Silesia who was called simply 'Fraülein' and, as far as I knew or know, had no other name. She was a peasant, simple, kindly, hard-working, making no distinction between English people, who were all strange to her in their various ways. Her English was not good; nor did it ever get better, as my grandparents habitually spoke German among themselves and their children were bilingual. After my grandparents died in 1928 and Oaklea was sold, she returned to Silesia and may, a poor old woman, have lived long enough to cry 'Heil Hitler!' and later be driven from her home, raped, slaughtered or all in turn by the advancing Red Army and its Polish supporters, bent on blind revenge.

Where and in what circumstances my father met my mother

round about the turn of the century I cannot say. But I can imagine the loud Germanic ructions which must have ensued in the gloomy halls of Oaklea, particularly in the fabled 'morning-room' with its glass-fronted bookcase of brown-bound German classics and engraving of Böcklin's 'Toten-insel' on the wall, when their acquaintance became known to his 'Pater' and 'Mater', as he called them with some fear and trembling.

My mother, Bertha Wharton, was born at Gomersal near Mirfield in the West Riding, one of a large family belonging to the lowest fringes of the lower middle or small shop-keeping class. My maternal grandparents are no more than shadows to me: my grandfather, Charles, only a dim, bearded face with a melancholy look, in a yellowing photograph on the mantelpiece of the 'front room' of their terraced house somewhere in Bradford; my grandmother not even that. After my mother married into a world entirely strange to her and them in terms of class, race and money, she must, of necessity if not by choice, have moved away from them. I doubt if my mother's parents, or their other surviving children, Joe, Herbert, Percy and Gertrude, ever met my father's parents. If they did, my grandfather, a kind and, within his old-fashioned limits, rather easy-going man, would have received them with decent courtesy; my grandmother, sharp-tongued and snobbish, would not.

To judge from her photograph my mother was a small, well-rounded, dark-haired, very pretty Yorkshire girl, whose attraction for my father is obvious enough. It is possible that they 'had to be married'. Whether this was so or not, my father's marriage immediately distanced him from the rest of his family and their friends and thereby distanced my brother, my sister and myself. We became outsiders to people who were themselves outsiders.

I have vague memories of compulsory Sunday luncheon at Oaklea, of the uncomfortable atmosphere in that place of fabled splendour close to the gates of Lister Park, with its big, soot-blackened garden and croquet lawn. My mother complained that her parents-in-law sometimes spoke German between themselves at table, perhaps in order to make adverse comments on her. There was certainly an unspoken assumption that a mistake had been made. My father, unlike his sisters, who made 'good' marriages into the English middle class, one to a Holmes, a member of an important wool family, the other to an Ambler, land agent to Lord Scarbrough, was continuously made aware of this; though there was no doubt one mitigating factor in my German grandmother's eyes: at least her foolish son had married a Gentile.

My mother, whose first-born, a boy, arrived in 1903, was Board School-educated, unlettered, almost illiterate. She now found herself visiting France and Switzerland. Her comment, made in her strong native accents, on the Alpine scenery, 'It's just like Todmorden', was received by my German grandmother with malicious satisfaction and endlessly retailed among her circle.

My mother stayed with my father, on his business trips in the prosperous reign of King Edward, at the best hotels in Paris, Madrid, Berlin; she even went with him to Buenos Aires. Everywhere she remarked on the oddity of all foreigners, the insolence of Spaniards, the fatuously small hats of Frenchmen. For her those were days of ambiguous glory. It might be thought that my father would 'raise her to his level', as the saying used to be. But in fact he had no level to raise her to but that of money, expensive clothes, 'champagne wine', asparagus, hand-made chocolates, Havana cigars and coloured bathsalts in huge glass jars. He was, by birth, a stranger himself; she, as a native Englishwoman, had her own kind of superiority.

He was a weak and amiable man of suppressed charm and humour. Though fluent in four languages, he spoke them all with a Yorkshire accent. He had no interest in books, art or even in his parents' German music, except of the most elementary kind. What happened was that rather than raising his young wife to his own 'social level', he tended to decline to hers. This he did in a certain masochistic spirit very characteristic of him. The more he felt the disapproval of his parents, the broader grew his West Riding accent. At the same time he introduced German words into his own growing family's vocabulary, which turned on my mother's lips into what I now know were amazing distortions but then seemed only a puzzling element in daily life. In effect they both lost their levels and we, their children, never had any. Here lay the source of much anger, much disruption, much misunderstanding, much bewilderment and strangeness. We had never heard of 'alienation'. But had some wandering psychologist climbed down from the clouds he would have rubbed his hands and eagerly reached for a new notebook.

There was one exception to the unspoken rule which virtually excluded my mother's family from our own. This was her younger sister Gertrude. She was a plain woman without hope of marriage, what was then called 'simple'. She had a small collection of books – a prayer book, a Bible, a herbal, a few late Victorian bestsellers like *A Peep Behind the Scenes, Froggie's Little Brother*, Marie Corelli's *Sorrows of Satan* and *The Master Christian*. She was addicted to 'Extra Strong Mint Imperials'. She could play simple hymn tunes on our out-of-tune upright piano. And she could work. Gradually she became incorporated into her sister's household as a kind of serf, butt of incessant jokes from my father and the elder children which she took uncomplainingly except for occasional outbursts of futile anger. She lost her own name and became known simply as 'Aunt', even referring to herself by this name and writing it in the flyleaves of her precious books.

She was an indifferent cook, whose rock buns and Eccles cakes were notorious for their leaden quality; her rice-pudding and bread were indistinguishable and her tea was disliked because she often forgot to put any in the tea-pot. But she was a great hand with the mangle, the bed-making, the dusting and the carpet-sweeping, and carried out all tasks which her elder sister set her as well as she knew how.

There was nothing particularly good about her except her almost infinite patience, but there was nothing at all bad about her either. She was a holy innocent and as she was more in evidence and more indispensable in my own childhood than in the growing time of my much older brother and sister, she became, in a curious way, a strong influence in my life.

She was there, no doubt, at the scene of my earliest memory, the beach of St Anne's-on-Sea, where, when I was about two, we spent a wartime holiday. She was there in 1916, when my grandmother held in her hand the telegram from the War Office which announced that my uncle Percy, a private in the West Yorkshire Regiment, was missing on the Somme. She was certainly *not* there when a similar telegram arrived to announce the same news of my paternal uncle, my father's youngest brother Leo, a second lieutenant in the same regiment, to say nothing of the fate of various unknown relations who must have fallen in the German army.

Her strange locutions ('Gnaw's Zark', 'indegredients', 'lozenger' and 'galosher' – back-formations from the plural – are examples) and individual phonetic system may have had something to do with my early interest in words. She extended and elaborated the West Riding practice of using voiced sounds where standard English has unvoiced ('buz' for 'bus', 'uz' for 'us') in the most amazing way; and systematically interchanged plosive, fricative and velar sounds. She not only called me 'Mytle' and said 'goddles' for 'goggles' and 'rackle' for 'rattle' but even 'sithers' for 'scissors'.

Meanwhile, in other realms, great events were going on, no less than the transformation of the world. But they scarcely affected me. By the end of the Great War I was five years old. I can date an early memory to 1917, when I sat quietly looking at the pictures in the *Chatterbox Annual* for that year as the German Zeppelin which had been trying to bomb Hull passed harmlessly over Bradford (my mother, who was already beginning to be resentful of her strange situation and to hit back, said there were so many Germans in the city that the enemy naturally let it alone). I can date another memory precisely to 11 November 1918, when I waved a small Union Jack among crowds cheering our victory. Among the voices which resound from that period, all in the ponderous accents of the West Riding, are some which say 'Ireland? There's only one thing to do with it. They want to tow it out into the middle of the Atlantic and sink it', and others which say 'I'll tell you one thing. In t'next war we'll be fighting the French; they're nothing but a nuisance and always have been.' When there was talk of the League of Nations and the 'war to end war' my mother invariably said: 'There'll always be wars.' Nor, as far as I know, did anyone dissent from this opinion.

As the youngest child, I was thoroughly spoiled and something of a milksop. I cannot remember playing with other children. I doubt whether my brother and sister, though less spoiled than I was, played with any either. My parents, partly because of their peculiar position in life, partly because of the way this must have affected their attitudes to other people whether they knew it or not, seemed to have few if any friends whose children their own children might have played with. We were cut off from our cousins on my father's side, who were of roughly the same age, by snobbery on the one hand and by my mother's resentment and distrust on the other. As for the neighbours' children, my mother's general attitude may be summed up in the phrase 'You never know where they've been'.

Even our surroundings seemed – or so I think now – to reinforce the feeling of not belonging anywhere. There were parts of Shipley which were neither town nor country. There was a functioning farm, with real cows and sheep, among new-built villas. Sandy tracks led from abandoned mills, where mist rose from green-scummed mill-ponds, to wooded hollows where sour streams ran down past rows of terraced houses to the River Aire. A long steep path between high walls led to an empty villa in an overgrown garden, called the 'murder house', though nobody would ever tell me why. Near a collapsing hen-house in Nab Wood was a small, scrawny grove of trees. One particular hollow tree stump was invested with mystery. It contained secret messages, I believed, though I could never find them. This was my first intimation of the numinous, a momentary sense of awe and mystery, indescribably delicious. Not far away, at Cottingley Bridge, was the place where Sir Oliver Lodge, the once famous scientist, photographed the last fairies to be seen and the first to be photographed in England.

Further off, approached by a perilous railway-crossing ('don't forget to look both ways,' my mother and 'Aunt' always said in unison) was Shipley Glen, with its gas-tram and ginger beer in those bottles with glass marbles in the top which are now to be found only in the downstairs lavatories of modish publishers. I was not, of course, allowed to go to these places by myself. If I was not with my brother and sister, 'Aunt' would go with me, wearing her 'helmet' hat and one of the two 'costumes', one in 'nigger brown', one in 'navy blue', which she invariably wore. These, like most things about 'Aunt', were family jokes (there is nothing like a state of siege to encourage such cruel behaviour). While on our walks she would keep a look out for the herbs she had painfully read about in her herbal, particularly comfrey, which, she maintained, 'cured everything'. I cannot remember that she ever found any. This was another running joke.

So, as a family, we drew together in uneasy alliance, if it could be called that when our parents' almost continuous quarrelling and bickering (or 'fratching', as it was called) was becoming a part of daily life. This is not to say that my father and mother were not fond of each other in their own way. They were deeply attached. The idea of infidelity, if not unthinkable – there had once been a Miss Litchfield, governess to my brother and sister, who, it was whispered, 'had to go' – was certainly an idea only. And of course there were happy times amid the 'fratching'. It was in 1919, I think, that we first spent a holiday at Arncliffe, then a remote village in a remote part of the Yorkshire Dales, reached by pony-and-trap on a rough, stony road from the nearest station, Grassington, on the now long-abandoned branch-line from Skipton.

We stayed at first in The Falcon Inn, later in holiday cottages. Every day, if the weather was fine enough, we took our tea to a certain place on the left bank of the River Skirfare, where the water ran swiftly among limestone boulders, forming little beaches and pools for paddling which were deep enough for mild adventure but perfectly safe. Sometimes my father and brother went shooting the rabbits which lived in thousands on the limestone hills. My sister learned to ride a pony. I learned nothing except to keep quiet and observe the behaviour of others. Because of my silence, my German grandfather had nicknamed me 'Moltke', after the famous general who seldom spoke and was said to have smiled only twice in all his life. Because of my solemnity a business acquaintance (perhaps even a rare friend) of my father called me 'Canon Fletcher', after a local clergyman notable for his serious mien. Even 'Aunt' commented that I 'liked to sit'.

My parents, though they had been baptised into the Church of England and my mother had been confirmed, showed no interest in religion, apart from having their own children baptised at St Peter's Church in Shipley, on the uphill road that led to the ogre's wood. 'Aunt' occasionally went to church and once, when she had been goaded by my father's jokes about her gloves, rock-cakes or habit of reading Zadkiel's *Guide to Palmistry* (another volume in her small personal library) upside down, accused him of being an 'atheest'. My mother also pronounced the word in this unusual way.

Whether as Moltke, Canon Fletcher or mother's boy, I already began to show signs of habitual melancholy and of a certain torpor, an inability to take a normal, active interest in life which, had my parents been less conventional (within their unconventional situation), more imaginative or even more plain sensible, would have worried them more than it did. There are certain people who are born old. Hardy's 'Old Father Time', the child who hanged his half-brothers and sisters and himself out of despair and a conviction, shared with his creator, of the uncaring cruelty of the universe, is no myth. I know this because as a child I sometimes felt like that myself. At the age of eight I vowed to myself, after due consideration, not to commit suicide right away but to do so when my mother died. She was the only being, apart, perhaps, from my sister, whom I loved. She lived to be ninety-seven. I have not kept that vow.

Born to function, as it were, on one cylinder only, I had to make that one cylinder work overtime. I was much more intelligent than my parents or my brother and sister; I had a precocious fondness for words. Although I did not go to school until I was seven (my mother had somehow convinced herself that I was too delicate or sensitive, though there was no particular evidence of this delicacy except a dislike of games rougher than tig, pat-ball, snap or beggar-my-neighbour), I had already taught myself to read and even write after a fashion. I invented stories and histories of the dynasties of our dogs and cats. A little later I began writing plays in which our few friends or acquaintances appeared as grotesques. So began or first appeared a lifelong addiction to fantasy.

I have mentioned my first remembered experience of the numinous, the mysterious tree stump in Nab Wood. As time went on this indescribable feeling, one of intense pleasure, came to be attached to other features of the neighbourhood – a clump of trees on a ridge against the skyline on the road to a fabulous region, 'Chellow Dene', I had heard mentioned but never visited; a soot-black mill seen against the sunset; the movement of leafless boughs in Lister Park in winter; the sham stained glass in the fanlight of our front doorway. By sitting on the stairs and looking through this I could change the outer world at will into various forms of coloured illusion. Soon this feeling of disembodied ecstasy would visit me without apparent reason. I looked and hoped for its inexplicable onset and the few seconds it lasted – though perhaps it could not be measured in time, being outside it. I had another occasional sensation, neither pleasant nor unpleasant, but also, in its way, one of disembodiment. Lying stretched out on my back in bed before getting up in the morning I would suddenly feel that I was made of stone and of gigantic size. The sensation lasted only a few seconds and I felt it only over a short period of what must be called my childhood. I have never felt it since.

My first school was the kindergarten department of the Bradford Girls' Grammar School (my brother and sister were already pupils at the respective senior establishments). I remember nothing about this except the arrival of my first short school report. 'His application and ability to learn are excellent. But he is too passive and lacks initiative.' After my father had consulted his dictionary, one of the few books in the house apart from my fairy tales, my brother's and sister's adventure stories and 'Aunt's' personal library, there was a long discussion leading to a blazing row in which my mother condemned the teacher who had written this report in unmeasured terms and even talked of 'having it out with her', while my father, after accusing her of 'spoiling the child', slammed the door and cut off the rest of the conversation from my calm, impartial listening ears.

Later I went to the Junior Department of the Bradford Grammar School proper, a malodorous place smelling of ink, sweat and, faintly, of horses, in Fountain Street (I liked the name) in the central part of Bradford near the main school, a soot-black, towered building opposite the Yorkshire Penny Bank at the junction of steep, tram-groaning Cheapside and Darley Street which I was to know well later on. I remember nothing much about this junior school except bursting into tears in a 'nature study' lesson, losing my first brief fight (with a disagreeable Jewish boy I had tripped up on an irresistible impulse) rather ignominiously, and being called for at the end of school one afternoon by my father in a taxi, a cause of awe among my fellow-pupils, who were almost all of a class which did not take taxis. Normally, of course, I was taken to school on the tram by 'Aunt' and taken home by her. I dare say this was the cause not of awe but of derision among my fellows. I made no friends during the short time I was there.

A change now came over my family's fortunes. My father, though no 'hard man who looked as if he had done well out of the War', had shared, perhaps more by luck than good management, in the boom in the wool trade. So we moved from comparatively humble Shipley to proud Harrogate, where the rich people lived. Our new home, a large, irregularly-shaped villa portentously called Duchy Grange, had been built about the beginning of the century and so was old enough to have partly ivied walls. It had a terrace, lawn, winding paths, flower-beds, a big kitchen garden and a garage, though we had no car, still in 1920 the perquisite of the very rich and fashionable.

Already averse to change, I did not like the move, even though it was so obviously for the better. But my parents did. For a time they were much preoccupied with moving in and beautifying their new home with a fine big Persian carpet for the drawing-room, Dresden figurines, standard lamps, engraved steel fenders and other expensive objects of hideous art nouveau design, as well as Chippendale chairs and a splendid mahogany dining-room table with a sheet of heavy plate glass to cover it. Canteens of heavy silver appeared and a fine pair of Georgian silver candlesticks (pronounced Georgeéan by my mother) as well as hundreds of elaborate appliances such as card tables with inbuilt ashtrays and hinged rings for glasses.

Cards, which then meant 'auction bridge', were an important

preoccupation in the evenings when some of my parents' scarce friends came in for a few rubbers. My mother, unfortunately, was very bad at the game. Even though my father, who was reasonably good at it, was not, of course, partnering her, he still flew into the astounding rages which were becoming habitual, rising from the table to bang his head on the wall in only nominal mock despair, shouting at my mother in German and getting xenophobic shouts in return. I have abhorred bridge ever since, though I am fond of card games in general.

We had two servants, a cook and a housemaid. But my mother could not or would not maintain her new social status, now moved one notch higher. She would not trust the servants to carry out their duties and was for ever interfering with them, convinced, perhaps rightly, that she could do better herself. But whenever my father found her dusting, carpet-sweeping, cooking or, worst of all, washing up he would fall into one of his more and more frequent rages.

He travelled by train to Bradford most days to work in what was mysteriously called 'the Warehouse'. When he returned to his uneasy mansion in the evenings, irritated perhaps by racing losses (he was becoming an inveterate gambler) or faced with the worry of a housemaid's pregnancy, my mother would exclaim 'Here comes the Fleyboggard!' – a West Riding bogey – so as to get the children on her side. This often led to another blazing exogamic row.

At the same time my mother, angered by the Nathans, was beginning to brood more and more about her own family, the Whartons. A shadowy greatness gathered. She hinted and more than hinted at connections with the Whartons of Wharton Hall in Westmorland. For two hundred years they had been one of the greatest and most powerful families of the North. Their last, foolish, drunken head, Philip Wharton, had been created Duke, squandered his fortune, turned Jacobite and Catholic and fought with the Spaniards against his own countrymen at the Siege of Gibraltar,

forfeiting title and estates and perishing miserably, to be com-
memorated by Pope in a famous passage of vitriolic eloquence:
'Wharton, the scorn and wonder of our days . . .' I don't think my
mother had ever heard of Pope. But encouraged by my brother,
who was interested in heraldry as well as golf and stamp-collecting,
she took to remembering how her father was said to have come to
Yorkshire from Westmorland as a child. She even hinted at a
Missing Will. I listened and pondered.

One of the results of our move to genteel Harrogate, where 'nice
people' lived and there were expensive shops for the adornment of
my mother with fine clothes and enormous emeralds, was that my
brother and sister were removed from their respective Bradford
grammar schools and sent, not to English public schools like their
cousins, but to schools in Switzerland, by the Lake of Geneva,
where they mingled or at least met with other scions of the rich
manufacturing class and also exotic foreigners, often Argentine.
The general idea was that they should learn manners and French.
The latter would be an asset for my brother when in due course he
entered the wool trade.

As for me, I was the clever one. I was intended for public school
and so was sent at the age of nine, in the first place as a day boy,
to a prep school not more than half a mile from our house. Not
liking the prospect, I arranged to get acute appendicitis just before
my first term was due to begin in September 1921. I was rushed to
a nursing home (there was no lack of them in Harrogate) and
operated on, then tended by a pretty nurse with whom I fell in love,
my first experience in that line.

My status as 'delicate' established to my mother's satisfaction, I
enjoyed a prolonged convalescence. On the advice of the good Dr
Nimmo-Watson, once a noted enthusiast for lemon juice, my
mother took me to Brighton for a fortnight. I felt an access of the
numinous, still faintly remembered now, amid the strange sea
smells. Then we went to London, where we stayed at the then

expensive and fashionable Piccadilly Hotel and were joined by my father, who had been on one of his business trips to Leipzig or Barcelona. My parents, for all I have said so unkindly about them, were fond of each other in their way. Their reunion gave me what may have been my first experience of jealousy. But in the reserved first-class carriage of the train which took us back to Harrogate, as the telephone wires dipped and rose past the windows and the big advertisements for Carter's Paints appeared rhythmically in the fields, they soon took to quarrelling again.

The quarrel may have been about a new pregnant housemaid or the jobbing gardener, a dour Yorkshireman called Lund. His bill was thought excessive, including as it did the wages of his assistant, the boy Norman. As a final move in a bitter campaign, Lund sent in a long, indignant letter. The concluding section of this began: 'And now as to Norman . . .'

This became a catch-phrase. It was a peculiarity of my family, particularly my father, to seize on such things as this and make them into the stock family jokes, quite unintelligible to other people, which relieved our endless dilemma of exclusion and rejection. My father had only to enter a room, pronounce the word 'Lund!' or 'Jessica Mumby!' (a particularly awkward, owlish, bespectacled housemaid) or 'Mrs Wertheimer!' (a bridge-playing neighbour who was suspected of cheating and figured as a grotesque mass murderess in one of my satirical melodramas) to bring the house down.

My mother, who had no sense of humour, was vaguely puzzled by these formulae which contained a world of comic meaning for the initiated. But they must have had something to do with the emergence in myself of that 'sense of humour' which, though it has helped, against all the odds, to keep me alive and even to earn me a living, is not a thing I can really approve of. There was cruelty in it. It reduced Lund, Jessica Mumby, Mrs Wertheimer and, amid a growing collection of such figures, several of the inhabitants of

Arncliffe, where in spite of our new grandeur we still spent all our holidays, to mere things, comic cut-outs with no claim to humanity. The putative psychologist would have been interested. He might even have made a note: 'defensive hysteria'.

'Aunt', who soon joined the Harrogate household as an all-purpose serf, was of course a primary character in this strange shooting-gallery. So were others of my mother's relations, particularly Aunt Annie, who lived with her husband, Uncle Herbert, in a terraced house in Manchester. He was a clerk, I think, a man of no particular note, humble, God-fearing, providing little or nothing for stock-jokery. Aunt Annie provided plenty. Troubled by constipation, she was said to resort to a legendary 'black draught' of prodigious power and was therefore known to my father as 'Black Draught Annie'. So 'Black Draught Annie!' or better still, 'Jallop!', a horse-drench said to be the main ingredient in the draught, became one of those key locutions and signals for general merriment.

My father himself took a keen interest in his bowel movements. Sometimes, when he had had a particularly satisfying one, he would announce the fact for all to hear. This growing 'vulgarity' was, I think, a form of defiance of his parents and of the superior social pretensions of his brothers and sisters, of whom we saw little even after our translation to Harrogate. It was part of a delight he had in self-abasement. He encouraged my brother, now back from Switzerland, to join him in these intestinal interests. Their farting competitions, I remember, were a feature of a motor tour we made one summer in a chauffeur-driven Daimler to the Scottish Highlands. Together with billiards, card-games and ritual pronouncements of 'Lund!' or 'Mrs Wertheimer!', they must have been, though deprecated by my mother, a relief from the incessant rain and misunderstandings about hotel-bookings.

At Strathpeffer a particularly spectacular farting competition – a fastidious observer, I took no part in such things – almost got us expelled from our gloomy hydro. At Braemar I became fascinated by the labyrinthine passages of the Invercauld Arms – material for many a pleasurable nightmare ever since – and for a time was pronounced 'lost'. Did I wish I had been?

The family 'sense of humour' stood me in good stead when the dreaded time arrived for me to join my prep school, Belgrave House. It was a curious kind of school in some ways. It was run, for a start, not by a headmaster but by two sisters, the Misses Nightingale, whose deputy-head, Mr Routledge, supplied the ogre figure of games-crazed disciplinarian I had been particularly dreading. He took an immediate dislike to me. By a strange chance, he died suddenly and most unexpectedly (he was about thirty, I suppose) of a heart-attack, not long after I joined the school. I was delighted.

Apart from my sense of humour, my main asset, if it was one, was a precocious intelligence. Excused games and gym in my first term because of delicacy, I shortly found I was exceptionally bad at both and though taking part half-heartedly in cricket and football, able to do somersaults of formal elegance and climb wall-bars as fast as anybody else, I was soon given up as hopeless. As for learning, although there were no books at home apart from bestselling novels (*Peter Jackson: Cigar Merchant*, *Blood and Sand* by Blasco Ibañez, the works of Sheila Kaye-Smith and Edgar Wallace) I soon got hold of some for myself and by the age of ten was probably as academically advanced as most of the teachers at Belgrave House, none of whom had university degrees. But the geography master, an amiable young idiot, had a sports car, and the English master, who practised sarcasm in a big way, once made the fearful prediction that I should live to be editor of *Punch*.

Another occasional teacher was Percival Hale Coke, a drawling, languid man with a monocle, who wore a pork-pie hat and was a local poet and man of letters. I was a pretty-looking boy and he took a special interest in me. He was sympathetic, for instance, as well as intrigued when, one autumn evening during a scripture lesson, he handed me a box of matches and asked me to stand on my desk and light the gas. Alas! I had led a life so sheltered that I did not know how to strike a match! His monocle fell from his eye and he looked, as he often did, most quizzical.

Perhaps to smooth over the contretemps, as well as out of interest, he said, in his slow drawl and 'upper-class' lisp, 'But why are you in this lesson anyhow? Aren't you Jewish?' 'He is by rights,' said a big, forthright boy, Theakston, perhaps, the brewer's son, in a reasonable, tolerant sort of way. I cannot remember what I said. Nothing, perhaps. Already conscious of so many differences between myself and others, I did not think of this dubious one as particularly important. It was not talked about at home, where the Vicar of St Wilfrid's, the big, rich Victorian parish church, was an occasional baffled visitor.

After a time, to make me more fit to stand up to public school, I became a boarder, though only a weekly one. It was my 'sense of humour' that got me through the mild bullying, the games, the crocodile walks, the toothpaste or wet knotted towel tortures and other conventional features of prep school life even in this peculiar and rather crummy specimen. There were even moments of enjoyment – one in particular on a summer evening after cricket when, for no reason at all, I suddenly felt for a moment that I was redeemed from singularity and an accepted member of the human race. It passed, but the feeling seems significant even now – an earnest of what might with luck and insight have been nourished and made habitual; even as things fell out, it stands as a pledge of something which cannot be destroyed.

Apart from my 'sense of humour' my intelligence helped. I found learning absurdly easy and was avid for knowledge. Finding among my brother's books (he also had his singularities, as will appear) Sir Wallis Budge's text and translation of the Egyptian Book of the

Dead, I became fascinated by the hieroglyphs and resolved to master them. I even persuaded my mother to take out a subscription for me to the *British Journal of Egyptology*. Suddenly, growing afraid of that cold, huge, monumental civilisation – was it the source of my own stony sensations? – I lost interest, declared myself, self-consciously and in due form, freed from the 'bondage of the Egyptians' – and switched to Assyriology and cuneiform. Would I have gone on to Aztec if more conventional studies had not intervened?

I can remember making only one friend at this school, if you could call him a friend rather than an acolyte. He was a small, fat, idle, rather stupid, dark-haired boy called Haigh; and for a time was my constant companion or attendant. 'I can't make out what you see in him,' said the English master in a friendly way. What did I see in him? Subservience, perhaps. To be most at ease with inferiors – or supposed inferiors – is not uncommon with those who lack assurance. But perhaps there was something else in Haigh that made him interesting to me. He left the school before I did. I wonder whether he was the same Haigh – the physical features certainly correspond – who thirty years later was to make his mark in the world as the murderer of Mrs Durand-Deacon at the Onslow Court Hotel?

The time was now approaching when I was due to sit for a scholarship at a public school. I doubt if such a scholarship, even of the humblest kind, had ever been won by a pupil of Belgrave House in all its history, but in my case Winchester was the first school suggested. I was to have special tuition in Greek! Immense excitement seized me. Long before my first lesson with the sallow, strange-faced Mr Pereira, notorious for his bad breath and unpopularity with the other masters, I had learned the Greek alphabet, could decline the present tense of 'luo' and had a considerable vocabulary.

All the same I did not succeed in winning a scholarship either at

Winchester or at Shrewsbury, where my eldest cousin, son of my father's bossy elder sister Gertrude Ambler (the antithesis of 'Aunt'), who was particularly fond of squashing my mother, had been some years before, later proceeding to Oxford. What was the reason? 'He is too passive and lacks initiative'?

This was the time when our family fortunes began to collapse. The climax of our fortunes must have been that Christmas when on three successive nights, my father and his two sisters and their families entertained each other in turn, vying in their hospitality. Aunt Gertrude Ambler, whose husband had disappeared mysteriously from the scene, now lived at Oaklea itself. She had lost her independent base at Stone Grange – a real grange on Lord Scarbrough's estate at Sandbeck near Roche Abbey, and to me a place of romance and mystery – and was only marginally an Ambler. But this did not prevent her from eyeing our arrangements at Duchy Grange with a patronising eye or criticising my mother's hospitality as crushingly as she could manage. We were still made to know our place.

One exotic at these celebrations was Irene, whom my tiny uncle Julius, a judge in Malaya, was said to have met on board ship, and, after an attack of infatuation, married. She had been a youngish widow, with dark good looks, suspected of being both a 'siren' and an 'adventuress'. She was certainly accustomed to more sophisticated company than the Nathans or even the Holmeses (though not necessarily the central Amblers) and so though less respectable, had an advantage over my overbearing Aunt Gertrude or my sharp-tongued Aunt Marian.

She was shingled, could Charleston and shimmy, used a long diamond-encrusted cigarette-holder and could manage some fashionable small-talk. She embarrassed my brother, then approaching his majority, fascinated my sister, now in her late teens, and took, or affected to take, a great interest in myself, both for my prettiness and my mimetic talents ('he'll sit there saying nothing and taking it all in,' my mother would explain, 'and then, when you've gone, he'll do a perfect imitation of you'). Irene said she would like to adopt me. But the offer, serious or not, was declined.

That Christmas, with its round of hospitality, was the bright end of the old order. The slump was on its way. My grandfather lost money; my father, with less to lose, bad at managing his affairs and with a growing addiction to gambling and other kinds of extravagance, of which expensive chocolates from Charbonnel and Walker were only a symbol, was not exactly ruined but was certainly brought down in the world. Duchy Grange was sold amid violent recriminations, and we moved to a tall semi-detached house, servantless except for 'Aunt', in a less select part of Harrogate.

A little after this my sister, who had begun to have a reputation for being 'fast', asserted her independence and after furious rows and accusations, made her escape. She had become a great dog-lover, was given a beautiful Irish setter for her twenty-first birthday and through this became fast friends with a formidable lady Alsatian-breeder, a well-to-do scion of an ancient Scottish family, who had bought a derelict old water mill and other properties in a Dales village. With her my sister, breaking with my parents, took refuge in a canine paradise, shared with the dog-fancier's only son, who later married her. My brother was despatched to get my sister back, but failed in his mission. 'Words were said which could never be forgotten or forgiven.' My father, never one to assert himself, shrugged his shoulders hopelessly. 'Aunt' recommended comfrey. The atmosphere became sulphurous.

I overheard my mother and brother concocting a secret plan. They would leave my father, the Fleyboggard, take my mother's name of Wharton and, presumably with me in tow (or was Irene's offer still open?) settle in Bedford and, after selling my mother's jewellery, make an entirely fresh start. Why Bedford? I never knew.

In any case the scheme came to nothing. Soon afterwards my brother made his own escape, both from our strange family and from the collapsing wool trade.

His own way of escape was into sheep farming, first as an apprentice to a farmer in Upper Wharfedale and then as a shepherd in Waldendale, a tributary valley of Wensleydale and as remote a place as any in England. Has there ever been another shepherd in the Yorkshire Dales called Nathan who was educated at an expensive boarding school in Switzerland? He always sought out the most remote places he could find, and when he married a Swaledale girl and took a farm of his own it was high up among the wild moors at the head of that northern-most of the Yorkshire Dales, an isolated starvecrow place approached only by a boulder-strewn road, in winter a torrent. The domestic water supply came from a moorland stream bubbling into a rough stone basin.

Soon he became more of a Yorkshire dalesman than any ever born. He changed his modified West Riding accent for the more attractive North Riding one. He went to market, bought and sold, could talk of 'clipping' and dipping and cairds and ticks with the best. A lean, very energetic man with saturnine good looks, he spent his days alone with his flocks on the wild moors. He was probably the last sheep-farmer in England to wear clogs. He was also one of the last to cut and stack peat for fuel in the immemorial way. For all I know he may, in his lonely fanaticism, have counted his sheep by the old Celtic numerals he had read about in the countryside-crazed books of the Leeds topographer Edmund Bogg. He had a good wife, a genuine sheep-farmer's daughter, to share this hard, dedicated, yet in a typically Nathanian way, essentially make-believe existence. I do not think he made any friends among his fellow farmers, or wanted any.

Meanwhile, in Harrogate, life was changing for me. I had reached the troubled age of puberty with its half-understood and confused desires which I, a shy, withdrawn boy with no close friends of either sex, learned all too well to satisfy in secret after the customary fashion. Nobody told me the 'facts of life'. I found, hidden in a drawer in my parents' bedroom, a copy of *Married Love*, by Marie Stopes, wrapped in brown paper inscribed *My Travels in Canada*, by the Bishop of Birmingham, together with *The Picture of Dorian Gray*, similarly wrapped and inscribed *My Travels in Australia*, by the Bishop of Liverpool. But a hasty glance at both works merely confused me further.

With puberty came a loss of reasoning power and concentration, perhaps not unusual in very precocious children. There was now no hope of my going to a public school. It was decided that I should go to the Bradford Grammar School, travelling there and back by train every week-day, escorted to Harrogate station and back by 'Aunt'. I was now among a rougher sort of boys, some of whom mimicked my 'improved' Yorkshire accent and tended, though without malice, to set my hair on fire or interfere with my share of the appalling hash and custard served every day for lunch for boys who for various reasons did not go home for it. The meal was superintended by Mr Pallister, the head laboratory assistant, who with Sergeant Sugden, the dreaded gym instructor, formed the NCO element of the staff. The school was divided into five departments, Classics, Mathematics, Science, History and Modern Languages. Classics, to which I adhered, was acknowledged, though grudgingly by some, to be by far the most respected discipline. The headmaster, Dr Edwards, like many of the masters a Welshman, occasionally took classical periods himself. He was a fussy, rather weak man with a walrus moustache, not greatly respected except for his office.

I now found myself taught by masters very different from the drop-outs and farceurs of Belgrave House. Even the humblest was a graduate and my own shortcomings became more obvious. I usually had only a medium position in the various classes through which I passed, eventually to reach the Classical Sixth, the apex of the school, where Mr Lionel Pelling Lewis, a most remarkable Welshman, presided, with Mr Robertson, a lovable Irishman, as his second-in-command.

Mr Lewis had cultivated a schoolmaster's eccentricity to a point bordering on madness. A small, fierce-looking, bald, grey-bearded man who always wore a pale blue tie passed through a ring, he came rushing through the door to his desk without a pause, sat down, pinched his nose and cheeks and scratched his beard in a ritual manner, adjusted his gold-rimmed pince-nez and then shouted in a high, sharp, harsh voice like a demented parrot: 'Waterhouse!' or 'Sutcliffe!' or 'Murgatroyd!' or even 'Nathan!' – '*Prometheus Desmotes* – line 102 – construe!'

Should there be hesitation, his high-pitched 'next, next, next, next, next', uttered with extreme rapidity, had a paralysing effect. But sometimes he would rush to his desk at the beginning of a period and, without even alluding to the classics, recite, in the same harsh, absurdly mannered tone (a gift to schoolboy mimics – I can still do it without effort) 'The Hunting of the Snark' or other poems by Lewis Carroll.

But he was an excellent teacher with a true love of language. His methods were as eccentric as himself. To illustrate precisely the alternative uses of a Greek preposition he would make groups of boys stand at different levels, on benches, desks or even on top of a tall cupboard. Sometimes, during one of these noisy charades, the headmaster would put his head round the door, then withdraw it with a deprecating cough. A look of subtle, indescribable complicity passed between Mr Lewis and his class. They never forgot the uses of those prepositions.

I was an indifferent worker. But I soon became, even without Mr Lewis's influence, a lover of language, as in a childish way I had always been. It had been music which invaded my soul in the first fervour of adolescence. There was no music at home except for my sister's jazz records or my father's 'Liszt's Hungarian

Rhapsody No 2' – sole sad relic of his parents' standard German-Jewish culture. Brahms, my grandfather's favourite, was always said to be 'too heavy'. Now I began saving up my pocket money to buy records, progressing very rapidly from Ketèlbey's 'In a Persian Market' to Beethoven's Symphonies and Debussy's 'L'Après–midi d'un Faune', which I played ceaselessly on the big, mahogany cabinet wind-up gramophone which had somehow survived from Duchy Grange.

Soon, poetry superseded music as my primary passion, though without supplanting it. Palgrave's *Golden Treasury* was always with me. I could repeat 'Lycidas' by heart. I began to write poetry myself, adolescent stuff with Keats as first model, then the earlier Yeats. It was sad stuff indeed. All the same I was beginning to learn how to write. I stood top of the class in English though in nothing else. As for maths, I was so hopeless, so unable to see 'what it was about' (nobody ever told me that it was not 'about' anything) that I had to have extra tuition in it to get me through Matriculation, an exam for which elementary maths was obligatory. That hurdle once passed, I never had to look seriously at a number again in all my days at school or university. Now, unable to do the simplest sum and almost incapable of abstract thought, though hopelessly fascinated by astronomy, I know what I have missed.

Games were not compulsory at the Bradford Grammar School. In my spare time I mooned about, read voraciously and at week-ends explored the pleasant, secluded country north-west of Harrogate in an obsessive way, tramping every lane and field-track in a romantic fervour. I had a fiercely protective feeling for these places, resentful of any change in them, whether pylon or metalled road or any other sign of 'progress' – a 'conservationist' before the time. Among those woods and foothills on the edge of the Pennine moors momentary experiences of the numinous were frequent and more intense than ever. Even the fact that 'Aunt', on my mother's insistence, had to go with me in case I should fall down a hole or be kidnapped by gypsies, did not spoil my ardour. A strange pair we must have looked as we walked the green lanes or ate our symbolic sandwiches under a beech tree – she vacant and silent with her unvarying 'helmet' hat and 'costume', I with wild black hair, repeating poems or gabbling a spell I had got out of Eliphas Levi's *Transcendental Magic*. I do not think I was very kind to her.

In 1929, when I was sixteen, still Aunt-ridden but consumed with music, poetry and ineffectual lust, there was a further decline in my father's fortunes. Bouts of 'fratching' had reached a new intensity after the escape of my brother and sister and their mutual estrangement. My father had become addicted to 'having a gastric ulcer', sometimes rolling on the floor and groaning in agony in a manner so theatrical that the poor man's genuine pains, augmented and perhaps originally produced by a sense of failure in life, got little or no sympathy. Even 'Aunt' told him not to be a baby. During one of these amazing exhibitions, our neurotic Aberdeen terrier, Bodo (named after Bodo von Elstein, a real person as well as a character in one of my satirical dramas, who once, looking back lasciviously at a pretty girl in the street, had fallen over a passing dog and broken his leg – a great family 'joke') – this unlucky animal began running round in circles, foaming at the mouth and 'encapsulating', as some might say, the strange lunacy of our lives.

When we moved from Harrogate to a semi-detached house in Nab Wood, not very far from where I was born, my mother, resentful of this decline, brooded more often on the Missing Will, the Wharton Inheritance and all that might have been. Now that Oaklea was gone and my father's remaining family, firmly part of the English middle class, ceased to have much connection with him, he became even more deliberately plebeian, acquiring furtive gambling associates in Bradford and wasting what remained of his inheritance on the horses. My mother's reproaches, for all the genuine affection they still had for each other in spite of the violent rows, had no effect. Her growing tendency to recall past days of grandeur, of rich hotels and foreign journeys, of fine clothes and jewellery and bathsalts, which grew ever grander in her confused recollection, did not help to keep the peace.

We now spent our holidays, including Christmas, on my brother's farm, Fell End, in Swaledale. As part of his sheep-farming character he had developed an exaggerated meanness, conscious and half-theatrical. He would go to a certain cupboard and return smoking a cigarette. Up on the moor he had a small personal coalmine – a mere hole in the ground, with a ladder, pickaxe and bucket. The coal it yielded was of wretched quality, but it cost nothing. So he insisted on using it for the grudgingly lit fire in the parlour, where it smouldered sulphurously, occasionally exploding and showering the room with fragments of shale and slate.

'If you want proper coal, you must bring your own,' he told my father. So it was a strange party which alighted from the bus, after the twenty mile journey from Richmond, at the end of the steep, rough track to Fell End. We staggered up the hill, burdened not only with chickens, potatoes and other kinds of food, as well as boxes of my father's favourite *marrons glacés*, the one feature of his luxurious past he could not bear to do without, but also with heavy sacks of coal, 'Aunt' and myself carrying one between us.

It was difficult for my father to slink away from Fell End to place bets. The nearest telephone was several miles away. His lust for gambling had to be assuaged by games of Parcheesi, a form of Ludo, for which he gave small prizes. The game became a passion, with me as with the rest. Great tournaments were organised – marathon sessions of a dozen games or more, in which even my brother sometimes joined, shaking the dice-box vigorously with his lean, hard, bony hand and moving the counters while an occasional sheep-tick fell upon the board. My father was a bad loser, not because of meanness – he was a very generous man – but because he was the butt of all the jokes that were going, throwing more than his share of 'three sixes' (which meant that your counter was sent back to base) to roars and screams of demented laughter. Once, teased beyond endurance, he seized the board, tore it to pieces and flung it on the fire, which immediately exploded, covering him with debris as he rolled on the floor in a positively blood-and-thunder demonstration of his gastric ulcer, while Bodo had another of his fits.

'Domimina Nustio Illumea,' said a voice one day as we assembled in the school hall for morning prayers. I saw a short but compact and muscular boy, or rather, young man, two or three years older than myself, with a pale, square face, dark copper-coloured hair and greenish-brown eyes. There was something very unusual in that face. To call it merely elfin or mischievous would not do justice to it. It was watchful and somehow not quite of this world. The words – which were, of course, simply produced by a horizontal reading of the school motto on its two-paged open book high up in the window behind the dais where the masters sat – made a strong impression on me, both solemn and absurd. As we sang the hymns – 'casting down their golden crowns upon the glassy sea' – the words chimed through my mind with magical effect. They corresponded exactly with my own love of all that was odd and strange.

This was the first time I met Alan Robertson Davis, to give him his full name. He was a noted, even famous figure in the school, a good classical scholar, already in the Sixth and preparing for university while I was still in the Remove or 'Transitus'. He was a wonderful speaker in the Debating Society. He was a member of the O T C. He was also a member of another kind of army. His father, now dead, and his mother and only sister all were or had been officers in the Salvation Army. Alan played a trombone in the band and spoke of the 'glory' of marching along in the rain through the slums of Bradford where the Army worked to feed the poor and bring sinners to the Mercy Seat. 'Glory' was a word which was often on his lips, and not only in that connection. He seemed always to be aware in a direct way, as I could only occasionally be, of the glory of the World and of the Word, and of worlds and words beyond these. One of his heroes was Rudolf Steiner, the founder of anthroposophy and of a discipline which could give experience of those other worlds. He was writing, as well as curious poems, a novel – 'the novel' – in which such unearthly matters were combined with fantastic absurdity.

Alan Davis – and we became friends immediately and remained so, with intermissions, for the rest of his short life – was the only man of undoubted genius I have ever known intimately. He was to be killed in action against the Japanese, an officer in the West Yorkshire Regiment, in the retreat from Burma in 1942. Had he lived he might have done great things, not necessarily as a writer, but in spheres I cannot even guess at. I say 'might', because there was, if we are thinking of worldly achievement even of the highest kind, a lack of effort in him, a drifting, a vagueness. It was as though he already belonged to another world and could not take this one seriously.

Meanwhile our friendship prospered. We were complementary to each other – he of Welsh and Scottish birth, entirely 'Celtic', I of curiously mixed origin but needing a focus for loyalties which I had already found in the dubiously 'Celtic' world of Yeats. Both devoted to languages, the more outlandish and useless the better, we studied Welsh, Irish and Scottish Gaelic together. He introduced me to the world of George Borrow's *Lavengro* – a whole enchanted realm of scholarship and adventure. We began to invent a private language on complex grammatical principles – its nouns, I remember, with their eleven cases and nine declensions, had not only a dual but a triune number.

We used to meet after school most days to drink cups of tea – alcohol was yet unthought of – in the steamy refreshment room at the Midland Station in Forster Square, hard by the grand, marble-infested Midland Hotel, haunt of rich woolmen. There, in its 'French Restaurant', with its *flambé* fires suggesting, with the absurd incongruity I loved, Homeric sacrifices to the gods, my father occasionally treated me to a meal which to him must have suggested, most sadly, the glories of his past.

But that was a different world. In 'Fingal's Cave', as we called the station refreshment room because of its fluted pillars and dim, mysterious atmosphere, with a suggestion that the sea was breaking outside, we talked no end of wonderful nonsense. 'The Prometheus Club', a conspiratorial organisation dedicated to our particular kind of visionary enlightenment, was one project. As far as I know it never had more than two members. For the rest, there were Celtic matters, mingling incongruously with the elaborate mythology we were building out of the dark, rainy streets of Bradford itself: the great soot-blackened Victorian Gothic Town Hall with its bell-booming towers; Darley Street with its statue of the great Richard Oastler, noble-hearted Tory Radical; and its public reference library which we believed was haunted by the ghost of Edmund Bogg.

But all Bradford and its surroundings, half town, half country, had become magical, fulfilling those numinous intimations I had had from the beginning. There were giants in those days, enchanters in the decaying wool magnates' houses among the overgrown gardens and straggling groves. To ride on the groaning trams, jangling their earnest bells, was a majestic privilege, particularly when they took us to the far-off Cross Flatts Terminus, beyond Bingley, from which we could soon reach Ilkley moor. But the moor itself, though good for 'a health-giving walk', lacked the magical incongruity of Bradford itself.

It did not occur to me, or to my friend, to wonder what others made of our friendship. Very little, I imagine. It was totally innocent. Neither I nor any of the people I knew had ever heard of homosexuality, or if they had would not have dreamed of speaking of it, except in shocked hints when some wretched clergyman or cinema organist was mysteriously disgraced. We sometimes talked of girls, of those unimaginable goddesses we would one day love. Alan claimed to be in love with Olive, a tea-shop waitress, and even to have borrowed half-a-crown from her. But in such matters we were backward, in my case, at least, from shyness and a devotion to the ideal.

I never met Alan's mother and sister. To Alan, I suppose, brought up in strict and respectable poverty, my family must have seemed rich. He came to our house once or twice, making a good impression, and must have noticed the signs of wealth, though diminished, in its incongruous furnishings.

We had lives, of course, apart from each other. I had other friends among my contemporaries – mostly the middle-class members of my form who shared my interest in literature and 'intellectual' pursuits and my lack of interest in games, and may even have written poems as bad as my own or worse. But they are, by comparison, shadowy figures in my memory – Bell, Waterhouse, Preston, Pendlebury, Rushworth: what became of them? And making their way upwards in the school, though junior to me, were such pupils as Alan Bullock and Denis Healey, already bent, I dare say, on making a name for themselves in academic and public affairs. My own purposes were quite other. I thought nothing of such things then and think little enough of them now.

Alan Davis became head of the school and a very popular one. For all his peculiarities, neither the headmaster nor others in authority could ignore his outstanding qualities. He had also won an Open Classical Scholarship to Lincoln College, Oxford, and there he went in the Michaelmas Term of 1930, ending this short epoch in my life and leaving me somewhat disconsolate. I had now passed my Higher School Certificate Examination, with distinctions in Latin and English. It was the latter, I think, which won me a

West Riding County Major Scholarship, worth £50 per annum. I now set about working for a Classical Scholarship myself. Incited by the delights of Oxford life which Alan described in his letters and at our occasional meetings during his vacations and my holidays, I resolved to follow him, as he urged, to Lincoln.

Along with my coevals I travelled by train to Oxford several times in the university vacations to take the scholarship examinations of various groups of colleges, when we naive provincials stayed in undergraduates' empty rooms – the cause of wonder and envy. Those were strange journeys in a strange country – since my childhood I had scarcely ever been out of Yorkshire, and never in the south of England. I looked at Oxford and the flat countryside, with its sluggish streams, pollarded willows, neat woods and glimpses of ancient houses in parks still unravished – a kind of English life then near its end – with bewildered eyes.

On one of these visits – I cannot remember (or do not want to remember) in which college I was staying – I met an anti-semitic demonstration for the first time in my life. It was only a matter of a few drunken 'hearties', staying up, perhaps, for extra study in the vacation, invading my allotted set of rooms and braying a few insults. But I was no less shocked by this experience for being surprised and hardly knowing what to make of it. I did not think of myself as Jewish and was in fact no more than a quarter Jewish by race. I was angry and disturbed to have this label – by these English bullies so abhorred and despised – stuck on me willy-nilly. It made me think; not happily.

Meanwhile, though one by one my contemporaries were winning scholarships and exhibitions at various colleges, I made no progress. My mind, bemused by adolescent fantasies, was not working well. And perhaps there was another reason for repeated failures. I did not shine at the personal interviews. 'He is too passive and lacks initiative.' That was a bad time for me. My natural indolence and torpor had returned. For days on end I would moon about, stare out of my window at Nab Wood with a blank mind, or slump in my chair, thinking of nothing, my books unread.

At the same time I had got into the habit of playing the fool in the school classes from which I should soon, had all gone well, have had the prospect of an honourable delivery as an undergraduate-to-be. I began writing a fantastic story about a novelist, Egbert Masterman, author of a puritan romance, *Billiards and Sin*. One day, while I was thus engaged in class, I received a stinging blow on the cheek from an exercise book. 'What are you doing?' roared the new young English master, scarcely older than myself, and evidently ignorant of my greatness. 'Writing a novel,' I explained. He sent me to the headmaster, who chided me in his mild manner. It was a low point in my schooldays.

At another time I grew a moustache and, seeing no reason to stop, a full beard. This made me, I believed, the only bearded schoolboy in the West Riding, perhaps in the British Isles. The headmaster, evidently thinking I should grow out of these idiot vagaries, did not trouble to reprimand me or order me to shave off my beard. In this he was wise. I soon decided it did not suit me, removed it and have never seriously grown one since. When a more eccentric and amiable young English master replaced my enemy, he found me writing odes in class and said: 'You aren't making much of these. You must be one of those writers who will be remembered only for a few divine fragments.'

In the spring of 1932 I was nineteen. There was now no hope of my winning a scholarship to university. But I must now leave school. What was to become of me? Unfitted for business or for any useful occupation, I was in the situation of the young Borrow – but without his prodigious energy, physical stamina and giant courage. It was my County Major Scholarship which saved me. I was offered a small supplement to it and my father agreed, out of his dwindling resources, to supply enough money for me to live at Oxford, barely but no worse than some. Lincoln College agreed, on the score of my past work, to give me a place. And there in the Michaelmas Term of 1932 I went as a Commoner of Oxford University.

2
Whining and Dining

It was not, I suppose, until I went to Oxford and so, as far as such a thing is possible, escaped from my family as my brother and sister had done before me in their different ways, that I realised how extremely odd they all were. This realisation did not, of course, come all at once but gradually, as I met various people, both dons and undergraduates, who might be described as 'normal', with more or less 'normal' parents, with roots in life which they took for granted and a recognisable place in the world. The realisation that I was irredeemably odd myself and could not be otherwise, came later. The realisation that many if not all of these supposedly normal people were quite as odd, in their own perhaps less complicated ways, as my own parents and myself came later still; it is hard to grasp even now.

Being odd, I gravitated towards other out-of-the-ordinary people. Most, if not all, of the friends and close acquaintances I had at Oxford were out-of-the-ordinary. My initial attempts to 'fraternise' with the general run of undergraduates at Lincoln, who worked reasonably hard, rowed or played other games, generally met with rebuffs, for reasons which I did not care to analyse (my surname was obviously one of them). Once rebuffed, I did not try again. Once hurt, I would not risk another wound. I became expert at knowing exactly what things could be said to what people. So with most people I tended to be silent. I did not like this myself and the knowledge that most people did not like it either made my self-conscious agonies of silence even more painful.

The world I entered at Oxford was entirely different, I found (and here at least I was the same as others) from the world I had come from. I had often wondered what it would be like not to have been born Michael Nathan in the West Riding. It seemed inconceivable in those early days that there were any other places in England, let alone the world, where it would be possible to have been born. The very thought brought on a feeling of vertigo.

So I settled into my rooms at Lincoln that first autumn evening (they were on the top floor of the first staircase on the right as you passed through the porter's lodge), and arranged my few belongings, mostly books, amid the meagre furniture of my 'sitter' and 'bedder'. Why do I dislike these terms so much that I find it hard to write them? Why do I dislike writing 'the Corn', 'the High', 'the Broad', 'the House'? Why is it that whenever I visit Oxford now, the needle on the dial of my pocket angstometer flickers upwards? The reason will become clear.

I was very much alone that first term. My idol Alan Davis was the only person I knew from school. Lincoln was a small college, though ancient, and ranked rather low in the hierarchy of colleges in those days (it has come up in the world since), and most of my fellow Bradfordians (apart from those like my old friends Waterhouse, Bell, Rushworth, Preston and Pendlebury, who had, I think, all got scholarships or exhibitions at Cambridge) were at other, larger colleges. Many from the North, particularly from Yorkshire, were at the Queen's College. There was a legend, founded on fact, that they occupied the Back Quad there *en masse*, forming a sub-culture of their own. They retained their native accents unimpaired, followed the fortunes of Bradford City, Huddersfield or Leeds United and even had copies of the *Bradford Telegraph and Argus* sent to them in big bundles every week, reading them aloud to each other every Saturday evening when other undergraduates were getting drunk, at sessions which lasted far into the night. These strange creatures never left their college except to go to lectures. They would have been fair game for persecution by the public school boys who were then the majority of undergraduates had they not been both tough and incomprehensible, obstinate as toads. So they were left alone to their strange rituals.

Alan Davis, whose rooms, much larger and more pleasant, as befitted a Scholar, were below mine on the same staircase, took me under his wing. We went for walks in the Parks or to a strange hamlet, Woodeaton, which he had incorporated into his mythology. There was a shuttered, deserted manor-house in a neglected park and a small, ancient church which always seemed to have a bird trapped inside it. We could never release it for all our efforts. We climbed up perilous ladders to the birdlimed, spider-webbed belfry and once, by kicking, brought a sound, deep-toned and strange, from the single great bell. Our shared world of fantasy was still in being, a consolation to me in my general loneliness. But Alan was two years older than myself, he had already taken 'Honour Mods' (again that twinge), was an important figure in the life of the college and had friends of his own year who did not greatly take to me.

I remember very little of that first term except the melancholy feeling of Oxford in autumn: the drifting leaves in the cobbled lanes, the dank mists which rose from its two rivers, the sound of bells which filled the air on Sunday evenings. Sam, my 'scout', who made my bed, cleaned my rooms, brought my coal for the tiny fire and my lunchtime 'Commons' of bread and cheese, must have thought me a quiet, well-behaved person who would give him no trouble. He soon had reason to change that opinion. He was a ruddy-faced, rather sly Oxfordshire man who had once worked in a lunatic asylum and used to tell his fellow-scouts that most of the young gentlemen (of whom I was one by courtesy) were much the same as the inmates.

I read my books, went to the prescribed lectures, had weekly tutorials with the bursar, a bumbling, amiable man whose reading-room was always in a state of indescribable confusion. He took up a lot of time scrabbling vaguely among the mountainous masses of paper on his desk. I did not mind this. I was gradually sinking into a familiar state of torpor. I often felt, as I tried to read, in my rooms or in the Union library (I had joined the Union on Alan's recommendation), a pervading sense of unreality, accompanied by an aching of the joints. One evening towards the end of that first term I sat in the one meagre armchair in my room, devoid of thought or hope, with an uneaten slice of chocolate Swiss Roll on the table beside me. I had not even the energy or interest to light the fire or turn on the light. I may have spent an hour or so sitting there in the gathering dark when a fellow-undergraduate whom I hardly knew even by sight came in on some pretext. 'I say, are you all right? Don't you even want the light on?' 'No,' I said. 'I don't.' 'Are you sure you're all right?' 'No.' After a while he left, baffled and vaguely worried.

Then one evening – I think it was the last evening before the end of that first term – all was changed. I don't know quite how it was, but I found myself, after dining in hall and perhaps drinking more than my usual modest amount, milling about with a crowd of my fellows who were singing, shouting and joking inanely. Most likely I had made some joke, out of that latent 'sense of humour' of mine, which took their fancy. They were already drunk; accepted into their company, I became so. I discovered the pleasure of drinking. I rampaged about with the rest; played the fool; made friends who at the time seemed lifelong; was sick into somebody's fireplace; and at last staggered up my stairs to bed, to wake next morning with my first hangover, feeble enough, but a pleasant accompaniment for my new companions' talk of the extraordinary doings of the previous night. When, later that day, I boarded the train at Oxford Station en route for Bradford (change at Rugby) I had acquired a different view of the place.

My course was set. My career at Oxford (contrary to the high hopes of my parents and of the West Riding education authorities) was to be, at the very best, undistinguished. In fact I learned very little there except to drink, to be idle, and how to live, with some help from like-minded companions, 'in a world of my own'. To be an undergraduate at Oxford in the Thirties with very little money, among those (though few at my college) who had a great deal, was not necessarily a happy experience unless you had ambition of a conventional kind or social graces, and I had not much of either. So I have little to say of days of golden youth, of triumphs in Union debates or at the OUDS, of afternoons spent with beautiful girls in punts on the Cherwell, moored under the willow trees, of conversations about the nature of reality protracted far into the night in panelled rooms, of roaring off in sports cars to London, of listening on May Morning to the choir singing on Magdalen Tower – all those things which make up the sentimentally nostalgic idea of being an undergraduate at Oxford in the Thirties.

My own experience – no doubt this was partly my own fault – was not like that at all. But there were, of course, pleasant times among the boring and the bad. I learned to enjoy a lot of music on my portable, wind-up undergraduate's gramophone, and although I did not read the books I was supposed to be reading and soon stopped going to lectures, I read and absorbed for myself, in a desultory way, more literature than I realised. As a youth, before going to Oxford, I had read large parts of the *Encyclopaedia Britannica* (11th edition) leaving out the articles on science and mathematics, except those on astronomy, and in this way acquired an enormous store of disorganised knowledge on all kinds of subjects from the origin of the letter A to Zymotic Diseases (a term all the more attractive for being described as obsolete).

During my second term at Oxford I got to know other under-graduates who were 'wasting their time' and taking no part in university activities almost as determinedly as I was. Some of them were the companions of my initiation into the pleasures of drinking, and considering our generally meagre financial resources we got through so much drink in that term that my staircase became known among the scouts, thanks to Sam, as 'the boozing staircase'.

As well as Alan Davis and myself, one of its occupants was David Thomson, who was to become a talented writer and, although we could not have foreseen this, an important figure in my life. He was then and remained afterwards a man of remarkable sweetness of character. He seemed entirely without self-consciousness. He was one of the few people I have known who were completely without pretence; unlike myself, who tended to be a different person with different people, he seemed not to take the slightest interest in who was who or how important or unimportant any particular person was or appeared to be; he was always himself.

This did not mean that he was free from nervousness. He often chewed up handkerchiefs without being aware of it. He was extremely short-sighted, but, physically as well as morally fearless, rode a bicycle though he could scarcely have seen beyond the handlebars, with an individual, zig-zag motion, a strange-looking figure in a thick white jersey and pebble glasses. He liked my jokes and fantastications. I was probably a bad influence on him; but for all his air of 'holy fool' he was no fool, though possibly holy.

Another friend or acquaintance at my college was a strange, flamboyant White Russian, Alexis Saburov, who wore bright blue silk shirts and affected homosexual leanings (then fashionable at Oxford) which I did not believe in. Even now, in spite of all I know to the contrary, I can hardly believe in the actual practice of sodomy and other perversions – I have always kept an element of West Riding commonsense, warring perpetually with other elements of my inheritance.

Saburov, who was much more a 'man of the world' than the rest of us, with more money and a background of mysterious grandeur, had a talent for getting systematically drunk in the Russian manner and organised our drinking in a most efficient way, making what might have been a mere barbarous enjoyment into a sophisticated entertainment. He was, of course, an extreme reactionary in politics as in everything else and introduced me to the dangerous writings of de Maistre and Houston Stewart Chamberlain, giving me a taste for geo-political speculation, one of the few proclivities I share with Adolf Hitler. He also confirmed and encouraged my own already reactionary views and consuming hatred of 'progress'.

He used to have 'self-pity hours' every Thursday afternoon at the Cadena Café in the 'Corn', with its wicker chairs, ladies' string trio and 'set teas' (the 'Lansdowne' or the 'Windsor' – 'pot of tea, bread and butter, scones, jam and slice of Genoa cake'). There he would sit for a whole hour by himself, the sentimental music in his ears, recalling in detail the humiliations and imperfections of his life until a satisfactory number of tears had run down his broad Russian cheeks; then, purged of all self-pity until next Thursday, he would rise, pay his bill with a lavish tip and bound into the bright, transfigured outer world, filled with self-confidence and satisfaction.

Saburov was a History Scholar, with an impressive library of his own which included many unusual, even exotic books. He was a dandy, wine-bibber and gourmet. Seized by a sudden desire for lobsters, he would buy a few, shut himself in his rooms ('sporting his oak') and consume them all by himself, with a bottle or two of champagne, emerging later with a catlike, satisfied if rather bloated look. Often drunk, he took pride in being able to sober up immediately if occasion – such as the sudden appearance of the Rector – required, becoming, in his own florid language, 'pale, grave, composed and noble' in an instant. To Sam he was a wonder and a mystery, 'a foreign young gentleman with a lot to say'. According to a story I heard much later, when we had both left Oxford, his end was premature and remarkable. Found in the gutter in Piccadilly, drunk or suffering from a fit brought on by over-eating, or both, he was carried into the Ritz to die (a rare realisation of the catch-phrase 'he died as he would have wished').

Another friend and drinking companion at Lincoln at this time was Denis Hills, a big, handsome, fair-haired young man, a History Scholar from Birmingham, very charming and amusing, who was to have an eventful life in the Second World War and later as a wanderer about Africa, where he nearly met his end as a prisoner of Idi Amin, the tyrant of Uganda, saved at the last moment by James Callaghan, later Prime Minister.

It was about this time that Alan Davis's behaviour began to give the college authorities concern. Though senior, and reading for his Classical Finals, he was still, as a Scholar in his third year, living in college and on the boozing staircase. Always fond of drink, he was an occasional member of our circle, to which he contributed some of his store of mysterious knowledge. But anthroposophy does not go with alcohol, and it was alcohol which began to get the upper hand. Already, he claimed, he had been 'excommunicated' from the Salvation Army but *kept his trombone* (later on, as he sat playing it by the fire in some dismal bed-sitter in London, he related, an emissary of the Army who had tracked him down arrived to reclaim it, leaving a receipt).

He began to write and sing what later came to be called 'surrealist hymns' to Salvation Army tunes. I can still remember fragments of them. Here is one:

> 'I with my brand-new Belgian ophicleide,
> Took it to church with me at Walrustide.
> For the Holy Ghost is fond of toast,
> And he brushes his hair with an old umbrella.'

Others were improvised from a single word or phrase, spoken or read in a newspaper, which his curious mind would seize upon:

'That he can;
In the Vatican
There are books of all sizes.
Some are the Pope's own Sunday School prizes.'

Or, more obscurely:

'What is a Stimfig?
A Stimfig is a man.
Billiards, he laiketh* billiards
For the North Ward Liberal clan.'

I remember one or two complete works:

'In the days of Fulke the Red,
The nuns all went to bed
With the mouth-organ hidden in the clothes;
And the Nonnë Priestess said
From the middle of the bed:
"Hark, hark, how soft the mistral blows".'

We spent quite a lot of time playing a game with very complicated rules: West Riding Knife Throwing. This involved throwing and catching by the handle, at high speed, a long, sharp kitchen knife. Our hands were often heavily bandaged. The college authorities seemed (though I don't suppose this was really so) to take no more notice of this than they did of any other features of what may be called an unremitting war on reality. There is no doubt that had we been undergraduates behaving in such a way fifty years later the authorities would have packed us all off to the psychiatrist; but as far as they were concerned psychiatry was then only just beginning to come in.

* 'Laike': West Riding dialect for 'play'.

However, Alan was sent out of college into lodgings. This did not improve matters. According to his own story his landlord took to persecuting him, writing anonymous letters to the college and following him about on a rusty old bicycle wherever he went. At last the college did take action, sending him off to the Littlemore Hospital to see Dr Neumann, a refugee from Germany who later, as a Flight Lieutenant in the Medical Branch of the RAF, had the task of attending every performance of Terence Rattigan's wartime play *Flight Path*, noting the reactions of the audience and producing statistical tables for analysis (I am not sure whether he got a medal for this, as he certainly deserved).

On a call for help from Alan, who feared he might be shut up in Littlemore by the sinister doctor, David Thomson and I set off to rescue him. We found him sitting in a nearby pub where, he said, he had taken refuge after distracting the doctor by telling him that smoke was coming out of his bookcase and then jumping out of the window. We thought the safest way to evade pursuit by the doctor and his white-coated assistants was to go to a small neighbouring railway station which was left mysteriously unmanned. We found a railway engine and actually contrived to make it travel over a short distance before we were spotted and ran for it.

But the college had had enough. Alan's scholarship was removed, which meant that he had to leave Oxford for good. It was a sorrowful business. At the time the college was installing a new organ in the chapel, and he composed a moving threnody to the tune of 'my bonnie lies over the ocean':

> 'My emoluments went into the organ,
> My emoluments are under the key . . .
> Bring back, bring back, oh bring back my
> emoluments to me . . .'

So he left to make his fortune in London, wearing his black

Homburg ('Anthony Eden') hat, which we called the 'Hat of Peace', a pun on the Irish words 'sidh' and 'sioch' which anybody can work out for himself, and carrying a battered suitcase and a packet of cheese and tomato sandwiches as he walked away jerkily with one foot on the pavement and one in the gutter.

Meanwhile, in other realms, Hitler and the Nazis had risen to power. At that time I don't think I was greatly interested, regarding them at first as fabulous monsters and material for fantasy and later as unmistakable harbingers of war who provided another good reason for regarding Oxford, examinations, careers and 'all that sort of thing' as futile. None of my friends had any interest in politics except Denis Hills, who was at first attracted by the Nazi movement, though not for long, and Alexis Saburov, whose chief political aims, if he had any, were the restoration of the Tsar and the recovery of his own fabulous family estates in the Province of Orel.

We had a great contempt for the embryo politicians of the Oxford Union, in particular for one member of my college who talked of nothing but politics, hoped to become an MP (I dare say he did), and was once heard to boast: 'I left the debate just behind Michael Foot, and do you know, he let me help him on with his overcoat!'

I never asked myself what I would do when I left Oxford. It seemed inconceivable that we should ever leave it, or even that there was a world outside it. Whole days and weeks seemed to pass in idleness, in tiddleywink marathons or cricket-darts test match series, varied by occasional parties given by 'socially prominent' undergraduates where, sometimes as gatecrashers, we would pose unconvincingly as professional footballers or chemists' assistants.

Were there no girls in this curious, dreamlike existence? There were girls, but they belonged to a different order of things. From time to time I thought myself in love, sometimes extravagantly so, and even invited girls to my rooms during the permitted hours, up to 6 p.m., which were rigidly enforced by the porter, a saturnine man of splendid military bearing, whose eye nothing escaped. But I was shy and backward. I could not interpret the most obvious signals. I was also afraid of girls I thought beautiful and more at ease with those I did not, making the common mistake of the immature of supposing that attractive girls could not be intelligent or interesting to talk to.

As for going to bed with any girls, beautiful or otherwise, I doubt if I would have known what to do if I had ever got any to that point. Though considered very good-looking, I was or came to believe myself unattractive through rebuffs real or imaginary. Perhaps I was. I was ill-dressed and rather dirty, taking baths infrequently because I did not like the boisterous bathrooms of the college with their shouting and horseplay.

As for my studies, I took a poor Third in 'Honour Mods' in 1934, with an alpha in one paper only, on the satirist Juvenal. For 'Greats', my final examination, which I was due to take in 1936, I had to read philosophy and go to tutorials with the Rector himself, the bearded, precise and highly rational Dr Munro. We did not take to one another. I have a mind unapt for dealing with abstractions – perhaps unapt for sustained logical thought – and philosophy was not for me. After one term of hopeless floundering, I switched to what some called the 'soft option' of English (I have always had a passion for languages and Anglo-Saxon encouraged the interest I already had in the other, older languages of the British Isles). But I can't say I worked very hard at that either.

Although I went to very few lectures I did, of course, still have to visit my tutors from time to time to read essays to them aloud; I usually copied them almost verbatim from fairly obvious sources at the last possible moment, working far into the night. I could summon up enough impudence to read these wretched productions only after fortifying myself with two or three pints of strong ale. When the ordeal of reading was over, I scarcely listened to the long-suffering dons' comments before shambling from the room.

I had grown very far apart from my parents. But having no money or invitations elsewhere, or the hardihood to tramp the roads or join the Foreign Legion, I had to spend the greater part of my vacations with them. Their fortunes had now taken a curious turn. About the end of my second year at Oxford my father, although he could not have been much over fifty, decided to retire from the wool trade and, using most of what remained of his money, join my brother and his wife in a sheep farm bigger and better than Fell End, though even more remote.

It was in the wild upper reaches of the River Rawthey, on the border between Yorkshire and Westmorland, just within the former but with a postal address in the latter – 'near Ravenstonedale' (how proudly I had this romantic address engraved, in Saburovian splendour, on my visiting cards!). It was on the western side of Wild Boar Fell, a place to suit my brother's obsessive love of distancing himself from all the human race except his admirable wife, and, as far as I was concerned, a place where I could wander in solitude as I pleased, in glorious contrast to my life at Oxford.

There my father and mother, attended by 'Aunt', who after a brief escape into employment with the wife of the Vicar of Shipley, who thought her ill-treated, had been summoned back to serfdom, moved with the remnants of their impedimenta – the Chippendale chairs, the mahogany sideboard with its silver candlesticks, the Dresden figurines, the bridge tables, the art nouveau chromium standardlamps, the dining table with its thick slab of plate glass. Never can a rough Westmorland farmhouse have been so incongruously furnished. And never can there have been an arrangement, even among my family's arrangements, so obviously doomed to failure.

It was not long before my father got Bell's Palsy, an ailment usually associated with worry, which caused the left side of his face to drop and gave him a strange appearance which aroused shouts of laughter whenever he appeared. He seemed an old man already, partly because he liked, for his own masochistic reasons, to pose as old, and partly because he was continually told so. The only duty about the farm he was thought capable of was feeding the hens which clucked about in their small field beyond the muddy, cow-mucky back yard and the outdoor privy. A scene comes to my mind's eye from that time: my father, tottering along (or 'crammling' as 'Aunt' called it in her personal dialect) towards the front door of the house with his empty hen-food bucket, entering and putting it down on the mahogany sideboard between the silver candlesticks, with a look half rueful and half satisfied at his absurd abasement.

This set off a row in the old style as my mother began upbraiding him for 'spoiling her nice things'. There were a lot of rows, and although my brother did not like them he was at least used to them, and may have thought them a price worth paying for the possession of the farm. His wife, unused to the exotic goings-on of exotic people, was upset by them; and even more upset by my mother's attitude to her, which became, as memories of past grandeur grew ever grander, the attitude of a fine lady to a humble farmer's daughter. The resulting troubles were always blamed on my father. At the time I accepted this. But, as I later realised with remorse, that ineffectual and kindly man was hardly at all to blame. Nor was my poor, deluded mother. It was all an 'inherent contradiction'.

My brother, for all the element of desperate play-acting in his role of sheep farmer, was, I think, a very competent one. He certainly worked hard enough for two; he even contrived to put twice as much energy into whistling at his sheep dogs as any indigenous farmer would have done. At haytime he turned into a positive tyrant in his determination to get his one big field of hay into his barns – rising at dawn to beat the weather and using the uncertain headlights of his ancient Riley car to supplement moonlight. The hay was mown by a horse-drawn mower. Then it was spread in long rows across the field and had to be dried by a laborious process of raking over by hand. The poor old horse was managed by Old Jack, our 'hind', or labourer, a solitary man who looked as if he were made out of the rocks of his native Westmorland. He seldom spoke, but incessantly chewed tobacco, regarding it as unworthy of a man, indeed almost effeminate, to smoke it. He refused my father's offer of a Havana with scorn. My father bravely accepted his offer of a plug, but turned green after a few minutes' chewing.

'I'll have no passengers on this farm!' shouted my brother in his ever more convincing Westmorland voice, as he urged on his labour force whenever the weather was suitable for turning the hay, and sometimes when it wasn't – a gleam of sunshine between showers was enough to produce a frenzy of activity. So my mother, my father, 'Aunt' and myself toiled away with our rakes in the sun, helped by one of those Irishmen, all called 'Paddy', who came, often from the poorest and most remote parts of the West, to supplement the haytime workers on all but the poorest farms. Our wild Westmorland must have seemed a tame and highly civilised place to these temporary migrants from their land of rocks, potato patches and straggling fuchsia hedges. To my brother's fury, our own 'Paddy' was delighted when it rained. He could spend his time sleeping in a barn or playing ha'penny Nap with Old Jack, and still get his few pounds' wages at the end.

When the hay was dry it was heaped up in haycocks (I enjoyed constructing these) and then came the last frenzied operation – loading it on a cart and leading the horse to the barns where we, the menfolk, that is, forked it in with pitchforks, my brother making the final adjustments within. My father's ineptitude with the pitch-fork was remarkable and the cause of endless mockery. Once, when he was wielding his fork and smoking one of his last Havanas – a decidedly foolhardy thing to do, since it might have sent the precious hay up in flames and, though this might have been thought of less account, burned him to death – my brother angrily snatched away both fork and cigar. He kept the cigar butt for making one or more of the hand-rolled cigarettes he kept in a secret, personal store.

It was, of course, traditional to provide 'drinkings' for the toilers in the hayfield – the Irishmen would not have worked without it – during their brief periods of necessary rest. The 'drinkings' my brother provided were not lavish – a few stone jars of cider, which my father supplemented with some bottles of Grand Marnier, Cointreau and other liqueurs he had salvaged from his Harrogate cellars. It was pleasant, on a hot summer's day, to sit drinking in the long grass in a shady corner of the field. With my superior Oxford expertise I drank more than anybody else, sometimes linger-ing overlong while the rest were at their ancient, backbreaking task, and even daring to defy my brother's angry eye before joining them with infuriating languor. Because I lived there only part of the time I was a liberated serf.

One very hot day, when we were working in the field, 'Aunt', who had been sent to the house to get some bread and cheese – because of her notorious rock-hard buns and coagulated puddings she was not trusted with anything else – suddenly rushed out and shouted the single word 'Joescum!' What had happened was that my mother's bother Joe, who lived in Manchester and was something of a ne'er-do-well, the black sheep of the Wharton family, had taken it into his head to pay us a visit, walking ten miles from the nearest station, Kirkby Stephen. He was said to 'like a drink' – a sure sign of depravity in my mother's family. He was parched. But with scarcely a word said he had a rake thrust into his hand and was propelled into the field to join the line of rakers. 'It's like t'Khyber Pass here,' he said, looking round at the wild surroundings in amazement and adjusting a knotted handkerchief on his already reddening bald head. Henceforth – and, bearing no ill-will, he made several uninvited appearances – he was always known as 'Joescum'. This became another of those arcane terms particularly relished by my father, which had only to be pronounced, à propos of nothing, to have everybody falling about with amusement. Even my brother would take a moment off to smile.

But hard as he worked and hard as he strove to be like them, the neighbouring farmers – there were three or four other farms scattered within two or three miles – did not like him. What could people called Fothergill or Metcalfe, whose forebears had lived in this rough place for hundreds of years, make of a newcomer called Nathan, who arrived out of nowhere with a strange, incongruous entourage?

What could they make of my father, with his habit of rolling on the floor in simulated agony and his fondness for expensive chocolates and marrons glacés, which still arrived occasionally from a shop in Harrogate or even, for all I know, from Fortnum and Mason? What could they make of 'Aunt', who in her meagre spare time still searched the pastures for comfrey and sometimes, out of habit, tried to accompany me on my wanderings on the fells? What could they make of me? 'Thoo's a big lad to be still at school,' said Old Jack.

The landlord of my brother's farm and a few others was Dr Frankland, who lived at Needlehouse, a picturesque place, quite large but of no great age, down in the hollow by the rushing river, surrounded by gloomy pine trees. He was a learned man and a romantic, and his romance was Norway and the Norsemen who had colonised this neighbourhood, perhaps by way of Ireland, a thousand years before. He rode a fine black fell pony, with a big knife in an ornate scabbard of Norse design at his side. His children, then quite young, have made some mark in the world since; he had named them Raven, Noble and Helga, names resonant of the hard, bitter north which belonged to the people he loved, the colonisers of Iceland and Vinland.

What the Franklands made of our ménage I cannot say. One day Mrs Frankland invited us all to tea – except for my brother, who was too busy for inessential things. It was a strange occasion. We sat in her pleasant middle-class sitting-room, with its 'good' furniture, which looked out on the small lawn, with a few flower-beds, in the narrow space between the house and the river foaming among rocks – my father, my mother, my brother's wife, 'Aunt' and myself. Although Mrs Frankland must have known I was at Oxford she did not mention this, perhaps regarding it as something too absurdly incongruous to accept. I did not speak but rudely fell, as I often did, into a sort of waking dream, in which the sound of the river merged with the murmur of voices. My father, who was wearing one of his old Savile Row suits, did not speak much either.

My brother's wife – apart from Mrs Frankland perhaps the only sensible person present – talked of the affairs of the farm and of the small flower-garden she was trying to create in a corner of the garth. But her remarks and Mrs Frankland's were gradually overborne by a dialogue between my mother and 'Aunt'. My poor mother was doing her best and producing, in her efforts to assert herself, some remarkable phonemes. But by some mischance 'Aunt' had begun to talk about the mysterious symptoms her sister, 'Black Draught Annie', had developed lately – red spots which appeared on her forehead whenever she drank tea. 'It was on a Wednesday.' 'Aunt' recommended comfrey. My mother brushed this suggestion aside, recalling Dr Nimmo-Watson's panacea, lemon juice. 'Besides,' she said, 'they want to get rid of that dog, Spot – I'm sure it's unhealthy – only Herbert won't hear of it. It wants putting down at that age,' she said, appealing to Mrs Frankland's commonsense. 'Aunt' began muttering about a neighbour of Mrs Hall, the Shipley vicar's wife, who had suffered from *blue* spots after drinking tea.

Although there had been no mention of 'Black Draught Annie's' digestive troubles, my father suddenly exploded in helpless laughter. My mother rose to her feet in indignation and alarm. Anything could have happened. But at that moment Bodo, the now aged Aberdeen which was one of our remaining links with 'Duchy Grange', rushed past the window in one of his hysterical fits, pursued by a sheep dog. The party broke up and as far as I know there was no second invitation.

Our strange ménage was now under many tensions. My brother's wife was quite often in tears, her flower-garden belittled ('Lund!' my father would say to offset my mother's references to her Harrogate parterres, but even this magic formula for relief by laughter failed to work, for lack of a quorum which it could act on), her supposedly lowly origins in Swaledale contrasted with her husband's expensive education in Switzerland. Threatened with a miscarriage, she had to go to the nearest suitable hospital, in Preston. We all piled into my brother's car, which smelled strongly of the sheep he often carried in it, and he drove us erratically southwards (his driving was like everything else about him, energetic to the point of frenzy, involving much agonised grinding of gears). On our return the engine boiled on a steep hill and when we were nearing home on the rough farm track one of the back wheels came off, rolling in front of the car in a way which surprised us all. Finding that the car remained stable, my brother, I think, might not have troubled to put the wheel on again if my father had not insisted, maddened by bleating noises from the back of the car, coming either from a sheep which had got into the party without being noticed or, more likely, from 'Aunt'.

The ménage was becoming intolerable. There was trouble with a neighbouring farmer who, finding some of my brother's sheep intruding on his land, cut off their toes. There was a court case. My brother was awarded damages, but this did not help him in the eyes of the indigenous farmers who may, for all I knew, have thought this primitive brutality quite excusable, even laudable. Did Dr Frankland, dreaming of Viking days, wonder whether there were grounds for a blood-feud, a fight to the death with axes, while overhead the eagles screamed? My own cruel fantasies certainly ran on those lines.

Many years later I found among my 'papers' a photograph, already turning brown, which seemed to sum up our life at that time. It showed (I no longer have it; it has mysteriously disappeared) a group of us lined up in front of the door of the farmhouse on a gloomy October day. There was my father, a short, paunchy figure with a kindly lop-sided smile, clutching his hen-food bucket; my mother, also short, dressed in town clothes, wearing a pearl necklace and a large emerald ring; my brother, his lean brown face full of impatience at this waste of time, dressed in farmer's gear and carrying a shepherd's crook, topped with a ram's horn, which for all I know he had made himself; his wife, smiling a pleasant smile and standing out among the rest by her wholesome, natural appearance; 'Joescum', evidently on one of his periodical visits, looking as if he could do with a drink; 'Aunt' staring madly at the camera with folded arms, wearing what looked like a flattened fireman's hat; and myself, sinister in an idiotic way, with long, untidy hair and stubbly cheeks, holding a large, late mushroom. We looked like a group of partisans – hopelessly inefficient ones – rounded up by the Germans in the Second World War somewhere in the forests of Volhynia and about to be herded off and shot. Who took this photograph? Perhaps it was a passing sheep.

It cannot have been long after this that my father decided to cut his losses (among other things he had had a bath installed at great expense, though there was still no indoor lavatory) and moved with my mother back to Bradford, where he took up a rather humble job in some old friend's wool firm. Apart from the absurdity of this attempt to live an impossible life with a daughter-in-law my mother could not get on with, that was a bad time for farming. His losses must have been considerable. But he was able to afford a pleasant enough flat in Manningham, near Lister Park and not far from Oaklea, symbol, to him sad and majestic, of a life which had gone for ever.

Back at Oxford my life of mingled torpor, drunkenness and general oddity had lost some of its flavour with the departure of Alan Davis. He now lived in London, supporting himself or being supported as best he could. At one time he lodged in a tiny, totally unfurnished room in a flat in one of the less socially acceptable mansion blocks in Prince of Wales Drive in Battersea, one of those London streets which 'everybody' is said to live in at one time or another (and where, many years later, I was to live myself). His landlord, typically enough, was a religious maniac, a former contemporary of his at Lincoln who had left after trying to commit suicide in his rooms in an unusually elaborate way. He rigged up a hammock between a bookcase and the cupboard where he kept his fruitcake and supply of mineral-water, drank half a bottle of whisky, swallowed some aspirins, climbed into the hammock and set fire to it. He had overlooked the matter of smoke, which at once alerted the porter, who removed the babbling man calmly and efficiently, with a piece of advice: 'Take my word for it, sir, a carving knife is the best thing. But do try to make as little mess as possible. It's not fair on the scouts.'

The 'boozing staircase' was not so agreeable as it had been. One evening, a group of public school freshmen, annoyed by our unacceptable attempt to combine boozing with poetry, the fascist philosophy of Alexis Saburov and the incessant playing of Mozart's chamber music on my gramophone – they believed, perhaps rightly, that undergraduates should be 'hearties' or 'aesthetes' but not both – attacked my rooms. Their idea was to put Saburov, a foreigner, reputed homosexual and therefore the most objectionable member of the gang, under the pump in the front quad – a traditional punishment. I produced an antique horse-pistol which some girl had given me as a token of esteem and, pointing it at the leader of the lynch party, put them to flight (they returned later on, of course, and gave Saburov, who screamed in an unseemly foreign manner like a stuck pig, a thorough sousing).

Summoned before the Dean next day to account for my horse-pistol – the use of firearms in college, particularly for such a purpose, was a serious offence – I pulled the weapon from under my coat. 'Don't point that thing at me!' he shouted. 'It might go off!' I showed him that it was impossible to fire it. After warning me against such breaches of discipline, he let me go. But it was another black mark to add to my dossier of offences – some comparatively conventional, such as letting off fire-extinguishers – others less so, such as carrying about a large brass doorknob and letting it fall to the ground with a mysterious clang during lectures or even tutorials, then disclaiming all responsibility.

I was moving away from my boon companions (or, more likely, they from me) and becoming more and more of a solitary creature. Sometimes, in the evenings, I used to wander into the part of Oxford called St Ebbe's (it has since been flattened to make car parks, council flats, 'precincts' and supermarkets), a mysterious place, the dankest, most permanently autumnal quarter of that dank, autumnal city. I had discovered, somewhere in that maze of undistinguished streets, a small, shabby, wholly undistinguished pub. Here, in a brown parlour with a cracked, out-of-tune piano and dusty photographs of long-dead jockeys on the walls, I played a simple variant of dominoes for half pints of beer with undersized, secretive men who sometimes changed the rules, such as they were, in mid-game.

Some of them, men with flat, opaque eyes in sallow faces, descended perhaps from the marsh-dwellers of Otmoor, may have been related to college servants, judging from the bags of assorted

food – mostly curling anchovy toast or, in summer, lobster mayon-
naise and strawberries – they often had with them. Their conversation was about missing bicycles, varieties of soap or the best ways
of catching rats.

It was hard to say if these strange people accepted me. Sometimes,
bemused by beer and dominoes, I passed into a trancelike state in
which they seemed not so much human beings as a crowd of
rain-worn sundials and clock-faces, whose sighing breath lifted the
frayed linoleum at my feet with a soothing, rhythmic motion. They
did not seem to mind.

One summer vacation, after I had come into a tiny legacy, I spent
almost all of it on a solitary three weeks' walking-tour in the West
of Ireland. Horribly sea-sick on the night boat from Liverpool to
Dublin through drinking Guinness all night with a crowd of people
who looked at me with suspicion because of my Oxford 'aesthete's'
purple shirt and green velvet tie but were willing enough to accept
rounds of drinks, I staggered into bed at Jury's hotel, then spent a
few days wandering about Dublin before catching a train to Sligo,
sacred birthplace of my hero Yeats.

From there I walked by stages through Mayo to Galway, thence
by train to Dublin and so back to England. I can remember every
detail of this trip – the hotels, dirty and primitive, with little but 'fry
ups' to offer by way of food; the fine, wild country, with its daily
stint of rain and multiple rainbows; the mountains – one, Nephin
in Mayo, made a peculiar impression on me, though I was riddled
with flea-bites from the hotel on the shore of Loch Conn – the
places by the wayside where I rested with my stick and knapsack
among the rocks.

Did I enjoy all this? It is hard to say. I hardly spoke to a soul
except in the way of asking directions or blunderingly seeking a
bed for the night. It was a kind of escape, but I cannot say what
I was escaping from unless it were myself. There was a certain
self-consciousness in my progress through these regions, so long

imagined from my addiction to the illusory 'Celtic' world. I took a bus from Galway to Gort and stood in ritual homage by Yeats's Tower, with its stone bridge over the gliding stream, then, after a statutory time, walked back. The poet was not there (it did not look as if anybody at all had ever lived there). If he had come out and spoken to me I doubt if I could have thought of anything to say.

On the day I took the boat back to England, I had a solitary luncheon at Jammet's, then the most famous restaurant in Dublin, perhaps the only one worthy of the name. In a ritual, self-conscious manner, I ordered an absurd, Saburovian and very expensive meal, accompanied, I think, by the *wrong kind of wine*, and finishing with a large Havana cigar. Without knowing it, I was falling into the very same state of incongruity which annoyed and embarrassed me so much in the case of my own family. Back at Oxford, Saburov was abandoning his humbler friends, myself included, for what he called, with an outrageous flourish, 'birds of finer feather', the cosmopolitan people of the continual parties, the 'celebrities' who figured in *Isis*, the Oxford magazine. Unequipped either with money or social ease, I tried to emulate him. It is a time I cannot recall without shame – the rebuffs, the awkward silences, the absurd snobberies which I tolerated, even tried to share in, the foolish pursuit of smart, sophisticated girls who, if they noticed me at all, looked through me, the rejection of pleasant, unsmart girls who were no doubt just as good to look at and much more agreeable to talk to than those female chimeras.

A perceptive young French Jew at my college called Reinach, member of a distinguished family, said to me after we had both been at one of these parties so coveted by me, but to him, no doubt, a matter of course: 'You are a strange person, Michael. I cannot understand how anyone can be at the same time so civilised and intelligent and yet so stupid and boorish.' It would certainly have been hard to explain this to him, even if I had understood it myself.

Would a visit to Bradford or Westmorland – supposing such a thing were conceivable – have enlightened this well-mannered, handsome young man who was often to be seen that summer lying in the cushions of a punt on the Cherwell, while some adoring young woman of the sort I lusted after so vainly poled him gracefully along? A dark thought sounds like a harsh-toned bell through this trivial chronicle – what became of young Reinach when, six years later, the Germans conquered France?

At the end of my second year I moved out of college into lodgings. I chose some rooms in Holywell Street, just opposite what were then the Oxford University Music Rooms. They were pleasant rooms on the first floor, much better than my rooms in college and, in accord with my general defiance of reality and attempts to emulate Saburov, more expensive than I could afford. The landlady, Mrs Gems, a widow who lived in her own mysterious quarters below with her elder sister, was heard to say I was a very quiet, pleasant young gentleman. Before long, like Sam, she had cause to revise her opinion.

Partly to get away from Bradford and partly with the idea of turning over a new leaf and actually doing some work for my Finals, I arrived a week or so before term started. On a fine, sunny October morning I sat down to the first of Mrs Gems's breakfasts, rather more content with myself than usual, and read in the morning paper which she had brought – it was *The Times*, my reaction to my parents' invariable *Daily Mail* – that King Alexander of Yugoslavia and the French Foreign Minister had been assassinated at Marseilles. This meant little to me. I had no great interest in politics, though next year I was to be indignant at Mussolini's invasion of Abyssinia, perhaps the first and only time I have ever felt any twinges of liberal feeling. Was it because Abyssinia and its Emperor, the Lion of Judah, the strange, savage mountain monasteries of the Coptic-descended church, the Amharic language and its peculiar alphabet, the exotic rituals of a barbaric court had somehow become a cherished bit of the knowledge-hoard accumulated through all that reading of the *Encyclopaedia Britannica*?

My resolve to work did not last long. Soon I was drinking as much as ever. My sitting-room overlooked the street and had a pleasant window seat, a strong temptation to sit doing nothing except stare out of the window at passers-by, turning them into the creatures of comic fantasy I liked so much. I was already convinced that I would become a 'great writer', both poet and novelist. A habit of turning real people, even people I liked, into fictional characters was, of course, deeply rooted in me from childhood on -- it was one of the things that separated me from people, and made me a sort of emotional cripple. It was defensive and essentially feeble, but to many people it made me seem arrogant, haughty and even, absurdly enough, mature beyond my years. My friend David Thomson wrote at this time in some notes for a novel I took a look at one day when he was out of his rooms: 'He seemed to look at people as though they were animals at a fair.' This was true and perceptive. But did he realise what lay behind this unpleasing attitude?

Soon I was at my old tricks again, playing my personal game of social snakes and ladders in which there were only a few short ladders and many long snakes. I drank a lot, sometimes with my old college friends, who were all in lodgings themselves in different parts of Oxford; sometimes alone. Towards the end of that term I was 'gated' for the rest of it – confined to my lodgings after nine o'clock at night. I cannot even remember what offence I had committed – perhaps it was persistent drinking in pubs, which undergraduates were then forbidden to visit by the university rules. I had become friendly with a girl who was studying at the Ruskin School of Art and lived with a woman friend in a curious shanty, liable to flooding, by the Cherwell. On the last night of the term I 'broke my gating' by climbing out of my lodgings – it was quite easy, a simple jump from the broad lintel over the front door – to spend the night with her.

It was the first time I had been to bed with a girl. In a technical sense it was a chaste occasion.

Next day I found that Mrs Gems, who had been eyeing me more and more malevolently, and with good reason – she had amended her original impression of me to 'a quiet gentleman but he has such noisy friends' – had informed the Dean of my college that I was absent. It was the day of 'Responsions', a short, intermediate written examination taken in the college hall. I turned up looking tousled and wearing – a silly badge of bravado – a girl's 'kirby grip' stuck in my hair. Soon I was summoned to see the Rector. His manner was cold, his words few. 'You have a good brain but you refuse to use it. You are rusticated for the whole of next term. You will leave Oxford immediately. I cannot say what attitude the – er – ' he consulted some notes with distaste, his pointed beard quivering slightly – 'I cannot say what attitude the West Riding Education Committee will take in the matter of continuing your scholarship.' He obviously hoped they would discontinue it. I left, and as I crossed his small rectorial garden, deliberately walked on the dewy grass and left my evil trail on it. Though slightly stunned, I laughed. Wasn't this what always happened to great, romantic writers in their youth?

Unwilling to go back to Bradford to face my parents with my disgrace – I had long assumed that although my mother would not hear a word against me, neither of them would understand anything I did or why I did it, and therefore never told them anything – I did not leave Oxford immediately either. I stole a few books and sold them – another romantic gesture of genius. With my girl I spent several days and nights living in the rooms, mainly in New College, I think, of undergraduates who had gone down for the vacation, occasionally entertaining such friends as David Thomson and Denis Hills. It is amazing that we were not detected. There was a popular tune of that time, 'Lost in a Fog' – other favourites which come to mind now with unearthly, nostalgic force are 'Stormy Weather' and 'The Last Round Up' – which expressed our mood completely. I was lost in a fog, not so much of love – though there was love, certainly on her part – as of romantic illusion.

We travelled north and spent several weeks in a tumbledown cottage in Yorkshire which some kind friend had lent us. We had little enough to eat, but the howling gales and rainstorms suited our mood. Sometimes there were wonderful days of winter sunshine and diamond frost, with icicles inside the small panes of the cottage windows. We would walk for miles in the lonely countryside, eating and drinking supplies of expensive food and wine in the Saburovian tradition which I ordered on the various accounts I had at shops in Oxford. Boxes of Havana cigars and of the then fashionable black Russian cigarettes were delivered. We had my portable undergraduate's gramophone, but all my records had been lost or stolen during our adventures – except one, Brahms's String Quartet in C Minor, with its sad, hesitant slow movement which my girl said was like a bird with a broken wing. She often said such things and I did not count them against her.

One day I was summoned to Wakefield, the headquarters of the West Riding County Council, to explain myself to members of the education committee. The Rector of Lincoln's hopes were not realised. The committee were surprisingly sympathetic, obviously puzzled by a paradox: that I, who looked so bookish and seemed so quiet, should go in for such harum-scarum doings as spraying fire-extinguishers and climbing at night over college roofs. They evidently thought I looked – as I probably did – like the sort of undergraduate, with a Jewish name into the bargain – who would get fire-extinguishers sprayed over *him*. They forgave me, exhorted me to do better and be myself in future. I said I would try. But how could I be myself? It was the very last thing I wanted to be.

Next term – the summer term – was windy and sad at Oxford. By courtesy of Mrs Gems, I was back in my old lodgings. I made one or two new friends who, though they did not belong to Saburov's 'lofty circle', as he called it, were sometimes mentioned in *Isis*. I also genuinely liked them. Saburov once said, in his flamboyant way, when, having drunk too much, I was about to vomit with as much neatness as I could manage into a large magenta-coloured vase, 'the cold white serpent coiled about his heart has risen to his cheeks'. Whatever he and others might say, I was not incapable of human feelings.

One of my new friends was the kind, clever and attractive Sally Graves, niece of Robert Graves. Another, also at Somerville, was Eithne Wilkins, a big, blonde girl with a delightful, deep, affected voice, who, crippled in one hip by polio, walked with a strange, swaying motion. She was well thought of as a poet at Oxford in those days, writing under the name of Eithne nic Liamóig – 'Eithne the Daughter of Little William', an ingenious Gaelicised version of her name. Her poems were eloquent and extremely obscure, making my own seem simple-minded and derivative. She found my fantasticated jokes amusing, and thus encouraged by somebody I could both like and respect, I became good company for her, though instantly lapsing into painful silence when her 'important' friends were present.

Eithne was, I suppose, in love with me. But she did not mind that I was only a friend in return. Years later, at the end of the war, she was to marry a German-Jewish refugee, Ernst Kaiser, like herself a genuine intellectual, no pseudo-intellectual like myself. Together they translated the works of the unreadable Robert Musil and became the greatest authorities in the world on his life and work. Such was to be Eithne's niche in literature, and not the poet's fame I supposed would certainly be hers.

What did we talk about, what did we do in those concluding days of my time at Oxford? I can hardly remember. At the beginning of my final year I moved from Holywell to new, humbler lodgings in Wellington Square. I had a sitting-room on the ground floor from which I could see across the square the room of an undergraduate unknown to me – he was one of those who wore yellow shirts with blue ties and vice versa, one of those I thought most enviable – who constantly entertained girls of the kind I always wanted and never got. How often, as I sat at my desk, reading *Beowulf* or Spenser, or trying to read them, did I watch in jealous anguish the arrival of these girls, whether small and boyish or tall and elegant! Why did they seem so infinitely more desirable than any girls I knew myself? Perhaps they were. But, as I recall those futile afternoons and feel again the rigidity which was the physical expression of a locked and paralysed will, I think the fault was in myself and in my own perverted eyes.

I did not spend all my time in such futile ways. I read a great deal, learning to enjoy – it was almost the keenest enjoyment I knew – English poetry which was not on my set books – Hopkins, Pound, Eliot. And, sometimes alone, sometimes with friends, I made excursions on foot or bicycle into the haunted countryside round Oxford, to Otmoor or Wychwood Forest, one of the ancient royal hunting forests of England whose largest remnant, still magical and mysterious, is within the big park of Cornbury House, the one house in all England which I most covet and would choose should a grateful nation ever ask me what reward I wanted for my services. There were many times, amid the boredom and jealousy, when the old sense of the numinous, springing from some combination of light and colour, or contour of fields, woods and hills, assured me that all was not lost.

At the end of that last Hilary term of 1936, I quarrelled with my girl – I had met some other girl I found attractive and who showed signs of not rebuffing me – and went off to Bradford to stay in my parents' flat and make a last desperate effort to catch up on my work so as to get a degree of some sort, however lowly. I felt relieved at the break, then guilty. So when my girl rang up one day and asked if we could make it up and could she come to Bradford, I did not demur. My mother, ever indulgent and liking the girl, did not demur either. My father, who was sinking into an apathy which only furtive betting and the company of low companions could relieve, made no complaint.

There was nothing much to do in Bradford and I could not settle to my books. It was late March; the trees in the park were leafless; their smoke-blackened boughs were set against a dead-white sky; gardeners were busy among the still wintry paths and beds; we read; my girl did some sketching and painting; we walked about the peculiar half-country on the edge of Bradford, looking towards the moors. Suddenly I began writing a 'novel', typing a few pages as I had so often done before on my big, solid portable before giving up. This time I did not give up.

What I was producing was a nightmarish vision of a city in the West Riding, based on Bradford, of course, whose civic leaders suddenly decide to declare its independence. The central character, a retired army officer who has formerly travelled in Tibet, is visiting the city to give a lecture on that country and is caught up in the collective fantasy of the independence movement; he tries to leave but finds it more and more difficult until at last he is completely trapped. The book, in fact, has a moral lesson against getting involved in fantasies which are really of your own making. In a way it described my own condition. But I did not think of it in that way when I was writing it. I tried to mingle Gothic beauty with grotesque humour.

Once I had got beyond the first chapter, I worked on, day after day. Never in my life, I think, before or since, have I been so completely absorbed in any task as I was in writing this book. It took me about six months of concentrated work. Back at Oxford my Finals, which came when I had written about three-quarters of the book, seemed merely a nuisance and intrusion. I did not even bother, when sitting the examination, to answer the questions but answered others which I made up to pass the time.

In fact I was only allowed to take the examination at all by what I now see was the extreme good nature of the authorities. I had been technically sent down just beforehand, partly for the mass-destruction of crockery and throwing a Scotch egg at the high table in hall, and partly for an unusual offence which compounded those rather commonplace ones: dismantling a huge old Victorian sofa in order to throw it out of the window of an empty room in my college. I spent a whole day on this task, while various undergraduates looked in from time to time to see how I was getting on or ask if they could lend a hand. This I declined.

The defenestration of the sofa, like the writing of my book, I saw as my task alone. I had got the back and legs off and had the main bulk of the thing half out of the window when the authorities intervened, indicting me for what was, though not so described at the time, the culmination of a whole series of unprovoked attacks upon furniture. The incident has found its way into fiction and memoirs, sometimes attributed to others. But whether it is a matter for pride or shame, or both, or neither, I claim it as my own.

When the farce of the examination was over, I took leave of Oxford under the statutory cloud (seen off at the station by my only remaining friend at Lincoln, David Thomson, with his habitual air of rueful, puzzled concern and goodwill), and went to Bournemouth, where my girl had taken a job as a waitress. I hired a bed-sitter in some tree-lined road, finished my book, typed out three copies of all 120,000 words of it, sent one to a London literary agent I had met on my journey in Ireland, then got married to my girl at the local registry office with two taxi drivers for witnesses. We returned to Oxford, where I was due to take my 'Viva', immediately after-wards.

In the train I glanced at the stop-press in a newspaper. It mentioned, among the racing results and cricket scores, that a

Spanish general, Francisco Franco, had started a revolt against the Socialist government. When I took the 'Viva' next morning, quite early, I realised that I had over-prepared myself for this nerve-wracking event. I must have been one of the most drunken undergraduates ever to appear before the examiners. Next day we bought bicycles and set off from Oxford, I for the last time *in statu pupillari*, in a north-westerly direction.

That we should make for Wales was natural enough, for I had long been interested in it. I had read Borrow's *Wild Wales* too (he has always had a subversive, unsettling influence), but there was a good deal of difference between the middle-aged Borrow who tramped through Wales with his big green umbrella in the 1850s, asking all he met what various monticles and precipices were called, showing off his Welsh and searching out the graves of famous Welsh poets, and the young man and woman who wandered about the beautiful wild recesses of Wales in the summer of 1936.

We soon ditched our bicyles, perhaps because of mechanical defects, and took to walking. I cannot remember what my wife wore. But I myself, in order to cope with all kinds of weather, wore a thick black overcoat and a black 'hat of peace'. For luggage we both carried stout shopping bags with a few pairs of socks and other odd articles of clothing. We were determined, I suppose, not to be taken for hikers or to be conventional in any way. Heaven knows what romantic nonsense we talked as we crossed the Cotswolds as quickly as possible, then made for Ross-on-Wye and our first objective, the Black Mountains, whose name had long intrigued me.

We stayed in the Abbey hotel at Llanthony, where Landor once had lived, then crossed over the Bwlch yr Efengyl by what was then a rough, stony track (it is now a traffic jam at week-ends) into the Wye Valley. We laughed, we sang, we quarrelled sometimes, made up, grew browner every day as we crossed the great 'Welsh Desert', then a wonderful empty expanse, a place of freedom, with not a single sitka spruce tree in sight. Those green and golden hillsides were alive with larks and grazed by innumerable sheep. We reached the sea at Aberystwyth, then turning back with an instinct for solitude which, though I did not realise it, was not unlike my brother's, crossed over the hills again.

One night we slept in the haunted park of Hafod, huddled together for warmth and waking to find my hat full of snails, the next in some wayside pub under the shoulder of Plynlimon, then turned north-west again towards Machynlleth and the sea, then zig-zagged back to Bala. We stayed that night at the best hotel in that intensely Welsh town, then turned resolutely west towards the higher mountains.

We meant to spend that night in a barn in sight of Arenig Fawr, a wild, unvisited mountain which seemed and still seems (and not for me only) to have a special, magical essence more powerful than the more famous mountains of Wales. Escaping from a fierce stallion in a field by sacrificing our last scrap of food, a banana, we stumbled across the cottage where, unknown to us, Augustus John had stayed before the First World War, and met with true Welsh hospitality – a feather-bed, a good breakfast and no questions asked of this odd pair as we set off again next morning through the solitudes of Migneint towards the mountains of Gwynedd.

What use is a catalogue of places? I remember now our innocence and health, our immersion in the world of the senses in jewel-bright Wales. We met various odd characters, genuine tramps, people (mostly English) who wondered what we were at and, once, a stern Welsh minister who gave us a lecture, not on morals (though I doubt he believed the evidence of my young wife's wedding ring) but on the glories of the Welsh nation and on the foolish Saxons who held it of such small account. I listened, not telling him that he was preaching to the converted. I was silent and withdrawn with strangers, dependent on my wife's easy chatter. Sometimes she would tell me I should smile a bit more. I tried it once or twice, but soon forgot – a joke which fortunately we could share.

Sometimes I would fall into sadness, and knew that she neither shared nor understood it. Could this sadness, which came and went without apparent reason, have been brought on not only by my innate melancholy but by ghosts from the future, ghosts of myself, who was to visit these places so often long afterwards, in different circumstances, when the rough tracks had turned to metalled motor-roads and the green paths were classified and waymarked, no tramp or pseudo-tramp, but in comfort, with money in my pocket, but without her?

This aimless wandering might have gone on for ever, or at least until winter came. But a time came when we turned, without quite knowing why, back towards England. We settled down in a fusty old furnished cottage with a fine big orchard we found on the Herefordshire border. There on an evil day, with autumn coming on, the typescript of my book came thudding through the door – rejected, even by the literary agent! This was a terrible blow. In my arrogant simplicity I had never even thought of such a possibility. I fell into one of my fits of miserable torpor, a particularly bad one this, and even took to my bed. Always able to produce symptoms of illness at will, I ran quite a high fever. My wife, alarmed, sent for the doctor from the nearby market town.

Dr Kingdom, a portly, middle-aged man with a black bag, eyed me, took my temperature, hummed faintly to himself, then stood for a long time staring out of the window at the copious apples hanging all red and enticing in the neglected orchard. 'Who gets the fruit?' he said at last, then left, with a few perfunctory words of advice, none too sympathetic. The question he had asked of no one in particular seemed somehow profound and resonant. I have never forgotten it, and even now will occasionally pronounce it, à propos of nothing, to the puzzlement of all. Who gets the fruit indeed?

But now the little money we had was running out. It became necessary to earn, or at any rate get, some money to live on. We went to London, picking up our few possessions in Oxford on the way, and began living from hand to mouth in Chelsea, moving from one bed-sitter to another, often in different parts of Oakley Street, another of those streets of which it was said that everybody in the world lived there at one time or another. There were times when we had no money at all. We became expert in the well-known trick of lying on the floor when landlords, milkmen or other creditors called, scarcely breathing as they hammered on the door and shouted through the letter-box like cops in a film: 'I know you're in there!' All sources of borrowing temporarily exhausted, we spent three whole days without eating, drinking only water. It was an interesting experience. After two days a certain light-headedness set in. We began drawing food on sheets of paper: chops, plates of bacon and eggs, a magnificent game pie.

Later on somebody gave us a few bits of elementary furniture and we rented an unfurnished room. I spent an interesting morning in the public library studying all the laws on distraint until I burst out laughing and the lady librarian hissed 'Quiet, please!' It seemed that bailiffs wishing to 'effect entry' into your premises were not allowed to force their way in; but if they found a window or skylight ever so slightly open they could enlarge the opening and so get inside. When distraining on goods and chattels they were obliged to leave the bare necessities: bed, chair, table, frying-pan, kettle, mug, plate, knife, fork and spoon. They could not remove the essential tools of a man's trade, which meant that my solid old black portable typewriter was safe. They were obliged to leave parrots (to give an example from the section about pets) an adequate supply of seed. They could not remove animals if by so doing they might cause injury to the person or a breach of the peace – for example, they could not remove your horse from under you.

At one time I had a job in an antiquarian bookshop, the only job

I have ever had, I think, at which I was expected to keep regular hours; but after a few weeks I was sacked, partly because I could not make up parcels with the primitive brown paper and string then used and partly because I had been found by the proprietor, entertaining, quite innocently, as it happened, a young woman in the basement. But it might not have been innocent. The sort of people we associated with and belonged to (if we belonged anywhere) were what were then called Bohemians. Our sexual morals were what would now be called 'permissive' and have become commonplace.

Former friends at Oxford such as Eithne Wilkins, who moved in a more respectable world, recommended me to several publishers; two or three, and those not obscure, showed a strong interest in my novel; but it seemed to evaporate when I went to see them. The book was eventually published twenty years later in a shortened form; but alas! the shadows of surrealism and Kafka – bane of English writers in the Thirties – lie all too heavily on it.

My wife was now getting occasional work as an artist's model. One of those who employed her was a rich amateur, Gerald Reitlinger, who appears in Anthony Powell's early novels and is pilloried in Wyndham Lewis's *Apes of God*. He was to die, many years later, in a tragic way after the burning of his house and porcelain collection. He read my book, praised it highly and told my wife I should 'shake my shaggy locks' and write another. I set to work in another burst of energy but with less enthusiasm, and produced, in a very short time, about 40,000 words of a second, Kafka-free novel and sent it to one of the interested publishers. They praised its 'atmosphere', but ... well, it has never been completed and almost certainly never will be.

Poverty led us into absurd adventures. Visiting some friends at Oxford – there was a new generation there who seemed to me more agreeable in some ways than my own coevals – I overstayed my welcome. Finding I had nowhere to sleep I climbed through the window of a store-room. There was nothing in it except hundreds of orange-coloured paperback copies of Gollancz Left Book Club publications piled on the floor. It was a warm summer evening. Making a nest among the books I fell into a sound and – considering the nature of my bed – a curiously dreamless sleep. I left at dawn before the keeper of this high-piled granary of Leftist propaganda could arrive. Can this experience, working through my dreaming mind, have reinforced and confirmed for ever my already strongly right-wing views?

Meanwhile I tried to shake my shaggy locks and wrote short stories and articles. The first piece of writing I ever had printed and paid for was an article about Welsh nationalism. It appeared, oddly enough, in the *New Statesman*, which also gave me a few books to review ('Nothing over 7s. 6d., mind!' shouted Raymond Mortimer quietly, as I looked over the shelves). Kingsley Martin, the editor, asked me suspiciously, 'Are you sure these Welsh nationalists aren't Fascists?'

This interest in Welsh nationalism (I had been greatly moved and impressed when the writer and scholar Saunders Lewis, with two other unlikely and unviolent people, set fire to an RAF training school in Llŷn, the very extremity and refuge of Welsh Wales, whose language I had studied after a fashion) shows the kind of politics which attracted me at that time, when Europe was moving towards a war which was to make them seem temporarily irrelevant. At Oxford I had occasionally been to meetings of the Chestertonian Distributist Club. I was particularly impressed by Father Vincent MacNab, a saintly man so hostile to machinery that he had even made his own fountain-pen. Later, in London, the Social Credit or 'Greenshirt' journal, the *New English Weekly*, printed some of my short stories, though as its editor Philip Mairet, a pleasant, quiet, pallid man who suffered from intestinal rumblings, explained, it could not afford to pay me anything. Was he, I wondered, listening to his own words and the words of his stomach, as hungry as I was?

I had developed, partly because of my general loathing for 'progress' and technology – I can claim to have been what is now called, somewhat nauseatingly, a 'friend of the earth' thirty years before the Environment was invented – an extreme hatred of Communism which has never left me. I was, if there can be such a thing, a 'Tory anarchist', an admirer of Cobbett, Ferrand, Oastler, Parson Bull and the great Bishop Philpotts of Exeter, of the 'Young England' party and of all who spoke out in early Victorian years against the factory system and against the 'Manchester bagmen and their calico millennium'. There was something of this strain, of a return to 'rural values' in the early days of the Nazi party, deceptive though it proved to be; and (although I had no love for either, to say the least) I would, I suppose, have had to say that I preferred Hitler to Stalin. I certainly hoped for Franco's victory in Spain, and this, of course, did not endear me to the intellectuals of that time.

Among such people, adherence to the 'Red' or 'Republican cause' was unthinking and automatic. They thought (just as the corresponding people think now, in different contexts) that an apparently intelligent person like myself must be posing or trying to be annoying when he expressed opposing principles. They were, I think, genuinely incredulous that I should not at least pretend to be trying to join the International Brigade.

One evening I was in a pub in what came to be known as 'Fitzrovia' – The Wheatsheaf, to be exact, once famous as a favourite haunt of Dylan Thomas – when I found myself talking, for no particular reason, to a tall young man who was wearing a beret and smoking French cigarettes. He was also holding forth volubly about anything or nothing. He was Constantine FitzGibbon, a man who was to become a firm friend and a strong influence in my life, though he was in almost all ways the opposite of myself.

75

He was of the Anglo-Irish 'ascendancy' on his (divorced) father's side; patrician American on his mother's. He had been on a precocious 'grand tour' of Europe, learning French and German, frequenting Paris cafés and who knows what inconceivable places. He was rich – at least his mother was – and even though he was then only seventeen, already had what seemed to me an air of great sophistication. We took to each other at once, discovering that we liked the same kind of jokes and fantastical conversations – of which we both had an inexhaustible supply – that we were both fond of drinking and that we had, surprisingly, much the same political opinions. It had not taken him long to shed the 'fun-Communism' which had got him expelled from Wellington.

He also had a mistress, if not two, and was at that time living with one of them in a bed-sitter in Oakley Street not far away from us, though at the more expensive end. The four of us became great friends. It was not merely that I liked Constantine and that he liked me. He offered a glimpse of a world I had never entered – the world of the upper class whose members, even if they were passive and lacked initiative, which he at least certainly did not, yet had an absolute confidence that whatever others might be, they could be themselves, with the right of entry to any place they chose.

Constantine 'seemed to know everybody'. At any rate he knew people like Dylan Thomas, Nina Hamnett, William Empson and Norman Cameron, as well as Count Potocki, with his long fair hair and velvet cloak, the self-styled King of Poland, a person of extreme reactionary views who insisted on marching at the rear of Blackshirt demonstrations, greatly to the Mosleyites' embarrassment.

Under his tutelage I began to meet people I would certainly not have met otherwise, though it is true I did not feel comfortable with them, and tended to hover in batlike unease on the outer edges of their tremendous parties. All the same, I drank, laughed, talked agreeable nonsense. I even went to a few night-clubs and in the afternoons, to those most agreeable of drinking-clubs with very few customers, where, as the pianist tinkled away, I could sink into a mild alcoholic trance, as if into a feather-bed where I would be visited by the strangest dreams, glorified versions of those distortions of the real world seen through the many-coloured glass fanlights of childhood.

I was at the celebrated opening of the London Surrealist Exhibition, with its underwater piano and cup and saucer made of fur, when Dylan Thomas, after going round inserting various objects such as carrots and pencil-sharpeners by way of improving the exhibits, smashing a picture over some art critic's head and leaving the frame stuck round his neck, was eventually flung out. A very beautiful German countess, seeing me standing wistfully in a corner, declared that she was in love with me and invited me to call at her flat in Hammersmith next day. I did so but found there was no such address. Such idiocies were not uncommon. And there were occasions when I did wake up in women's beds uncertain of how I had got there. I also had that sinister experience, familiar to drinkers, of waking up alone in a strange room after a prolonged drinking bout, uncertain whether it was early morning or late evening and waiting for the light to fade or brighten as the case might be, and thus set my uneasy mind at rest.

I heard the chimes at midnight. But it would be misleading to describe my life at that time as totally worthless and disgraceful. It is no bad thing for a young man who is going to be a writer or any sort of artist to spend a few years of his youth doing nothing in particular, except absorb impressions both from life and books. One day, in the Chelsea public library, I came by chance on Rimbaud's *Illuminations*, borrowed it and read those magical prose poems over and over again in transports of delight. I had never before come across any writing which gave me so exactly what I wanted. My wife had been away for a few days, perhaps trying to raise money from her relations; when she got back she could not make out what on earth had happened to me. She assumed I had fallen in love, as in a sense I had.

Another 'seminal' book I read about this time was *Mystics and Magicians in Tibet*, by Alexandra David-Neel, the first European woman to enter Lhasa, who died in 1969 at the age of 100. I was fascinated by her account of life in Tibetan monasteries, the festivals, devil-dances, exhibitions of butter sculpture; the annual psychic sports, when the monks would compete in levitation, in moving objects at a distance (or telekinesis as it is now called), in the production of thought-forms, and in the generation of supernatural body heat, where the competitors had to strip and sit naked in the snow all night, the monk who melted the largest patch of snow being the winner.

There were the splendid ceremonials, when the great nobles and abbots appeared in their ritual garments of silk, brocade and gold; at the New Year, at the beginning of February, there were the epileptic writhings and obscure pronouncements of the State Oracle before the assembled multitude. All was unchanging ritual, an unchanging hierarchy from high to low. Whether I believed every word – or even many of the words – of Mme David-Neel's highly wrought account, it seemed then – as it seems now – to portray a most satisfactory form of what is boringly called social organisation. There were only two possible answers to any query: 'It is the custom', or 'It is not the custom'. Life in Tibet was harsh, cold and uncomfortable, even for the rich. The peasants were poor and unimaginably dirty, but – other travellers and witnesses confirmed this – they seemed always to be smiling. If they stank, they stank of happiness.

Now it has all gone, destroyed by the Communist Chinese conquerors (or, perhaps, rightly regarded, from a Tibetan viewpoint, it is all still there). I have read many books about Tibet since then. But I am grateful to Mme David-Neel. Apart from influencing my 'political ideas', her book gave me for several nights a series of coloured dreams which I have never forgotten; even after all these years they can still flood my mind with wonder.

My political ideas, indeed! Could they or can they be called ideas? Chiefly they amount to no more than a conviction that in the age I have lived in all change is for the worse. It is said that anyone who is not a Socialist at the age of twenty has no heart and that anyone who is not a Conservative at the age of forty is a fool. I have always been a Conservative. I have always hated 'progress'. I have always been a pessimist.

Now the wandering psychologist I have occasionally mentioned might well say that I held these opinions because of a reaction against myself and my own character and antecedents. A person of contradictory background, both of race and class, a person without roots, unsure of his own place in the world, I ought by rights to have been a rabid revolutionary, bent on destroying our existing society. Instead, I was a passionate upholder of the status quo; a passionate defender of the very people, the middle and upper class, with whom, a few excepted, I could never feel at ease and who, perhaps for that reason, had little time for me.

A person of melancholy, retiring nature, I most admired those who were exactly the opposite – outgoing, sanguine, confident. Lacking in self-esteem, I admired those who stood up for themselves, particularly against the odds (the White Rhodesians and South Africans were to prove good examples later on). Above all, I would choose the losing side, and there at least, as an instinctive loser, I had a kind of consistency. No wonder I supported Franco when all my generation held him in execration; and even felt a perverse sympathy with the Nazis and the Italian fascists. They may have looked like winners in 1937. But I knew that they, with all they stood for, were doomed to be defeated. If I was a passionate anti-Communist, it was partly because I felt that Communism was going to win, that in various forms and guises the barbarians, the materialists, the atheists, the levellers, the worshippers of perverted science, the destroyers of hierarchy and ritual splendour would take over the world – though not, of course, for ever. To believe that would be ultimate despair.

Irreligious by nature, with no more than a social parody of a Christian upbringing, I have always hankered after the unchanging certainty of the Roman Catholic faith as it was before the Second Vatican Council destroyed it. But for that I should undoubtedly have been a Catholic. Would it have been its rituals, incense and sonorous Latin that attracted me? Not entirely. Still unable to believe in the essential Christian doctrines – the Incarnation and Redemption – I know, all the same, that this is not the only world there is.

Was it, the wandering psychiatrist would wonder, 'merely' awareness of my own irreligious nature that made me disbelieve in the supremely irreligious Marxist concept of Heaven on Earth? Was it, to some extent, awareness of having Jewish blood which made me reject, with horror and outrage, that secular, 'Jewish' vision of the future? It might be so. But even if it were so, that would not mean, of course, that I was wrong to reject it.

This is a digression, perhaps a confusing one. I cannot remember much discussion of political or religious matters among my friends at that time. We were mostly intent on enjoying ourselves before the deluge. Constantine was due to go to Oxford in the autumn of 1937. In the meantime, like many young people of his class and habits of life, he decided, that summer, that it would be a good idea to go and live in the South of France with his current or principal mistress. So off they went to Cassis, near Marseilles. It was arranged that we should join them there. But whether owing to my habitual torpor, or lack of money for the fare (life in France at that time was, of course, incredibly cheap for English or American people), or a feeling that actually to 'go abroad' was something which so far exceeded my low expectations in life as to be out of the question, we stayed in London, still living from hand to mouth and moving from one lodging to another.

There were other friends to replace Constantine and his associates, most of whom we did not really fit in with. There was David Thomson, my friend of Oxford days, involved, though I did not know it then, in a hopeless love affair in Ireland which he was to make, years afterwards, into a fine book marred only by a misleading though typically generous view of Irish history. Alan Davis turned up from time to time, as poor as we were or even poorer, living I know not how or where, but still a figure of magic. On the tin whistle he was a virtuoso. He could play not only the two octaves of its normal range but also in what he called the 'spectral tone', an eerie sound he had discovered by experiment. It seemed to come from another world. I was a fair player myself and we used to play duets, mainly Scottish airs such as 'Ye Banks and Braes o' Bonnie Doon', with quite ravishing effect. We occasionally played for money in the street, mainly in the Fulham Road on rainy nights, when we collected a few pennies but were not a great success.

We decided to write a bestseller and set to work industriously, writing alternate chapters. It was a preposterous romance about a Welsh colony on an island somewhere in the Pacific, with a beautiful heroine called Branwen and assorted cardboard characters such as 'the ticket-of-leave man, Ransom', heroic, self-sacrificing Ifan Cadwallader-Jones, the villainous Dr Crevasse and others. It was, of course, hopelessly unpublishable. Alan, partly from having a practical, even surprisingly cynical streak ('all that fuss about a bitch in a black dress') and partly from unreliability, gave up half-way, leaving me to complete the remaining chapters in a dogged, obstinate, masochistic way. Sheets of this ghastly romance, which I typed out in triplicate, kept turning up even twenty years afterwards and were useful for writing on the back of.

Alan had new surrealist hymns to sing to us, too. Here is one, perhaps the longest fragment still remaining in my memory:

'The singing of the dentist's wife,
As I lay in my bunk,
Brought me fresh liberty and life,
Though she was rotten drunk . . .

I saw His boots, I saw His feet,
I chased Him all down Oxford Street,
I dined with Him at Marble Arch
On damson shillebeer and starch.

He is the shout, the victory
By thirteen goals to nil;
Moly and febrifuge is He
When folks are taken ill . . .'

There was also a beautiful song which began:

'Back in the old village band,
With a lemon cheese tart in my hand . . .'

The rest is lost, unless by chance some survivor of those days who knew this strange and wonderful man can supply more, and help, perhaps, to produce the memoir he deserves.

It was now clear to all except the blind and deaf that war was not far off. We got used to hearing, with a kind of horrid fascination, the voice of the Führer on the wireless as he went into the *hwyl* – I had a theory that he was really a Welshman, an Alpine Celt such as the Nazi racial theorist Rosenberg might have dreamed of in an unguarded moment – and the disciplined howling of his people. The Sudeten Germans came into the news; Czechoslovakia, a distant country of which I knew something – that it was an artificial

creation – was now the object of Hitler's attention. He declared or
was said to have declared that it was his last.

Now came conscription, slit-trenches in the parks, sandbag-
filling, gas-mask-fitting in Chelsea Town Hall, hard by the old Six
Bells and Bowling Green where I had so often sat joking and
fantasticating, or on days when we could afford only one glass of
beer, drooping listlessly and watching the old men who had 'been
in the last lot' at their bowls. And now came fear.

Another factor had entered our lives. My wife and I had discovered, some time in the year before, how to make love properly
and she was promptly pregnant. The baby, a boy, was born in
February, a healthy specimen enough. Thanks to the bounty and
help of a woman doctor, a friend of one of my cousins, the only
member of my family, apart from my parents, whom I was still on
terms with – and that not for long – Nicholas was born in a
nursing-home in Putney and duly came home with his mother to a
flea-ridden, barely furnished flat somewhere near the Fulham Road.
It is worth mentioning that I had not told my parents of my marriage
at the time, nor did I tell them of the baby's birth until it became
impossible or pointless to conceal it.

It was at this time, in any case, that I decided to 'make a new
start in life', not precisely to 'go straight' or 'become respectable',
but to become more responsible, soundly based and honest, now
that I was a father. One step I took, to assume my maternal name
of Wharton, may seem to some people to be dishonest rather than
honest. But I did not think so then and I do not think so now. I
wanted to escape once and for all from the oddity and even absurdity
of my early life and one symbolic way of doing this was to remove
a label which did not suit me or, quite apart from its immense
potency in the eyes of others, rightly belong to me. Years later my
son, himself one of the reasons for the change, decided, in a burst
of Jewish romanticism at the time of the Israeli victory in the Six
Days War, to change his name back, though in fact it belongs to

him even less, by precisely half, than it belongs to me. 'Would you', he asked me, 'really rather belong to generations of English North Country clod-hoppers and dolts or even landowning bullies and villains than to the ancient people of Heine, to say nothing of the people of Goethe and Beethoven?' I thought for a long time about this, then answered 'Yes.' But of course it was neither a straight question nor a straight answer. Having no choice, I belong to all these disparate worlds at once.

When the baby was born, we decided, like a lot of people, that London was not a good place to be. 'If there is another war,' people had been saying ever since I could remember, particularly old men in the West Riding, where they knew everything, 'if there is another war, we' – and they obviously thought *they* would survive whatever happened – 'shall all be living in caves afterwards.' Because the First World War was not all that long ago – in fact the Second, as it turned out, was merely the continuation of it – the terror of another war was probably much greater than it is now, nuclear weapons and all. Most people believed that London and other cities would be obliterated within hours ('the bomber will always get through') and that poison gas would be used immediately on the largest possible scale.

If we were not exactly heroic, we were not alone in that. Nor did I believe, before the Nazi-Soviet Pact of August 1939, that it was our necessary duty to go to war with Germany, or, after the German invasion of the Soviet Union in 1941, to prosecute such a war to the point of Germany's total destruction and the partition of Germany and Europe. With hindsight, I now believe it even less, knowing what I then only guessed from hints and rumours, that there were men and women in Germany who, if they had been given due support, might have overthrown Hitler and the murderous gang who had imposed their odious system on a great nation. This was not a popular view of things then, nor is it, strangely enough, acceptable even now, when we know so much more of the truth about both Nazi Germany and Soviet Russia. But I am not ashamed of it. If it had prevailed, how different our unfortunate country and the whole world might be now! Such speculations, of course, were and are completely futile.

After Munich we left London and moved into a cottage I had found, after some false trails, a few miles from Appleby in the valley of the Eden in Westmorland, in that bounteous region I had glimpsed years before in my wanderings along the summits of the barren Pennines from my brother's farm at Fell End. It had looked like paradise then and so, in a curious way, it was to prove.

The county of Westmorland had long been endeared to me in a hundred ways, in particular the Valley of the Eden. I remembered, in a half-mocking way, my mother's hints, gradually turning into positive belief, that her father's people had come from there. And wasn't Wharton Hall, seat of a once powerful family, only a few miles further up the valley, near Kirkby Stephen, whose red sand-stone church even had a Wharton Chapel, with recumbent effigies of the first Lord Wharton and his two wives? The Hall itself was ruined now, its courtyard, chapel, great hall, terrace and parapets incorporated into a farmhouse. Perhaps the Missing Will itself was hidden somewhere in its ivied crannies? And, as a voice from Shipley said in a flat North Midland accent quite different from the sharp, attractive sing-song of the Westmorland people, who spoke a true North-Western dialect: 'Aye, and perhaps not.'

There were certainly plenty of people called Wharton in the neighbourhood where we settled. But none of them claimed re-lationship with the great family of the Hall; nor, I suppose, did they claim relationship, however distant, with myself. Yet I felt at home in the Valley of the Eden. Our cottage, I felt, was the first settled home I had ever had, and I cherished every part of it.

We had moved in, with a few bits of furniture and books – chiefly the twenty-four volumes of the *Encyclopaedia Britannica* and my well-loved typewriter which had been through so much – at the end of 1938 and awoke on New Year's Day, a fine, frosty morning, loud with the baby's cries, in a dank house quickly drying out with the enormous fires we had lit in every grate. I stepped out on to the narrow flagged pathway outside the front door, feeling dejected for myself and apprehensive for my wife and baby in the uncertain future. But the sun was coming up gloriously on the right hand above the flat top of Wildboar Fell. I felt reassured as we had our first breakfast and arranged our small effects.

The rent of this quite roomy cottage was 10s. a month. It had no electric light and only one cold water tap, connected to the mains for our arrival. It had a huge copper in one of its capacious kitchens for washing clothes and taking baths. Hordes of migrant rats visited it at intervals, some of them big enough to defy the big brindled cat a neighbouring farmer's wife produced, struggling in a sack, soon after we moved in ('Ye'll be wantin' this, I'se reckon').

Some nights we could hear these rats scampering overhead; it was as if they were holding sports meetings or even moving their rat-furniture about. I got quite fond of them. One particular rat I had got to recognise would come quite close, staring at me without fear with its bright eyes as I sat reading about Ballistics or the Punic Wars by the light of four candles stuck in those cheap round tin candleholders which must then have been counted in millions throughout England. Where are they all now? They have the curious pathos of things, once familiar to everybody, which all at once vanish from memory.

One of the chief subjects of discussion at the small pub about half a mile away through the fields was the best way of catching rats. Some recommended long planks placed against the wainscot ('he likes a tunnel, like, to run along, dosta see?') with a trap at the end. Others suggested elaborate devices involving cardboard boxes, balanced weights and pails of water. Others believed in poisoned sandwiches ('cut triangular. He likes 'em all dainty, like'). But I was not too keen on catching them at all. One night later on, a friend who was staying with us went to bed early with his supper – a pint of beer and a pilchard sandwich, a great standby for cheapness and nourishment. He fell asleep and woke with a scream to find a big rat dragging the sandwich off his chest. We thought this very funny at the time.

What did we live on? Well, I had discovered about the time we left London that as well as doing 'serious' writing, which brought in hardly any money (though I did get a short story called 'The Bitter Lozenge' – an unkind bit of writing based on 'Aunt' and her herb book – published in the very first issue of Cyril Connolly's *Horizon*), I discovered I had a knack of writing short pieces of humorous fantasy for which *Punch* was willing to pay about £12 a thousand words. I sent these off to London most weeks under the pseudonym 'Simon Crabtree', often writing them at night, with the rats' eyes on me, at the last possible moment for next week's issue – it was often almost as bad as writing essays for my Oxford tutorials, but at least they were paid for – bicycling into Appleby next morning to post them and then, with great relief, do some shopping and drink a pint of beer.

With its broad, sloping main street, the Castle at the top, the Moot Hall down below and St Lawrence's Church at the bottom, and its fine, solid houses, Appleby, the county town of Westmorland, was and still is, for all the cars that choke it now, one of the most perfect and delightful little market towns in England. In those days Lord Hothfield, a big, tall man, every inch a Peer of the Realm, still lived in the Castle. He was, I think, perpetual mayor – who would have ventured to oppose him? – and an imposing figure in the mayoral procession at times of the Assizes, when the Judge invariably got his traditional pair of white gloves since there were never any cases to be tried.

There were nine pubs in Appleby to choose from. I generally took my pint of beer either in The Crown and Cushion or in The Hare and Hounds on the opposite side of the main street. I sometimes had a game of dominoes in The Crown and Cushion, where there were regular habitués whose faces and names I have forgotten, though they sometimes detained me with beer and dominoes longer than I had meant to stay. If I was not feeling particularly sociable I went to The Hare and Hounds, where I was usually the only customer. The landlord, a taciturn elderly man, was also a carpenter. After he had drawn my pint from the barrel he would retire to his back yard, leaving me alone in the stone-flagged, barely furnished room to drink my beer and listen to the sound of his sawing and hammering. What was he making? A coffin, I imagined. It went well with his grave manner. And sometimes his equally taciturn and elderly wife would come and sit by the fire without speaking, knitting away at what must surely have been a shroud.

On something like £30 a month my wife and I and the baby could live quite easily. My wife was a good manager, with what I called a very high 'nidification index' – that is, she was expert at converting the bare cottage into a simple but comfortable home. She could sew both curtains and cushions. She sometimes went to auction sales, returning with amazing bargains – a small sofa, a fine scrubbed table, wheel-backed chairs, rugs. Idle though I was by nature, I did my best to live up to my new role. There was quite a big plot of garden in front of the house, looking across the valley towards the Northern Pennines and the flat top of Crossfell. Here I set to, with my gleaming new spade, to dig up the whole plot. I worked at this for two hours on most mornings, taking about two months to turn over an area which an expert digger – or even an average one – would have managed in a week – even allowing for the frequent pauses I made, resting on my spade, looking with pleasure at the woods and hills and watching the numerous birds which began to appear as the year advanced and spring came on – greenfinches, bullfinches, goldfinches. Once, I convinced myself I had seen a pair of hawfinches, largest and rarest of their tribe.

Then came planting, seeding the strip of ground by the flagged path in front of the house with a few simple flowers and the rest with rows of potatoes, cabbages, carrots, onions and turnips. To my amazement – I had never grown anything before – these, or most of them, actually came up. We lived quite well. I shot an occasional rabbit with my airgun. Nettles, when young and green, are at least as agreeable as spinach. A friendly gamekeeper, whom I occasionally drank with at the pub, would sometimes leave a brace of pheasant hanging on the back door, where we would find them when we got up. One habit we kept from earlier days was late rising.

As spring advanced we began to explore the neighbourhood, propelling the often complaining baby along rough tracks in his push-chair. Soon he began to crawl, then stand up in his play-pen, pushing it round the room and in this way learning to walk. Most interesting was the development of his speech. All infants, before they learn to copy the 'recognised pronunciation' of their parents, construct their own phonetic system and follow its rules for a time with inner consistency. This baby's temporary phonetic system was unusually elaborate.

He could not pronounce words beginning with a sibilant followed by another consonant, so he used nasals in their place. For 'spade' he said 'made'; for 'stone' 'none'. I did an experiment, asking him to repeat the word 'skate', and sure enough out came a perfect 'ngate'. I wrote this down and my wife said she couldn't pronounce it. I was sorry when this individual phonetic system, which even produced 'mlice' for 'splice', disappeared. But later, when, knowing the words 'bee' and 'motor', the child looked up at an aeroplane overhead – a rarity, even a troubling portent – and at once cried 'motor bee' I began to think we had produced a prodigy.

This was a dreamlike time which now seems one of undiluted bliss. It was not, of course; I had not ceased, even in Westmorland, to be a state-registered melancholiac, and even in that spring and summer, particularly in wet weather, would have black moods which lasted for days on end, as I sat in our only armchair with closed eyes, refusing to speak, while my patient, sensible wife went busily about her tasks. Such moods might sometimes be resolved by bouts of love-making. But not always or even very often. I did not love my extremely lovable wife as I should have done, hankering foolishly after girls more beautiful, more strange, more eccentric or even – ultimate stupidity on my part – more clever.

But the summer of 1939 was fine (or was it? we can take it that it was) and while the news from the outside world crackled more and more violently and threateningly from our wireless set we were, on the whole, happy enough in what was then an escapist's dream, a really sequestered part of England, with hardly a car on the roads and not a single tractor in the fields. On many mornings we would cook and eat our breakfast out of doors, either in our orchard, which grew not only apple trees but the finest damson trees, the local women said, in all Westmorland, or by the small, stony, strong-running beck – there was a kingfisher there – a couple of fields away from our cottage.

We were all the more happy – or so it seems now – because we knew that very soon – one year, two years? – this kind of life must have an end. We had felt something like panic just before Munich, and a momentary relief – after all, we were not professional politicians – when the Prime Minister returned with 'peace in our time'. We knew very well that there was not going to be peace in our time. But in a curious way (I can speak only for myself) I had worked the fear out of my system at the time of Munich, and when, eleven months later, the next and final 'crisis' came, it did not return. I even had moments of bravado, quoting from my favourite Yeats, whose strange, much-derided book *A Vision* I read over and over again, that message from his spirit communicators: 'Dear predatory birds, prepare for war. Prepare your children and all that you can reach ...'

That last summer of the old world the beauty of the countryside intoxicated me. When I was not doing my weekly money-making stint for *Punch* or other 'serious' writings which for the most part have never been completed or seen the light of day except in transmogrified form, reading the Encyclopaedia from A to Z, not necessarily in that order, tending the garden, playing with the baby or otherwise employed, I spent whole days alone, on foot or bicycle, exploring near and far. There were moments of that paradisial experience which Wordsworth knew; whose gradual loss he mourned; that feeling of the numinous I had always known since childhood, but now intensified and prolonged to the point of ecstasy. Now that it has utterly gone from me – or is it waiting somewhere to be retrieved? – it is hard even to believe in the sweet, enormous joy which seized me in those luminous evenings of May.

On one such evening I stood in the winding, stony lane which led from the main road to our cottage; the soft, suffused light of the sun going down, the smell of may blossom, the calling of birds, the rustle, almost imperceptible, of the trees and tall grasses by the wayside filled me with serene delight. I leaned on my bicycle, waiting for my wife to come from our cottage to meet me, and thought: supposing it were some girl I truly loved, as I loved with holy fervour this natural world spread about me on every side! That would have been a perfection of life in which the erotic and the numinous, the human and the inhuman, would have been joined together in an experience I have never known. Not having known it, have I ever lived? Did she repine, as I did, at the incomplete beauty of such evenings? Was that why there was nothing to say as I laid my bicycle on the verge and we walked on with a sense of something lost or missing, never to be attained?

However, there were many consolations. Who that has sat, when young, in an outside privy in Westmorland on a fine June morning, with the door wide open, watching the procession of the clouds across the sky and listening to the songs of the birds, with a big slice of currant pasty in his hand, can say that he has never lived?

Friends from London or elsewhere would sometimes arrive

without warning, but there was room enough for all, provided they did not mind the rats and scarcity of washing arrangements. Alan Davis stayed for a few days in the course of a pilgrimage he was making to Iona on a borrowed motorbike. It was the last time I was to set eyes on this extraordinary man.

One afternoon, to our amazement, Constantine FitzGibbon came loping down our lane. He had left Oxford, quarrelled with his rich mother and was temporarily 'penniless', a comparative term. We agreed that time was short. Hitler ranted nightly about the provocations of the Poles, while we talked, drank, gathered mushrooms in the fields (it goes without saying that there was a stupendous crop of them that year), played darts or dominoes in the pub and discussed the situation with men whose views and opinions, still to a large extent their own and not imposed by centralised 'media', were often, to say the least, strange and far-fetched.

This pub was a small, narrow building with a kitchen at one end from which, on many mornings, came the delicious smell of baking, and two tiny bars, the larger given over to darts and dominoes. It smelt of generations of beer-drinking. To enter it was like going inside a rich plumcake. Every man in it was what would now be called a 'character', from the landlord, an edentate man with slight sadistic tendencies, to the various farmers, labourers and gamekeepers, each with his own peculiarity. There was a good deal of the rustic humour which cannot have changed since the middle ages – verbal jokes which would seem innocent enough in our time of electronic pornography, and practical jokes of immemorial antiquity, such as tying a curly pig's tail to a man's coat – a slightly 'simple' man called Frank was usually the victim. There was also a mythological cycle about a local character nicknamed 'Wufflicote' because of his tousled, Old English sheepdog appearance, an elderly man (I suppose he was about forty) who was notorious for propositioning women, invariably without success, though this did not save him, later on, from a well-deserved beating from some local girl's brother. 'Wufflicote' had once appeared at our door when I was away on one of my rambles, and when my wife appeared, at once offered to mend an undamaged slate on the roof. He did not get inside, but the incident, I suppose, was incorporated in the mythological cycle, decorated and expanded. It was all very harmless and amusing.

On Saturday evenings we would walk, either by road or by the field path which led over the beck, through Bandley Wood – favourite resort of lovers – and past the brand-new Observer Corps post into Appleby. To make a ritual pub crawl, we were obliged to drink in each of its nine pubs – not only The Crown and Cushion and The Hare and Hounds, but The Tufton Arms, the principal inn of the town, with its Crimean War daguerrotypes and slightly superior air (it closed its doors at times of the New Fair in June, when knife-carrying gypsies and other troublemakers were about), The Golden Ball, The Chequers, The Aboard, which was so narrow that only one man could enter it at a time, The King's Head by the river, The Grapes, The Royal Oak in Bongate, haunt of malignant dwarfs, and even the gloomy Railway Inn, where even on the finest evenings a gritty feeling, brought all the way from London, seemed to lurk.

Towards the end of August Constantine came to stay with a new, delightful girl whom, as so often, I coveted myself, but in a way so obviously hopeless that the friendship of the four of us was not marred. News came that the Nazis had signed their pact with the Russian Communists. To us, as to Evelyn Waugh, this was a kind of relief. War was now certain and until 1941 it was to be, beyond question, a war against the right enemies, a conjunction of evil monsters; in Waugh's own phrase, we 'faced the modern world in arms'.

We woke on the morning of Friday, 1 September to the news that the Germans had invaded Poland. Two strange days of waiting

93

followed. I doubt if we were ever entirely sober. There was a great deal of love-making too; there is nothing like a 'crisis', a feeling of excitement and apprehension, to induce a state of priapism. The political discussions in the pub, which we visited as often as there was time to spare, became more and more outlandish; one man thought the danger was not so much from the Germans (whom he had fought in what was still 'the War') as the Japanese. He maintained, looking up uneasily at the sky for weird oriental-looking planes, that they were importing into England large quantities of extra-strong mint imperials, which, when swallowed, would explode inside you, not violently enough to blow you to bits, but enough to make you fall downstairs or stagger into the road and be run over by a lorry. 'They're coonnin' devils, tha knaws,' he said. He claimed, when the landlady, a magnificent Westmorland woman with the face of one of the better Roman emperors, put a finger to her forehead, to have seen one of these diabolical sweets in a pub in Penrith. 'Didst eat it, then?' 'Nay, they'se noan catchin' me that way.'

There were troops moving on the roads; there was a rumour that parachutists, not yet the sort disguised as nuns, had already landed at such key points as Crosby Ravensworth and Temple Sowerby; a strange blue light had been seen over at Keisley, away on the other side of Appleby, where the helm wind sometimes blew; an unpopular old lady in another part of the county was said to have hedges in her garden in the form of a swastika, unrecognisable from the ground but useful for the Luftwaffe. Not only that, but she was said to have a Nazi flag all ready in her linen cupboard. Even my own addiction to apparently motiveless bicycling and my collection of large-scale maps of the district came in for teasing accusations of espionage and, later on, brought a visit from the police, tipped off, some thought, by the disappointed 'Wufflicote'.

By night, marring that perfect darkness which nobody can ever see in England now, searchlights appeared far away over the

Pennines, guarding the north-eastern coasts, as good a sign as any that our private paradise was lost. And so, at noon on that fine morning of Sunday, 3 September 1939, we listened to its death-sentence in the voice of Mr Neville Chamberlain, hoarse, paper-thin yet determined, sounding more disappointed than angry, from our ancient wireless-set: '. . . consequently this country is at war with Germany . . . it is not the German people . . . but evil things we shall be fighting against . . .' I am told that in a burst of inverted bravado I declared I would go to bed and stay there till the war was over. But that was not the way things turned out at all.

3
Saluting on the March

I did not go to bed 'for the duration', but unlike Constantine, who left very soon to join the Irish Guards, while his girl enlisted in the Women's Auxiliary Air Force, I carried on through the 'Phoney War' and the summer that followed, awaiting my call up in an unheroic manner. When the Russian Communists invaded Finland and there was talk of forming a British Expeditionary Force to help the Finns, I wrote to the War Office to inquire about volunteering. But nothing came of that. It was naive of me to think (if I really did) that when the Russian Communists, as arranged by their pact with the Nazis, occupied large parts of Poland, the country on whose behalf we had ostensibly gone to war, we should automatically have declared war, or at least been in a 'state of war' with Communist Russia as well as Nazi Germany. What a glorious, noble, quixotic war that would have been – and what a gloriously hopeless one! Or would it have been hopeless? We cannot tell how events would have interacted and alliances reshaped themselves.

We went on with our usual pursuits. Apart from some night-scented stock beneath our windows, the garden grew only vegetables that year. I went on writing my articles for *Punch*; I went on playing dominoes in The Crown and Cushion and meditating on mortality in The Hare and Hounds; I bought a map of Europe and some pins to stick in it; one fine spring day, which we had spent lazily by the beck side, we returned to the cottage to find that the Nazis had invaded Denmark and Norway; I could now begin to stick in my pins and, next month, on another beautiful day, I had need of a fresh supply. The Nazis had begun their blitzkrieg in the West and the real war had begun.

97

My call-up papers arrived. Anticipating matters, I went to Carlisle and enlisted in the Royal Artillery, thereby ensuring that I should know the precise date of my call-up and have a short time to put my affairs in order, as the saying is. My affairs were few and soon put in order. On a gloomy late afternoon in November I took leave of my wife and child, and bidding them stay in the cottage, walked along the winding lane for what I supposed might be the last time. As I stood waiting for the bus which was to take me to Tebay Junction (as I lived in Westmorland, the Army had arranged for me to begin my training in Exeter), our friend the gamekeeper joined me. He remarked, as well he might, on the suitcase I had with me, which was to be used, as Army regulations laid down, for returning my civilian clothes. It was a heavy leather suitcase which had belonged to my father and was stuck all over with the labels of foreign hotels – the Hotel Bristol in Dresden, the Elephant at Zagreb, the Grand Hotel at Riga and so on – all symbols of that Europe which was now to be destroyed.

I broke my journey and stayed that night at Shrewsbury, clinging, I suppose, to my status as civilian to the last and next day watching to the last the passing fields and woods of Herefordshire, where I had walked and bicycled only a few years before. When the train arrived at Exeter I had ceased to be a civilian and had become one of the month's intake at Topsham Barracks, to sleep that night with my fellow-recruits in the old stables, to shave and wash in cold water next morning as best I could and then spend several days being classified, numbered, documented, issued with various items of uniform, medically and dentally checked, intelligence-tested and absorbed into what might have been called the 'military machine'. But machine was just what it was not.

The most unmilitary of men, I had assumed that I should spend my career in the Army, if I was kept in it at all, cleaning latrines, collecting and sorting waste paper and performing various humble tasks of that sort under the bulging eyes of ferocious NCOs, lashed by their pitiless tongues. It was not so. I made several discoveries in that first week. One was that in any representative group of men, such as an Army squad, there will always be one or two who are quite easy to get along with. Another discovery was that life in the Army – at any rate as a Gunner – was hilariously funny. What could be funnier, to begin with, than being known as '1083777 Gunner Wharton MB'?

That first month of marching, counter-marching, turning right, turning left, saluting on the march, with rifles or without, of PT on the chilly playing fields with the soft woods and hills of Devon to look at – I had never before been in the West Country – now seems like a comic dream. Quite a lot of the men in my squad came from the slums of Liverpool and had never left them before. Their incessant, monotonous use of the common expletives was comical in itself. Comical was their bewilderment at the train journey from Liverpool to Exeter ('animals in the fields – miles and miles of fuck all'); comical were their stories of life in Liverpool, with its gruesome incidents of German bombs, its larger than life characters, the mere mention of whose names, as with my own family, was enough to raise tremendous guffaws ('Farting Liza! Remember those pies she made out of old tram tickets?'): all this was novel and fascinating.

This worked both ways. The green pyjamas I wore when we kipped down on our blankets on the floor around the glowing coke-stove in the Nissen hut were a matter of wonder to my fellow gunners rather than scorn. My way of talking, far from being an offence, was also a matter of wonder. If I had worn spectacles I should have been called 'Prof.'. As it was that nickname was reserved for a former schoolmaster, the one man in our squad who took everything with deadly seriousness and was therefore thought much more odd and even ridiculous than I was. The spirit of class deference was still gloriously alive in England. I was its unworthy beneficiary.

We were a very mixed lot. But in those early days we had one overriding interest. No, it was not beating Hitler and suppressing the Nazis. I doubt if I ever heard, either then or later, any such sentiments expressed. There may have been soldiers who talked in such Churchillian terms. If so, I did not meet them. There was merely a sense of being part of a great Necessity, whose purpose, neither questioned nor spoken of, was to prevent our country from being changed by foreigners, whoever they might be, into something different from what it was. There was a great and wonderful innocence about these men, an absence of envy and mean class hatred. There were those, as I know now, who saw in the war a means of changing that innocence and decency and to a large extent succeeded.

Our overriding interest, in those early days, was to put a fantastic shine on our boots. This, our sergeant, a handsome, smart-looking Irishman, had indicated, was a primary duty in that first month. He gave several hints, such as the use of bones, on how this was to be done. There was great competition for shining our boot-caps 'till you could see to shave in them', and although the word 'bullshit' was often used, nobody, except a few amiable, illiterate men already earmarked for transfer to the Pioneer Corps, thought of not competing. One or two of us, who had more money than the private soldier's 10s. a week (about 7s. 6d. after deductions for haircuts and 'barrack-room damages') paid the odd sixpence to a wizened, elderly recruit (I suppose he was about thirty-five) to keep polishing away at our boots so that we could spend more time drinking beer and eating chips in the Naafi while listening to Gunner Harrison tinkling out tunes on the cigarette-blistered piano. The elderly recruit had formerly been in the army of what was then the neutral Irish Free State. He could hardly believe in the sybaritic comfort, lavish pay and generally 'cushy' conditions of the British Army.

I do not think my boots, even with this Irishman's help, were the shiniest of all, but they would pass. My buttons, too, thanks to hours with Brasso and button-stick, were reasonably bright. My kit, laid out for Saturday morning inspection in a rigidly traditional pattern which gave me, a natural Tibetan, intense pleasure, was as satisfactory as the next man's. Once, forewarned in a dream that the metal rings round our water-bottle corks would be the object of special attention (this was technically called 'a blitz on water-bottle corks'), I earned good marks from the inspecting officer for being the only man who had thought of polishing this most obscure item of equipment. My fellow-recruits (we were yet far from being soldiers) did not mind. They had learned to take an interest in my dreams. As we lay, dog-tired after a day's drill, round the stove in our hut, the snoring and groaning – it was Rayner Heppenstall, another literary recruit then training somewhere else in England, but less cunning and adaptable than I was, who wrote the memorable line, 'I hear the khaki beast grieve in his stall' – this collective bombination would sometimes take an articulate form. One man habitually sang hymns in his sleep and was cursed for it. I sometimes shouted out: 'I did not do it! I tell you I did not do it! I am innocent!' Next morning my comrades would ask me, with wonder, almost with admiration, 'But what *did* you do, mate? It must have been something fuckin' terrible.' They may have been right.

Although I was inclined to flat feet and tended to clash my rifle against my tin hat when marching with rifle at the slope, I enjoyed the drill, while grumbling with the rest at being spilled out from warm and frowsty beds on to the vast barrack-square at an hour when the stars were not yet fading in the sky. I liked the ritual patterns and was particularly good at 'rhythm' drill, when only parts of the words of command were shouted out and our feet had to complete the correct movements of this leaden yet fast-moving dance.

I even liked the nights when I was on sentry-duty ('eight hours on and eight hours off') with its ritual of changing guard; and once claimed, when I had been on duty at the main gate of the barracks, that a mysterious civilian had approached and tried to sell me a bren-gun carrier. My tendency to fantasy gained immense impetus in my early days in the Army. I am amazed at what I got away with. Suppose my tale of the bren-gun carrier had been reported to Colonel Sunderland, the stiff, wooden-looking CO of this important training regiment? Once, when I saluted him on the barrack-square with a lighted cigarette in my mouth, the heavens fell.

At Topsham Barracks the comical could be found combined with the mysterious. Why were we sometimes ordered to change from one kind of uniform, from battledress to denims, and then without any apparent reason, back again? Sometimes we had to wear denims *over* our battledress; one man, misunderstanding the orders, tried to wear battledress over his denims instead. He was, I think, the only man in my time who got the coveted 'ticket' of discharge ('lucky sod') which was always being discussed with an envy which in most cases was quite insincere. Why was a certain sergeant-major known as 'Grandma'? Once, on some fatigue duty or other connected with the disposal of waste, I found, in a remote part of the barracks, a mysterious hut made out of piles of solidified cardboard, waste paper and flattened salmon tins. An elderly soldier, who looked as though he had been made out of the same materials, lived in it and, it seemed, slept in it. How long had he been living there? Did the Lieutenant Quartermaster of the Regiment, another elderly man who was very good on military songs – my favourite was 'The Quartermaster's Stores', whose plaintive notes still ring through my head from time to time, inducing hopeless nostalgia – did this important and reputedly unscrupulous officer even know that the mysterious hut and its occupant existed?

What did we do when we were not marching about, doing PT under the direction of men known as 'bloodshot wasps' because of their red and yellow striped jerseys and thought, because of their high voices, to be 'queer'; eating disgusting yet welcome meals at times which would have seemed unthinkable to me in 'civvy street', supplemented by buns and bottles of Bass in the Naafi? A scene in our Nissen hut comes to mind. Half a dozen men are sitting round, some on the floor, some on packing cases, shining their boots or buttons or oiling their rifles. From time to time a melancholy, wavering chant arises: 'South of the Border, Down Mexico Way ... Der der der der, der der der der ... South of the Border ...' Suddenly a single voice says in a flat tone: 'Fucking arseholes!' Nobody takes any notice whatever. All know exactly what he means. He is expressing a feeling of disgusted yet cheerful wonder. Why are we here? What are we supposed to be doing? Is it a dream?

For me this life as a gunner, a private soldier in the proper sense, sceptical and ironical, yet doing whatever I was told to do, however absurd, was over all too soon. The British Army was supposed to be a democratic army, in which all, whether they were dukes or dustmen, served initially in the ranks. So (with obvious exceptions) they did. But those who appeared intelligent and 'educated' were very soon plucked from the ranks and formed into a special squad of 'potential officers' (the 'PO Squad'). I was one of these.

Thenceforward life at Topsham Barracks, though still amusing, became less continuously so. We were expected to work harder than the rank-and-file we had left behind, to take training more seriously. Those who did not or could not or would not, soon found themselves back with the rank-and-file again, or, in the case of the intelligent but unsoldierly, were made 'specialists' in signalling or the other primitive electrical skills which were all the Army knew at that time.

I was quite determined not to be returned to the rank-and-file or to be made a 'specialist' (being weak to the point of imbecility in mathematical or engineering skills, I would not have made even a tolerable one, anyhow). What kept me in the 'PO Squad' for all those weeks of training and retraining which were to lead in due

course to the interview board at Taunton, the OCTU (or Officer
Cadet Training Unit) at Catterick and then to a commission? The
mutual support of all the friends I made? An obstinate, even
ratlike attitude, learned perhaps, from the rats of Westmorland? Or
something about me which convinced the authorities that, however
hopelessly unmilitary and even eccentric I seemed, I could not but
be, if I was to be anything, an officer?

We were training on real guns now, the once famous 4.5 howitzer
'artillery pieces'; every day of the week except Saturday (because it
was inspection day) and Sunday (because it was Sunday) we did
gun-drill in teams of six men, changing round for the various duties
from the most intelligent duty, that of No. 3, who sighted the gun,
to Nos. 5 and 6 who passed the ammunition (wooden shells at this
stage) to be shoved into the breach. We also had to be expert at
setting up the 'director' on its surveyor's tripod, which gave the
guns their angle of fire. We had to dismantle breach-blocks and
put them together again as fast as possible. I thought (and probably
said) that these beautiful artefacts of shining steel, with their inter-
locking sections, pins and bolts, would make delightful Christmas
presents. We went out on map-reading expeditions into the beautiful
country which lay all round Exeter, sometimes shining all glorious
in the snow. I was very good at map-reading, sometimes correcting
the errors of the instructor as tactfully as possible. I enjoyed days
out on the rifle range, being a reasonably good shot. I was less good,
to say the least, at the parts of artillery training which involved
elementary mathematics. Was the real reason why I stayed the
course that I made remarks which amused our Sergeant
Blastfurnace, a huge, red-haired Durham man, with a reputation
for ferocity and the heart of a child, by their outrageous pedantry?
'Puts it very nicely, doesn't he?' this redoubtable, much-feared man
would say. 'Come on, Gunner Wharton, say something else. I could
listen to him all day – but *we haven't got all day*,' he suddenly roared,
turning mock-savage in a moment. 'So get fell in! Right Dress!

Number off!' etc. etc. I was for a time, when he would constantly threaten me with relegation to despised 'specialism', a kind of pet or freak. I took full advantage of it.

When, after about six months, I got a statutory week's leave and went back to Westmorland (the journey from Exeter took about twenty-four hours in a blacked-out train and was enlivened by a sailor from Plymouth trying to open a tin of sardines with his teeth and bare hands), I felt a sense of something lacking. It was not that I was not glad to see my wife and child, glad to have a rest from Army life (to sleep between sheets had become an immense pleasure in itself), glad to wander about the familiar lanes and woods and hills. But some meaning had gone out of them. All these things belonged to a phase of life which was now receding into the past beyond recall.

So, putting sadness aside, I was not altogether displeased at getting back to Exeter and its life of organised, dutiful absurdity. It was good to enjoy better physical health than I have ever had before or since; good to have friends to share a whole new world of jokes and technical pleasantries; good to meet women and not think them out of reach.

I think of what may, most improbably, have been one of the longest periods of sustained happiness I ever knew in my life, in a fine week of early summer in 1941. Although the invasion scare was over, perhaps *because* it was over, our battery, including the 'P O Squad', were sent to establish gun positions on the top of some cliffs near Torquay. It was glorious weather; for four days we dug, we fixed up camouflage nets, we ate Army stew out of our mess-tins and drank some Devon cider which we had secreted; and at sundown we went back in our trucks to barracks, singing those melancholy songs. One luminous evening, when the scent of may seemed to pervade the whole world and the evening star had a supernatural brightness, the truck I was in broke down somewhere in Torquay and we stumbled into some 'posh' hotel, all sweaty and dirty as we were in our mud-stained denims. I spoke some German and very soon became an object of suspicion to some officious R A F policeman. Threatened with arrest, I produced my soldier's pass-book, that AB64 in whose convenient back-flap it was the done thing in those days to keep a single French letter, symbol of sophistication. The R A F man seemed mollified, but still suspicious. Perhaps he was right to be so. We got back to barracks at three in the morning, caring nothing that we had to be up again by six.

Soon after that all those who had passed the selection board at Taunton (how much better in every way was that interview, from the first smashing salute I made on entering the room, to the second, even more smashing salute I made when turning on my heel to leave, than the wretched, craven, drunken 'Viva' at Oxford, only five years before!) were made up to Lance-Bombardier, so that before proceeding to O C T U we could learn some of the elementary habits of command. It was the proudest, most improbable title I have ever borne. That evening, after sewing on my single stripe, I entered the bar of The White Lion for an evening's celebratory drinking. But I had been upstaged. An hour before, the news of Rudolf Hess's flight from Germany in search of the Duke of Hamilton had come over the wireless.

How could anyone talk or think of anything else? It was the moment when, after the conquest of the Balkans and Crete, the Nazi Empire in Europe was at its zenith, as yet one long triumph without a single setback. We talked, wallowing in ignorance of what all this might mean. Wisely, no doubt, I kept my own opinions to myself. But I could not see then, and cannot see now, why it would have been more disgraceful for us to make a pact with the Germans in May 1941 than it was for the Russian Communists to make a pact with the Nazis in August 1939. We do not know what the consequences of doing so would have been. But we do know what the consequences of *not* doing so have been. We have only to consider the world as it is now.

I did not go on thinking much about these things at the time.
As a Lance-Bombardier I now had to drill new recruits, both in
rifle and gun drill. I shouted the commands which not long
before had been shouted at me – and sometimes, while thus
engaged, I caught the sardonic eye of Sergeant Blastfurnace upon
me and heard his encouraging roar: 'That's it, Bom, gi' 'em a
good bellow!'

So far the Army had treated me with unexpected kindness. It
had also made me physically healthy and driven out my tendency
to melancholia, though not my fondness for curious fancies, for
which material lay about me in quantities greater than at any time
before or since.

The Army, of course, moves (or moved then) in a mysterious
way. Because of some error of computation, a 'back-log' of
cadets had built up, and I and my fellow temporary acting
lance-bombardiers were kept kicking our heels, fulfilling no really
useful function, for about two months before we were posted to
OCTU. We were a mixed lot indeed: a Cary, belonging to a
Somerset farming family who were said to be the most cunning
people in England; Harry Rée, a brilliant, energetic, very brave
young man, trilingual, part-Jewish, who left suddenly one day to
join the Intelligence Corps and later became a hero, much
decorated, of the French resistance; an Oxford don; a Lancashire
manufacturer; patrician young men who, starting as Gunner
Fitzhardinge-Berkeley (a particular butt of Sergeant Blastfurnace)
or Gunner Skaife-D'Ingerthorpe, soon found themselves lance-
bombardiers, with styles and titles of extravagant fantasy.

But it was not a good time for morale. Something of my old
torpor began to come over me; I drank too much (I was still slyly
supplementing my income of 7s. 6d. a week by writing occasional
pieces for *Punch*, drawing on the fantasies of Army life. One piece,
about Sergeant Blastfurnace and RSM 'Grandma', who had asked
me to teach him Greek and oil his cricket-bat, was 'brought to their

notice', by Harry Rée, I think, and they became puzzled and less friendly).

We were sent on leave quite a lot, and I was able to show off my stripe in Westmorland. On one of these leaves, on a beautiful midsummer morning, we heard the news that the Germans had invaded Russia. Like many people, I thought the German army, undefeated after two years of war, would make short work of the Russian Communists. I was German enough, and, more to the point, anti-Communist enough, to hope so. This may sound outrageous, but the diabolical nature of the Nazi doctrines was not so apparent then as it is now. The Germans, too, had better uniforms and a suggestion of romantic evil which had a certain sinister attraction for people like myself. There is no doubt which side Alexis Saburov, Russian though he was, would have been on in this campaign.

It seemed to me that to have been a German tank commander on that first morning, waiting on the fragrant turf, with the larks singing, for the order to advance into the blue distances of Russia, would have been to experience true military glory, perhaps for the last time in the history of the world. Were not the German armies, as they advanced through White Russia and the Ukraine, welcomed at first as liberators, with flowers and crucifixes? And all this glory, through perverse stupidity, they were to throw away. It does not do to think of these things.

Recalled to Exeter from one of these frequent leaves, I was ordered almost at once to proceed to the Artillery OCTU at Catterick, not a great way from our cottage in Westmorland. So a much more serious phase of life began. Catterick had the reputation of being a 'hard' OCTU, with a higher proportion of men made 'RTU' (returned to unit), as not being 'officer material', than most. I needed all my cunning to survive. But here again some obscure spell seemed to be working. Men who would obviously have made much better officers than I were '

RTU', often to their great resentment. In 1941 the class system was still in being. I did not really belong to any class. But I looked and talked as if I belonged to the officer class. And so I somehow *had* to become an officer, even though I could not really understand the elementary mathematics involved in gunnery and was probably the worst driver who was ever reluctantly passed as fit to hold a driving licence by Bombardier Lewis, my patient young instructor. He was a Welsh-speaker and was therefore so amazed and gratified by my knowledge of the language that he overlooked my inability (never overcome) to start a vehicle on steep hills or bring it to a standstill within five yards of the point desired. I have always found it difficult to do more than one thing at a time and driving a car, like playing a piano, involves this very common ability.

However, even if I was unfit to drive I was capable of studying the working of the internal combustion engine. I found it fascinating. It was no abstract thing, but a complicated toy with, it seemed and seems, a crude, even fanciful and intestinal mode of operation. In the written examination we cadets had to take on this subject, I got a mark of 96 per cent. My diagrams of the gear-box were very beautiful. A month later I could not have told anyone a single thing about it.

The Commandant at Catterick was a pleasant, genial gentleman, Colonel Waller, a landowner with an estate quite near Catterick, over in County Durham. One of his specialities was a short written general knowledge paper which he devised himself. It was evidently designed to test the cadets' fitness for a commission. One of the questions in my own paper was: 'What is the female of a blackcock?' I was the only cadet in my battery who got the answer right (it is, of course, a greyhen). It is possible that I owed my commission to this bit of information, picked up, I think, from a Westmorland gamekeeper.

Soon after this general knowledge test there was a big batch of 'RTUs'. There were some angry looks among the rejected ones as they packed their kitbags and prepared to leave. There was a good deal of muttering ('If your face fits, all right') and a general determination to wring the neck of any greyhens they came across in future. I believe it was about this time that some democratic rag, perhaps the *Daily Mirror*, got up an agitation about people like Colonel Waller ('Are these the men we want to train our Officers ...?', 'Britain's Snob Army ...' and so on). It may have been no coincidence that the good Colonel Waller left soon afterwards and was replaced by Colonel Jackson, a very different kind of man who may not even have known or cared what a blackcock was, let alone a greyhen. This newcomer took an instant dislike to me and would, I think, have dearly loved to 'RTU' me (he once found me reading Virgil, a writer Colonel Waller had been fond of and had discussed with me). But by then I had reached the last month of training. I wore the magic double white tapes on my shoulder-straps which confirmed my selection for a commission and put me beyond the reach of the new CO's dull efficiency and egalitarian malice. My officer's uniform was measured and made and the great morning came, a fine frosty morning in January 1942 – my 'training' had certainly been a long one – when I and my coevals dressed up like so many actors for the Passing Out Parade.

After a statutory week's leave, which I spent partly with my wife, the baby and my parents in their flat in Bradford and partly in Westmorland (that was a good leave; we were more pleased with each other than we had been for a long time and my wife, though perhaps secretly surprised, was proud of my new status), I was ordered to report to the firing camp at Trawsfynydd in North Wales. It was strange to travel on the little railway line which crossed the mountains between Bala and Ffestiniog; to pass, by night, the enchanted mountain, Arenig, beneath whose crags, only a few years before, we had tramped the roads and fled from a fierce stallion. Alone in a first-class carriage, creaking in my new uniform, I savoured this contrast with pleasure and sadness. What on earth would happen next?

I was surprised to wake next morning in a Nissen hut as a voice said 'Where are we? It looks like the Wild West.' Out of the window I saw the beautiful snow-covered mountains of Ardudwy. It was a sparkling winter day. All that week we drove about the mountain tracks, positioned our guns, checked parallelism, fired off live shells (my first experience of this) then returned to a highly civilised mess where I realised fully the advantages of being an officer. The week was over too soon. It was followed, after the peculiar fashion of the Army, with yet another week's leave.

'He is too passive and lacks initiative.' These negative qualities, which enabled me to float along with the moment, had helped me to become an officer. They also ensured that I did not get a very good first posting. It was to an old yeomanry regiment which had been converted to medium artillery. I had been trained on field artillery – the famous 4.5 howitzers – and knew nothing of medium artillery, except that it was larger and worked in much the same way. This did not seem to matter. The battery I was assigned to was stationed in the southern part of the West Riding. I was billeted in a tiny room at the top of a local magnate's house in a region not unlike the place where I was born, though less hilly, neither town nor country and with collieries and slag-heaps instead of mills. My duties were slight; my fellow officers nondescript and rather boring, except for the commanding officer, a foppish Welshman who always took his corgi dog with him wherever he went. He was not popular; nor was his dog; and I was amused to notice, one day, when we were on some incomprehensible exercise, that when the Colonel's back was turned and he was fiddling pettishly with his binoculars, my sergeant, noted for his sense of humour, shoved the dog into a muddy pond, then rescued it and handed it to its master with a stupendous salute.

I can't say I was kept very busy. I spent a good deal of time walking down the main street of the village where the men of my section were billeted and then walking back again. Nominally I was supposed to see that they were busy at their duties. But they could have got along quite well without me. I spent the rest of my time reading in my billet and in the officers' mess, a very different one from that of Trawsfynydd and with a very different class of officer.

It was not long before I met, at a regimental dance, a tall, fair, spoiled, attractive girl, only daughter of a rich local manufacturer. She supplied an interest in life which might otherwise have been lacking. 'Didn't take you long to get your feet under the table,' said one of my fellow subalterns without much rancour. He had somehow got the idea that I was an actor in civil life. I did not contradict this. But in fact I was more of an actor in military life.

My regiment, which was on vague garrison duties, soon left South Yorkshire and during the next two or three months changed its location several times. This gave us all something to do. As it moved about in a fairly small area in the East Riding and Lincolnshire it was not difficult for my girl friend and myself to snatch occasional meetings, usually in hotels where many of the other guests were probably occupied in much the same way.

I had a remarkable capacity for avoiding air-raids, not by any calculation but by odd coincidence. On the night after I had spent an afternoon in bed with my girl friend in York, it was heavily bombed in one of the 'Baedeker raids' – retaliation for RAF raids on historic German towns and cities – which incidentally reduced many of my old haunts in Exeter to rubble.

It was a time of waiting. My battery was continually going off on inexplicable exercises to places which I would never otherwise have visited: the Yorkshire Wolds; Lincolnshire; the Wash. Certain sights and sounds are vivid: Lincoln Minster, huge at foggy nightfall as we returned in convoy from some exercise or other; a bivouac in straw in a barn down by the Wash at some out of the way place like

Leake or Wrangle, after a day spent firing shells into the mud-flats under a leaden sky; the moaning and whining of the shell fragments; waking on a morning of early summer in my tent in the garden of a magical grange in Tennyson's Lincolnshire, with the birds all singing – a place I have often tried to find again, in vain. And indeed to find it now would mean nothing. I am not the same person who was then bewitched.

It was now May 1942, the mid-point of the war. All this time, while I was going through the motions of training, marching about, returning salutes with my little stick under my arm (British officers still carried them at that time, though they tended to be mislaid and not replaced) or contriving furtive assignations – all this time the most horrific events were taking place in what must be called the real world: men were being blown to bits, burned to death, drowned, buried alive, hideously mutilated; women and children were being dismembered from the air, squashed, eviscerated, plastered like so much bloody jelly on the sides of collapsing buildings. The world was screaming with man-made, God-ordained suffering. What did I and my fellow-soldiers in an England scarcely touched, living, on the whole, better than most civilians, think about all this? The answer is that we scarcely thought about it at all. It was somewhere else; it was the News (at that time almost uniformly bad) on the wireless in the mess, preceded or followed by 'ITMA'; we had been lucky so far (were we even thankful for that?); but our time would no doubt come.

As a rather useless and idle subaltern I tended to be sent on 'courses', in effect a week's leave in some novel or unvisited spot. This could be useful for meeting my girl friend and it was surprising how enterprising we became. A week spent on instruction in 'tropi-cal hygiene' in the park of some big house in the Home Counties comes to mind – the lectures when drowsiness was hard to over-come, the strolls among the shrubbery, the demonstration, which nearly caused a chain-reaction of disasters, of how to make an 'oil and water flashfire' to dispose of rubbish in jungles yet unvisited. I have never to this day had occasion to make one.

I had just learned that I was to be sent on a heavy tractor driving course at Prestatyn when, in the manner of the Army, everything was suddenly changed. I and a fellow-officer were posted to a field artillery regiment which was mobilising to go abroad. So, abandoning plans to get my girl friend from Yorkshire to North Wales, I found myself in Northumberland, with the proud rampant lion badge of a Scottish division on my arm. The regiment I was joining was a very different outfit from the yeomanry. It was efficient and keen and its officers were of a better class, though not, in general, less boring. The CO belonged to a landowning Anglo-Irish family but, mysteriously, had a Swedish title. He was a mild, social man with no fire-eating characteristics.

My battery commander, Major Crick-Balderton, had plenty. He was a small, energetic, fierce-looking man with sharp features, not, I imagine, unlike Montgomery, at that time about to take over the North African campaign. He was full of what he called 'wheezes', and knowing that I was a bookish sort of chap, asked me if I thought it would be a good wheeze to run off a few dozen copies of Kipling's 'If' and have the officers read out the poem to their men every morning on parade. I said I did not think it was a good wheeze. But he went ahead with it all the same. When my turn came to read 'If' to my section I only just managed to get through it without laughing. Several of the men did not manage it and technically I should have put them on a charge. I did not do so, thinking it unfair unless I could put myself on a charge as well.

We were due to embark for an unknown destination in about six weeks' time, and were extremely busy counting and checking our stores. I was first billeted in the regimental headquarters, a fine old house north of Alnwick, not far from Chillingham, where Lord Tankerville kept his herd of white cattle, descended from the wild cattle of ancient times. Later on, my battery was stationed nearer

Alnwick, around a smaller but still acceptable country house which made a pleasant officers' mess; the other two batteries were stationed around other country houses, in which Northumberland abounds. Once again the Army had brought me to a part of England I had never visited before, and a very beautiful one. It was early summer and I welcomed the expeditions we made in the surrounding countryside. I was sent on various errands which involved driving an Army truck. I did not thereby get much better at driving, reversing tactlessly on to a trim lawn at our battery headquarters rather than knock down the stone gateposts with their heraldic gryphons – a difficult choice.

Once I was sent with a party of men all the way to Newcastle to collect some stores or other (we were always collecting stores). The errand, whatever it was, did not take long, so, as we were not due back before nightfall, we occupied ourselves in getting drunk in different hostelries (as an officer I could not drink, let alone get drunk, in the same places as the men). By the time we were due to return we were all drunk, but the men were drunker than I was, particularly the driver. So there was nothing for it but to drive myself. It was probably my greatest military achievement up to that time, particularly as the truck was of a new American type then beginning to arrive in England and had its steering-wheel on the 'wrong' side. Did these men realise what danger they were in? It was lucky they were anaesthetised by drink. As their lingering songs turned to snores I did my duty and, to my own amazement, delivered them safely back to camp, prudently stopping the truck about fifty yards from its proper place, where I should almost certainly have crashed it into a wall.

One day we were all issued with tropical kit. This, I said in the mess, obviously meant we were bound for Iceland. Major Balderton gave a sharp, barking laugh. But I could see he was not amused. He was, in fact, coming to regard me with suspicion. Next day the whole regiment, wearing the new tropical kit, paraded before the

CO. In our pith helmets and knee-length, buttoned-up khaki shorts we looked ridiculous and knew it. The Colonel looked as ridiculous as any, though he had had his shorts tailored and his pith helmet, unlike mine, seemed to be a reasonable fit. He gave us a gentlemanly pep-talk and dismissed us to our never-ending checking of stores, with its accompaniment of traditional Army jokes ('piss-pots, rubber, lunatic officers for the use of, six,' etc. etc.).

During these activities I got to know some of the NCOs rather better than I knew the officers. On the whole they were much more interesting people anyhow, with greater maturity and experience of life. So I quite enjoyed being duty officer at nights, walking the paths among the trees with Sergeant Smith or Sergeant Budgen and talking about all manner of things, from marriage to the scarcity of glow-worms (there were a few in the tall grass, however, and Sergeant Smith, a particularly interesting and agreeable man, greeted their tiny, intense green lanterns with as much delight as I did). One day, during a roadside stop on some exercise or other, Sergeant Smith produced a pocket chess set and we started a game which was not finished, though he was getting a slight advantage, when we had to move on. Later Major Balderton, who had noted this unseemly behaviour, gave me a good ticking off and after that I was constantly given the boring duty of pay parade, handing out 7s. 6d. (or whatever it had become by this time) to long lines of men, each of whom had to step one pace forward, salute, take the money, salute again, about turn, take one pace back and retire. Once, to save time, I arranged to have my hair cut while paying the men. Major Balderton gave me another ticking off for this early example of time and motion study.

For a few days we all went to the firing range at Otterburn. This, in spite of heavy rain, was pure delight. The rolling moors of Northumberland, stretching unfenced all the way to the Border and beyond, with their copses and green mosstroopers' tracks, were then all beautiful open country, not yet blanketed with the huge, horrible parody 'forests' of Sitka spruce which have turned their Border poetry into Canadian prose. We lived in tents (I had a batman, Gunner Runcie, who had the knack of seeing that I was as comfortable as possible. He was, I think, a bigamist. This is beside the point). At the end of the week we officers went to The Redesdale Arms in the village, dined well by wartime standards and got ritually drunk, some of my fellow-officers turning out to be more interesting than they had seemed. I was late on parade for our return journey next morning and, what made things worse, had put on my smart officer's raincoat, with its warm lining, against the cold, wet weather. I was improperly dressed. 'Take that thing off,' said Major Balderton, 'and wear your greatcoat like everybody else.' It was another black mark for my mounting score.

The time of leaving for a destination unknown but guessed at (our tropical kit had not been replaced by arctic fur and skis) was near. I had ten days' embarkation leave. I spent the first few days with my girl friend, staying in the North Yorkshire moors; the rest in Westmorland with my wife and child. We went on foot or by bicycle about the familiar haunts, the lanes, woods, becks and hills for what we knew would be the last time. There was a certain place, on a well-known path by a woodside, where we took our leave of the last vestiges of that life in Westmorland. It was a bright June day with a mild breeze. A bough creaked, over and over again, with what seemed to me then (I have never forgotten it) a musical, elegiac note. Then came the parting at the station, the last sight of my wife and child, the sad settling back in the railway carriage, watching all that had been familiar slide away. It was a scene which must have been going on at that same moment not only in England but in all parts of the warring world. Back in Northumberland there was more checking of stores; a day when our country house headquarters became empty of the soldiery who had briefly occupied it; and then, on a late afternoon of midsummer, green and golden, the last parade.

A corner seat in a compartment of a blacked-out train full of troops and equipment; a journey with many stops throughout the night; occasional distant explosions which I had learned to ignore; then grey morning light revealed what could only be the waterfront of Liverpool and the great buildings I had last seen only eight years before on my solitary foray into Ireland. Now I was not to know solitude for a very long time. I was a subaltern in an artillery regiment bound, as we now knew, for India, a very small part of the Army indeed but carrying, as Major Balderton had told us in one of his shrill pep-talks, great responsibilities. I had no great sense of this, only of being myself, in an extremely strange situation. Unlike my fellow subalterns I was playing a part, a part which had become second nature by now, but a part nonetheless. Passive and lacking initiative, I was carried along in the stream of events.

After a time – I have no idea how long– all military activities, particularly the movement of men and stores, are very confusing – I found I was looking at the waterfront of Liverpool from the deck of a great liner. It was the P & O liner *Orion*, converted to a troopship, but, as I soon found with pleasant surprise, only partially converted. The officers' quarters were positively luxurious. I shared a smallish cabin with three other subalterns, none of them particular friends of mine but possible to get along with (they were a bit put off by the books I had brought with me: Yeats's *Last Poems* and *A Vision*, which I read constantly, believing it to be a key to much that was going on in the world, and Volume One of Spengler's *Decline of the West*, which I had found, as an other rank, fitted neatly into my 'small pack'). But the bunks were comfortable and the washing arrangements satisfactory.

The ship still had civilian stewards. It still had, for the officers, great dining-rooms with separate tables, snowy white tablecloths and gleaming silver. There were five courses for breakfast, including kedgeree and eggs done in any way you chose. In the bars and the great saloon where we spent much of our spare time, stewards were on hand to serve unlimited amounts of pink gin at about 5*d*. a go, as well as most other drinks you could desire. Not finding any very congenial drinking companions among the officers of my own battery, I found some among others of the numerous units – mostly tanks and artillery – on board. I made one faithful friend, a young signals subaltern who seemed to find my continual fantasising about the ship, the people on it and the voyage itself, quite irresistible. We often sat at a table in the centre of one side of the great saloon, immediately underneath the legend, set out in large gilt letters on the wall, 'Fear God and Honour the King', and, as somebody told me later, became known by those nicknames.

The contrast between the officers' comfortable quarters and semi-civilian life and the quarters, if such they could be called, allotted to the other ranks below decks was staggering. As I found – it was part of my duty to descend to these nether regions to see to the welfare of my men, though how I was to do that was not clear to me – they were crowded together like convicts, some sleeping in hammocks, some on 'biscuits' and blankets on the deck itself. It was appallingly hot down there even before the ship began to move; later it became an inferno, stinking of unwashed bodies and in rough weather of vomit. But I heard no complaints, except the habitual, half-jocular grumbling of the British 'khaki beast'. They accepted their lot without question. It seems incredible now that they did not mutiny. But even if they knew the full extent of the contrast between their sweaty hell and the comfort up above – and it is possible that they didn't – I don't think they would have been outraged. They knew their place. I knew my place – for while I was in the Army I had a place, identifiable by uniform and badges of rank, temporary and unlooked for as it was. I was not outraged by the difference, as Harry Rée, the heroic socialist of Topsham

Barracks days, would have been. He would not have tried to organise a mutiny. But he might have organised – as he once did at Exeter – a 'voluntary compulsory' concert of classical music for other ranks in the officers' saloon, which would have been cleared of drinkers for the purpose. He would thus have annoyed everybody for their own good.

The *Orion* stayed at Liverpool for an inexplicable length of time. But eventually she cast anchor and began to move. Through a haze of pink gin I saw the sea. Next morning I looked out of the porthole and saw, instead of Liverpool, unknown Scottish islands with green hills, brown moors, white sands and here and there white crofts. This was the last of home. We headed out into the Atlantic to join a very large convoy bound for South Africa. It was the end of June, but it was something like a month before we reached our destination, taking a circuitous course which brought us almost to the coast of South America to avoid the German U-boats, then at the height of their campaign.

In this convoy the *Orion* had its own allotted and unvarying position, somewhere in the middle, I was glad to note, of several lines of ships great and small. So every morning I woke to see this steady progress through waters at first grey and gloomy-looking, then, as we steamed south-west, turning blue in ever warmer weather. I had several turns on night watch – the only time I was alone – and searched the sky as the familiar constellations dropped away and stars unseen before appeared to my wondering, would-be astronomer's eyes. I saw Canopus, second in brightness only to Sirius in all the sky, and then the great stars of the Southern Cross. What I did not see or even hear of throughout the entire voyage was a single U-boat. Aware that one of these might be lurking about, that at any moment a rending explosion might hole the great ship, I simply did not think about the matter at all.

It was a pleasant voyage. My duties were slight. There was occasional drill and PT. I had got hold of an Urdu textbook and knowing that I was 'a bit of an intellectual' Major Balderton set me the task of giving volunteers among our battery lessons in the language. I worked quite hard at this, keeping two or three jumps ahead of my pupils, who, of course, had no textbooks. They learned a bit of the language in a lackadaisical way, all except one lance-bombardier, a future Communist shop-steward perhaps, who would resentfully argue with me about points of grammar and syntax.

One of my other duties was to censor the men's letters home. Some of them were writing roughly identical letters to several girls at once; one man, a big good-humoured gunner with every reason for good humour, as many as five. Another man, a dark gentle-faced young gunner, just married before embarkation, was writing love-letters of great tenderness and even beauty to his young wife; in fact they were so well-written that I was tempted to tell him so. I had a feeling (though I do not know if it proved so) that he was one of those fated to be lost and that he would not see his grieving bride again.

As I could read Welsh I was given most of the Welsh letters of all units to censor. I noted, with some asperity, that they were not usually written in very good Welsh; some contained a good deal of 'OK' and 'blydi well'; the Welsh language is short of swear-words, ferocious as it can be made to sound.

So the time passed: the sun, straight overhead, showed we had crossed the Equator; it grew hot; we sweated at our PT; the wretched soldiery below decks sweltered away; there was a falling off in attendance at my Urdu lessons. We turned eastward. For a time it grew colder; there was a swell of great waves as I went on watch one sunset and knew we were rounding the Cape, with nothing but the Antarctic to the south. On a certain day birds appeared. Soon we were docked in the port of Durban. Here we parted company with most of the convoy, which was bound for Egypt.

For a week we stayed in the Imperial Transit Camp, ten miles or so from the city. We smelt the curious peppery smell of Africa; saw strange flowers and trees; we were allowed to go into Durban on pass, in the afternoons and evenings. Most of the white people of Natal (and at that time we hardly noticed there were any other people, apart from the extortionate Indian taxi-drivers) were friendly enough. Once in an hotel ('the hotel') I saw a group of white people looking at us in a hostile way. They were the dreaded Ossewabrandwag, we were told, the pro-German, anti-British Afrikaaners.

Meeting an attractive and intelligent girl in a night-club called the 'Stardust', of which officers in transit were made temporary members, I arranged to meet her next day on the steps of the General Post Office. To my surprise and some alarm, she turned up, and in an hour or so I had fallen in love with her. Sophie was a small, fair, graceful girl, Scots of Natal, sympathetic and willing. I spent all the rest of my available time with her, much of it in the 'Stardust', a strange South African version of the clubs Constantine had introduced me to in London. We had a hasty parting. I did not want to be posted 'absent without leave', though tempted to risk it. Later on I wrote love-letters to her, but got no answer. There would be other transient subalterns for her in the 'Stardust'. But being seen with this surprising beauty made my stock rise sensationally with my fellow officers when we resumed our voyage. Escaping from the other half of 'Fear God and Honour the King', I was even invited (only think!) to play poker with Old Etonians.

Now, all about us, the Indian Ocean smiled and smiled, exactly as I had imagined it. We saw dolphins, beautiful, iridescent flying fish. Although the Japanese whom we were going to fight were then at the height of their success (there were reports that they were going to invade Ceylon and even had their eyes on Madagascar), we had no cause to fear their submarines. On a day in early August we saw birds again, perhaps the dreaded 'shitehawks' we were told were one of the horrors of India, which, according to the general view, was an utterly horrible country. 'You can smell the fucking place miles out from Bombay,' I was told by ancient quartermasters. In fact, the smell, smoky, fragrant from burning dung and quite different from the smell of Africa, seemed languorous and not unpleasant.

4
Adrift in India

As it happened, we reached Bombay on the very day in August 1942 when the leaders of the Congress party, with Jawaharlal Nehru at their head, were arrested. Small, excited but aimless-looking mobs of brown people dressed, if they were dressed at all, in dirty white, were roaming about, crying 'Quit India' and throwing stones. But, busily transferring ourselves and our stores from ship to train, working at night by arc-lights, we thought little about them, if at all. On an afternoon of great heat our train set off inland. India, brown and green, looking more like an enormous golf-course than anything else I had ever seen before, swirled about us, dusty, inexpressibly alien and strange.

We seemed to spend weeks in the train, waking, sleeping, doing nothing in particular, as it slowly puffed across the middle of India, sometimes stopping, for no apparent reason, among bright-green paddy-fields where skeletal figures stooped, or at a wayside station with its name-board in English and in the thick, overlined Nagri characters I had not yet learned to read, where a few people strolled aimlessly about or slept in the shade. While we waited, a bullock-cart creaked slowly over a level-crossing. In the unfamiliar trees small monkeys chattered and busily flea'd their young, or fought over a scrap of bread flung to them from the train. Sometimes, after going rapidly and purposefully forward for several miles, the train slowed down, stopped, went a few miles backwards, then forwards again.

An American officer on his way to some liaison post in Calcutta, perhaps, hatless in the sun and in long trousers, scornful of the lectures we had had from medical officers warning us to wear our pith helmets ('Bombay bowlers') or risk dropping dead within minutes, forced me to play liar dice with him for several days on end. It is a game I have disliked ever since. We crossed great rivers, shrunk to small channels among sand and boulders, on which brown, slender women, rousing a faint impulse in men long celibate, were bashing their meagre, coloured cloths. We passed through great stretches of open grassland with groves of broad-leaved sâl trees; denser jungles, isolated rocky hills of fantastic shape, some with what looked like ruined forts or temples on their summits, and, further off, higher ranges fading into blue distance. At night small fires broke out in mud villages; groups of people, chattering, gesticulating and spitting the crimson juice of betel nut, came together, dispersed, reassembled, sat down, fell asleep. There seemed no reason why this journey should ever end.

It ended, at last, at the smallish town of Ranchi in the Province of Bihar, an impoverished, densely forested part of India which had many Army training camps. In one of these, a few miles out of the town, we found ourselves, after a period of indescribable confusion, installed in tents in an open part of the forest. I write 'found ourselves' because I have no recollection, myself, of doing anything to bring this about. At one moment I was getting out of the familiar train into glaring heat which, as I knew it would from my reading, 'hit me like a blow': I was aware of passing in a truck, with others, through a dusty street crowded with shouting people (one, bolder than the rest, may have shouted 'Quit India!' and received from some sardonic NCO the unintelligible reply, 'With pleasure, mate!'); of seeing incomprehensible shops full of broken objects, jars, ancient gramophones, piles of fly-infested sweetmeats, bottles of virulent green and purple mineral water, an enormous pair of false teeth painted on a board, signs – 'Ayurvedic medicine, egg and chips, lemonade, spectacles, food'; and finally of sitting in my officer's tent, one of a long row, which was just big enough to contain my folding

bed (with mosquito net) and my tin trunk for sitting on. The
legs of the bed were built up on bricks standing in tins of shallow
water, to prevent white ants from eating the bed itself. In their
search for food and other necessities these ants, which operate
in darkness, were swiftly constructing raised tunnels in the
earth-floor of the tent; observing them provided something to do
until the next event occurred.

At nightfall, dutifully putting on my pith helmet, I walked to the
larger mess-tent, where Major Balderton never failed to tell me I
looked just like a character from 'one of Noël Coward's plays about
life out east' (which were those?). Mad on salutes, he rebuked me
several times for failing to salute him. Once, having to wait on him
when he was taking a bath in his tent, I saluted so vigorously that
part of the tent collapsed. It is fair to say that instead of being angry
he gave a shrill, mad cackle. 'Wait for the rains!' he shouted.

Soon after we arrived in this camp the rains, eagerly awaited
in the outrageous heat, suddenly broke one afternoon when I
was sitting in my tent, wondering, as so often, what on earth I
was supposed to be doing. The rain began to come down in
what seemed a solid mass. A shrill scream of joy told me that
Major Balderton had rushed out of his tent in his underpants,
which he had often told us was the custom when the rains
arrived. We soon had more serious things to attend to, digging
channels round our tents to prevent the water washing them
away. Steam rose from the ground with a strange, rich smell. It
was as though we were inhaling curry. Thunder rumbled about
in a splendid way and as night fell the sky was lit by glorious
violet lightning. I have always enjoyed thunderstorms. This was
a storm of the highest quality.

The same performance went on for several days, the rain descending punctually at exactly the same time in the afternoon, then
easing off for a display of distant lightning. The temperature fell to
a bearable 95 degrees or so at midday, making it possible to think

of doing some 'training'. The surrounding area west of Ranchi, beautiful hilly jungle and open woodland, was very suitable for this. The inhabitants were aboriginals, dark, graceful, shy people dressed in nothing but small loincloths and beads, with scarlet flowers of 'flame of the forest' in their hair. Sometimes by day, as I was saluting Major Balderton or checking some stores, I would be aware that one of these grave, quiet people, carrying a bow and a few arrows, was passing softly over the grass a short way off among the trees. Once, in evening twilight, I saw one raise his bow as if in salute, though neither to Major Balderton nor myself but to the crescent moon.

Quiet and furtive as they went about their business during the day, these people seemed to spend their nights in endless festival, to the sound of drums, flutes and wild singing. Their villages or settlements were, of course, strictly out of bounds. Many soldiers (and even officers) said they envied this carefree way of living, which certainly seemed to me both happier and better than ours. But Major Balderton, a teetotaller and lifelong bachelor (he once described, at breakfast, in apparent innocence, a 'curious dream I had about being in an absolute sea of naked women'), warned us against the potent 'jungle juice', a kind of rice beer, which the natives drank at their orgiastic festivals. It was said that one man, not in my battery, had been severely disciplined for trying to gatecrash, and another, unable to resist following one of their undoubtedly lissom young women into the jungle, had disappeared altogether.

One by one, as gleefully predicted by Major Balderton, we succumbed to dysentery, which ruled out all activities except excretion and left the sufferer weak, limp and careless whether he lived or died. None died, but several had a few days in hospital in Ranchi, to be dosed with caolin – a not unpleasant spell off duty. I was one of them. Major Balderton, on a routine inspection of the slit trenches, then in constant use, discovered that one sufferer in extremis, finding no other material to wipe his bum, had used pieces of a large-scale ordnance map of the district. The culprit was, of course, myself. This amused him hugely.

Ranchi itself, for all its initial strangeness, seemed a dull little town. It had a small club, however. All officers were made honorary members, and we were generally allowed to go there for the Saturday evening dance. There was only one attractive girl among the Europeans who went there, the dark-haired daughter of a local tea-planter. I met her again, by chance, when after quite a short time, in the curious manner of the Army, I was given a fortnight's leave in the nearest hill-station, Darjeeling.

The long journey there by train and funicular was strange and dreamlike. I woke one morning to find the train had stopped (as usual, for no particular reason) on a great dusty plain. Small boys stood by the line holding bantams' eggs in thin brown palms. 'Boil egg, sahib! Boil egg!' I bought one or two, though advised not to eat them, and, being now immunised against dysentery, took no harm either from them or from the small earthenware pipkins of tea and horribly sweet and sticky buns older vendors were offering. Suddenly I noticed, to the north, a high bank of cloud lying over wooded hills. But it was no cloud. It was the range of the Himalaya.

I had never seen high mountains before. The effect was stupendous, and later, when we reached Darjeeling, I could hardly take my eyes off the great mountain Kanchenjunga all the time I was there. As was the custom, I toiled up Tiger Hill, breathless in the rarefied air, and saw, a hundred miles away, the peak of Everest, with its eternal plume of snow blown by the wind out of Tibet. It was, of course, the most wonderful thing I had seen since the total eclipse of the sun in 1927 – we had been given a school holiday to see that – could it possibly have been only fifteen years before? Did I feel, when gazing at Kanchenjunga and Everest, the numinous sensation of my youth?

I doubt it. I believe that even then – I was only twenty-nine – I was beginning to feel its loss, that indescribable 'feel of not to feel it' which Keats could do no more than state, though Coleridge, in his ode 'Dejection', comes closer to putting it into words. The tea-planter's daughter was fond of poetry and I used to read it to her. Once Major Balderton saw us in a rickshaw together, moving down a tree-lined road in the cantonment of Ranchi. 'I see you're a bit of a poodle-faker, Wharton,' he said later in the mess, with his mad, screaming laugh. It was another black mark.

His opportunity to get rid of me came fairly soon. With some other young officers I was asked to a party at the tea-planter's bungalow and, drinking too much, fell asleep in one of the bedrooms, to wake in the morning much bitten by mosquitoes and technically absent without leave. Back at the camp I was relieved of my revolver, put under arrest and escorted by two fellow-officers to receive a reprimand and seven days' confinement to camp. A little later came a request from Corps HQ, under whose command, though a British regiment, we came, for an intelligence officer. I was supposed to be intelligent, was certainly a bit of a nuisance, and so, by no means unwilling, was seconded. Major Balderton's farewell was surprisingly cordial and accompanied by an exceptionally fine mad cackle. The CO seemed genuinely sorry to lose me. Always gentlemanly and mild, he wished me the best of luck.

Corps HQ was in a neighbouring rajah's palace, with marble floors and bathrooms, all marble and gold, of remarkable vulgarity. It was good to sleep under a roof and to take a hand in marking up the maps in the War Room, where they were inspected by the Corps Commander, General Slim, himself. Slim, who though perfectly English, looked like a caricature of a good kind of Australian, was very different from any senior officer I had come across before. He was both intelligent and amiable. He inspired respect, even devotion, and later on, of course, was to prove himself most worthy of them.

I particularly liked marking up the map of the Eastern Front according to the daily reports. The Germans had reached the Caucasus. Did I secretly wish them to advance further? Did I even stick a swastika-flagged pin in Astrakhan on the Caspian Sea, advancing the German Army to a point it never in fact reached? If so, nobody noticed.

There were congenial officers among my fellows in GS(I). One of these, Dick Storry from Doncaster, shared my liking for fantasy and was to become a lifelong friend, turning up at odd moments during my wartime service both on duty and on leave, and always making life more agreeable. With his co-operation I could make the rather pompous and disagreeable head of our intelligence section, Major Caird-Smith, into an amazing figure of fun.

Our headquarters went out on numerous field exercises into the beautiful hills and jungles of Bihar. These were most enjoyable. At least they seem so now, when seen through the wrong end of a telescope, jewel-bright and with all discomfort smoothed away. Certain scenes remain vivid in memory. I am trying to shave in the wing-mirror of a truck at dawn, while a shimmering mist of delicate pink, green and amethyst rises from the ground as the sun comes up, quickly strengthening and dispersing those veils of dreamlike beauty. I am in the back of a truck bumping along dirt roads that connect remote villages, covered from head to foot in the choking red dust of our progress and rejoicing in the prospect of a good soaking in a canvas bath prepared by a willing bearer.

I am sitting by myself on a boulder in the jungle, not far from a small village where the smell of wood-smoke is strong and fragrant and women can be seen rolling out chapattis on flat stones with their feet or making cakes of buffalo-dung for fuel. There is a sudden trumpeting and swishing noise on the jungle track and there, only a few yards from me is an elephant, no zoo-bound beast but a genuine working elephant with a great load of logs on his back and his master by his side, urging him on with unearthly cries. I am so surprised that I stand up, with an absurd impulse to salute this wonder. The Indian laughs, showing red, betel-stained gap-teeth in a fine, friendly smile. Does the sahib seem as strange to him as the elephant does to me?

Strangest of all, I am lying on my canvas bed, looking at the big clear stars overhead through the meshes of the mosquito net secured for convenience to the tailboard of my truck, and listening, without fear, to the incessant slithering and whispering of countless snakes moving about among the coarse grass and large pink and blue flowers which grow everywhere in the sandy ground.

These were long, copper-coloured snakes, quite harmless. There was another kind of snake, however, which I had already heard a lot about when I was with the regiment. This was the banded krait, which looked like a short length of string on a dusty road. Its venom, according to the excitable Major Balderton, would 'have you whirling round like a catherine wheel and dead in six minutes' – or was it six seconds? The only thing to do, if you were bitten by one of these killers, was to cut out the affected part with a razor-blade. Major Balderton accordingly issued razor-blades to 'all personnel'. According to rumour, one man, thinking he had been bitten by a krait, immediately cut his finger off, only to find later on that what had bitten him was not a krait at all but some relatively harmless reptile. This was generally thought a great joke, though Major Balderton, mindful of his status and authority, refrained from the screaming laugh he must have felt welling up inside him.

After a time I was selected for a course at the Army Intelligence School at Karachi. This meant a three-day journey by train all the way from Asansol on the main line, a centre of the strange Bihar coalfield, worked by sad, tamed aboriginals from the forests, tricked or forced into exchanging their bows and arrows and flowers and all-night parties for money-wages, their graceful nakedness for horrible little khaki shorts. We saw Benares and the great Gangetic Plain, the Indus, the Thar Desert – too many wonders to take in on one journey without suffering visual surfeit and mental indigestion.

The weather was now perfect. In the winter of Northern India, every day between November and February is like a hot English summer day and the nights are cool enough for fires. On a certain pre-determined day in January it rains a little. It is also supposed to rain a little, for reasons acceptable to Christians, on Christmas Day by way of celebration. I am not certain that this is true.

I did not care for Karachi. Even its European Club, though palatial compared with that of Ranchi, seemed rather boring. So, on the whole, did the Intelligence School, in spite of its Commandant, an Ulsterman who, most unsuitably, would shout 'Hi!' as he appeared at his lecturer's desk in the morning, the assembled officers being required to answer 'Ho!' He was like an eccentric schoolmaster dressed in uniform, and many officers laboured hard to perfect their imitations of his voice and stiff, pedantic manner. It would not have been surprising if, at the end of the course, we had all been tested for taking him off accurately and awarded marks accordingly.

This was the time of Stalingrad, of Alamein, of the turning-point of the war, when the defeat of Germany, and consequently the defeat of Japan, was already a foregone conclusion. But most of the exercises we did on the Intelligence course, both in the lecture-room and 'in the field', were still based on the assumption that the Germans would break through the Caucasus, occupy the Middle East and Persia and then try to invade India. Some of the more enjoyable parts of the course were simulated intelligence exercises based on this already far-fetched hypothesis. There was a good 'scenario' or charade in which the German invasion of the Indus Valley was supported by a Muslim uprising and a re-run of the

Indian Mutiny. I was responsible for the role of the Pir Pagaro or some other specimen of those fanatical religious leaders who were always about at that time, rallying ferocious tribesmen, disappearing and re-appearing in a bewildering way, always 'with a price on their heads' and described as 'a thorn in the side of the British Raj'. I invented the Thargs, a fanatical sect who lived in caves in the Sind Desert but were in wireless (or perhaps telepathic) communication with the German High Command. As the first panzers appeared on our side of the Khyber they were ready to 'rise as one man', sacking the bazaars, wrecking trains and sniping from mosques at the British and those Indians who remained loyal to us. As these Thargs had red or even blond hair and blue eyes (they were, of course, direct descendants of Alexander's soldiers) the Germans regarded them as Aryans and Dr Rosenberg, the Nazi racial theoretician, had suggested to Hitler that a Greater Thargia, under German protection, should be set up in most of what is now called Pakistan – an entity not all that much more absurd. I became so enthusiastic about these imaginary Thargs that I was ordered to abolish them.

We also went out on exercises. One of these, which involved wading through foul-smelling mangrove swamps on the Indus Delta, was particularly nasty and dangerous. One officer, who could not swim, was, I think, actually drowned. My own request for a taxi to take me back to dry land and beat the steadily rising tide which was flooding these muddy, noisome creeks, was ill-taken by the directing staff. On another exercise in the Sind Desert, which at least had a definite purpose, map-reading, I found myself separated from the rest by being the only man to read the map correctly. Alone in this barren country, which yet seemed able to support a few goats (since there was no vegetation, what on earth did they feed on?) I sat down on a stony hillside, wondering, as so often, what I was doing here in this improbable place. The winter sun shone in a perfectly blue sky, enough to warm me most pleasantly but not to burn or turn me much browner than I already was; I looked about me into this stony nothingness and felt a surge of that 'oceanic' feeling of inexplicable happiness which even at twenty-nine, as I have said, I was beginning to fear was lost for ever. I felt I might just as well stay where I was, letting this feeling flood over me and through me, as go anywhere else or do anything else. I had an absurd feeling that 'Aunt' might appear. But when some of my fellow intelligence students appeared instead, fiddling with their maps and compasses, I joined them just the same.

There was much that was absurd about the course. It is not really very difficult to be an Intelligence Officer, unless you are concerned with coding, cryptography and all those techniques which in other theatres of war were already beginning to have decisive importance. But we in India and on the borders of Burma were, as the English newspapers put it, 'the Forgotten Front'. As the German offensive into India never materialised, it was to remain forgotten for some time.

One day the Commandant, after going through his 'Hi!' and 'Ho!' procedure, announced that we were going to have a lecture on some of the main races of India – Sikhs, Mahrattas, Punjabi 'Mussulmen', Bengalis and so on. Specimens of various races, dressed in appropriate costume, were paraded before us as in a 'mannequin parade' while an officer pointed out their characteristics with his swagger stick – the last time, I think, I saw this profoundly undemocratic artefact actually used (I had long ago lost mine). As the assorted Indians, smiling in an obliging way, paraded before us, there were some ribald comments from my companions. But only the specimen Sikh looked at all angry. It was as well he had no sword with him.

On the whole it would be true to say that except for those in the Indian Army, who came into personal contact with Indian troops, mostly of the favoured 'martial races', some of whom were now being commissioned, most English (or British) people in India regarded Indians as patently inferior and even ridiculous. When I was with my regiment Major Balderton had ticked me off for speaking Urdu with an authentic accent (though without any real 'gift for languages' I am exceptionally good at mimicking accents). As Major Balderton explained, it was simply not done to speak any Indian language unless with an English accent, preferably that of Camberley.

English women, as is well known, were more habitually rude to Indians than English men. But it was easy to get into the habit of treating them with disdain, of shouting at them for their inefficiency, procrastination, vagueness, weakness in spatial relations or sense of time. Most people found that characteristic oblique nod of the head, which seems to indicate 'yes' and 'no' at the same time, particularly infuriating. I found it delightful and convenient for expressing various shades of unmeaning. I soon found myself, now there was no Major Balderton about to tick me off, using this gesture myself. I still do. I also occasionally use that curious spiral upward movement of the hand and wrist – so attractive in the narrow-boned Indian – which, especially in conjunction with the oblique nod, expresses the complex ambiguity which is said to lie in the very soul of India.

The Intelligence course finished (I had learned a lot without being aware of it), we returned to our units – in my case, the 15th Indian Corps in its rajah's palace in Bihar. It was, as it happened, on the point of moving forward towards the frontier of Burma, where our troops confronted the Japanese in small concentrations in mountainous, jungle country inhabited by non-Indian aboriginal tribesmen such as the Karens and the Nagas.

Nothing much was happening on this 'Forgotten Front' except for a little desultory shelling and patrolling. It was the spring of 1943 and the Japanese, already beginning to be pushed back from the extreme limits of their 'Greater East Asia Co-prosperity Sphere', had no time to spare for their Indian Front. As an intelligence officer I worked on information concerning the Indian National Army which Subhas Chandra Bose, the 'Bengali Fascist', a remarkable and, as it was to turn out, tragic figure, was recruiting from Indian prisoners of war taken in Malaya, Singapore and Burma, and preparing for an eventual invasion of India. I also studied the Japanese-occupied railway system in South-East Asia, with particular attention to making lists of locomotives. But my most interesting work, on the whole, was a study of the private lives of important Japanese generals. Information on this, as on other subjects which concerned military intelligence, was graded in degrees of reliability ranging from 'A' – 'information from very reliable sources' – to 'G' – 'bazaar rumours'. I have since found this system of classification valuable in civilian life. As for the Japanese generals, they did not seem a very exciting lot. Perhaps there was simply not enough information about them. So I invented one – let us call him General Yamaha Mitsutachi – a one-eyed man in his late forties who had spent some of his early years in Bradford, learning the textile trade, whose inmost secrets, needless to say, he discovered in typical Japanese fashion, at once sending them back to Japan for imitation. He had also discovered the secret formulae for Doncaster Butterscotch, Pontefract Cakes, Harrogate Toffee, parkin and Yorkshire pudding and thought up the brilliant idea of building factories in Japan to manufacture these articles, calling the associated workers' estates 'Doncaster', 'Pontefract', 'Harrogate' and so on, so that 'Made in Pontefract' would be a legitimate description of the contents of green-lettered tins which yet had something odd and obscurely Japanese about them.

While in Bradford Mitsutachi had been insulted by Willy Gaunt (a legendary Bradford magnate notorious for his meanness who, though a millionaire, still lodged with his mother for a small weekly rent) in the 'French Restaurant' of the Midland Hotel, where he was entertaining Gaunt to a sumptuous luncheon. He returned to

Japan with the words 'little yellow monkey' festering in his soul and with a burning lust for vengeance. Joining the army, he soon rose to general rank, mystifying his fellow-officers by shouting, in the English he had learned in Yorkshire, 'Bah Gum, I'll get my own back if it's the last thing I do' in a ferocious way and poring over Japanese military maps of the West Riding in which such places as 'Frizinghall', 'Cleckheaton' and 'Gomersal' were ringed with angry scarlet, prime targets for his revenge.

For a few weeks or months I passed my time in such harmless pursuits, enjoying the open air life and the beauties of the jungle until I was recalled and attached to the newly formed Indian Army Public Relations Directorate, which had been invented, elevated into a Department of the General Staff and rapidly expanded into an 'empire' by a remarkable, energetic, red-haired Scot, Brigadier Ivor Jehu. Its officers included, besides myself, some remarkable drop-outs and eccentrics who gave me a lot of material for a fantastic novel which, though I made copious notes, never got written.

One of the main characters was an officer who, while on a motiveless tour of Southern India, got so drunk that he fell out of a train in a remote jungle and was picked up by some kindly aboriginals who nursed him back to health with magical herbs. In return he had nothing to offer except some handouts issued by the Directorate about new types of light tank operated by paraffin which, it was hoped, would strike terror into the Japanese. Delighted, these kindly people tore them into small pieces and sowed them in one of the fields they roughly hacked out of the forest (they used what is called 'the slash and burn' type of cultivation). Soon a miraculous kind of giant maize sprang up. The aboriginals, regarding Captain Snoddie as a minor deity, implored him to stay with them for ever.

This he was glad to do. But on an evil day, tiring of the rice beer which was their only form of intoxicant – he had to drink it in such prodigious quantities even to approach his normal alcoholic intake that he was in danger of becoming dropsical and immobile – he set off for the nearest town, many miles away, in the hope of getting a bottle of whisky. There he fell in with a treacherous ayurvedic dentist, who detained him with flattery and atrocious home-distilled spirit, took his money off him and eventually handed him over to the local magistrate, the hunchbacked Dr Sen, who informed the military. Taken back to Delhi under escort, he was given such a terrible dressing down by Brigadier Jehu himself that he burst into tears and was at once promoted major on compassionate grounds. Another character . . . but enough of these fantasies . . .

The function of the Directorate was supposed to be 'liaison' with the Indian Press, both English and vernacular, and the incessant feeding of Indian journalists with material presenting our forces in a favourable light. It also arranged visits by Indian journalists and public men to Army, Navy and Air Force units and formations and dealt with parties of visitors and 'VIPs' from England, observers from allied and neutral countries and other such matters. It also had other, less publicised functions. When I joined it I did not cease to be an intelligence officer.

Although I am very cowardly by nature I do not think this move, which placed me many hundreds of miles further away from the Japanese, was deliberately contrived by me for that reason. It was one of those chances by which, as I have mentioned before, I found myself, for instance, leaving a particular place just before it was heavily bombed. Nor was my subsequent life in the Army entirely without danger, physical and mental. What my new role did involve (and in this I was greatly privileged) was the opportunity to travel, often entirely alone, to almost all parts of India during the next three years, and to meet more Indians than was at all usual for a British officer.

My first posting was to Agra, headquarters of Central Command, to which I was attached. There, in the spacious cantonment, I was allotted a billet appropriate to my new rank of Captain, a small apartment in a row of brick huts along one side of the maidan, a large square open space recalling part of the Stray at Harrogate rather than anything else. It was, however, mid-June, in the very hot season, with shade temperatures reaching 120 degrees, dust storms, prickly heat, dhobi's itch (an unpleasant eczema of the crotch which the good medical Captain da Cruz treated with the well-known Army cure-all, gentian violet) and, during hours of duty, a condition of lassitude which made it difficult to do anything much except sit at a table in my office hut sifting through papers on every conceivable subject. A punkah waved backwards and forwards overhead, operated by a string held in the strong big toe of an elderly Indian (aged about thirty, I suppose) who sprawled outside on the verandah. In addition, two younger Indians occupied themselves all day in throwing buckets of cold water over the wicker screens, called *khus khus tatti*, which leaned against the outer walls.

What emerges from this haze of lassitude? Now that the German threat to invade India, if it had ever really existed, had receded, probably for ever, now that Mussolini had fallen and the Italians, or most of them, had surrendered (many Italian prisoners were beginning to arrive in India), HQ Central Command at Agra was just about as far as it was possible to get in the Northern Hemisphere, apart from Siberia and North America, from the conflict which every day and night was killing and maiming thousands of people, tearing historic buildings apart and filling the world with grief and hatred. The fact is that we at Agra thought very little about these things. What I was seeing there was a rather obscure corner of the British Raj still in being. The malis still tended the fine lawns and brilliant flower-beds of official bungalows. At night the chowkidar, or night-watchman, still went his rounds, coughing horribly at intervals and feebly tapping his stave on the ground. The dhobi plied his trade. The darzi, or tailor, still sat cross-legged at the door of his shop, obsequiously taking orders for bush-shirts or pyjamas of heavy Indian silk, promising to have them ready without fail within a week and still promising the same after a week, two weeks, three weeks.

The memsahibs, whether they were officers' wives, in which case many of their husbands were away in Africa or Italy or on the fringes of Burma, or the wives of officials of the Indian Civil Service, in which case their husbands were with them when they were not on tour, lived very much in the old style. They gave dinner parties as they had always given them. The port circulated in the proper manner when the ladies retired and the men were left to talk about whatever they had always talked about: promotion, demotion, the impossibility of Indians being able to rule themselves ('give them independence and within a week there won't be a rupee or a virgin between Peshawar and Delhi'). As I was thought to be quite amusing, I was occasionally asked to these dinner parties. Once, when I had had a good deal to drink, no very uncommon thing, I said, à propos of the Russian campaign, that the Russian Communists were not really our allies and that we should not be helping them in any way, since it was better that the Germans should weaken their odious regime and if possible destroy it. There was a bit of silence at this. A Major Atherstone-Smith, rising from his place and going scarlet in the face, said I ought to be court-martialled. I heard nothing further, but noticed his face bulging slightly whenever I came across him afterwards. I wonder whether he still believed in our gallant Communist allies ten or even five years later?

The monsoon, my second in India, broke soon after this, cooling things down a bit to the great relief of all, and once again rain came down not only by the bucketful but at least once in the form of large jagged lumps of ice which probably killed a few Indians. Indians, as everybody knew, could be killed very easily, which was one reason, Major Balderton had often mentioned with his mad cackle, why you had to avoid striking servants, however maddened you might be by their dim-witted incompetence.

At about the beginning of September I took a period of furlough in Simla, the nearest sizeable hill-station. In peacetime the Government of India moved up there en masse in the hot weather. In wartime they stayed in Delhi, but most of their wives and daughters still went to the hills. As young or youngish officers came and went, the more personable of these ladies found themselves greatly in demand and able to pick and choose. After a few days I 'found myself' having an affaire with Margaret, the pretty, fair-haired, blue-eyed wife of an ICS official. She was not, perhaps, the most stunningly beautiful or lucidly intelligent of the European women in Simla, but she was not without admirers. I was soon in love, and so, she told me, was she. I was the more innocent of the two. But at least she made me feel as happy and contented during that leave in Simla as it was in my nature to be.

We met in the mornings at the Green Room Club, part of the Simla Amateur Dramatic Society which at that time was rehearsing *Young Woodley*. We walked about the Mall or among the forest paths on the steep slopes of the spur of the Himalaya on which Simla is built. A Scotch mist, the mountain equivalent of the monsoon, wavered and floated among the pines and strange-looking, rambling bungalows. At certain points, when the mist parted, you could look down beyond the precipices to where, thousands of feet below, the great plains burned in the heat.

Quite by chance, while I was in Simla, I ran into Richard Storry, who had helped me to make Dickensian grotesques out of some of our seniors at Ranchi. He was studying at the Army School of Japanese studies in Simla, and so absorbed had he become with Japanese matters that already his square, reddish, very English face was beginning to acquire a Japanese look. He asked me to dinner at the School, where there was an interesting assortment of officers. One was a man who later on became a best-selling novelist. Another was a huge, moustachioed, bearlike White Russian, born at Mukden in Manchuria. He bent a few iron bars for our amusement (he claimed to have been a strong man in a Korean-owned circus), then bellowed songs in Russian and other languages. We played several traditional mess-games, such as climbing round the walls without touching the floor and billiard fives, a painful, taxing game which involves batting billiard balls about with your bare palms, until we were too drunk to continue.

When the end of my leave came soon afterwards Margaret and I took sad leave of each other, promising to write continually and meet again at the first possible opportunity. Delhi, after all, was only about 150 miles from Agra, quite near in Indian terms. We met only once again, about two years later, and could think of nothing whatever to say to each other. But in the meantime, at odd times and places, I met several officers who had met her on their periods of leave. What we all shared had become, sadly, an unspoken joke.

My fellow staff officers at Agra were a mixed lot. Some were remarkable drop-outs, regular officers like the nominal head of my own department, Lieutenant-Colonel Huzzifreak, a man wizened and prematurely old from service in India. He had been with the 'Piffers' or the 'Paffers' or some such regiment on the North-West Frontier. His main purpose in life was to do as little as possible, which at moments of highest achievement meant absolutely nothing. But he was friendly and amiable enough, his main cross being the third officer in our department, an Indian who was both eager to please and resentful of us two Europeans. When thwarted in any way, such as having his suggestion of going on a tour which would include his native city of Nagpur turned down, he went grey in the face with frustration and anger. But Colonel Huzzifreak dealt with him most effectively by his favourite method of doing and saying absolutely nothing.

Perhaps the most remarkable of my fellow staff officers was Major Charles Rankin, a very good-looking man of upper-class background, not more than two or three years older than myself. He was delightfully urbane and amusing and never at a loss. He was exactly the sort of person I have always (well, sometimes) wanted to be. What his real function in the Headquarters was I never knew – it may have been as ambiguous as my own – but his style and title was General Staff Officer Grade II (Chemical Warfare). Since there was not the remotest chance that chemical weapons would be used in the area of Central Command this meant that he appeared – whatever the real truth of the matter – to have absolutely nothing whatever to do. A good deal of paper came to him daily from GHQ in New Delhi. A lot of it was about defence against mustard gas, phosgene and other substances used on the Western Front in the First World War, or about the use of bleach, brown paper and other things I had last heard of at Topsham Barracks in Exeter. He threw away most of this paper but kept a single large blue file marked 'Most Secret' (the vulgar, ungrammatical, objectionable American 'Top Secret' had not yet been introduced, and was perhaps never to be used in Central Command, that castle of indolence where only rumours penetrated from the tiresome, noisy outer world).

Major Rankin, whose social contacts were obviously on a higher level and often took him away 'on tour', did not attend the Saturday evening dances at the Agra Club, a commodious and agreeable building in one corner of the maidan which for certain purposes also functioned as an officers' mess. Here was a bar, a billiard-room, a dining-room, a small, variegated library which contained, as well as the works of Maud Diver, many of the novels of William Gerhardi, such as his best one, *My Wife's the Least of It*, which I read several times, and a ballroom. It had pleasant gardens, a capacious verandah and terraces where, now that the weather was turning into the wonderful North Indian winter, it was pleasant to sit drinking glass after delicious glass of fresh lime juice, gin and soda.

At the dances a small string orchestra of Indian musicians played such numbers as 'As Time Goes By', 'That Lovely Week-end' and even, by request, 'Begin the Beguine', 'Sand in My Shoes' and 'Stormy Weather' (my own favourites, heavy with nostalgia no more than four years old) in an odd, unreal style. Were these musicians more at home playing authentic Indian music? I never found out and in my early days in Agra I scarcely knew this music existed. I had heard only the debased film music played on raucous gramophones in the bazaar.

The Saturday night dances were mainly an occasion for getting drunk, playing billiards or both. But they also offered an opportunity to meet European ladies who were not, I think, socially of the best class, that is, the class of those who gave dinner parties, cocktail parties and, on occasion, dances of their own. At one of these dances in the Club I met a woman whose husband was said to be a prisoner of war. I had been told, I think by the Station Staff Officer, a man of homosexual temperament, that she had a bad reputation and should be avoided. He even told me he had thought of having her expelled from the cantonment. But in fact he never carried out this threat because he was shortly afterwards required to leave himself.

Harriet was a very small, gamine woman of about thirty, not particularly good-looking but most attractive because of her vivacity, intelligence and the pale reddish hair which is found only among Scotswomen and goes with that white, slightly metallic, freckled skin which for me has always transmitted a sexual current of very high voltage.

We got into conversation, laughed, drank (she turned out to be one of those women who can drink most men under the table) and danced or pretended to dance (I have never been able to dance, but on a small, crowded dance-floor could go through the required

motions), under the reproving eyes of several of the officers' ladies
who, perhaps for reasons of their own, may have shared the Station
Staff Officer's opinion. We slipped away from the Club, crossed
the dark maidan to the small bungalow where she lived. I had
seldom, if ever, enjoyed such pleasures. I left by climbing through
the window in the early hours of the morning, almost bumping into
Major Atherstone-Smith whose billet was in a nearby bungalow
and whom I had noticed earlier on playing billiards and getting
ritually drunk. We did not speak, but I could see he had registered
another item to add to my anti-Soviet remarks.

I saw him again next day at the Club where, after sleeping off
the various exertions of the night before, it was customary to drink
an enormous amount of gin, followed by a huge Sunday lunch
of curry, followed by another spell of sleep. Forgetting or only
half-remembering Margaret of Simla, I was now in love with Harriet
as well. She was quicker, more amusing, better able to share my
fantasies and jokes about the denizens of Central Command. She
could drink like a man, liked music; and she was not respectable.
That was the first of many nights, either in Harriet's room or in my
billet, where my quiet Hindu bearer, sleeping on his charpoy or
string-bed just outside the back door, must have heard those lovers'
gasps and moans, but gave no sign next morning.

What was I doing when I was not making love, drinking,
talking nonsense or shuffling papers in an Army hut? 'Staff work'
in Central Command consisted mainly in distributing memoranda,
the chief amusement in that being the concept of distribution
itself (should a copy of this or that go to 'Chaplains' or 'Education'
or 'Welfare'?). Many were the flashes of colour which relieved
the khaki monotony of the well-cut 'bush jackets' and long
trousers which had now replaced the ludicrous uniform that had
made Major Balderton regard me as 'a character from Noël
Coward'. I wore the red armband of the General Staff myself.
But there were other armbands of different colours, as well as

coloured tabs and hatbands marking the rank of full Colonel and above – purple for medical, green for dentistry and pale blue for education, the last two being real collectors' items. Not many people, I imagine, have ever met a full Colonel of the Education Corps. Even in remote, obscure Central Command that organis- ation was beginning the work of indoctrination among the forces which was to help, later on, to secure a landslide victory for the Labour Party and the sensational ousting of Winston Churchill. Even then, I think, it was clear to me what these people were up to. It disturbed and alarmed me. So, in the larger world, did the close collaboration of Churchill, Roosevelt and Stalin and the enormous amount of support the Western Allies were giving the Russian Communist forces, enabling them to turn the Germans back and go on to an offensive which was not to end until they had occupied the eastern half of Europe. But on the whole I kept my own counsel. I had no more scenes with Major Atherstone-Smith. He would probably have refused to stay in the same room with me now that I was offending him not only by my political views but by my low moral standards.

The second winter of my life in India was beginning. The perfect weather came round again, as regular as clockwork. The nights were cold enough for fires (an additional charm for love-making). It was also a good time to go 'on tour' and that is what I was now doing, visiting subsidiary headquarters and units throughout the area which stretched from Lucknow in the United Provinces to the borders of Hyderabad in the south and included, in the Central Provinces, the enchanted jungles and mountains of the Vindhya and the Satpura. My work – whatever it may have been – also meant that unlike most British or even Indian Army officers I met a great many Indian civilians. Ordered by Major Balderton and others to regard such people as not merely unspeakable but almost nonexistent, I now found that I could get on very well with them. They were fond of jokes, for one thing. They were not so much conservative as immovable, taking it for granted that as far as their daily lives were concerned nothing would ever change.

This applied particularly to Hindus, who, however westernised, still observed the ancient ceremonies and lived by the intricate rules of the caste system, with its multitude of sub-castes and sub-sub-castes underlying the pattern of the four great castes which, originally based on *varna*, colour, the light-skinned ancient Aryan conquerors of India had devised (or had it devised them?) to keep themselves aloof from the dark-skinned aboriginal inhabitants.

Just as Catholics can joke about their religion so, I found, could Hindus joke about their caste system. It is not, of course, a class system, nor is it based on money. This means, in principle, that it can never change, and it explains why, even now, Hindu India still has the only social system in the world which has not been absorbed or taken over by western liberalism and technology. No wonder I found it so attractive. And the system, so abhorrent to progressive people, had odd results which amused and enchanted me as much as the Hindus themselves.

One day, the Indian officer in our castle of indolence in Agra, now free of its wickerwork cooling apparatus, asked a clerk who was a Brahmin and of higher caste than himself to get him a glass of water. This he did unthinkingly. The officer, taking the glass, burst out laughing. 'Now you have defiled yourself! You, a Brahmin, have brought me, a Vaidhya, a glass of water. Now you must go to the temple and pay ten rupees to get yourself purified!' The Brahmin clerk, though somewhat mortified, also laughed and for a few moments the pair of them went through an elaborate ritual of oblique head-movements and spiral motions of the forearm. But the clerk, although he appreciated the joke, certainly did go and get himself purified. It would have been unthinkable not to do so.

When I think of that time, a multitude of dreamlike scenes come into my mind. With a congenial fellow-officer, who belonged to a

Gurkha regiment but was on attachment to the staff and became, for the time he was in Agra, a good friend and companion, I bicycled the short distance to the Taj Mahal several times and saw its ivory splendour, already familiar, perhaps too familiar, by moonlight and by flaming sunset. For all its beauty it did not produce the always hoped for numinous feeling. I was worried about this. Was this the end of youth? I was now in my thirtieth year, and to a man of thirty that already seems the beginning of age.

I peer through the wrong end of the telescope again. Now I am in Lucknow, city of poetry, music and gardens, drinking tea with a mysterious Muslim merchant in the main room of his big, yellow-brown mansion, hidden behind high, dung-coloured walls and a thick, iron-studded doorway in an obscure alleyway smelling of mingled urine, incense and wood-smoke. We talk, and as we talk there is a continual giggling and whispering behind the elaborate lattice screen which runs along one end of the room. 'Please pay no attention,' he says. 'It is the women. They are curious about you.' He gets up now and again, excusing himself with elaborate courtesy, goes behind the screen of the zenana and bids his wives – he has four, the maximum allowed by Islamic law, denoting that, unlike most Muslim, he is rich enough to maintain them – remember their manners. But the giggling and whispering soon begin again. I have an impression of dark eyes peering through the interstices of the screen.

Later that evening we dine in my hotel, set in splendid gardens and with as fine a collection of turbaned, soft-footed servants as any old-fashioned novelist could imagine. Then he takes me to a concert. It is in the open air, in a garden where the faint splash of fountains can be heard in the background of that music which is like no other. Strange, soothing, hypnotic, the concert goes on all through the warm night, under the big stars, as various players of sitar, dilruba, tablas and so on, as well as singers and reciters, come and go, and members of the audience also come and go. Vividly coloured mineral water, bright green, scarlet, purple, orange but all tasting the same, intolerably sweet, as Indians like it, are on sale, together with sugar balls, pan, betel nut and various other substances which Indians maintain, no doubt rightly, are 'beneficial to blood'. It is as unlike a European concert as can be imagined. Listening to the sonorities of that music, insidious and seductive, making our Western music seem, for the moment, noisy and square-cut by comparison, and even crass, I am enslaved. I am still there as the subtly coloured Indian dawn invades the sky and the sun rises quickly for another hot English summer day.

Now I am in the big tent, carpeted like the tents of the Mogul court as it made its way from Delhi to Kashmir, of an officers' mess in some training area in the jungle, enjoying the drinks and jokes – some at the expense of 'staff wallahs' – and surprised, perhaps, to find that some unlikely Indian Army officer has not only done some quite tolerable water-colours in his spare moments but has a copy of 'A Shropshire Lad' in his pocket and knows most of it by heart.

I stop my truck by the roadside in some remote place in the jungle in order to relieve myself among the trees. I hear a flute playing in the distance. There is a fine waterfall, sunny glades, fallen leaves. A path leads down into the forest. I follow it a short way, tempted for a moment to go further, find the flute-player, join the aboriginal tribe which lives somewhere in this paradise, wed one or more of their slender women. What an utterly stupid idea! I go back to the road and my driver looks at me curiously as I order him to proceed. To him this is the abode of savages, deadly snakes, wild beasts, the terrible wild bees which nest in the crevices of the red, sandstone cliffs – a place to get away from as soon as possible.

Now I am walking in some godforsaken military camp somewhere in the great Gangetic Plain, talking to who knows what bewildered brigadier about the state of public opinion (what can that possibly mean in Indian terms?) in Cawnpore or Allahabad; about the Indian National Army; how many people have heard of it or sympathise with it; how, if at all, they get news of it (I have been listening, perhaps, to English-language broadcasts by the Japanese radio in Burma and heard a march-past of detachments from the nations of the Greater East Asia Co-Prosperity Sphere, 'Eight Corners under one Roof', which sounds like a parody of a Nuremberg rally coming from another planet); and my eyes stray to the great river with its shoals and sandy islands, whose further shore, two miles away, I cannot distinguish from the mists of evening.

I am accompanying a party of visiting Afghan generals round military installations and ammunition factories. None speak more than a few words of English. Some have done a course at the Potsdam Military Academy and speak some German. Had the Germans entered India, as it had seemed they might have done less than a year before, these well-mannered Afghans would have raised no great objection; now they know which is going to be the winning side. One speaks of his love of Persian poetry; invites me, when the war is over, to stay with him in Kabul and see his rose gardens. What Communist gun-emplacement occupies those gardens now? And what would he have said if he had known that many years after, one of the results of the war would be the destruction of his own country?

Towards the end of February 1944 I went with a party of Indian newspaper editors to the 'Forgotten Front' on the border of India and Burma. It included one Englishman, the agreeable editor of the *Civil and Military Gazette* of Lahore, Kipling's old paper, among a dozen or so Indians, mostly editors of vernacular papers. We foregathered in Calcutta; then travelled by a very slow train to Dimapur on the Ganges, crossing the great river (I did not fail to remind myself that it had flowed out of Tibet) by ferry and staying in a base-camp which because of the great number of *lingams*, stone phallic symbols, to be seen round about, was called by the British soldiery 'Penis Park'. From there we went by road to Kohima and Imphal, headquarters of the Fourth Indian Army, a beautiful place in a lunar crater surrounded by forests and jagged mountains. To reach it we had to drive perilously on serpentine roads hacked out of precipices by gangs of tribal labourers who worked continuously to repair sections cut by landslides. At certain places could be seen, a thousand feet down, the rusting burned out wrecks of trucks just like our own.

I got on pretty well with these Indian editors, who, though at first suspicious, responded well to teasing and fantasy. There was trouble one morning when one of them came to me complaining that one of the others had stolen his watch. I ordered them all to 'parade' before me, then told them that if they did not behave themselves I would have them all taken to a quarry and shot. This greatly amused them. But it was not long before the editor whose watch was missing told me that it had mysteriously reappeared. One of the others looked sheepish and avoided my eye. What, I wondered, would Major Balderton have said to this? Would he have given his mad, cackling laugh? I doubt it.

The weather was still quite cool and the mountain air intoxicating. We drove eastward, over roads even more hair-raising, to Tamu, just on the border. It was deserted. All around were mountainous green forests of paradisial beauty. To the east those forests held the Japanese enemy.

Back in Imphal I found my friend Richard Storry, now attached to headquarters as a Japanese expert and interrogator of such Japanese as allowed themselves to be taken prisoner. At the moment there was only one, a wounded man brought back unconscious from a patrol. I looked at him with curiosity. He would say nothing, but only demanded the means of killing himself to avoid dishonour. We dined with the amusing Resident in Imphal, a 'Native State' with an eccentric Rajah; it was all immensely civilised, in a remote part of the Raj, where not even rumours of possible independence had penetrated and the names of Gandhi and Nehru were scarcely known.

We flew back next month in a rickety old Dakota from the Imphal airstrip. As we waited to board the plane I noted that it had brought, on its flight from Calcutta, an eminent personage. It was Orde Wingate, newly created Major-General, Churchill's protégé, inventor of the Chindits, the Long Range Penetration Groups which operated far behind the Japanese lines, with the loss of many lives and with dubious results. The General did not know it any more than we did, but he was on his last journey. A little later he was fated to die in an air crash in the Burmese jungle – his disappearance not entirely unwelcome to the orthodox generals he had overridden with what they thought of, perhaps rightly, as his hare-brained schemes.

I watched this famous personage with fascination. He looked every bit as eccentric as his reputation had it: a tall, gaunt figure in a pith helmet (was he the very last soldier to wear one?); a book (the Bible? Clausewitz? *The Oxford Book of English Verse?*) under one arm; in one hand a blue flower of a species unknown to me. All went in awe of him. He was said, among other things, to sit outside his tent in the evenings shooting at wasps with his revolver. I was glad I was not under his command, I reflected, as we flew creakingly westward over the floodlands of East Bengal (the pilot could not resist an ancient joke at the expense of non-flyers: 'Hold on to your hats; one engine gone; but I think with a bit of luck we'll just make it').

Back in Agra, in the dreamland of Central Command, tired and dirty from the journey, I was met by eager Harriet as if I were a hero. I had hardly time to take off my revolver-belt before she had got me into bed. Next day there were two items of news. One came from my mother, a telegram dated a month before, telling me that my father, who had been suffering from leukaemia for several months, had died. The other news was that the Japanese, in those beautiful jungles I had just been looking at, had started their long-prepared offensive, their last throw of the war, as it turned out, and had begun to cut the roads leading to Imphal. 'Bad luck, Wharton,' said some aged Brigadier, 'you've just missed all the fun.'

It was not long before Imphal was almost surrounded, unreachable except by air, and the bloody battle of Kohima, where I had sat not long ago admiring the scenery from the balcony of the comfortable *dak* bungalow, was providing all the fun of that sort which anybody could wish for. The 'Forgotten Front' was forgotten no longer. But once again, by a curious chance, I had just left a place where the most horrific things were about to happen for a place where nothing much happened at all.

Now it was March and the fine North Indian winter was over. It grew hotter and more trying every day. As it grew hotter Harriet grew colder, to me at any rate, for I think this fickle and animated woman had not been without suitors during the month I had been away. Her first warm welcome turned to tiresomeness and recrimination, then to positive aloofness. She had taken up with some young major or other and although I did not love her or value her very much except as an agreeable bed and drinking companion, I felt pangs of jealousy greater than I have ever felt before or since. I debased myself, made myself foolish, lost my temper in public, wept in private, knowing, of course, that if I had any hope of getting her back this was the most certain way of losing it. There was, of course, though I did not think of it at the time, an excellent remedy for this humiliating experience. I could have 'wangled' my way back to my regiment, then in the thick of the fighting on the Burma Front. It was what the heroes of romantic novels did, and what was sometimes done even in real life. But I was no hero.

Instead of being a hero, I went on a month's leave to Kashmir, pining at first and caring nothing for the privilege of being in a place which to people back in England and Yorkshire was a fabulous paradise ('Pale hands I loved beside the Shalimar' – Mrs Woodford-Finden's 'Four Indian Love Lyrics' were one of the very few pieces of recorded music in my parents' house). I thought about my father, of how I had been brought to misjudge a man whose bursts of lunatic bad temper were perfectly explicable and whose underlying goodness, generosity and even humour I had understood so little. I had a thoroughly morbid time.

After a bit I bestirred myself, went out to see the sights of the place (including the Shalimar Garden with its stone pavilions, formal flower-beds, fountains, rills and strutting hoopoes). I consoled myself as best I could with an officer's wife I can hardly remember. It was not a good leave. My pretence to myself that I was gathering material for a novel about the Public Relations Directorate was not convincing, though I made a lot of notes of oddities of behaviour, coincidences and inane remarks. I also thought of writing an *Anatomy of Boredom*, on the lines of Burton's *Anatomy of Melancholy*, and made some notes on this fascinating subject on which I was so well qualified to write. But the more I thought about it the more mysterious and unfathomable it seemed. It would be necessary to trace it back to the time, if time it could be called, before the Fall of the Rebel Angels. It would be necessary to deal with all aspects of Accidie, the deadly sin of which, out of all the deadly sins, I was most guilty. The prevalence of Accidie in mediaeval monasteries, where the monks must have drowsed away on summer afternoons, fuddled on the strong ale of which, according to the records, they had such a generous allowance ... no wonder the manuscripts they were supposed to be copying were full of textual corruptions which hundreds of years later were to delight the rigorous mind of Professor Housman ... The sin of Accidie, alone, I thought, was a lifetime's study, and that was only one strand in the great *Anatomy of Boredom* ...

When I returned to the intolerable plains of India and to what must, I suppose, be called the real world, the war had moved into a new phase. D-Day had come and the Allies were in France. The Japanese were in retreat and our own Army, commanded by General Slim, the admirable soldier whose maps I had once had the privilege of marking up with my chinagraph pencil, was on the offensive at last. It was fortunate that Wingate, favourite of Churchill, that very bad judge of men who had taken against the admirable Auchinleck and Wavell, was not around to interfere and even, it might be, oust the admirable Slim and claim the credit for victory. For once justice prevailed and the credit went to the one man who deserved it.

From Europe the news was both good and bad. It was good that the Nazis were being defeated. But it was bad, I thought, that the Allies were insisting on 'unconditional surrender'. We heard, perhaps some time after the event, details of the Plot of July 20, of Hitler's escape, of the hideous fate of Stauffenberg and the other heroic Germans who had tried to save their country not only from the Nazis but from the Russian Communists. Was I the only officer in the whole British Army in India who raged against their betrayal, our own failure to help the German Resistance, our rulers' refusal, for whatever reason, even to admit that there *was* a German Resistance?

Soon I was posted to Eastern Army HQ in Calcutta and took my torpor, melancholia and occasional bouts of activity to a billet in the Great Eastern Hotel in Chowringhee, the main street of that atrocious city, with its pullulating slums, its trams hung with white-clad clerks like swarming insects, its sacred cows nuzzling among the vegetable stalls to claim their portion (and what Hindu dare deny them?) and flop down in the middle of the street, obstructing the traffic until they chose, perhaps to oblige some soft-voiced, exceptionally pious devotee, to move; its two fantastic railway stations, Howrah and Sealdah, whose platforms were the only home of thousands of near-starving people, their innumerable children, the brass pots, ragged pallets and images of monkey or elephant gods which were all they owned.

To me, as to most Europeans (and not a few prosperous Indians) this world of fearful poverty and aimless bustle, of continual birth, sickness and death, was simply something 'given'. I did not grieve or agonise over these innumerable wretched human beings; I did not feel ashamed, when eating chocolate cake in Firpo's, the famous tea-shop, when a beggar woman held out her brass bowl. I would give her a few annas, fighting back the hideous joke which forced itself into my mind – to give her chocolate cake instead. I did not even blench when I saw dead bodies by the roadside, any more than did the Indians walking or bicycling past (sometimes, such was the sinuous agility of these narrow-boned people, with three or four on the same bicycle). To them it was a common sight. Next day the bodies would have been removed, not perhaps before the kitehawks always circling overhead made their obscene investigations.

Most of my time in Calcutta seemed to be spent in pointless conferences on this and that. With the end of the war now clearly in sight, the question of India's future began to emerge and become inescapable. I learned something of Indian opinion from people who often showed an uncanny prescience of what was going to happen. I did a half-hour weekly broadcast commentary on the progress of the war. Whether anybody listened to it I never discovered.

My Gurkha friend at Agra had given me an introduction to an agreeable English family, whose father was in the I C S. There were two beautiful and intelligent daughters. The younger was about twenty years old, a student of Indian dancing and music. I grew particularly fond of her and would have been madly in love if she had given the least sign of encouragement. But I was never good at seduction, except of women I had no respect for. Her wise, half-laughing gravity delighted me, but I would not have dreamed – at least do anything more than dream – of laying a finger on her. Now thirty-one, I thought myself far too old for this magical being.

So we were friends. I even found I could tell her about the secret of the Missing Will and the mysterious Curse of the Whartons. She came to dinner with me occasionally at the Great Eastern Hotel, which as well as billeting staff officers, was also the main hotel of Calcutta, full of bustle and confusion. I felt the absurd pride of being seen by fellow-officers with this beautiful young girl.

That May the war in Europe ended. As the hot weather drew towards its intolerable climax I was posted to GHQ New Delhi and employed on propaganda work as well as editing an Army magazine, in which I printed some of my own surrealist stories. Here I found some congenial people in the great, swarming anthill of GHQ not far from the Viceroy's House in Lutyens's glorious, spacious capital. My old acquaintance Major Rankin, he of the chemical warfare, was now an assistant secretary to the Viceroy, the admirable, eccentric Lord Wavell, whom Churchill had treated so badly, evidently mistrusting an obviously honest man. So I did not want for dinner parties and drinks parties with some of the great ones of the earth, from the Viceroy, the amiable and civilised Wavell, downwards. But for the drink which the overwhelmingly charming, well-mannered and mischievous Rankin thoughtfully provided in admirable quantity, these people would probably have terrified me to death.

As usual, I often wondered why I was here and what exactly I was doing. It was my passivity, my tendency to drift with the stream, to take the easy way, to be acted upon rather than act which had brought me here. But I could hardly complain or say I found it intolerable when, on a clear, starlit night I sat with Rankin and other friends in the Mughal Garden of the Viceroy's House, hearing the splash of fountains and the distant rumble of the city, drinking delicious drinks, talking agreeable nonsense and in the end – I was addicted to the habit – falling asleep.

There were many other transitory friends – George Wyndham of the ICS and his wife, the artist 'Haro' Hodson, his cousin Anne

Richmond, an intelligent, attractive girl with remarkably fine green eyes and some literary talent, who had joined a special corps of women designed to operate in the recaptured territories of the Far East as the Japanese were pushed back. She was a heroine indeed. Her reason for joining the corps was to be able to greet her fiancé, David Piper, when he was released from the Japanese prison-camp where he had been since the fall of Singapore. All turned out as she hoped and their story had a happy ending.

Meanwhile preparations were going on at GHQ for the British part in the final act of the war – the comparatively humble one of retaking Singapore, Malaya, the Dutch East Indies and Indo-China. One of those who were working on these plans was Brigadier Enoch Powell, already a byword for his terrifying and meticulous efficiency and his habit of wearing service dress, Sam Browne belt and all, in the hot weather, after the fashion of his predecessors in the Army of the East India Company. To the majority of the staff, who were flopping about in bush shirts, he seemed a formidable eccentric. It was rumoured (correctly) that he read Thucydides and that his ambition was to be Viceroy of India (which, if there were any justice in this world, he would have been). But there was to be no British attack on the Dutch East Indies, or anywhere else. One August evening news came over the wireless that an atomic bomb had been dropped on Japan.

The war was over. It is hard to remember what I and the people I knew felt about the way it ended. There was both shock and relief – relief that the war was over, and shock that technology had moved into another, even more utterly inhuman dimension. There was a victory parade for 'VJ Day' in Delhi as elsewhere. But there was no wild rejoicing. The dismantling of the European empires (with the exception of the Soviet Empire) was about to begin, eagerly abetted by the Americans, whose late President Roosevelt had not been one of my favourites, and the British Raj was clearly high up on the list. Bad news came thick and fast. At the General Election in England the Labour party had won a landslide victory, bemoaned by me and my friends but, as I could not help noticing, received with glee by many of my fellow-officers. They were of the sort who, through the Army Education Corps and other agencies, had been working away steadily throughout the war to bring about this outcome. I learned of it with despair, believing, in my pessimistic way, that there could never be another Conservative Government in England. Nor was there, in my own sense of the word 'conservative', which my experiences in the Army and my 'reactionary' views, reinforced by contact with intelligent Indians and others, had confirmed.

I was offered the choice of going to Japan for a year as part of the somewhat pathetic British contingent of the slightly less pathetic Commonwealth contingent of the Allied but almost entirely American forces of occupation, or taking my turn to await demobilisation, which would mean another six months or so in India. Unenterprisingly, I chose the latter. Or perhaps I was not being entirely unenterprising. I had been in the Army for five years and was beginning to have the feeling I had had about Oxford, that I had always been in it, always would be and that there was no world outside it. It was necessary to realize that there was. It was time I got back to England and decided what to do with the rest of my life.

I was made up to Lieutenant-Colonel (Temporary) and sent to join the staff of Southern Command at Bangalore. The next six months would have been a sort of prolonged holiday if it had not been for the fact that the Indians, both Hindu and Muslim, were now beginning to press for independence with the certainty that in some form or other they were soon going to get it. The 'Quit India' movement revived. Even in Bangalore, an agreeable place where I soon found agreeable company, I sometimes came across small groups of Indians carrying banners and saying politely 'Quit India, please'. Averse to change of any kind, I was not in favour of this but believed the Raj should go on for ever, if only on the grounds that it was much more agreeable for everybody than anything likely to succeed it. My Indian friends did not agree. Even the Begum ————, a member of an ancient landowning family in the North-West Frontier Province who had angered them by leaving her husband, did not agree with me on this point, though she did on many others. She was a Junior Commander (equivalent to Captain) in the IAF and occasionally wore a khaki-coloured uniform sari which became her only a little less than any of the dozens of beautiful saris she possessed.

I had originally met her through my friend Stuart Daniel, who was also a Staff Lieutenant-Colonel at the Southern Command H Q. I had known him vaguely at Oxford. At week-ends, with other congenial people, British and Indian, we went for elaborate picnics in the country around Bangalore, which was flat, with sensational rocky outcrops about as high above the plain as the hills of the Lake District are above sea-level, often with temples on top. We climbed some of these, bravely careless of thorn-trees, snakes and wild beasts. The Begum, whose duties in the Army seemed to be purely ceremonial, had two family retainers with her. One was a fierce-looking man who, had she ordered it, would have instantly cut a man's head off without more ado, and a serving woman almost as fierce-looking, who always carried an enormous iron spoon for dealing with beggars and other importunate people.

One week-end we spent in a comfortable bungalow on the Nandi Hills, where Tippoo Sahib had had an almost impregnable fort, as well as a convenient precipice for dropping prisoners over. It was said that one prisoner, a Scottish soldier, had survived the 500-foot drop to tell the tale. Now, on this shady hill which was like a small garden of Eden, we ate, drank and talked next to the very wall which must once have heard the screams of struggling victims.

When not engaged in these parties of pleasure I went on tours which took me to Madras and various other places including, for some reason I cannot remember, Golconda and the small French colony of Pondicherry, where I met the Governor, an impenetrable Frenchman in a superb uniform of a fashion already doomed. Beneath the surface of this life of Reilly, violence was lurking. The Indian National Army, which had surrendered on the Japanese defeat, was granted pardon en masse (to the great indignation of many), but its members, even if they merely returned to their native villages, had learned the lesson that the British could be defied. At the Bangalore headquarters we practised revolver-shooting.

It was in February 1946, when my time in India was running out, that news came of the Indian Naval Mutiny at Bombay, where the ratings, disarming their officers, had taken over several ships and *had actually turned their guns on the Bombay Yacht Club*. 'Beggars couldn't hit a gasometer if they were standing inside it,' said some old colonel. But he was speaking out of a world which had already passed away. Rioting broke out in Bombay, where, as in all Indian cities, there were masses of people with nothing much to do who always welcomed the chance of a good riot. These *goondas*, as they are called, made a point of seizing mineral water factories for the sake of their bottles of fizzy drinks, which had excellent fragmentation on impact. For a day or so the city was in their hands; the Congress leaders themselves became alarmed at the demon they had raised up; and finding their appeals in vain called on the Army to restore order, which it did with much greater loss of humble lives than ever was reported in the Press.

When I flew to Bombay to join the emergency headquarters which had been set up the worst of the trouble (of course) was over. Proceeding in convoy from the airfield to headquarters (I had been asked to take special care of some cases of whisky for the General) we came under a certain amount of stoning, and I even felt called upon to fire my revolver in the air, more in surprise than anger. After a day or two of intensive conferences, map-marking, drawing up contingency plans and other military activities, the city was pacified, the mutineers disarmed.

I returned to Bangalore and cancelling a projected 'tour' of Ceylon, set off with Stuart Daniel and the Begum for a fortnight's holiday in Ootacamund. 'Ooty' was, and no doubt still is, a place out of a fairy story – a region of rolling hills very much like the Wiltshire Downs as they must have been at the beginning of this century, but on a vast scale and including curious waterfalls and exotic flowers not to be found in Wiltshire. Being about 5,000 feet above sea-level, this paradise had the climate of a perfect English summer. The Begum had several English friends here and my friend Stuart soon contrived to captivate one of their attractive young daughters. It was typical of me that although the Begum was more interesting and in her own way quite as attractive, I hankered after this other girl and was quite put out when the time came for us to leave. Stuart decided to stay on for another week with his new sweetheart. The Begum and I, with her two servants, the serving woman brandishing her iron spoon more fiercely than ever, took the bus down the mountain in a sensationally coloured sunset to the railhead for Bangalore.

But now all was changed. The date for my departure had been fixed. Amid some lamentations I sorted out the clutter of objects I had accumulated during the last five years, took leave of my fellow-officers, shook the General's hand, had ritual garlands of jasmine draped about my neck by Indian clerks and servants and then on an appointed night boarded the train which was to take me and others to the transit camp at Devlali, famous for inducing the special brand of lunacy called 'Doolali tap'. Heaven knows what promises I made to the Begum, who proposed in due course to follow me to England. All proved false.

Devlali did not make me any more lunatic than I already was, but the fortnight or so I spent waiting there, eating appalling food and drinking appalling liquor, relieved only by a visit to Poona, to whose magnificent club I still owe twenty rupees for unredeemed bar-chits, was trying enough. The next stage was Bombay, where I somehow contrived to stay at the Taj Mahal Hotel, sitting alone on its westward terrace which looked over the sea, drinking gin and reading with complacent sadness a book which suited my elegiac mood, Cyril Connolly's just published *The Unquiet Grave*, bought at Tapoorewala'a bookshop for four rupees. Now India and everything I had done and seen there began to recede, grow small, closed off, turn into material for nostalgia: the forests, the mountains, the mad laugh of Major Balderton, my Muslim friend in Lucknow, with his wives and music, the corpse in the bazaar, the eyes of a magical girl, Wavell the deaf and agreeable Viceroy, soon to be succeeded by the preposterous Mountbatten, the snows of Kanchenjunga, Wingate with his book and flower, the lunar landscape of Imphal, the elephant in the jungle, the furtive loves of Agra and Simla, Mitsutachi the imaginary general, the wide streets of Imperial Delhi with their hundred thousand bicycles ...

All was reversed: my arrival at Bombay in 1942 became my departure in 1946. I went aboard, but the ship was no civilised, class-divided *Orion*. Something had been happening in the world while I had been away. It was the irresistible advance of democracy. No longer were the soldiers battened below decks. Now they would have mutinied in earnest. As it was they grumbled, not with the old grumbling but with a new rancour. Their womenfolk, many indoctrinated in hatred of the 'officer class', did more than merely grumble. All ranks in the crowded ship messed together in relays. I had left England a Second Lieutenant, sharing a comfortable cabin with three others. I returned a Major, sharing an uncomfortable cabin with half a dozen others. And, since America had conquered and imposed its will on England in small matters as in great, there was not in all that troopship a single drop of alcohol to drink.

What did I expect to find, or expect to do, as we crossed the

Indian Ocean, entered the Red Sea, with its dark green waters and jagged mountains, almost the only potent image which stays with me from that voyage, so much shorter yet more tedious than the voyage out; moved through the phantasmagoria of Port Said and into a calm, misty, ghostly Mediterranean; glimpsed the Rock; passed into the Atlantic where U-boats lurked no longer, saw the first of England, the Isle of Wight; landed at Southampton on or about my thirty-third birthday?

5
Attlee and After

The docks looked grey and battered and shabby; the people too. Not a single family, I found, was living among brass vessels, brightly-coloured cloths and household gods on the platforms of Southampton station. Not a single coolie hung dreamily about, waiting to carry something or perform some other service for an anna or a farthing. At the tops of walls there were a lot of elementary, childlike drawings of the same round face – 'Chad', the character who seemed to stand for England in its present state, with chalked slogans: 'Wot – no cigarettes?' 'Wot – no women?' It was all extremely strange. After a period of confusion, compounded of the Army 'fuck up' I was accustomed to and a new kind of civilian inefficiency, a party of us, still in uniform but already feeling the bewilderment of change, entrained, travelled with many unexplained stops – that at least was like the country I had come from – through a damp, green, miniature landscape to Tilehurst near Reading, where we were to spend the night before dispersing to various demobilisation centres. We drank beer in a pub and felt like ghosts.

As the only address I had to go to was in Dublin – my wife, who had a married sister in the neutral Irish Free State, had moved there some time before – my demobilisation centre was at Ashton-under-Lyne, near Stockport in the Manchester Conurbation. After a day's travelling through more of this unfamiliar miniature country full of houses, I reached that unattractive place. Next morning I filled in a lot of forms and collected some 'demob' clothes – I noted that they were the same for officers and men. I chose a tweed jacket, grey flannel trousers, brown shoes with bright brass eyes. In a few minutes, as it seemed, I was a civilian again. But I still wore my uniform, unwilling to take the final step into a confusing world where I had no definite, acknowledged place, as though my time in the Army had never been.

Feeling more than ever like a ghost, I spent the night at an hotel in Chester after a day of aimless sightseeing in that city, where I had never been before. In the cool, grey spring weather I walked by the Dee, watched at a certain place how the swans came sailing over the green water to where the dustmen of Chester had stopped their lorries and were throwing handfuls of stale bread to the beautiful, greedy birds. I made a note. I was always making notes for future books; but where was the will to write them?

It was late on the following day when I reached Dublin. The station seemed deserted. Holding my suitcase – the rest of my baggage would (or would not) follow later, I stood irresolutely. Then I saw a single horse-cab waiting. My wife and son – now eight years old – were there. What did I feel – what did she feel – what, for that matter, did he feel – at this statutory moment of reunion? Very little, I think. We went back to the flat she had, somewhere near Merrion Square, talked, I suppose, ate some supper, I suppose, and went to bed. I tried to make love to her. It was a failure.

I spent a few weeks in Dublin, living on my gratuity, which then seemed quite a respectable sum. I had a growing feeling, and so, of course, had she, that this would not do. I was bored, ill-tempered, tried to write, failed. We quarrelled a good deal and I decided to leave for England. I had nowhere to go except to my brother's farm near Ambleside in the Lake District, where my widowed mother was living. She seemed much older and smaller when she met me at Windermere station, resplendent in my uniform with a major's crowns still on my shoulders. My brother, who seemed to have done quite well out of the war – he had a much more civilised farmhouse in a not particularly remote place and even had a sign in the window: 'Teas' – soon cut me down to size. 'It's always the useless ones who survive,' he muttered. He may well have been right. But what, I wondered, had become of my *Encyclopaedia Britannica*, my bicycle, my maps and my Greek lexicon, the only things of value I had left behind?

The atmosphere was not congenial. The old antagonism between my mother and her daughter-in-law had not changed. 'I won't be treated like a servant', 'that clock is really mine.' Such remarks as these were common. My mother told me, not once but many times, that she had sold much of the remaining treasure of Duchy Grange – the silver, a fine emerald ring she had – to help my brother stock his farm: 'and look at all the thanks I get'. After a bit I felt I could not stand any more of this. I would give Dublin another try. I sent my wife a telegram to say I was coming back. The sweet, romantic soul replied with a telegram in overwrought, romantic terms, which, intercepted by my brother, greatly embarrassed me. But off I went.

This time it did not take me long to realise I had made yet another mistake. It would not do. I had grown so far apart from my wife and had so little feeling for her or my child that I must leave. On a fine day of midsummer I crossed the Irish Sea once more and this time caught the express from Holyhead to London. An Army friend – a 'mad Irishman' with an MC and two bars who, angry at not being awarded the DSO, had once upset the mess dining-table over his CO – had arranged a room for me in a bed-sitter house in Ebury Street. It was a tiny attic, with just enough room for a narrow bed, a table and chair and a spluttering gas fire. I was entirely alone.

Now began a very dreary and depressing time. I walked the Chelsea streets, hoping, perhaps, to meet someone I had known who would somehow lead me back to the old life. I ate abominable meals – they had the very taste of 'austerity' – in abominable pubs or in cheap cafés. I went to The Antelope, off Eaton Square – it had been a favourite haunt in what had become 'the old days'.

There, for want of anyone else to talk to I fell in with a set of men and women – the men, like me, were living on their dwindling gratuities – who had little in common with me except a liking for drink and a feeling of being lost in the civilian world.

My money was running out. It was necessary to get a job. I applied for various posts, including one as a Public Relations Officer with the new National Waste Paper Board (can this be right?). I have never been good at interviews. This one was particularly farcical. As I sat before the interviewers, answering various questions, I could see their puzzlement that I, who had lately held the rank of colonel, should seem so totally unfitted for any job at all. My handkerchief had escaped through a hole in my pocket. As I rose to go ('we'll let you know soon') I made a grab at the handkerchief through the hole and seized it, but then, trying to withdraw my arm, found my cuff caught in the hole. I scrambled crablike to the door, and as I closed it behind me, heard the roar of laughter from the other side. A good film sequence, I thought, and even made a note.

Other interviews were less amusing. A terrible torpor fell upon me. I spent hours lying without thought on the narrow bed in my attic hide-out. I even wrote a letter to my wife in Dublin, suggesting that we should get together again. Wisely, she declined. Chance led me, one despairing evening, to the pub in Rathbone Place, off Oxford Street, where I had originally met Constantine FitzGibbon. Perhaps I hoped to meet him again. Instead I met the instrument of my deliverance, my old friend of Oxford days, David Thomson.

He was still the same delightful, vague, generous and unselfconscious man he had been then, though he was more mature and confident from experience, as I may have at least appeared to be. He was with three beautiful Irish sisters and seemed to be in love with all of them and they, perhaps, with him. Because of his bad sight he had not served in the forces but had done farming and later joined the BBC. He was now a producer and writer in its 'features' department, which was responsible for documentary programmes. Finding that I was looking for work, he suggested that I should write a programme in a series he was producing by writers new to the 'radio medium'. Any subject I liked, he said in his vague way. I chose the Reading Room of the British Museum and with much toil and agony (I have always greatly disliked writing) eventually produced a somewhat over-poetic script which was broadcast, complete with sound effects, background music from Holst's 'Planets' and so on, towards the end of the year.

Very soon my deliverer introduced me to his colleagues and friends. The BBC then, as now, was distributed all over London; the Features Department had its offices near 'BH', as I soon learned to call the shiplike building, huge by the standards of that time, in Portland Place. The Department, whose chief was Lawrence Gilliam, a big, powerfully-built man with grey hair curly as a negro's, was then at the height of its fame. It was regarded by other parts of the BBC as something of a spoilt child. Because it included people of talent and was headed by a man who was fiercely loyal to them and protected them, it was allowed to go very much its own way. It therefore got good results – 'classics' of sound radio which seem now to belong to a remote epoch. It provided writers like Louis MacNeice, Rayner Heppenstall and W. R. ('Bertie') Rodgers with a living wage. On the other hand it was a danger to them. It was easier for them to use their talents in the evanescent medium of radio than to write books. Much good writing must have been lost that way.

The Features Department's own pub was The Stag's Head, on the corner of Hallam Street and Great Cavendish Street. Here I met Francis Dillon, or 'Jack', as he was always called, a small, energetic, semi-edentate man who kept up a continuous quickfire of jokes, often very good ones, in a high, hoarse voice (he had been gassed in the First World War). Because of his shabby appearance and ungentlemanly accent I took him at first for an unusually privileged member of the manual staff, a driver, perhaps (the spell of the Army was still on me). I could not have been more wrong. He was a man of great talent, who put most of it into talking and singing in pubs (he was an authority on folk-songs) rather than into books, or even into his official work. At that time he was editing and producing 'Country Magazine', a popular programme which went out at Sunday lunchtime on what was then called (in contradistinction to the 'Light Programme') the 'Home Service'. It was full of country lore, poachers, eccentric beekeepers, fragments of a rural England which still, even in 1946, somehow survived.

Before long I was doing odd jobs for this programme, earning just about enough to live on by interviewing country characters, writing down what they would say on the air (there were no tape-recorders in those days) and generally fitting their contributions into the final script. I did other jobs for other programmes, too – anything that was going, in fact. I wrote scripts for the Schools Programme on the Luddites (a theme always close to my heart) and soon became familiar with the simple techniques of the studio from red light to stopwatch.

'*Narrator*: By 1818 the condition of the handloom-weavers, betrayed, as they believed, by the new machines, became desperate:
(Fade up murmuring crowd)
'*Voice 1*: Give us bread!
'*Voice 2*: We're starvin'!
'*Voice 3 (female)*: Our children are starvin'!
(Loud angry murmur, clang of mill gates)
'*Voice 1*: Smash the frames!
'*Voice 2*: Aye, smash the devil's frames!
etc. etc.'

I also wrote, on the other hand, scripts about modern industries and things of that kind, my greatest masterpiece being 'Focus on Waste Paper' – an important subject in the years of austerity, rationing, 'Work or Want' and all the drab, grey phantasmagoria

of Mr Attlee's Labour Government. The staff of the Features
Department, if they had any political views at all, would have
described themselves as mildly Socialist, I suppose, though there
was a Marxist element represented by R. D. ('Reggie') Smith, a
big, bearlike, kindly-looking man who had a neat trick of giving
bores a helping hand and then neatly unloading them on someone
else, occasionally myself.

As for 'austerity', why should a physically healthy man in his
thirties, just out of the Army, worry about that? I met, while drinking
in The Stag, an energetic, jolly, dark-haired, handsome Welsh girl
called Anne who produced programmes about films. We set up
house together in a flat in Hampstead conveniently offered by a
friend of mine from post-Oxford days. His wife had been Constantine FitzGibbon's girl friend when he came to stay with us in
Westmorland. The pair of them were on their way back to Nigeria,
where he worked in the Colonial Service. It was in this flat that we
lived through the dread winter of 1946–7, when the streets of
London were covered with waves of black ice and were impassable
to traffic for days on end. It was an 'offence' to use more than one
bar of an electric fire and we had to drag bags of inferior coal, when
we could get any, from the depot in Finchley Road up the slopes
of Hampstead Hill. All our water-pipes froze and we cannot have
had much to eat. But I remember nothing of this hardship; only
the exhilaration when the thaw came at last and the huge long
icicles which draped our walls, things of iridescent beauty, gradually
disappeared.

Wishing to get a divorce, I consulted Stuart Daniel, he of
Bangalore, now in chambers in London, and under his direction
wrote the statutory letter to my wife in Dublin, saying that I
had left her and was now living in adultery with so-and-so at
such-and-such an address. In due course, a small, furtive man with
a black notebook arrived one evening, just as in a thousand novels
of the age before divorce became commonplace. 'I'll have to trouble

you for evidence of co-habitation,' he said. 'If I could just look in the bedroom ... If you could just lay out your ... night attire on the bed ... Thank you. No, I won't stay for a cup of coffee, thank you. I've three or four more calls to make tonight.' So it was done, and about nine months later, I was a single man. 'How do you feel?' asked Anne. 'Alone in the world,' I said.

She was a very energetic girl, determined, until she decided the task was hopeless, to see me 'make something of myself' and my presumed talents. It was she who fixed up a holiday for us in a château in the Valley of the Tarn, where, in the hot sun of the Midi, I became almost as brown as I had been in India; she who arranged another holiday in the Dordogne, then unpeopled by English settlers; she who worked things so that we could see the paintings in the cavern at Lascaux, before they were closed because of the destructive breath of too many visitors; she who arranged a few days in Paris, of which I remember little except a scene at the Gare du Nord, when we found ourselves, with a group of other English people, on the wrong platform. ''Raus! 'Raus!' shouted a French porter, to the huge amusement of his fellow countrymen and the indignation of the English. I thought it funny myself; Anne less so.

We were not really getting on well together. She had little patience with my listless and despondent moods. Why should she? I felt the odds and ends of work I was doing for the BBC were using only a small part of my capacity. 'Then why don't you write? You're supposed to be a writer.' But I could not. Remembering those solitary walks on Hampstead Heath when Anne was working and I was supposed to be writing some stupid script which I couldn't get started, that feeling of hopelessness combined with a powerful charge of unreality – I had not yet learned to call this sensation, subsequently so popular, *angst* – I feel again the emptiness of a life she would have liked, if she could, to fill with that strong happiness in which she moved so effortlessly herself.

David Thomson thought, when he first introduced me to the

Features Department, that Gilliam would soon give me a producer's job. But this did not happen. We did not hit it off. I could not feel at ease with this apparently masterful, efficient, 'dynamic' man in authority. So I went on doing odd jobs as a freelance, a precarious life.

I met such great ones as Louis MacNeice, Dylan Thomas, Elisabeth Lutyens, the celebrated, somewhat shrewish composeress, the more acceptable composer Humphrey Searle and many others, and drank with them in The George and its convenient annex the 'ML' Club across the road, where we could carry on drinking through the afternoon until The George opened again. I occasionally stayed in what might be called the Features Department's 'safe house' on the river at Wapping, where 'Bertie' Rodgers acted as a sort of resident warden and all approved people could stay – a great boon to secret lovers. This alliterative poet, so out of fashion now and perhaps sunk for ever, provided much quiet amusement. He had been a dissenting minister in Ulster until MacNeice, discovering his poems, brought him into the convenient haven of the BBC.

Rodgers, though 'irresistible to women', still had something of a minister's gravity of speech. He specialised in gnomic utterances ('You know what's what and you know where's where and you know when's when; but you never know why's why'). He also had the gift, sometimes found among Irishmen, of being in two places at once. Inadvertently opening his bedroom door one morning I found him in bed with a woman and quickly withdrew to the bar of the neighbouring pub, where he sat quietly drinking a glass of Guinness and asked, vainly, if I could lend him 7s. 6d. Not long after this, he 'ran off' with the beautiful wife of the powerful Gilliam, who was thus shown to be less powerful than I had thought. 'Bertie' had to resign, of course, but continued, under MacNeice's aegis, to work as a freelance. But Gilliam had pronounced a curse upon him: 'You shall be happy, but write no more poetry.' I hope he was happy. It is true he wrote no more poetry of any merit after 'Europa and the Bull' – you are to imagine that pronounced in an Ulster accent – and some years after died of cancer in America. But Gilliam had died of cancer before him.

As for death, my brother had died in the great polio epidemic of 1947 – astoundingly, for his was the only case for fifty miles around his farm at Ambleside – but not before my mother, aggrieved and unable to get on with her daughter-in-law, moved to a cottage in the Yorkshire Dales, not far from the domains of my sister's formidable, Alsatian-loving Scottish protectress, who frightened my mother out of her wits. Her son, who had trained as an RAF pilot in Rhodesia, married my sister, and after he had taken a late degree in geology, they went back to that white man's paradise to live, she to breed pekinese dogs, he to become, in due course, Professor of Geology at the University of Rhodesia.

My former wife had now come to England and, I am glad to say, found a second husband, a good swashbuckling New Zealander, which took away whatever guilt I may have been capable of feeling. My son stayed with his grandmother in Yorkshire – a strange sort of upbringing indeed. But although he must have heard much talk of past glories, of the grandeur of Duchy Grange – a few Chelsea china figures, a glass-topped table, a few plates, said to be of inestimable value, still remained – of his grandfather's foolish behaviour which had reduced them to this humble plight, and, above all, of the Missing Will of the Whartons, he survived to go to Skipton Grammar School and Christ's College, Cambridge, and to keep an insatiable curiosity about his real, or in default of that, imaginary antecedents.

The break with Anne came when we moved from Hampstead (my friends, on leave from Nigeria, needed their flat). We rented, as a temporary base, a house in Holland Park belonging to a young film-producer and his wife. I fell for the wife, Laura, instantly and heavily. She was small, with a well-bred prettiness, fond of drinking and nonsensical jokes. Both, like almost all the people in the film unit he worked for, were 'fun communists', she entirely for the fun, he out of some curious conviction, perhaps connected with his having a very rich father. While they were away, Anne, not without complaints on my part, for I had got used to her and wished to eat my cake and have it, moved out. When they got back it seemed the most natural thing in the world to these agreeable, easygoing people that I should stay on in a basement-room they had made comfortable for some vaguely-projected lodger who never appeared.

We became great friends. The film-producer had, of course, noted that I had fallen for his wife, but, as he told her and she duly reported to me, he thought me much too shy and reserved to tell her so. This was not so at all. Now began the only experience I have ever had of true, romantic and what seemed perfectly requited love. I also found, as others have done, that I had less purely physical pleasure with a woman I loved and cared for than with other women, both before and since, whom I have not greatly cared about.

But this did not matter or cause me to repine. What mattered was the good, warm feeling of being together with this delightful woman. She was wayward, and this, by ensuring that I could never be certain of what she would do next, made her twice as fascinating. There was the attraction, too, of keeping the affair a secret. To arrange occasions for making love involved ingenious stratagems such as taking a room at the Great Eastern Hotel under a false name, or meeting at Rye on some pretext and staying in some freezing hotel, where, in those days of austerity, the food was appalling and the mattress damp and hard. At one time I rented a small room in another part of Holland Park and there we would meet for an hour or two.

There were misunderstandings, quarrels, delicious reconciliations, narrow escapes from detection. We communicated by leaving notes in an unused tooth-mug in the bathroom ('per mugpost') and this is how our affair was eventually discovered by the husband, as it was bound to be. There was a mild scene only – it was certainly not the first time she had been unfaithful; but, of course, I had to leave. I took another room not far away (in those days there were still plenty of bed-sitters to be had), and so my state of happy misery went on.

All this time I had to find money to live on. I wrote odd scripts for the BBC. One evening in 1949 I was sitting in The Stag drinking a pint of beer when a Scotsman whose name I have forgotten came in and asked if there was anyone there who would care to write a script or scenario for the electrical power generation section of the industrial section of the Festival of Britain. This, then in the first stages of planning, was due in 1951, centenary year of the Great Exhibition. 'Putting the "Great" back into Great Britain' and many other inane slogans were floating about. The fee for the script was £150. I accepted the Scotsman's offer at once.

I knew absolutely nothing about electrical power generation but was good at research, as I had proved as a cadet at Catterick. I was given a ticket for the Library of the Institute of Electrical Engineers. There I asked the librarian to recommend a few elementary works. He produced a few and I took them away to a remote desk. All were completely unintelligible. But I had noticed a shelf containing such books as *Every Boy's Book of Electricity* and furtively taking these, I began my research. Every time the librarian came near I had to cover up the boys' books with the books he had given me. It was like being back at school again. But I soon found I was getting interested in the history of electrical generation. It started with amber, the loadstone and the terrible iron mountain in the *Arabian Nights*, which sank ships by drawing out all their rivets if they came near it, and progressed by easy stages to Faraday, that saintly man who, if he could have foreseen the evils his electro-magnetic discoveries would make possible, from pornographic films to nuclear weapons, would surely have destroyed his laboratory and hanged himself. Soon I had mastered the basic principles. I worked on the project, on and off, for more than a year. Not being able to afford the rail fare to Glasgow, where this section of the Exhibition was located, I never saw the humming, clanking, booming end-product of my work. But even now I retain enough of what I learned then to be able to pose, if only for a few minutes, as an electrical engineer.

Another job I was working on at this time was editing the Football Association Yearbook, published by a small firm which had been infiltrated, for reasons I could not discover, by Marxists. One of them, a big, jolly, very agreeable man, was a friend of my Holland Park patrons, who (before the exposure) recommended me for the job. I did not know much more about football than about electrical power generation. But there was less to know. So for the earlier part of 1949 I was busy, when not at work on broadcasting scripts or electrical affairs, on pasting up 'dummies' of the Yearbook, checking lists of results and even writing contributions of my own. My short article, 'Some Aspects of the Offside Rule' (with diagrams), was thought at the time to be the most lucid and masterly exposition of the subject which had ever appeared. I also wrote a number of histories of football clubs, such as Accrington Stanley and Luton Town ('the Hatters').

This meant 'research'. For this I used to go, every now and then, to the Football Association headquarters in Lancaster Gate, in Bayswater. The President of the Association was then Sir Stanley Rous. I never actually met him but those below him in this curious hierarchy of football officials were greatly in awe of him. I heard many stories of his overbearing character. At one time he had declared that the badge of the England international football team must be eleven lions. The College of Heralds ruled that this was a heraldic impossibility. This threw Sir Stanley into such a titanic rage that he flung a heavy presentation inkwell at a subordinate and shut himself up in his personal music-room to play thunderous chords on the organ he had had installed there until his nerves were calm enough for him to enter the human world again. Did I invent

all this? Yes. But some of the minor officials almost believed it. I
was taking notes like mad at that time.

My contact for research purposes was the Archivist, a Yorkshireman who lived in a room full of books and memorabilia which
covered the whole history of football from its beginnings. He also
collected all stamps connected with football (as the game spread to
foreign parts more and more of these were appearing). His albums,
which he showed me with great pride in the intervals of putting me
right on some historical detail or other – who, for instance, played
goal for Bradford City in 1913? – must have been quite valuable. I
thought of knocking him out, seizing them and making a dash for
it. But the thought of the titanic Sir Stanley deterred me. One day
when I was with the Archivist, there was a prolonged pause in the
conversation (a common experience with me). I was going to say
something about Wolverhampton Wanderers when I noticed that
the Archivist's face had gone blank and stony. Suddenly, in a
strange, indescribable tone, he said: 'I hate Sir Stanley.' I thought
it best to make no comment, and in a moment he was himself again
and reaching for his stamp albums.

There was one item of unchanging ritual in these visits to the
Archivist. Each time, before I left, he told me a single dirty story.
Some of them were quite ingenious. Had he invented them himself?
Was this strange office the place where all these stories, told by
commercial travellers (as they were called in those days) all over
England, had their origin? I never found out.

So it was, in these humble, disparate and incongruous tasks, that
I kept alive. In desperation, I had also started writing short pieces
of humorous fantasy for *Punch* again (there was a whole series about
a surrealist boilerworks which I sent in week after week until the
Editor – I think it was the one before Malcolm Muggeridge – grew
tired of them). The fees, I noted, were somewhat higher than they
had been in my days in Westmorland. But living in London was
much more expensive. Though unbelievably lazy in retrospect, I

must actually have been working quite hard, if to no particular purpose.

Meanwhile I was making new friends and acquaintances in the pubs of the BBC. One of them was René Cutforth, a big man with a special kind of grating voice, one of the most entertaining people I have ever met, and, for all his vagaries, one of the most lovable. He was as fond of fantasy as I was and had invented a monstrous saga of his upbringing as son of a mine owner in legendary Swadlincote, in the Derbyshire-Leicestershire coalfield. But his real life was fantastic enough. He had had an adventurous war, in the Abyssinian campaign and elsewhere, ending up as a prisoner of the Germans. He was perhaps the best of the BBC's war reporters (he wrote a book about his experiences in the Korean War which is by far the best I have read on that subject). But because of his adventurous and irregular life the administrators of the BBC ('the greymen', as we called them) regarded him with suspicion. They did not realise, or if they realised, did not respect, his considerable literary talent. And René himself, when he could have been writing remarkable books, preferred to put his talent into talking, singing and entertaining (he was a prodigious mimic – his Australian and Ulster accents were unsurpassed in my experience). He was, in a way, a tragic figure. It still annoys me to think of all the little people who at that time and since made a reputation as writers with no more than a modicum of his talent. But perhaps – and this is a phrase that often comes to mind – it does not really matter anyhow. He was himself.

Another character of those days who was decidedly himself was Peter Duval Smith, a young man of South African origin, who, according to legend, had been found by Louis MacNeice asleep in a gutter in Athens and brought back to join the BBC. His unique, mischievous laugh was the outward sign of his character. If Bertie Rodgers and David Thomson were irresistible to women, Peter Duval Smith was more than irresistible. It was fascinating to watch the process at work: it never seemed to fail. I made several notes about it.

This man was also completely careless of convention, and there was nothing he liked better than flouting the 'greymen' and generally defying authority. It was possible, by making friends with some girl in the archives department of the BBC – easy enough for such as he – to borrow one of the 'personal files' which everyone connected with the BBC, whether on the staff or not, had to have. These files would be produced at the annual interview which everyone, including heads of departments, had with his immediate superior. Peter got hold of the personal file of Lawrence Gilliam, Head of Features, his own department.

At the next annual meeting Gilliam had with his Immediate Superior, the 'Director of the Spoken Word' or some such functionary perhaps, his file was produced. The Immediate Superior was dumbfounded. The file proved to contain, among the records of programmes produced during the year and so on, some unexpected notes: 'This man is not to be trusted with messenger boys'; 'the unfortunate incident in the public lavatory at Seaford, though due to a misunderstanding on the part of the police officer . . .' and so on. 'What is the meaning of this?' asked the horrified Immediate Superior. Later Gilliam called the whole Department together and told them that unless the culprit owned up, they would all be kept in indefinitely – or words to that effect. Everybody, including the victim, knew that only one person could have done such a thing. Peter had to resign, of course, but, as in the case of Bertie Rodgers, he still went on working for the Department. The BBC was then, in some ways, a mysterious and admirable organisation. Peter continued his adventurous life until, years later, he died mysteriously in Saigon during the Vietnam War.

Amusing though all these merry pranks could be and pleasant as it was to know such people and share their adventures if only by proxy, I could not claim that I was 'getting anywhere', though now approaching my late thirties. What had become of my ambition to be a 'great writer', to be rich and famous? I was reminded of this one day, when, opening a newspaper, I read a review of a first novel by Constantine FitzGibbon, *The Arabian Bird*. 'A new star has risen over the horizon of the English novel,' wrote the reviewer, giving some details not only of the book but of the author's varied life as an intelligence officer in the American Army, interrogating captured German generals by the score, and of his subsequent experiences in America, Bermuda and Capri, where he was said to be writing a life of his paternal kinsman, Norman Douglas. I was not so base as to be angry at my friend's success. All the same it made me uneasy. I had not seen or heard of him for about ten years. Obviously he had not been crawling about on the surface of the earth since he had left the Army, nor picking up a living as best he could, preoccupied with unsatisfactory love affairs. Far from drifting passively, trying feebly to locate some all too missing will, he had been working to some purpose. I wished I could say the same.

One gloomy morning in December 1949 I was feeling particularly despondent. I had been to see the Football Association about the early history of Nottingham Forest and was on the upper deck of a bus in the Strand, about to alight for a morning's research with the electrical engineers. Things were not going well between Laura and myself. There was a distinct diminuendo, a feeling that 'there was no future' in our affair, as indeed there was not. I had nothing to offer her if she wanted to leave her husband for me; I would probably have been alarmed if she had suggested it.

Afflicted by the sort of feeling I associate with going alone to a public library on a Saturday afternoon, I had just turned to get off the bus when a well-known voice hailed me. It was Constantine. 'Nice to see you again,' I said, amazed and bewildered by what seemed a reversal of the laws of nature. 'Quick, drop whatever you're doing and come and have a drink,' he said. We went to the nearest pub, Henekey's in the Strand, and drank quite a lot of

Guinness. 'I thought nothing pleasant was ever going to happen again,' I said, overwhelmed by this apparition from what I had thought a lost world. He told me he had taken a flat in Chelsea with his new wife, Theodora, gave me his telephone number and asked me to go round that evening.

I was not at first smitten by Theodora, who seemed older than I had expected and had an air of immense sophistication which made me feel distinctly small. Asked what I was doing, I could not say I was doing anything much. It seemed they knew Laura from wartime days in London and had a poor opinion of her. Theodora thought she was 'wet'. 'Why don't you get a proper girl friend?' she shouted. There were difficult pauses in the conversation. 'I'm told you're mad, brilliant and witty,' she went on. 'Can't see much sign of it.' Constantine summed it up: 'The war has driven him sane.'

However, in spite of this unfortunate beginning, we soon resumed our old friendship. Constantine was already working on a new book and they were looking for a place in the country, not too far from London, where they could live with their giant poodle, Minka, and entertain their friends. They introduced me to all kinds of people, mostly literary – Terence Kilmartin, Robert Kee, Admiral Fawkes, Oscar Kokoschka, Arthur Koestler, 'Bunny' Esterhazy, Brian Howard, ex-King Umberto (is this right? probably not). They seemed to have a poor opinion of the BBC people and advised me to escape from that milieu as soon as possible. 'You're getting on for forty,' shouted Theodora. 'Time you got a book published.'

The only book I had written was *Sheldrake*, by this time rather *vieux jeu*, but I still hoped to get it published. 'Write another one,' advised Constantine. 'I don't know anything about anything,' I explained. 'What does that matter? Write about badgers.' He was right, of course. Among the people he introduced me to were a pair of publishers, Anthony Gibbs and Charles Fry, who ran a firm called Wingate, for which Constantine, who had another, more important publisher for his own books, did translations, mainly of the memoirs of German generals which were just starting to emerge from the rubble of the war. Gibbs, son of the author of *The Street of Adventure* and other bestsellers, was a dandified man with an eyeglass and a Rolls Royce, and wrote or had written some really terrible novels himself. Fry, a man of homosexual temperament, was languid and unhappy (he later committed suicide). Owing to a misunderstanding he tried to seduce me in his melancholy box of a flat in one of those blocks in Chelsea which had a depressing service restaurant on the ground floor.

These publishers were not inclined to publish *Sheldrake* (it finally got published, in 1958, by Anthony Blond, a rich Jew who joined their firm and then took it over). What they did was to put me in the way of ghost-writing. It did not pay well, but I added it to my list of miscellaneous fringe occupations. I ghosted one book, *Dare to be Free*, by W. D. Thomas, an excellent story, when re-written by myself, of the author's adventures after his escape from a German prison-camp in Crete. It was quite a success. 'Reads in parts like an enthralling fairy story,' said one review. 'Here is that most unusual thing, a man of action who can write.'

Gibbs and Fry also introduced me to Helga Greene, the divorced wife of Hugh Greene, later to be Director-General of the BBC. She was rich (what was described as a 'real', that is, 'banking' Guinness) and then held strong Leftish views. She was rather stern, too, and put me through a cross-examination about my own views before giving me work (yet another subterranean, mole-like activity) in the literary agency she ran from her house near Eaton Square. When I told her my political views, which were as decidedly 'right-wing' as they always had been, she obviously did not believe me. She was one of those people whom I came to think of later as 'Hampstead thinkers'; it was typical of them that they simply did not believe that a person who seemed intelligent and educated could have opinions different from their own. This was convenient for me because she was willing to give me work to do, mainly reading manuscripts. Later on she got me the job of editing the transcript of the Hearing in the Case of J. Robert Oppenheimer, the American nuclear physicist who was suspected of being a 'security risk', on the whole, I think, rightly. This meant reducing about a million words to a book of 80,000 words. I found this task, gruelling though it was, quite fascinating; what I was left with, in the end, was a play. I was pleased with my work on this, and pleased also that the short introduction I wrote for it was described by a reviewer in the *New Statesman* as 'surprisingly right-wing'. It was surprising to him, all right; he was another 'Hampstead thinker'.

For all her brusqueness Helga was kind to me. She even lent me her house to stay in once or twice. It was extremely comfortable. But, fortunately perhaps, she had locked up all the drink and there was nothing to eat either for me or for some girl I took there once except strawberries and a large tin of those cocktail biscuits made in the shape of small footballs with cheese inside. During the night the doorbell had some kind of seizure and went on ringing for hours. My knowledge of electrical power generation proved useless. Fearing that policemen or others might investigate, we fled at dawn.

In the spring of 1951 Constantine and Theodora found the house they were looking for: an old converted farmhouse called Sacombe's Ash, roomy enough and with a pleasant garden. It was in a part of Hertfordshire between Sawbridgeworth and Much Hadham which, considering how close it was to London, was still surprisingly rural, with old-fashioned pubs full of genuine 'characters' and surviving examples of genuine folk art, such as four stuffed squirrels playing cards in a glass case. Constantine and Theodora soon became 'characters' themselves, as they effortlessly took over the local pub, objects of amazement to the rustic customers, who had never before come across people who seemed to belong to the middle or upper class, yet drank their pints of beer and gossiped with the rest.

The pair of them very soon took charge of my life, allotting me a room in their house to live in at weekends for a small rent or none at all; and, since I had to be in London some of the time, they even found me a lodging in a house in Chelsea belonging to the wife of an eccentric would-be author about ten years older than myself. We got on well until my tendency to hopelessness got on his nerves. The part of the house his separated wife allowed him had one unusual feature: kitchen, bathroom and WC were one. It was possible to make toast while sitting on the lavatory.

I spent most of my week-ends with the FitzGibbons. I would sit in my room with a typewriter for an hour or two in the mornings, but had little to show for it, except a large number of disparate Chapters One of my new novel. The house was full of comings and goings. Theodora was a superb cook (she later became a famous cookery writer) and a splendid homemaker and hostess. The FitzGibbons had a great many friends whom they had got to know in their wanderings. Some, like Manes Sperber, one of those central European novelists who had turned away from Communism and wrote novels about the process, were famous in their day; others, like Noel Annan, Patrick O'Donovan, John Raymond, Christopher Ewart-Biggs and Woodrow Wyatt, were to become well-known in different fields.

I have always felt uneasy in the company of famous, successful or powerful people (except in the Army, when I knew, by reference to my shoulder-badges what my own precise status was); later a percipient woman friend said she had noticed how I used to 'climb immediately into my personal dustbin' when such people were about. Theodora soon noticed this too and was inclined to tease me or, in her uninhibited way, call me 'idiot'. I did not like this much. Nor did I greatly like the violent rows the pair of them had together, though these had their amusing side. It is a fact, I think, that when working-class people throw bottles and crockery at each other they quite often score hits; middle- or upper-class people seldom, if ever. Bottles flung by Constantine and Theodora at each other almost always hit the wall behind the target area. However

187

there was the danger of fragmentation, and they usually made sure there was a first-aid box handy. In one of these rows, which were really like tableaux or short dramatic performances (recalling my father's, though on a larger scale), Constantine, after hitting his wife on the head with a heavy German dictionary, sat her on the fire. She came back strongly with a wine-bottle and later they administered first-aid to each other for the cuts and burns they had sustained, laughing heartily and quite good friends again.

There was a good deal of serious drinking, either at the pub, which had a pleasant green space in front of it, arranged with benches and tables, or at the house itself, or, occasionally, at a wonderfully seedy 'country club', a small, decayed house in an overgrown park a few miles off, where the manager, usually very drunk himself, took a tolerant view of drinking and amatory matters. Guests at the FitzGibbons' frequent, enjoyable parties were sometimes boarded out there.

Another agreeable part of life at Sacombe's Ash was croquet. Constantine was extremely good at this and almost always won, even with a weak partner. Though I am very fond of the game, I have never been very good at it; lacking a logical mind (it is a game which calls for intelligent planning ahead and a feeling for geometrical relations), I am decidedly erratic, sometimes abject, sometimes positively brilliant. One great advantage of croquet is that it is the only outdoor game which can be played while drinking and talking.

Both the FitzGibbons were great talkers – an advantage for me because unless I am quite drunk I tend to be tongue-tied or even unable to think of anything to say. Much of what they talked about – foreign places, famous people they had met – meant little or nothing to me. A good deal of what Theodora talked about seemed far-fetched, but was not less entertaining for that. Her father, it seemed, had been an eccentric Irish peer. She had been brought up in one of those great decaying Irish country houses – where it actually was in Ireland I was not and am not sure – with no less than nine gigantic Irish wolfhounds to protect her. These and other details I absorbed without comment, just as I absorbed the continual references to Picasso, Jean-Paul Sartre, Albert Camus and the painters Peter Rose-Pulham (a former lover of Theodora's) and Sir Francis Rose, a man of homosexual tendencies.

After a stay with the FitzGibbons it felt odd to travel north, as I occasionally did, to see how my mother was getting on in her cottage in Yorkshire. When I first went there, 'Aunt' had been sent for to keep her company and, to some extent, to resume her old role of domestic slave. There was no talk about Picasso there. Neither of the two women had ever heard of him, any more than they had heard of Wingate's the publishers, Jean-Paul Sartre, Sir Stanley Rous of the Football Association, Louis MacNeice of the BBC, my friends the fun-communist and his delightful wife, or any of the characters in the different spheres I was living in simultaneously. But my mother was pleased about my job with the BBC ('I'm sure you'll get to be an announcer one day, if you work hard').

'Aunt' was dying of cancer, and very soon had to keep to her room. One of the things in my life, and they are many, I am ashamed of is that I did not go to see her until it was too late – for the day came when an ambulance arrived to take her to Leeds General Hospital, where she died. This was a simple soul; she had no power to harm and so did none; but I do not think she would have done any if she had had the power. She had been kind to me. I never returned that kindness. It is, however, I who will have to pay for that, if any payment is required. Such people as 'Aunt', to whom nothing memorable had ever happened in all her sixty odd years of life, are as great a mystery as Theodora FitzGibbon, to whom amazing things never seemed to stop happening – perhaps a greater.

Life at Sacombe's Ash that summer was an idyllic time in many ways. Things improved for me after a day when Theodora and myself, leaving Constantine to work at his writing, stayed rather a long time in the pub and, returning with a load of vegetables which the locals had provided, fell off our bicycles at the bend in the road. Bicycles, vegetables and ourselves lay spilled in a confused heap and we could not stop laughing for half an hour. After that we got on quite well together. She became even more concerned, in a genuinely worried way, at my lack of a regular girl friend. My affaire with Laura was rapidly fading out. The FitzGibbons, in their kindness, produced several candidates for my love. But none of them appealed to me. 'You are hard to please,' they said. However, their wish for me was soon to be granted, though not quite in the way they might have wished.

Although they were unfailingly kind to me, I felt sometimes that I was outstaying my welcome. Finding that David Thomson, who had a flat in Portland Place, near 'BH' itself, had a couple of rooms to let, I left my base at Sacombe's Ash as well as my base in Chelsea and with my few effects – there were hardly more of them than when I left the Army – moved into a little attic space of two rooms, approached by a rickety old lift and a steep flight of stairs, high up above the roofs of London, in the autumn of 1950.

Work for the BBC, of the same nondescript kind as before, now took up more of my life. I saw more of David and his friends, spent more time drinking in The Stag and The Windsor Castle, a tiny pub in the mews behind Portland Place, and generally distanced myself a little, though by no means altogether, from the grander world of Sacombe's Ash, which scarcely touched the BBC at any point.

I was beginning to feel a curious restlessness and a deepening depression. When I was at Sacombe's Ash, where I still often went at week-ends, I wished I was in London, and vice versa. I went to Yorkshire to see my mother and my son, now thirteen. His own mother, my former wife, also stayed there occasionally (I am not sure how we all fitted in). She was soon to marry her New Zealander and I found we got on better than we had done before, in a perfectly platonic way, of course, but one which may have caused him slight uneasiness. But soon I found the same restlessness, the same wish to be elsewhere, the same depression. I had been intermittently depressed all my life. But this depression was subtly different. I seemed to be sickening for something, as 'Aunt' would have said.

One morning in November 1951 I was drinking in The Stag when a remarkable-looking girl appeared, a protégée of 'Reggie' Smith, a man of many protégés who is well described in the novels of his wife, Olivia Manning. This girl, whose name was Kate Derrington, had hitch-hiked from Birmingham, where her large Roman Catholic family lived, in order to meet people in the BBC and perhaps find writing work to do (she was a poet, I gathered). She was twenty years old, tall, blonde, with a slim, rather boyish figure and a wild, nervous manner. She smoked incessantly and her fingers were strongly stained with nicotine. Her fingernails were very dirty, and her shabby green corduroy clothes and general air of defiance and unconventionality anticipated the mass-hippie movement which was to come. But she was no ignorant hippie. She loved poetry and music and talking about them, and her eager manner was appealing. I felt there was something dangerous about her. That did not make her less attractive to someone who, though inherently cautious, was capable of impulsive acts.

After getting some promises of work from 'Reggie' and returning to David's flat for some more drinks with myself and others, she left as suddenly as she had come, to hitch-hike back to Birmingham and her disapproving parents. I was intrigued, but not 'in love'. But I did not forget her. It was not long before she paid a second visit to London and, without surprise, we found ourselves in my attic and in bed. She said she was in love with me. I did not say I was in love with her. But I found her very attractive and acted accordingly. Making love is a very good antidote to depression. There were other occasions. It was some time towards the end of February (to place it historically, it was about the time King George VI died) that she told me she was pregnant. She seemed, in her wild way, to be pleased. Did she expect me to be pleased? Possibly. But I was not.

A BBC friend of mine lived in a tumbledown farmhouse in the thickly wooded country north of Newbury which is still attractive although it has been bisected by a motorway. His wife, one of the three Irish sisters David Thomson had once been reputedly in love with, was away with their children for a time and he asked me and René Cutforth to spend the weekend with him and do some walking and drinking. In the ordinary way I would have found this enjoyable. But as I travelled in the train to Newbury, where I was to meet the others and then take a bus further on, I felt a deepening depression, deeper than any I had ever felt before. We met, went on to our friend's house, had some supper and a few drinks, then went to bed. It was a primitive old house, lit by candles and small oil lamps. It was cold, and the wintry woods pressed round it on every side. How much of this cold, this sense of pressure was within myself?

I blew out my candle and composed myself for sleep, thinking I would feel better in the morning. But in that instant my mind seemed to give way, to turn upside down and then become a void. Into that void, or out of that void, I could not say which, flowed an extreme terror which seemed to fill every part of my being. I sprang up, lit the candle with a trembling hand and flung open the small window, shaking and gasping. Did I hope to let the demon out? Had I gone mad? Was this what madness was like? Why had it seized on me, now, here? Was the house haunted? These thoughts passed rapidly through what I was trying desperately to hold on to: my conscious mind. I said the Lord's Prayer. I tried to remember some of the poems I liked best and force myself to repeat them. At all costs I had to regain control. At last – I do not know how long this struggle lasted – perhaps no more than a few minutes – I felt a little calmer, though my hands, feet and genitals were cold as ice – a sign, I remembered, of demonic possession. To be able to put a name to what I felt was some sort of help. I got back into bed, sat upright for a long time, staring at the flower-pattern on the peeling wallpaper, before venturing to blow out the candle and entrust myself to the dark. At last I fell asleep.

When I woke, I felt an indescribably leaden sensation, as though all meaning had been drained not only out of myself, but out of all the things around me, the whole world. I went downstairs but could eat no breakfast. If there was anything odd about my manner my companions showed no sign of noticing it. I have always been known for long periods of silence. Someone suggested, after a bit, that we should take a walk through the woods to the pub in the nearest village. I went along with them like a zombie, along those woodland paths which would normally have seemed so beautiful. Now they seemed not to exist, any more than I did. And in that void of no-feeling I felt, from time to time, the onset of invading terror. We drank some beer. I could hardly drink it. We walked back to the house. I could say nothing. I drank a little brandy and felt slightly better. But as night came on I felt worse and worse. I explained that I must leave, must get back to London. Perhaps they were beginning to understand. We walked to another village, waited in a pub for a hired car to take us to Newbury station. In the bar was a television set, probably the first I had ever seen. I stared at it without understanding; the flickering bluish light may have calmed me a little.

The car came; we got into the train; like a dead man I made my way to my attic in Portland Place. David was away. I was glad of that. I did not feel that anyone could help me. Totally exhausted, I crawled into bed and fell asleep.

Next morning, which was a Monday, the leaden feeling persisted. But the inchoate terror had receded. I was capable of thinking. I washed and shaved. I noticed that my shaving-brush had become evil. Evil, a feeling of meaninglessness which yet had a certain attraction, inhered in it. It was as though it had acquired a squint.

These thoughts, because they interested me, were helpful. It seemed good to be interested in anything. I found I was able to get dressed and go to my 'National Health' doctor somewhere off Great Portland Street. I had never consulted him before. He was Jewish, tired-looking and rather seedy. I explained what had happened to me. He did not seem to think it was anything out of the ordinary. 'Yes, run down, bit of an attack of nerves.' He prescribed some tablets – amphetamine, I suppose, the psychotropic cure-all of the early Fifties. I took them 'as directed'.

For several days I had the leaden feeling, though the terror did not return. Gradually I got back to normal, if that is what it can be called. But I have never been free since then of an awareness of that underlying void. It is close to the surface of my life and sometimes, at moments of weakness or tiredness, I feel the onset of that vertigo which, if not quickly brought under control, must break through, invade and possess my being. I have developed certain tricks, such as deep breathing, to repel that onset, not always successfully (I am reminded of the Tibetan saying that by 'method' a man can live quite comfortably even in hell). There are certain associated temptations. One is to invite the horror, to endure it because of the possibility, even the conviction, that what lies on the other side of that evil might be a counterpoising and transcendent good. But I have never had the courage to let go. The other temptation is less easy to resist: it is a certain pride at having sensations, however unpleasant, which are the 'privilege' of a few, the elect, marked off from those who 'smile and call life pleasure'. This pride is, I am certain, very dangerous; it is playing, not with fire, but with evil itself.

At the time of my apparent deliverance from this first experience, I had no such reflections. I was simply grateful to be delivered – by what? Amphetamine? The mercy of God? I told Kate what had happened to me. She told me she had had the same experience herself a year or so before. Was this simply an expression of kindness and love? Probably. It was certainly very good for me. But now the question of Kate and her pregnancy had to be faced again. I would have favoured an abortion – I have changed my attitudes since then – but she, a Catholic, though 'lapsed', would not hear of it. My friends, when I confided in them, gave conflicting advice. Some, in particular the BBC people, advised me not to marry someone they thought wild and dangerous. The FitzGibbons were in favour, especially after they had met Kate and could think of her as a 'child bride', with the 'beauty of the future'. Their friend and mine, Sally Chilver (the Sally Graves I had known at Oxford), who was childless, offered to adopt the baby. Kate, to her credit, would not hear of this.

As time went on, and I remained in a state of indecision, I was attacked by fibrositis, an agonising stiffness of the shoulders. I had read about the German psychologist Groddeck, whom Auden had enthused about in the Thirties; his theory was that physical symptoms corresponded to mental states or life problems and that popular phrases like 'cold feet' or 'can't swallow that' had literal application. I have proved the truth of this twice in my own life. The moment I decided to marry Kate – it was in a train when I was travelling to the village of Eydon, near Rugby, to write a script about some gamekeeper or other 'character' for 'Jack' Dillon's 'Country Magazine' – my 'pain in the neck', the burden on my shoulders, left me within seconds. Back in my attic in London, where Kate was already living, we agreed to marry. She said: 'I will make your life pure gold.' And what did I reply? Probably something like: 'That certainly sounds extremely nice, I must say.' She was young enough, in love enough, still to find such remarks from me endearing and amusing.

The baby was born in University College Hospital – a girl. We were married just before Christmas in the registry office in Marylebone Town Hall. As we dressed that morning, I mentioned that it would be handy for changing my library books. The

FitzGibbons were witnesses. We were all on the way to being drunk, so much so that the registrar, a true greyman, had to remind us that marriage was a serious matter. The honeymoon, if such it could be called, was spent at the house in the Chilterns of my old friends the film-producer and his wife, who had long since found another lover.

While all this was going on I had, of course, to go on earning some sort of living. Now it was necessary to earn more. I had met, some months before, Denis Mitchell, a features producer in the Manchester branch of the BBC ('the North Region') and had written scripts for him on such subjects as the centenary of Liverpool University and the re-opening of the Free Trade Hall, destroyed by German bombs ten years before. We became friends and he suggested, no doubt bearing my dilemma in mind, that I should join his department in Manchester on a year's contract. I did not much like the idea of living in Manchester, but it would mean a secure job for a year at any rate. I would also see more of my mother and my son, now thirteen and a weekly boarder at Skipton Grammar School. He stayed at weekends in my mother's cottage, absorbing from her rambling talk of past grandeurs and miseries some sense of his own peculiar background and condition. With the appearance of a stepmother only six years older than himself it became more peculiar still.

We arrived in Manchester in the New Year of 1953. I realised at once that Mitchell's attitude had changed. He had the conventional left-wing ideas which were then compulsory not only in the BBC but among all supposedly intelligent people (though there were a few exceptions even in the BBC, notably René Cutforth, who had seen too much of life, including liberation from prison-camp by the Red Army, to swallow all that bigotry and drivel). Mitchell must have been aware already that I did not share those ideas, but we had not talked about politics and so he had not realised how strongly I disagreed with him. He now had a prominent figure of the left, the ballad-singer and playwright Ewan McColl, a bearded man of ruffianly charm, staying with him and writing for his productions. On the evening we arrived, the conversation turned to politics. McColl made some standardised left-wing remark. I could not take it and contradicted him. It was as though I had shouted an obscenity in church.

From that time on, Mitchell's attitude completely changed. He could not, of course, undo my year's contract, since it had been ratified by the Controller of the North Region (CNR) and the Head of Programmes (HP), the diffident, rich, amateur poet and scion of one of the oldest families in England, Brian Cave-Browne-Cave. What he could do was leave me to my own devices. I spent a good deal of time in the Manchester Public Library, doing 'research' on the eight hundredth centenary of the Duchy of Lancaster for a programme which was eventually broadcast with obligatory background music (very agreeable and stirring, always described by the 'composeress' Elisabeth Lutyens, I recalled, as 'cowpat music') from Vaughan Williams's Fifth Symphony.

Meanwhile I was able to observe an interesting phenomenon: the formation, in the North Region Features Department, of a Marxist coterie. The leading spirit was Ewan McColl (a man of talent and ingenuity who, when asked for a bit of a folk-song to liven up some documentary about the Workers, could pop off to the lavatory and be back with a perfectly good one in ten minutes flat). It was noticeable that many of the actors and musicians engaged to take part in Mitchell's productions (one series was the very popular 'Rhythm and Blues', which owed a lot to the American Marxist folk-song expert Alan Lomax and the English A. L. or 'Bert' Lloyd) had the 'right', that is 'left', political views. Some may well have been card-carrying members of the British Communist party.

I put myself beyond redemption one morning in March, when, as was the custom, the BBC people went along at about noon to drink in Yates's magnificent wine-bar, a vast circular chamber like a small Albert Hall, where there were many bars or counters, each with its own set of habitués. I went up to the BBC's counter, where Mitchell and others were drinking and, noticing they seemed stunned and unhappy, remarked: 'What's the matter? What has happened?' Mitchell turned to me slowly and solemnly, and said: 'Haven't you heard the news? Stalin is dead.' I could not help saying: 'Pity he was ever born.' Even in 1953, when the supreme monster's crimes were beginning to be generally known, that might have been an unexpected thing to say even among 'ordinary' people. To these people it was simply blasphemous. They did not speak to me again for a fortnight, and ever afterwards avoided me and also Kate, who, as a wife should, had exactly the same views as myself. If I had gone to Cave-Browne-Cave and told him that a Marxist cell was being formed within his fief, he would have thought I was a madman.

At least things in the North Region were as easygoing in their way as they had been in London. I 'put up' a suggestion that I should write and produce a programme about Lead-Mining in Derbyshire. So for a few months I was able to explore a part of England I had never visited before, the limestone plateaux, hills and gorges of the southern Pennines. This was a district where lead-mining had been carried on from pre-Roman times to the latter part of the nineteenth century, when the seams of lead were exhausted down to a level where it was not economic to mine them because of the expense of pumping machinery. But the spoilheaps of the old mines were full of fluorspar, a mineral which was now becoming valuable. Prospectors were arriving who, by staking a claim under the ancient laws and registering it at the Barmote Hall in Wirksworth, could acquire the right to work them over.

So that summer I found the means of getting out of Manchester into this delectable part of England, full of 'characters' who became, as far as it was possible, my friends. One of them was John Mort, a Moravian and former mining engineer who held the office of Barmaster and presided over half-yearly luncheons in places like Youlgreave or Ashford-on-the-Water, where clay-pipes were smoked and there was heavy drinking. There were stories of eccentric prospectors who, believing that a thousand 'jeeps' in packing cases had been dumped down a certain disused mine, surplus of the wartime arms industry, staked a claim there, only to find they had no means of recovering the treasure. There were stories of a remote pub where women danced naked on the tables. There were long, pub-crawling journeys back to Manchester through those luminous evenings of May when, what with friendship, alcohol and the vestiges of nature-worship, those numinous feelings, long thought dead, revived. One evening, after we had been driving all day about the limestone country, questioning various people about what they remembered of the past, we came to the house of an old mining engineer, a blank, white-washed building in a grove of wind-worn trees. He gave us whisky in tea cups. He played hymn tunes, very badly, on his out-of-tune piano. Every nook and cranny of his house was filled with mineral specimens. The level evening light struck through the windows on these minerals, filling the house with prismatic glory. On the moorland road back to Manchester there were fireflies in the dusk.

Such was the 'work' I did for the BBC in Manchester. We lived, first of all, in a horrible hotel near the University; later, in a superior boarding-house in Fallowfield kept by a landlady whose husband had died of over-eating; finally in a house in Withington which a friend had found for us. Apart from the Marxist cell, we made good friends in Manchester, or rather my wife did, being better than I was at making friends. The house belonged to Professor Max Newman, who held the chair of mathematics at the university, a sarcastic, rather disappointed man, a fine pianist who would 'unwind' at night, after his mathematical labours, by solving chess problems. We and Jane, now a year old, a beautiful child of grave impassivity mingled with fun, had half the house in return for looking after Newman's housekeeping in term time, while his wife, who did not care for Manchester, stayed in Cambridge with their children. It was slightly humiliating to go into his library, crammed with several thousand books of which I could not understand a single word. He was fond of marmalade pudding and pedantic jokes, i.e.: somebody might say, 'I suppose nobody knows the times of the trains to London?' He would say, 'It is not true that nobody knows the times. It is true that nobody in this room knows the times . . .' This infuriated my wife. We set traps for him so that he might make these jokes. He realised this and made them no more. I grew rather fond of him. There were unexpected things about him. One day a youngish man on a motorcycle came to see him. He looked distressed. 'Do you know who that was?' asked Newman after he had gone. 'It was Alan Turing.' The name meant nothing to me. Now I know that he was the man who is supposed to have invented the computer, a man of homosexual temperament who killed himself, not long after this visit, by eating an apple soaked in cyanide. Such single sightings or meetings with the great or famous were typical of a marginal life.

At the weekends we went by train and bus to my mother's cottage. Those seem in retrospect good times when all or most (my sister's mother-in-law, the Alsatian dog-breeder, was an exception) were good and kind. We rode our bicycles about the country lanes where wild flowers – Canterbury bells, mallow, marigolds, bird's eye primrose, bog violet – were still plentiful. There were millions of rabbits, too, before the evil myxomatosis wiped them out. Kate, walking by herself on the limestone terraces, once saw a rabbit parliament, with hundreds of thousands of the harmless creatures in conclave, their rabbit-elders in the midst.

My programme on the lead-mines was finished at last and broadcast. Very few, I imagine, listened to it. It was the time when television was beginning to take hold. That June we watched the

Coronation of Queen Elizabeth, with everyone else in the village, on the first television set to appear there. Its owner, a shoemaker from Skipton, provided a gigantic tin of toffee for refreshment. Those were innocent times. Who would have guessed that within twenty years this magic lantern would turn into a monster, dominating the lives of whole communities, making people entirely and admittedly devoid of any sort of talent into celebrities, an instrument of evil and idiocy unparalleled in the history of mankind?

In the last few months of that year I worked on popular medical programmes, which enabled me, later on, to pass as a doctor, usually an oto-rhyno-laryngologist, with some success. In the New Year I was told my contract would not be renewed. I had not distinguished myself in Manchester, it is true. But there were other reasons. When I took my leave of Denis Mitchell he did not rise from his chair or make the least gesture of goodwill. Was I not a self-declared reactionary and enemy of the human race?

A low, passive and torpid period followed. For the first few months of 1954 we stayed with my mother. Her initial goodwill towards my wife and baby faltered. She began to remove lumps of coal I had put on the fire in the freezing kitchen. There were telephone conversations ('Yes, I'm afraid they're still here'). But it was only her Yorkshire way. She meant no unkindness. When the old dog-breeding tyrant had tried to bully her into leaving her cottage and taking a much more disagreeable one on her own shrinking estates in the neighbouring village, she had gone and torn wallpaper off the walls. The blame, through some manoeuvre or other, fell on me. While in the BBC in Manchester I received several open postcards saying: 'KINDLY STOP TEARING THE WALLPAPER OFF MY WALLS OR LEGAL ACTION WILL BE TAKEN.'

I applied for several jobs in the London BBC without success. I was extraordinarily bad at interviews. Was this because they, the interviewers at the curving desk, five of them if you counted the psychiatrist, wondered why I, an apparently intelligent man of forty-one, with a varied and not wholly undistinguished life behind me, was in need of such jobs? Did their own feeling that there was something wrong somewhere interact with mine? At last, towards the end of August, a friend of René Cutforth's got me a job in the Talks Department of the BBC, decidedly a step down from the Features, but enough to provide a living. It was a matter of reading manuscripts for their amateur short story programme 'Morning Story', occasionally helping with 'A Book at Bedtime' and 'putting up' and producing various miscellaneous talks. The work was not unlike that of an air hostess: checking the spelling and pronunciation of writers and readers, timing them with a stop watch and generally putting them at their ease. My colleague, James Langham, was one of the last gentlemen in the BBC, a sweet-natured, sad man and an agreeable drinking companion, one of those for whom the BBC provided a refuge from life, and he died, painlessly enough, I think, very soon after he retired from it some ten years later.

The Talks Department had a very different atmosphere from the Features Department, though even that, with the coming of television and the general creeping vulgarisation of the BBC, was beginning to lose its lustre. There was a good deal more politics in the Talks and they were the politics of the Left. The 'Head of Talks', Mary Somerville, was the epitome of such attitudes; if she had known of my opinions, or even of my existence, she would probably have sent me packing. One of the trials of the Department was an addiction to meetings and conferences. Everyone had to attend two or three of these a week. Those who enjoyed them, particularly the lady producers – a special kind of person instantly recognisable but not easy to describe – would have liked to attend even more. They loved minutes and agenda and arguments about inter-departmental rivalries and lines of demarcation. They loved writing little notes during these meetings, folding them up and pushing them to each other across the polished table with its note-pads and carafes of water.

I found these meetings, at which I never spoke unless spoken to, excruciatingly boring. So did John Davenport, who at this time had a brief contract with the Department. A man of note in his day and of considerable influence as a teacher, perhaps the greatest non-writing writer of the twentieth century (he had a literary reputation although he never published a book, and could truly be said to 'know everybody'), he had fallen on evil days. He was a very strong, barrel-shaped man with an incongruous, high-pitched voice of extreme refinement. He was a dangerous man to cross, being one of the few literary men, apart from Roy Campbell the poet, who also worked in 'Talks' at one time, who could and actually did knock people down. As far as I could tell, from the great number of stories about this literary pugilist and from my own observation, he never knocked people down unless they deserved it.

He abhorred pomposity and humbug. Once, at a party, when he was being bored by some high-grade legal personage, he picked him up and sat him on the mantelpiece, saying: 'There; you talk like a clock. You shall *be* a clock. Now tick-tock away.' One somnolent, sultry summer afternoon, when John and myself, after a certain amount of drinking, were at one of the interminable 'Talks' meetings and little scraps of paper were circulating in dozens, he suddenly fell asleep and rolled off his chair on to the floor. There he remained, snoring horribly, until the end of the meeting. Nobody took any notice. For the 'Talks' producers this tasteless incident simply had not happened.

Kate and I were hard put to find somewhere to live, moving from one friend's house to another with our meagre belongings until at last, as so often, the FitzGibbons came to our rescue. An elderly Irishman, Michael O'Connell, had built a roomy wooden house for himself in the woods not far from Sacombe's Ash, near Perry Green, the village of Henry Moore. O'Connell was an old Leftie and friend of old-time Communists. He had invented a special method of weaving and dyeing rugs and tapestries in the big ramshackle shed he had built next to his house. Irresistible to women, he found it easy to get girls in the neighbourhood to work as his assistants on the simpler parts of his processes; it was even rumoured that Swedish and German au pair girls, attached to the prosperous inhabitants of Much Hadham and its environs, had been lured to work for him.

He was just off to South Africa (not quite yet the unique land of white fiends it was to become soon afterwards for left-wing thinkers), so what more reasonable than that I, with my wife and baby, should take over his house in the woods? It was an agreeable place, with a big, gnarled sitting-room and two enormous fireplaces where logs were always smouldering or roaring. It was like Hunding's Hut in *The Valkyries* and it would not have been surprising if there had been an ash-tree with a sword embedded in it, in the middle of the room. It would not have been surprising, either, if some Siegmund had appeared, one night of storm, to carry off my wife. But I was no Hunding, she no Sieglinde, and when Siegmund appeared at last it was to be in another, quite different place.

As well as building his own house, O'Connell had wired it for electricity in a most frightening way. Wires led through holes in the walls to all parts of the house, which had an alarmingly unstable upstairs portion, a narrow gallery with a spare bed. There were several naked terminals which you had to beware of. There was only one master-switch so that you had to have the whole place lit up or have no light at all. In order to read in bed, you had to screw a bulb into a socket above it, removing it when you wanted to go to sleep. It was remarkable how soon you got used to sleeping with live terminals dangling over your head.

It was a pleasant place enough and the country round about was still pretty and unspoiled. It was a two-mile walk through woods and fields to Sacombe's Ash and there – or in the pub the

FitzGibbons had taken over so completely that the landlord was now reading Nietzsche – we spent many convivial hours. Friends came and went. One of them was a saturnine-looking man who was said to be completing a novel. He lived in a house in a wood the other side of Hertford and was a great gardener, fitting little green hoods over his splendid roses against the frost at night and murmuring to them encouragingly. This was Nigel Dennis, whose book *Cards of Identity* was published in 1955, after we had left the neighbourhood, and made him instantly famous. One reviewer, alluding to his exceptionally sharp observation of human fraudulence, said he 'would not like to find himself sitting opposite Mr Dennis on a bus.' But although he was an astringent, even cruel writer, Dennis himself was the kindest of men and looked upon us two and our child with the greatest benevolence.

Another man we met, though less often, was one who had been famous for many years: the sculptor Henry Moore. Unlike Dennis, Moore was a man of great simplicity of character, though there was Yorkshire stone beneath his surface benevolence to all. He had a Russian wife, Irina, a capable and formidable person who must have been a great help to him in managing his life, leaving him free to devote himself wholeheartedly to his work. Once, at a party, he said to me with comical ruefulness, in the Yorkshire accent he had retained, little modified: 'They say I'm a great artist. All these great artists, like Picasso and that, seem to have dozens of mistresses. Why don't I have a mistress?'

Week-ends were spent with the FitzGibbons and their innumerable guests, in talking and drinking to the accompaniment of their few gramophone records. Their musical taste was not advanced. But to this day I can never hear 'Mac the Knife' or other songs from *The Threepenny Opera*, or the songs of Burl Ives, such as 'The Blue-tailed Fly', or that most wonderful of all Irish songs of defeat, 'The Battle of Aughrim', without seeing in my mind's eye that sitting-room and those long-departed friends.

Most days during the week I went to London to carry out my simple duties at the BBC. At first I used to get up early, walk the two miles or so to the station at Much Hadham and catch the train from there, returning in the same way in the evenings. Later we met, through Henry Moore, two commercial artists, the Askews, a childless couple of Yorkshire origin who lived in a rambling old converted farmhouse with Muscovy ducks on a pond and a house-keeper called Cissie. They had a studio in St John's Wood where they executed paintings for various advertisers. Askew himself was particularly proud of his oil-painting of sausages frying in a pan. But his wife was the more gifted of the two, or at any rate more in demand with clients. She it was who painted those scenes of smart people at race-meetings whose purpose was to show off clothes; he was only allowed to touch up the blue sky and fleecy clouds. This led to a certain amount of tension between them, as on one rainy evening when we had supper at their house. Askew said: 'I'll drive you home in my car.' 'How do you mean, *your* car?' said his wife. An awkward silence fell. They used to drink fairly heavily, but were not so good at it as the FitzGibbons, or, to tell the truth, myself. One evening when we were at supper with them after a number of powerful drinks Mrs Askew fell asleep with her head in a dish of mashed potatoes, blowing a fluted channel in them with her snores. Askew looked at her with love, for they were very fond of each other, and said in an affectionate tone: 'Ee, Ah never married that!'

To the FitzGibbons they were a great source of merriment. In this we joined, ungratefully, for they were very kind to us. After a bit we came to an arrangement by which they met me at the end of our lane most mornings and gave me a lift as far as St John's Wood. During these journeys they ate a great many boiled sweets, Mrs Askew continually pressing a large jar of them on me. They were somewhat in awe of my 'education' and general knowledge and the time came when Askew made a regular habit of retailing his dreams of the previous night and asking me to interpret them. 'I dreamed of an old man with a beard and I was eating this beard with a knife and fork when suddenly a big snake . . .' I did my best to interpret them in a tactful way.

There was another way the Askews helped me, though unwittingly. They would sometimes let me stay at their big house in St John's Wood, full of Louis Quinze furniture and purple Venetian glass, when I was late in London and they themselves went back to the country. There were times when I did not stay there alone. Ours was a free-and-easy marriage. I was not the only unfaithful party. We lived in a style which later on became known as 'permissive'. This way of living, innocent enough by comparison with what was to come later, was acceptable when it was confined to a few people and taken for granted among them. It was only when it became democratised and was claimed as a 'human right' by all or nearly all that it became a danger to civilisation.

The time came when O'Connell returned from South Africa and we were homeless again. I did not want to live in London and we had various temporary homes, none for long. In the end we had to give up the pleasant life we had been leading (more pleasant for me, perhaps, than for Kate). We found a furnished 'maisonnette' on two floors in Downshire Hill in Hampstead, one of the prettiest streets in London, and moved there in the early summer of 1955. The house belonged to the painter Fred Uhlman and his wife, who themselves lived in the house they owned next door. We found Hampstead a great change. The Uhlmans did not drink (as far as we were concerned people were divided into those who did and those who didn't). Our first experience with them was an evening party with coffee and little Jewish cakes, at which Fred, who had just got back from New York, read out aloud and at great length an article about his paintings in an American paper. Later there were madrigals. Mrs Blanco-White, an elderly lady, formerly one of H. G. Wells's innumerable mistresses, lectured me on Fabianism, assuming, of course, that I was in favour of it.

Mrs Uhlman was a Croft of Croft Castle in Herefordshire, and therefore a member of one of the oldest families in England. It was interesting to observe how her marriage to the Jewish refugee from Germany had affected her. She was intensely shy and would often cross the road when she saw me coming, humming, quite loudly, vaguely Brucknerian themes. In her, pride of ancestry warred with libertarian and internationalist views. I suspect that if it had come to a real showdown, pride of ancestry would have won.

Our daughter Jane was now in her third year, a child of angelic beauty, capable (since she could not, of course, be faultless) of severe tantrums. Later on, when we took her to France for a holiday (our horizons began to widen) peasants by the roadside would exclaim 'Surely this is no mortal child!' or words to that effect. Meanwhile we introduced her to the sea ('I like him very much,' she said) and to the moon and stars and enjoyed that vicarious pleasure which small children can give by reviving our own sense of wonder at the universe. Perhaps I should say that they could give it; one of the most fearful of all the evils television has brought must be the destruction of the child's sense of wonder. What are called the 'best' programmes – such as those on natural history and distant lands – are for that reason the worst. I am glad my own children spent their earliest years without being exposed to this agent of destruction.

Although we were still visiting the FitzGibbons occasionally and staying with my mother in Yorkshire quite often – not over fond of girl children, she was not unfavourable to ours – we made some new friends in London – John Phillimore, who was to become a talented painter, and his circle, Nicholas Mosley, West de Wend Fenton, an eccentric Yorkshire landowner, and others. We gave noisy parties in Downshire Hill when charades and tableaux were enacted – one, the Battle of the Somme, brought Fred Uhlman out of his house and dancing with rage on the pavement in the early hours. He was beginning to realise that we were not really his sort of people. But we had rented the Downshire Hill house for three years and were safe there for the time being.

It was an idle sort of life. My duties at the BBC were not onerous, and always I had the nagging feeling that I was using only a small part of my abilities. I was supposed to be a writer. Why didn't I write? Constantine once said I reminded him of a dynamo which was working away without producing any power. 'Never mind; I will write your books for you,' he said. That was kind; but I would have preferred to write my own. Meanwhile I was amazed at his industry, the way he turned out books, translations, even a play, while at the same time leading his busy social life.

I was not entirely idle. I wrote several 'documentary' features on subjects of my own choice for the Third Programme, then at the height of its power and prestige. One of these was a semi-fictional account of my life in Westmorland just before the outbreak of war. Another was about Colonel Sibthorp, MP for Lincoln for some forty years until his death in 1855 – a man after my own heart, a landowner of the old school, xenophobe, enemy of any and every sort of change from railways to public libraries, and to his contemporaries a comic figure who was continually lampooned in *Punch* and laughed at whenever he spoke in the Commons, which was often and at great length.

Always fond of the British Museum Reading Room, I spent long hours there researching on the Colonel and, because research and note-taking are so much more agreeable than writing, reading everything which had ever been written about him. There, in what poor George Gissing called 'the valley of the shadow of books', I sat on autumn afternoons, distracted on one side by some Central European scholar working on the history of the Bulgarian Exarchate and sucking pungent eucalyptus lozenges, on the other by some tantalisingly pretty Annamite girl student. My head nodded over my books as the leaves of the great catalogue in the round central desk rustled and the fluting voice of Angus Wilson, then Keeper of

Printed Books, later a famous novelist, seemed to come from far away, until I had to jerk myself awake and go out to take a few turns up and down the colonnade with a cigarette.

Another script I wrote for the Third Programme was about the 'Young England' Movement of the 1840s, whose ideas of reviving the feudal system and resisting the 'Manchester bagmen' of Victorian industrialism appealed to me strongly. Oastler, the Tory Radical whose statue stood at the top of Darley Street in Bradford, close to Weir's teashop where Alan Davis and I had met to embroider our fantasies and artificial languages; Ferrand, the enlightened mill-owner of Bingley; fiery Parson Bull, denouncer of Mammon; the great Bishop Phillpotts of Exeter – these were my heroes; my enemies such admirers of the 'stream of tendency' as the bluestocking monster Harriet Martineau, who mocked the ideas of 'Young England' as a frail craft of sticks and paper launched by political children and driven into backwaters by the currents of that mighty stream.

I was pleased with the final narration of my programme: 'The "stream of tendency" on which Miss Martineau had lectured them was flowing on, ever more broadly, rapidly and irresistibly. But already, not far ahead, the thunder of unimaginable cataracts could be heard. Even if they had failed, at least they had tried to dam or divert that stream.'

Now it was 1956. Excited by a once famous book, *Outrage*, by Ian Nairn, in which he wrote, with copious examples, of the degradation of the face of England by the growth of what he called 'Subtopia', I 'put up' to my superiors in the Talks Department the idea of a series of six programmes on this subject which would deal with various parts of the country in turn. So for several months that summer I travelled to such places as Norwich (I had never been in East Anglia before and to my surprise was captivated by that antithesis of the North), Dartmoor, Lancashire, the North Yorkshire Moors and so on. Nominally the scripts were by Sir Hugh Casson, a witty gnome of immense charm and a most agreeable travelling companion. In fact I did most of the work (why not? he was a very busy man). By the end of our series of tours I thought I had made a friend, but never met Sir Hugh again. And why should he bother? He knew who was important and who was not; and don't we all, with few exceptions, keep league tables of this kind? Certainly Constantine did; and I, as a believer in hierarchy, had no cause to complain if my place was, on the whole, rather a lowly one.

The completed programmes were broadcast without anybody taking any particular notice of them. But they had been the means of expressing the Luddism and opposition to 'progress' which I have had ever since I can remember. I felt, as passionately as Nairn, a sense of outrage at the ugliness which was overwhelming our country then and has since spread so far that there seems no longer any hope of stopping it. All that is left is a long groan of despair; thankfulness to have been born in time to see something of the beauty and seemliness of England as it once was; and a duty to fight on even though defeat seems certain.

Now came the time of Suez; the preposterous conspiracy of England, France and the State of Israel, and the political humiliations that followed. The BBC people, then as always, were 'left-wing' almost to a man, and passionately against their own country. One evening The George was crammed with producers and other BBC people all buzzing away like furious wasps. I was amused to find that out of the whole crowd only three people had a good word to say for England: René Cutforth, who loved a fight; myself; and a Jewish actor, Anthony Jacobs, who was naturally thrilled by the lightning advance of the hosts of Israel to the Suez Canal. 'On, to Cairo!' he shouted, as others once shouted 'À Berlin!' or 'Nach Paris!' But his voice was lost in the left-wing hubbub.

Now came a great tragedy. It began with a sense of glory, as the Hungarians rose against their Communist rulers, hanged their secret policemen from lamp-posts and burned their torture-headquarters, toppled (most glorious of all, in symbol) the giant statue of Stalin so that only the stumps of the monster's top-boots remained. Then came the return of the Russian Communist forces; the treachery by which walrus-moustached Nagy and heroic Maleter fell into the hands of their enemies and died. In cosy Hampstead we listened on the wireless to those last pleas for help from the battlements of Europe: 'This is where we live; and this is where we die.' There was no help coming to those heroic people, as we knew well. We wept.

Things were not going well with our marriage. My wife was hurt by my neglect and lack of love – or, to be more accurate, perhaps, my perverse inability or unwillingness to express it. Wild and excitable, she made demands on life much greater than my own. For a time, I think, she felt something of that terror of the void which, as I know well, lies close beneath the surface of our lives.

She recovered. We went to Derbyshire for a week, revisiting some of those places we had known as a refuge from Manchester. We returned to spend a weekend with the FitzGibbons, whose own life was not running very smoothly. They had made, a year or so before, two new friends, Colin Welch, who worked on the *Daily Telegraph*, and his beautiful wife Sybil. Colin had started, about a year before, a column of miscellaneous comment, humour and satire, signed 'Peter Simple', the work of various hands, to which I had contributed occasional items (the first one I ever wrote was on the centenary of the death of Colonel Sibthorp). Colin was a very talented and amusing man, a brilliant mimic and of such ebullient nature that on the croquet lawn at Sacombe's Ash Theodora called him 'Spring-heeled Jack'. Through him I met various other people who worked in Fleet Street: Peregrine Worsthorne, Henry Fairlie, Paul Johnson. This was a new world again, quite different from the world of broadcasting in which I had spent ten not very inspiring or profitable years.

The 'Peter Simple' column seemed to me to have great possibilities as a voice of true Conservatism in the British Press, which was then, as now, dominated by the 'liberal consensus' and mostly written by people who held to the 'left-wing package deal', a phrase coined, I think, by the American William Buckley. This package deal included internationalism; faith in the United Nations, to me one of the most enormous frauds in human history; total condemnation of the White South Africans and a refusal to recognise that they were caught in a historical trap and were trying to extricate themselves by constructing a social system which, if it were applied with justice (a big if, admittedly), was not in itself immoral; egalitarianism; pacifism; hatred of the past; and a strange kind of inverted patriotism, an instinctive feeling that in any dispute our own country must always be in the wrong.

Many people who held to the package deal were 'Lefties' who openly or secretly supported the Soviet Union and its policies. Even those who did not had a lingering feeling that the Soviet Union, being 'socialist' must somehow be working on the right lines and offered hope for the future, even though its rulers had committed and were committing atrocities and massacres on a greater scale than Hitler's. They were still suffering too, even if they did not realise it, from the effects of that intensive propaganda of the war years about 'our gallant Russian allies' and the 'glorious Red Army' which still lingered even when the Red Army and the evil system it supported had become an unmistakable threat to what remained of our own liberties.

The 'liberal consensus' at its silliest involved a belief in human perfectibility and paradise on earth. It represented, in fact, everything I abhorred. Colin Welch and I were very much in agreement on most things, though he seemed rather less extreme in his 'reactionary' views than I and did not entirely share my hatred of 'progress'. He was less eager than I to unfurl the green banner of General Ludd (for I was a 'Green' long before the 'Greens' were thought of, and long before the 'Environment' was invented).

The moment of my introduction to the Press was, as it happened, the moment when the BBC was about to be transformed. Television had arrived. The brightest and most ambitious people in the BBC were beginning to 'go over' to it. Nothing would be the same again. That cosy camaraderie was fading. Cracks were appearing in the majestic fabric of 'BH'. Its majesty was soon to be challenged by the new, flashy, gimcrack structures at Shepherd's Bush and Lime Grove. Soon there would be few who could even translate the noble Latin inscription in the foyer of 'BH', with its formal flower arrangements in chaste white urns (the work of a special section of pious and devoted women) beneath the bas-relief of Ariel by Eric Gill: 'Hoc Templum Artium ...' Later there would be few who even knew it was in Latin.

I have mentioned that it was possible, if you made yourself agreeable to the girls who worked in the Archives Department, to get hold of your own Personal File and examine it. It was about this time that I contrived to get hold of mine. Amid details of the work I had done for the 'Corp' – it was only later that it became known to journalists as the 'Beeb' – I came upon this sentence: 'He is not really BBC material.' An alarm bell rang loudly in my mind. Not long after this I was summoned for an interview with an administrator, a 'greyman' if ever there was one, grey-suited, grey-eyed, grey-haired, grey-minded. He hummed and hawed a bit and then began to talk about changes in the Corporation, the impact of television, reorganisation, retrenchment. He could not undertake to say that my contract – I had never reached the status of 'established' staff, who were unsackable except for the gravest offences, and even so one producer, who had exposed himself in the lift to several women secretaries, only got a warning – it would not be fair for him, he said, to say that my contract would be renewed indefinitely. Had I thought about my plans for the future? He thought it only right ...

I had not thought about my plans for the future. It was not my habit to do so. But now I began to think, not about my plans, for I had none, but about the future. I was forty-three years old. I had done nothing much with my life; I had not 'made something of it' though many people had exhorted me to do so. Apart from my years in the Army (now a lost world, a book closed and sealed), it had been a precarious life in terms of money, status or achievement, a life of odd jobs, a life which when I thought about it, seemed somewhat futile (and so, in a way, appealing to the masochistic side of my nature). It had been a life of self-indulgence marred by an incapacity for enjoyment. I had made little use of such talents as I had. I was even beginning to accept that I had not got any talents to speak of. What had happened to those dreams of being a great writer, of becoming rich and famous, or at any rate famous? The more I thought about my future, as the 'greyman' had recommended, the more unpromising it seemed.

I was staying with Kate at the FitzGibbons' when Colin Welch, who had moved to London with his wife and five-year-old son – the same age as our daughter – arrived on a visit. He mentioned that he was thinking of trying to get a regular full-time collaborator for the 'Peter Simple' column. I made no particular response to this. It was good old Theodora, of course, who suddenly shouted: 'Can't you see, you fathead? He's offering you a job.' 'I never thought of that,' I muttered. 'I must think about it.' I thought about it and agreed to take it. It occurred to me that my humorous fantasies might be turned to better account.

Soon afterwards I had the pleasure of telling the 'greyman' that I had decided to leave the BBC and would be taking a job on the *Daily Telegraph*. He obviously thought it would be a great comedown (so did my mother, for whom, as for most people, a BBC producer, even of the most unimportant kind, had a far higher status than a journalist – I would never get to be an announcer now, and what, after all, was a mere reporter?). But he wished me all success in my new career.

So, on New Year's Day, 1957, after a sleepless night of confused celebration, I sat down for the first time at my desk in the *Daily Telegraph* with one of the most appalling hangovers I have ever had in my life, and without a single idea in my head. I would have been incredulous, if not appalled, if I had been told I would still be there thirty years later, still spinning the faded dream with which this book begins.

A Dubious Codicil

TO JANE

Contents

I
Beyond the Lodge

The marble entrance-hall and, the part standing for the whole, the mahogany reception desk of the *Daily Telegraph*'s neo-Egyptian building in Fleet Street – slab-faced, solid and lofty for those times before the London skyscrapers overtopped St Paul's and proclaimed the empire of imaginary money – was known to all the staff, of whatever degree, as 'the Lodge'. It was so called because it was the entry to the domain of the dynasty of newspaper magnates who had founded and still owned the newspaper, the Berry Family, originally from South Wales, the head of which had borne, since 1941, the title of Viscount Camrose.

The second son of the first Viscount was the Hon. Michael Berry, who now ruled as Editor-in-Chief in a suite of panelled, finely furnished rooms on the fifth floor (known to all as 'The Fifth Floor'), complete with office, study, library, dining-room, kitchen, bedrooms and everything else needed for a miniature gentleman's seat. There was even a narrow strip of garden, with real flower-beds, real shrubs and a real lawn, below the parapet outside the tall French windows, and a real gardener to tend it. If it had been possible (and there were times, later on, when I believed it was), there would have been an avenue, terraces, fountains, statues, a walled garden producing peaches and nectarines as fine as any in Fleet Street for the master's table, a lake, a deer park, pheasant coverts, a home-farm and a prospect of rolling, fertile countryside, most of it in the possession of the family.

Mr Berry (or 'Michael', as some of his employees liked to call him, not necessarily to his face) was a worthy proprietor of this establishment. He had two others, one in the Home Counties and one in Cowley Street, Westminster, where his wife, Lady Pamela Berry, presided over a famous salon. She was a highly fashionable and sociable person, daughter of the first Lord Birkenhead, whose supposed part-gypsy descent (he was a Smith, or Petulengro) was evident, so some thought, in her dark good looks, flashing eyes and animated manner. It was possible, certainly, to imagine her dancing by a gypsy campfire or sitting, dressed in the bright colours favoured by gypsy womenfolk, on the steps of a gaily-painted hooped wagon of the traditional kind, making clothes-pegs which she would later offer for sale to mesmerised, even terrified, village housewives, with curses if they did not buy, and a promise of cut-price fortune-telling if they did.

Mr Berry evoked no such old-fashioned fantasies. It was impossible to imagine him in the complementary role of a Romany *Chal* or even a Gypsy Gentleman. He seemed in every way the opposite of his wife. He was, at the time I entered his service, a tall, handsome man of middle age without a trace of grey in his jet-black hair, with pleasant good manners and an air of extreme reserve. His shyness was notorious. It was said that once, when as a young man he had to make a public speech, he fainted clean away. But by my day he had learned, by admirable application, to master his shyness and even turn it to an advantage, making his hesitant manner serve a special kind of edged and ironical humour, most enjoyable for those who could appreciate such nuances, provided they were not its victims.

For myself, I never was. But then, petrified with class-conscious dread of both Michael Berry and Lady Pamela, I

2

scarcely exchanged more than a few words with either of them during my whole thirty years of service. Michael Berry, whose shyness might in theory have made a bond between us (there is an Irish proverb, 'One beetle knows another beetle'), once invited me, along with other selected members of staff, to one of his regular small luncheon-parties; I was so nervous I could not lift a glass to my mouth, and had to explain to him that my doctor had forbidden me alcohol, a thing so obviously untrue that he must have smiled inwardly. About the same time, Lady Pamela invited me to one of her evening parties in Cowley Street; I was so nervous I drank too many champagne cocktails, encouraged by a sympathetic butler, himself apparently drunk, and becoming unstable, I trod clumsily and heavily on her foot. Neither invitation was ever repeated.

No such anguished thoughts as these, of course, were in my mind when, on the cold grey New Year's Day of 1957 I passed, for the first time as an employee, through the mahogany-framed revolving door of Peterborough Court, as the Berrys' domain was called. Vaguely, I noted the racks of newspapers round the walls and the bronze tablet with its roll of honour commemorating employees killed in the two wars. Vaguely I returned the greetings of the men at the reception desk and took one of the three slow, ancient lifts to the 'Way of the World' room on the fourth floor to present myself to my friend of two years' standing, and now my colleague, Colin Welch.

Did I have any coherent thoughts at all? I had had scarcely any sleep; I had passed the night in a drunken phantasmagoria, partly with my wife Kate, partly with others mostly unremembered, in pubs, clubs and other places barely identifiable at the time, now a confused blur. My head throbbed; and such was the force of this superlative hangover that it did not even throb in a regular rhythm, but with unpredictable, jerking agony. Stale alcohol pumped through my veins and seethed in every joint and ganglion. Through eyes three-quarters closed I peered at the pale grey world as though trapped at the back of a splintered mirror. My hands and feet seemed to disengage from my body as the great clock which hung over Fleet Street, below the window, began to strike the hour of eleven.

It was Monday, the first day of the columnar week. A column would have to be ready for the 'deadline' of six o'clock that evening for the following day's paper. It must have been obvious to Colin, a man well able to recognise the symptoms of hang-overs, but of robust constitution and resilient temper, that he could expect no writing from me. He must have wondered, on that first morning, if he had done the right thing in rescuing me from the BBC and bringing me on to the paper as a regular, salaried collaborator on his column, which at the time used many occasional contributions from various hands, previously including mine. But he showed no uneasiness, giving me a few 'files' to look over, explaining the organisation and timetable of the column and introducing me to those who worked on it.

He had started the column on 18 October 1955 (it is important to get dates right), with a staff of two editorial assistants and a secretary, Miss Thompson, a dark, well-built woman in her thirties, an expert at typing, filing correspondence and constructing card indexes of formal beauty whose scanty remains lingered in the filing-cabinets for years afterwards, hopelessly pleading reminders of a lost efficiency which came to seem pointless and meaningless and perhaps had always been so.

The duties of the two editorial assistants, Michael Hogg and John Herbert, consisted mainly of reading the day's newspapers and occasionally extracting possible subjects for us to write about. John Herbert, son of A. P. Herbert, the MP and comic writer, was a tall, agreeable man in his late twenties; he left, soon after I arrived, to better himself in the world of the higher auctioneering. Michael Hogg, about the same age, was equally agreeable, but already somewhat inclined to world-weariness and a fairly low view of people in general. He had an enchanting wife, Elizabeth, always known as Liz, daughter of an eccentric Herefordshire baronet. She was an accomplished musician and further endeared to me by her knowledge of those 'Celtic' legends and Dark Age Affairs ('the Matter of Britain') on which I have always doted.

When I first joined the staff, and before he left to take a job elsewhere on the paper, it was Michael Hogg's daily duty to 'put the column to bed' on the 'stone' down below in the basement, where the printers and compositors worked and where, every day, at about half past three in the afternoon, the great presses began to roll with a distant roar which pervaded and gently shook the whole massive building. There was a slight vibration, like a ship's engines; the promise of a voyage never fulfilled, let alone begun, but always mysterious and pleasurable to anyone as addicted to illusions as I was.

An indispensable part of the columnar 'team', as it would have repulsively been called if it had existed later on when journalists began to write about each other and become familiar figures on the television screen, was Michael ffolkes, whose real name was Brian Davis. He drew the one or two stylish little drawings which had appeared every day in the four-days-a-week column from its earliest days. Already a successful comic artist, with aspirations and talents for something more, he worked from a studio high up in Shaftesbury Avenue, a strange room of narrow triangular shape crammed with an astounding assortment of treasures, as well as with his artist's paraphernalia – masks, crystals, brass jugs and trays, completed or half-completed drawings and paintings, screens stuck with exotic odds and ends. A huge photograph of a painting by the nineteenth-century French Salon painter Bouguereau was pasted on one wall, showing a crowd of naked nymphs, all identical, perfectly shaped, white-skinned, and of ideal nubility. This stupefying work of painstaking bad taste and technical skill amused Michael greatly; but it would be hypocritical to say that he – or any other man – did not enjoy looking at it.

From this junk-shop of a studio he telephoned every day at lunchtime to discuss what he should draw, and showed remarkable rapport and skill in providing what was needed, often producing little masterpieces of elegance and wit which, when reduced to microscopic proportions on the printed page, might easily escape the readers' notice. It was an affectation of his to maintain that he had never met any people like the 'characters' who subsequently appeared in the column. Yet somehow he contrived to realise them in a few lines with remarkable accuracy. He would sometimes drop into the *Telegraph* office in the evening with the day's drawings: a stocky, dark-haired man of about thirty when I first knew him, some twelve years younger than myself, a man of complicated origins, jaunty and charming, with a good opinion of himself. And why not? He was a friendly, amusing man, good company, and a very talented artist.

In some ways he was more like my BBC acquaintances than the Fleet Street people I was now getting to know. He was fond of a drink and his studio was never without a good supply of it, including champagne, for he believed in a 'high standard of living'. In his liking for drink he was, of course, no different from the Fleet Street journalists or anyone else I could get on with; but he was what might be called raffish, an old-fashioned 'Bohemian' artist with a distinctly irregular private life made

6

possible by a respectable, domestically efficient Jewish wife who looked after their flat in Pimlico and their two young children.

Colin Welch, the man who had rescued me so providentially from the BBC, though I did not realise how providential this was to prove, now regarded me, on that first day of my new career, with what must have been dubious eyes, as he and his assistants went through the process of producing a column while I gradually surfaced from my hangover. He was a lively, learned man of about the same age as Michael ffolkes; he had served in the army towards the end of the war and was wounded in the Normandy campaign. After the war he went up to Peterhouse, Cambridge, along with his friend and coeval Peregrine Worsthorne, and read history and economics.

He was at this time a compact, strongly-built man with thick dark curly hair and an exceptionally fine set of teeth, enabling him to smile more often and convincingly than I, though he would almost certainly have done so whatever his teeth had been like. He wore spectacles and his face belonged to a certain unmistakably English type which can be found in all classes anywhere, any day of the week.

But *this* man could not be found any day of the week in any class. He had 'a first-class mind', and imagination and literary talent to go with it. He was a magnificent talker on many subjects and one of the finest mimics I have met, able to set me in fits of laughter even when doing imitations of people I did not know, such as the aged father of Desmond Williams, a legendary Irishman who had just failed to get a fellowship at Peterhouse and now taught history at the National University of Ireland.

Colin had a prodigious knowledge and memory of music, and should some favourite musical work come to mind, he was capable of whistling, note-perfect, long extracts, even, it

seemed, whole operas, persisting until even the most passionately musical begged him to stop. Fond of drinking as he was
and with certain traits of fascinating eccentricity (he had a
habit, for example, of picking his nose, occasionally tasting the
extracted mucus or 'bogey', without any attempt to conceal
himself, as most people would, behind a newspaper), we could
hardly fail to get on, even though this merry, energetic, public
school man (like Worsthorne, he had been at Stowe) with his
easy, agreeable manners and incipient fondness for powerful
motorcyles, was a very different person from myself.

On that first day and for the succeeding few days, when I
had got over my initial panic and began writing my share of the
column, at first hesitatingly then with growing confidence, I felt
slightly homesick for the BBC. I had expected to find a world
of dynamic, shirt-sleeved journalists in Fleet Street, with green
eye-shades, always working madly against the clock and continually talking on several telephones at once with their feet on
the desk.

In fact the office of the *Daily Telegraph* seemed rather like a
shabbier version of 'B. H.', with older, less comfortable furniture and inferior washrooms and lavatories, without carpets on
the floors or tastefully arranged flowers in the foyer. I had
exchanged 'programme', 'cue', 'script' and 'studio' for 'copy',
'deadline' and 'stone', and for 'the Corp' (as the BBC was
called by its employees before it became 'the Beeb') 'the office',
one of the many different newspaper offices which made up
Fleet Street, 'the Street of Shame', as some of its denizens
called it even in those days, long before it came to deserve the
name so thoroughly – and, in its later days, after the Great
Diaspora, a name worse than shame and almost beyond words.

I had exchanged the George and the Stag, and its ancillary
afternoon drinking club – the 'M. L.', with its agreeable ming-

ling of BBC people and members of the 'mantle trade' from neighbouring Great Portland Street – for the Kings and Keys, a long, narrow pub next door to the *Telegraph* and part of the Berry domains, where the company was made up of journalists and printers. Although I did not know it, I was to spend a good deal of the next thirty years in this pub and to elaborate, in these rather unpromising surroundings, much of what might be called the mature 'Peter Simple' column. So I must fix it in memory and describe it. When I first went there it was very much a 'basic pub': a rough, almost primitive place with a few old cane chairs arranged along the bar; if it did not have sawdust on the floor it should have done.

The greater part of it was an L-shaped saloon bar, with a small 'snug' in one corner near the door which was traditionally used only by the blue-overalled printers when they grew tired, on fine evenings, of leaning against the front of the building between shifts, gazing sardonically at all that went on in the street, hoping, perhaps, for an accident to happen. Observant, self-confident and well-paid, they were able, as they well knew, to enforce their will over the management at any time by bringing the presses to a standstill, and so thought themselves, not without reason, greatly superior to the journalists. About these, I felt, they knew much more than the journalists knew about them, stolidly sinking their pints of beer and listening with half an ear as the objects of their observation became more and more noisy, ribald, excited and recklessly indiscreet towards closing time.

The landlord, in those early days, was a middle-aged Irishman, Seán Macnamara, who was reputed not only to have fought with distinction in the Troubles and the Civil War, reaching the rank of Commandant, but to have been one of General O'Duffy's Blueshirts, one of those who volunteered to fight for Franco and were therefore on the right side in the Spanish Civil War as far as I was concerned. His tales of ambushing British soldiers during the Troubles went down much better then than they would now. He was a pleasant enough man of strong will-power, and a born landlord. He demonstrated both his military authority and his power of command, as well as his right-wing opinions, to notable effect one evening when I was in the bar and the bulbous, drunken face of Brendan Behan, then at the height of his fame, appeared round the door. 'Out! I'll not serve your sort here!' barked Macnamara, repeating the words in Irish for good measure, and the man who in any other circumstances would have begun flailing his fists, vomiting and breaking up the furniture – all perhaps at the same time (for he was a highly talented man in this department) – instantly disappeared.

I had exchanged the 'grey men' of the BBC administrative machine and the endless conferences of the Talks Department for the far from grey editor of the *Daily Telegraph*, Sir Colin Coote, to whom alone the column was responsible. He was inclined to distrust it. It had been the brainchild, in the first place, of his deputy editor, Donald McLachlan, a clever but highly eccentric man, formerly in Naval Intelligence, with a cryptographer's mind and a habit of making tangential remarks which sometimes made him difficult to follow. 'I've got an idea for you,' he would say when I encountered him somewhere in the building. 'Come into my room and I'll tell you all about it.' But by the time I had followed him into his room he had to admit, with a rueful look, that he had forgotten what his idea was. Sir Colin's opinion of him was obviously low. He showed this by a practice of referring to him in the presence of subordinates as 'Macglashan', 'MacCorquodale' or anything of that sort which took his fancy, always with a look of complicity for whoever else was present. (As I still had a vestige of Army feeling about what was and was not done, I found this disagreeable, even shocking.) He gave similar treatment to H. D. Ziman (always known as 'Zed'), the literary editor, who had been at Rugby with him but had earned his contempt for not being able to bowl overarm; a garrulous Jewish intellectual, he lived in Belsize Park and gave wine and cheese parties: none of these things can have endeared him to the editor.

Sir Colin was a portentous figure in his late sixties, large, rubicund and upright, very healthy-looking but with a hint of the sardonic and choleric in his expression. Later on, when Michael Hogg had left and, for a time, Colin and I took turns to 'put the column to bed', I had to face him across the imposing editorial desk in his panelled room where conventional portraits of previous owners and editors looked down from the walls. I found it quite an ordeal. Here was a man who had 'done everything' – fought gallantly in the Great War, sat in Parliament, raced at Brooklands, flown solo to Le Touquet and back. He had also had three wives and was, I had been told, a figure of high romance.

In hospital after being wounded in France, he had fallen in love with a beautiful French nurse, and she with him. But through the chances of war they completely lost touch with each other. Back in England and picking up the threads of his career, he married an Englishwoman of his own class and had several children. Then one day in the Thirties he was sitting in Brown's Hotel, having tea with his wife and family when, suddenly looking up, he saw his French beloved, older but still just as beautiful, crossing the room and making for the lift.

Without a moment's hesitation he excused himself, got to his feet and followed her into the lift. Between floors (I cannot say how many – they may have gone up and down the whole way several times for all I know) he pleaded with her to stop whatever she was doing – she may have been married herself – and run away with him. She agreed, they fell into each other's arms, descended to the ground floor by another way and disappeared. Divorced, they married. But their happiness was brief. She died soon afterwards, leaving him broken-hearted. For his third wife he took, in due course, a sensible Dutch lady, a magnificent cook and above-average bridge player.

The last part of this story was undoubtedly true, whatever might be said of the rest. I could not help thinking of it on evenings when it was my turn for the painful duty of sitting on the other side of his desk and watching him read the day's offerings: it helped me in a situation which was not unlike my encounters with my unfortunate tutors at Oxford twenty years before. But at least I was usually sober and did not have to read the stuff aloud; I was paid for it and on the whole it was of a higher quality than my Oxford essays. Not that this necessarily helped. Sir Colin's attitude was not encouraging (perhaps his suspicion of anything connected with 'MacGillivray' persisted) and never once did I notice even a hint of a smile. 'Not too many skits please, Wharton,' he would say when some fantasy of mine seemed to him to have got out of hand. 'I don't quite see the point of this bit about Alderman Foodbotham being too big to get into the tram terminus.' On these occasions he had something in common with the overpowering alderman himself. And once he asked of ffolkes and his drawings: 'Does he get paid for these sketches?'

For obvious reasons, he was a great francophile (his stamp-collection was said to consist only of French stamps), and excessively anti-German. Inclined to be pro-German myself for atavistic and other reasons, I now learnt to apply a trick I had acquired in the army: if you had not shaved very convincingly before going on parade, you would leave a button undone. When the inspecting officer came round this diverted his attention from the more serious fault, and could immediately be put right. So when I wanted to make sure of slipping some item into the column, perhaps a 'skit' too fantastical for Sir Colin's taste, I would write another item full of praise for the Germans. The decoy always worked. 'Can't have this!' he would say, good-humouredly enough, as he read something extolling German virtue. 'Can't have the Hun getting above himself, you know!' And so some new aspect of Alderman Foodbotham or Mrs Dutt-Pauker got into print.

For my knowledge of Sir Colin's private life, particularly the romantic side of it, I was indebted to Claude Worsthorne, wife of 'Perry' Worsthorne (I had met both of them occasionally in the FitzGibbon circle when the Welches were our neighbours at Much Hadham). After Miss Thompson left, Claude became columnar secretary. Known as Claudie, she was a skilled story-teller with a talent for scandalous embroidery which may sometimes have got her into trouble. A very small, attractive, blonde Frenchwoman born in Egypt (her father was a director of the Suez Canal Company), she had a fine command of English apart from a few Gallicisms and personal idiomatic eccentricities. But although some believed she did not have to do this, she always spoke English with a strong French accent.

She had been married when very young, just before the outbreak of the Second World War, to a young scion of the Welsh squirearchy who promptly joined the RAF and vanished, leaving her pregnant in a large dark house in Carmarthenshire to be cared for by two aunts, among people who scarcely spoke English, let alone French. She escaped and made her way to London where she joined the Free French and was said to have been photographed at the side of General de Gaulle ('Titch and Lofty'). Totally fearless, with marked scatological tendencies and, on the whole, a poor opinion of the English (her description of the smell inside a crowded London bus was a *tour de force*) she was now married, with a daughter of about the same age as mine, to one of those upper-class cosmopolitan Englishmen whose relations all have confusingly different names.

Perry Worsthorne was the younger son of Lady Norman (later married to the notorious Governor of the Bank of England and *bête noire* of my old comrades the Greenshirts) by the Belgian Baron Kok de Gooreynd. Lady Norman, herself part Belgian, came from an ancient Lancastrian family, the Towneleys, whose estates once included the town of Burnley (their house, Towneley Hall, is now the municipal museum). Adopted as Conservative Candidate for Burnley, the Baron shrewdly reasoned that the name Kok de Gooreynd might not appeal to the general run of the electors. So he took the name of Worsthorne from a small village on what remained of the Towneley estates. For all that, he was not elected. He then reverted to his original name. But of his two sons, the elder, Simon, took the name Towneley on inheriting the property, while the younger, Peregrine, who retained the name Worsthorne, inherited nothing.

Claudie, whether mistakenly or on purpose – I could never make out which – was addicted to getting English phrases slightly wrong ('Claudieisms'); later she used to say pityingly of her husband, 'Poor boy, 'e 'as not a pea to 'is name'. She also said ''e is as poor as a church rat'. Neither statement, to judge from the Worsthornes' manner of life, was strictly true; they moved in higher social circles than other journalists on the *Telegraph*, including the editor, and Perry's lofty, flamboyant manner was not popular with all of them.

When I joined the paper and secured, for the first time in my life, at the age of forty-three, a regular salaried job, I dropped, with relief, all the odd and disparate freelance activities – writing for *Punch*, editing the Football Association Yearbook, ghosting memoirs, rewriting other people's books and so on – which had furnished me with a meagre and precarious livelihood. I now had a contract and a salary of £1,600 a year, plus 'expenses'. This was more than I had ever dreamed of; indeed it was quite a long time before I stopped being surprised at being paid anything at all for what I was doing.

Cunningly, I kept one link with the BBC. I retained the part of my job there which entailed reading the manuscripts of about a hundred short stories a week – the work of amateur writers – and selecting about half a dozen of them for various actors to read on the then popular radio programme 'Morning Story', produced by my sad but lovable friend and drinking companion James Langham, one of the last gentlemen of the BBC. So innocent were those short stories; their plots seldom involved anything more exciting than a poor but deserving person unexpectedly coming into a fortune or the late-won love of some lonely widow or widower; innocent, indeed, was the BBC itself in those days, innocent and secure!

Yet at that very moment – the year 1957 was almost the precise turning-point, if there was such a thing – a movement was beginning, not only in the BBC but all over England, which in a few years was first to shake, and then bring down, that innocent security in ruins. It was the beginning of what became known, whether in approval or condemnation, as 'the permissive age'. I and most of my friends had always been 'permissive'; but here was a new kind of permissiveness, the low permissiveness of democracy; sexual freedom, once taken for granted by a few, was claimed by the too-many, and not

15

only claimed but openly preached as a 'right', a principle and before long, a duty. Reticence and modesty became matters for public ridicule. A certain amount of hypocrisy is necessary in any civilised society. Now it was shoved aside. The new reformers, who often had financial or political motives, or both, for hastening this process, had the way clear. Ironically, they might themselves have been shocked and horrified if they could have foreseen the outcome in England thirty years later.

In those days we saw only the first, feeble intimations of the horrors of today. 'Espresso bars' appeared, populated by dim young nihilists who had never heard the term; 'teddy boys'; 'guitars and skiffle-boards'; 'rock 'n roll'; and 'angry young men'. They jeered at stuffy old class-ridden England, sometimes, indeed, amusingly and justifiably. How far away it all seems now, and, considering all that has happened since, how innocent!

One small sign of decay I had noted some years before when a couple of intellectual Australians, he a physicist, she a would-be novelist with whom I had a brief, sad and remorse-ridden love affair, told me they regarded jazz as an important 'art form'. I had always enjoyed this kind of music as a background to getting drunk in night-clubs on the rare occasions I went to night-clubs with Constantine FitzGibbon, the only person I knew who frequented them. I was amazed and incredulous to come across intelligent people who took jazz seriously; and not merely that, but were themselves amazed and incredulous to find I didn't. It was the first time I had come across this phenomenon, later familiar in the writings of Kingsley Amis and Philip Larkin.

In the wider world other greater phenomena were becoming noticeable, and now that I was obliged to read the newspapers, unavoidable: the headlong advance of that science and technology I had always feared and detested, manifesting itself in such things as scientific farming; nuclear power stations; military rocket-ranges in, of all places, the Hebrides; chemical contraception (the application of technology to sexual love) and artificial insemination for human beings; the 'conquest of space', in which the Soviet Communists with their 'sputnik' took the lead and were the first to spout boastful nonsense about such technological conjuring tricks, 'signs and wonders' to delude simple-minded people.

Those were the days when the last remnants of the British Empire in Africa were liquidated and replaced by pseudo-states under 'black majority rule'; and, by a strange process of reversal, when the first batches of immigrants were arriving in England. Those were the days also, when television began to take a hold on minds and habits, stealthily growing from an ingenious toy into one of the greatest influences – and certainly the most evil – in the life of England. Bogus art and every sort of impudent imposture began to flourish as never before. Such was the rich and abundant material 'Peter Simple' had to work on. Like Juvenal who had written in the decadence of Imperial Rome, I found it impossible not to write satire. The difficulty was to find a way to do it: a column with fictitious 'characters' epitomising various types of detestable humbug seemed the best way.

Mrs Dutt-Pauker, the 'Hampstead thinker', the rich fellow-traveller and specialist in every kind of left-wing prejudice from adulation of the Soviet Union to virulent hatred of white South Africa, was, I think, the only important columnar 'character' who had appeared, in a rudimentary form, before I joined the column. Her name, invented by Colin, was, of course, an ingenious combination of Palme Dutt, the Suedo-Bengali theoretician of the Communist Party of Great Britain, and Anna Pauker, the post-war Romanian Communist leader who once complained that 'not nearly enough middle-class people were committing suicide'. This stereotype I contrived to flesh out, in the course of time, with details derived from some of the well-off left-wing ladies of our part of Hampstead.

It was not long before other 'characters' began to take shape. It was understood in the first place that for the most part Colin would write the 'serious' and polemical items of the four or five which made up the daily column (my knowledge of politics was slight in those days, and of economics, nil, as it has remained) and I the 'funny' and fantastical items. For these, in my early days on the column while I was still trying to adjust to my new life, Colin sometimes provided the germ (for example, he suggested the name of the fatuous soldier General Nidgett, who spoke like Montgomery, only more so); I had originally called the prodigious Bradford alderman (a version of one of my giant archetypal figures, along with Sir Marsden Braithwaite in my novel *Sheldrake* and, in real life, Lord Hothfield, the perpetual mayor of Appleby, and Sir Stanley Rous, the overpowering head of the Football Association) by the inadequate though authentically West Riding name of 'Alderman Sugden'. 'Foodbotham' was Colin's suggestion, a better comic name and one which would avert any trouble from the real-life Sugdens of the region. It was a curious thing that I was at first careless of possible libel; yet I still retained, from my training at the BBC, an instinctive horror of advertising; it was many years before I could write the words 'Guinness' or even 'Rolls-Royce' without profound misgiving.

By nature passive and lacking in initiative, and morbidly afraid, through inordinate pride, of failure, I could not, I think, have started the column myself from scratch, even if it had been purely humorous and fantastical, though I had found my gifts in that direction exploitable in *Punch* and *Sheldrake*. This was a pity because there was no reason, in principle, why I should not have secured myself a newspaper column long before, perhaps on leaving the army, and become reasonably rich and famous (though not in the way I originally hoped) and saved myself those years of self-indulgent obscurity in the BBC with all the troubles they led to. Such thoughts are of course utterly profitless.

However, given the impetus and example of a more vigorous personality, himself with no small comic talent, I soon began to discover a capacity for developing my inventions on my own lines. For a man lazy and apathetic by nature the routine of working four days a week to a newspaper deadline was salvation; capable of very hard work when given an incentive and with a very strong sense of duty and honesty springing from self-suspicion of being fundamentally irresponsible and dishonest, combined with guilt at the waste of my earlier years, I found myself, for the first time in my life, in a job I could actually do well and – a thing entirely new to me – get well paid for. Or so it seemed, with my low expectations at that time.

Colin had rescued me not only from the dead-end of the BBC but from my own sense of futility, my only too conscious failure to make use of whatever talent I may have had. For this I was deeply grateful. But needless to say, as with all my endeavours, a morbid doubt lurked. Could my work be regarded as a structure, however elaborate, luxuriant and transformed by my own personal idiosyncracies and talents it later became, raised on another man's foundations? And if so, was this an aspect of the Jewish side of my nature, the vestigial, thinned-out yet still troubling legacy of my part-Jewish paternal grand-parents?

In his book *Sex and Character*, published at the beginning of this century, the German Jewish writer Otto Weininger builds a great edifice of mad logic to show that all human beings partake, on a graduated scale which he demonstrates mathematically, of the masculine and feminine nature, the active and passive, the creative and derivative, and that only the most masculine people can possess original genius, the highest human quality. The Jewish nature, he holds, is essentially feminine, which is why there are no Jewish artists, writers or composers of original genius, only adapters and developers, however talented, of the ideas and insights of others. Knowing that as a Jew (and also a homosexual) he could not be a man of genius for all the fame his book had brought him, the wretched and despairing Weininger, epitome of Jewish self-hatred, shot himself at the age of twenty-three in Bonn, birthplace of Beethoven, the greatest genius and therefore the greatest man who ever lived. In one of his few jokes Hitler is reported to have said of Weininger that he was the only good Jew whom he had ever heard of and a fine example for all the others to follow.

Because of the book's supposed 'anti-semitism' – an objection which rests on the assumption that the Jews as a race are above criticism, an assumption reactively derived from Hitler's persecution – and also because of its 'sexism' and opposition to homosexuality, both attitudes unacceptable to present fashion (probably for the same reactive, anti-Hitlerian reason) – *Sex and Character* is now very difficult to find. There is an English translation, but the only copy I have ever come across is in the London Library, heavily annotated in the margins with many a 'true!' and 'excellent!' as well as stronger and more tasteless comments. It is one of the great 'forbidden' books of this century, along with Whittaker Chamber's *Witness*, and like that great testimony against 'liberalism', should be reprinted by some enterprising publisher, if only to tease and annoy established opinion and be dismissed as evil nonsense by pipsqueak reviewers in the Sunday press. I have read that Wittgenstein, who was three-quarters Jewish, had the same misgivings as I (and in crude statistical terms, with about three times as much reason) about Weininger's theories, which made him doubt whether he could be a truly original thinker. Sensibly, this undoubted hero of the mind decided that he would try to be as original as he was able to be. And that, I think, will have to do for my unheroic and comparatively mindless self.

Seen across the level prairie-fields of our denuded England thirty years later, by an old man beset both by the terrors of his own approaching death and by the multiplying terrors whose shadows are deepening over his country and the world, that distant time can sometimes seem like a lost dream of richness and happiness. It certainly should have been rich and happy in reality. My wife Kate and I had a pleasant furnished house – or rather half-house – in Downshire Hill in Hampstead, rented from the painter Fred Uhlman and his wife, who lived next door. It was one of the prettiest streets in London. We had our daughter Jane, a child of remarkable beauty and intelligence. We had our old friends from the BBC and new friends from the world of journalism; the FitzGibbons still held court at Sacomb's Ash, still gave their weekend parties for a strange assortment of people, some high in Constantine's social league-tables, some low, but all equally welcome. Among them were an agreeable couple, neighbours of theirs, Andrew and Elizabeth Foster-Melliar and their daughter Belinda, a year younger than Jane; they became lifelong friends. Elizabeth, née O'Kelly, from the County Kildare, was Catholic and helped to ensure that Jane was christened, somewhat late in life at the age of four, at the pretty Catholic church in Hampstead.

One of her godmothers was Theodora FitzGibbon and her

godfather Peregrine Worsthorne. The service was, of course, in noble Latin, and the sight of the small girl gravely holding her candle and promising to forswear the Devil and all his works might well have moved even a less facile heart than mine – that is to say, almost anybody's – to tears. Afterwards there was a party at our house. Kate was good at giving parties. Unlike myself, she was good at making friends, even if she did not always keep them (who, for that matter, does?). I sometimes felt that I depended on her for making contact with other people, and that this dependency was growing, distinctly to my disadvantage. Later on, when things had gone wrong, perhaps irremediably wrong, between us, she would remind me how one evening in the early days of our marriage, when we were in London on a visit from Manchester at the time the BBC employed me there, she had suggested looking up some old friends – René Cutforth and his wife Marguerite, perhaps. But I, looking dismally out of the window at the sun setting over the rooftops, had said, 'Oh, who on earth would want to see us?' Of course, when we met our friends, I was glad and so were they. Rightly, Kate had no patience with this miserable attitude. Not that it was anything more than intermittent, but it was always there under the surface like an evil spirit, blighting life and hope, needing only the least encouragement, such as any imagined slight, to reveal its dull and squinting face.

Were we happy? The thought is like a cloud stealing over the sun. We ought to have been supremely happy; certainly I ought to have been – possessor of this fine young girl, eighteen years younger than myself, intelligent, imaginative, humorous, responsive, on whom, I could not fail to notice, the glances of other men sometimes rested with unmistakable speculation. It may be that we should not have married; I am not the only man who has found, after living with a woman, that marriage subtly changed his feelings, however free of conventional morality he may have thought himself, making what was illicit into what was permitted and killing desire stone dead. How, even if I had fully realised this myself, which I did not, could I have explained it to my young, loving and eager wife, who had promised to 'make my life pure gold', this Nordic blonde who, when I 'confessed' to having Jewish blood, immediately claimed to have Jewish blood herself, a manifest absurdity?

It is true that she was wilful, egotistical, wild and dangerous. 'Jack' Dillon, one of the great BBC 'characters', had warned me not to have anything to do with her; he explained, in his best storytelling form, that she was a prime specimen of a teredo, the dreaded shipworm of old days which, once attached, would bore away until the timbers rotted and the vessel became unseaworthy and sank, preferably with all hands aboard. She was also extremely eccentric in many ways and this she remained after our marriage, though her proto-hippie get-up of pullover and corduroy slacks, supplemented by a personal shabby mackintosh, which she had worn when we first met in the Stag's Head in Hallam Street, gave way to smarter but still unusual clothes. But her fingernails remained movingly dirty.

This eccentricity had captivated me in BBC days, when, after eating mussel soup in the local Italian restaurant, we hastened to my attic room high above Portland Place to discard any clothes, eccentric or otherwise, we may have been wearing – and how these things tear at my heart with a terrible pang of regret! – to roll about on the floor or on the bed or anywhere else available.

Those days were long past. We had a marriage and no marriage – not, if the truth were told, a thing uncommon among the people we knew. We had the tie of affection and intermittent lust, and of a shared love of books, poetry, music, drinking and walking in the country. We were not faithful to each other; which of us was the first to be unfaithful I cannot say. We went our own ways, with occasional affairs of little consequence, so it seemed; we behaved as we had always done before we were married. But Kate was growing stronger. She was no longer the 'child bride' or 'beauty of the future' of the FitzGibbons' fantasy; nor the ephebic 'sonny boy' that Manchester shop-keepers, seeing only her top half over their counters, had some-times called her to our amusement. She was turning into a mature young woman, outwardly self-confident (for all those inward doubts about herself which never left her) with an assert-ive voice and manner which some people came to regard, a thing by no means unpleasing to her, as 'posh' or even 'upper-class'.

She seemed somehow to have acquired a family background which did not belong to other members of her family I had met. Dominated by me in our early days, she now began to dominate. This is not, of course, an unusual role reversal; indeed it may happen more often than not. But I resented it, wincing at her overbearing ways and, perhaps, envying them. The FitzGibbons, who still had much influence over me, were inclined to laugh at her. Over a *tête-à-tête* supper in a Soho restaurant, Theodora confided to me, in one of her favourite amusing catch-phrases, that she had 'taken an instant dislike' to Kate and advised me to divorce her on the grounds of adultery as soon as possible. I said I would think it over and let her know what I decided. On the way home to Hampstead in the tube I picked up a pretty Welsh girl called Glenys and gave her coffee at an espresso, but though she invited me to her neighbouring bedsitter, I declined the offer. Regretting this the next day, I rang her but found her decidedly less friendly. All this was thoroughly in character, or, as Theodora would have said, 'typical of you'. Such was the absurd frivolity we all affected, thinking ourselves invulnerable to time and chance.

When we spent a month's holiday that summer at the Uhlmans' cottage in North Wales, Beudy Newydd, a lonely converted barn in the hills a few miles from Penrhyndeudraeth, taking with us the delightful, rather melancholy Elizabeth Foster-Melliar and her daughter Belinda (Andrew, jokingly believed by the FitzGibbons to be a spy, was not available), it was Kate who arranged matters with Fred Uhlman, dubious though he was about us, and not without reason, considering our frequently drunken and rowdy behaviour. She had grown masterful; and it was she who organised the slow journey by the old Cambrian Express from Paddington through Welshpool and along the coast of Wales, glorious in the old June weather which – perhaps Kate had organised this too – lasted without a break for almost all our holiday. It was she who organised supplies of food and drink from the local grocer, an old-fashioned Welsh archetype who, gratified by the long list, asked subserviently when she had finished: 'And will that be all, madam?' in a tone which suggested that, had she said 'And your immortal soul', he would have written that down too.

Perhaps because I was interested in the Welsh language and could understand it to some extent, though unable to speak it, and was sympathetic to Welsh nationalism, she expressed a hearty English contempt for the Welsh. 'He seems to be half-witted,' she complained, in tones that may have owed something to Theodora, of the elderly farmer across the *cwm* who supplied our milk. In fact, to my extreme pleasure, I found he could hardly understand a word of English.

It was Kate, too, who made friends with some of the neighbours, not usually those the Uhlmans had recommended who were inclined to be too respectable and not fond enough of drinking, but an assortment of youngish English people who forgathered at the pub they ignorantly called 'the Ring' (*yr Inn*, i.e. the Inn) at Garreg on the edge of the Traeth Mawr, and who were often adversely commented on, as I secretly knew, by the affably-smiling Welsh-speaking regulars. This was the domain of the celebrated architect Clough Williams-Ellis, creator of the fantastic Italianate village of Portmeirion; an eccentric old figure in knee breeches and yellow stockings. Many of the people we met were summer tenants of his cottages, all painted peacock blue, scattered over the rocky, bracken-covered hills.

Many of these English people, who formed a little community, very typical of that period in that they adhered to the 'left-wing package-deal', were would-be writers or painters or both. Though they were not without money, some, particularly those of the upper class, lived in studied squalor. One called 'John Jones the Englishman' who had a strikingly beautiful pre-Raphaelite wife with long auburn hair and a string of beautiful children to match, was convenor of the Communist Party in Harlech, evidently not an onerous post. He seemed to spend most of his time asleep on a bench outside his house.

Another one, distinguished by having rather more 'reactionary' views than the others and an admirer of the 'Peter Simple' column, had a small sheep farm in the mountains near Manod, the hollow hill where the Crown Jewels and treasures from the national collections had been kept during the war; a tarmac road led to it, ending abruptly in a great steel door. But he spent most of his time looking after his powerful sports cars, which he drove expertly and terrifyingly at breakneck speed along the winding roads. He sometimes stayed in bed late, leaving his sheep to fend for themselves on the mountain or, dashing impulsively to London, ignored them altogether. They tended to dwindle in number: after one period of absence he found, to his evident surprise, that they had all been slyly incorporated into the flocks of his neighbours. 'I suppose I'd better go to market and buy some more,' he said cheerfully, at which his long-suffering wife, another pre-Raphaelite but pale-haired, sad and lily-white, hung her head over the kitchen sink.

All these part-time settlers, who would be going back to London when summer ended, expressed great dislike of their landlord, accusing him of meanness in demanding their rent and not looking after his properties; it was typical that although they had made them into pigsties they still expected him to keep them in good order. They scoffed when we hired a car to take us to dinner at Portmeirion. The driver, Mr Jones, would take us only a hundred yards short of the entrance, explaining that it was 'the gate of hell', an opinion confirmed when we staggered out in the small hours to his enrichment.

We took the children to the sea, walked over the hills to Maentwrog or Beddgelert, where at the Royal Goat Hotel we ate delicious Welsh mutton and, asking for brandy from a young temporary barman, possibly monoglot, were given half-pint glasses full to the brim. It was a carefree time, or should have been, when the sun shone every day on the green world of Wales. We spent a good deal of time drinking beer on the crudely-built terrace and admiring the mountains. The Uhlmans, who had wisely locked up most of their possessions, had left out a portable gramophone of the kind I had had as an undergraduate, but only one record with it, an LP of Dvořák's Seventh Symphony. So whenever I hear this tuneful yet slightly sombre work it unfailingly calls up the memory of those weeks of summer, my first visit to Wales since my time at the army camp at Transfynydd in 1942, not far away over the mountains of Ardudwy, and soon to be the site of an abhorred nuclear power station. But before this, though I might strive to ignore it, our lives had been irrevocably altered.

I had realised that Kate was having an affair in London, but thought little of it. It was nothing new; and, nothing new either, I was having an affair myself. My friend was a small fair-haired woman in her early thirties with a neat, pleasing body; not pretty but with fine grey eyes, and one irresistible attraction for me, slightly protruding, 'goofy' teeth. She was the English wife of a Sephardic Jewish anarchist bookseller, a friend of David Thomson, who was then still working at the BBC and still, in spite of having standard 'liberal' opinions for a particularly good reason – the natural generosity and kindness of his nature – on reasonably friendly terms with me. Both Penny and her husband were said to be Reichians. Perhaps that was why she was so good in bed; or perhaps that is simply a matter of a man and woman liking each other.

There was something mysteriously familiar about her anyhow; I felt I had come across her somewhere before, but could not tell where. Here is a good opportunity for implied sexual boasting ('He's had so many women he can't keep count') to which I am not entitled. In fact it was only after our brief affair was over that I suddenly realised where I had come across her before. It was ten years ago, and she had been standing two or three places in front of my BBC girl friend Anne and myself as we queued up outside the Everyman Cinema in Hampstead one summer evening. I was instantly captivated by this unknown girl, who was wearing a beret, the only attractive kind of female headgear, and had an air of interesting artiness as well as sexual appeal. I was vaguely annoyed and frustrated because there was no chance of speaking to her; and although I looked for her after the film I could not see her. I soon forgot her consciously. But without my being aware of it she had become one of those 'women I might have loved', glimpsed for an instant in the street, then lost, one of those phantoms which all men, I suppose, carry around in their minds as unattainable love-objects, so that any real woman can only seem second-best. That is all very well. But to have got to know her after all, to have made love to her, and not to know it! This is really carrying idiocy too far.

Thus preoccupied, I may not have realised for some time that Kate was not merely having an affair but was seriously in love. Yet a certain physical change in her, a blooming and softening which made her more physically attractive to me as well as to others, should have told me unmistakably that this was something more important than our casual affairs. Jealousy, which clinched the matter, did not arrive till later.

Not far from the Daily Telegraph, a few doors from the Kings and Keys, there was a rather sleazy café called 'Mick's' where Colin, I and others sometimes had lunch or, more usually, tea. It was frequented by partisans of CND, then beginning to make a name in the world, who provided ironical material for the column, notably old Peggy Duff and Pat Arrowsmith, famous in their day as leaders of the growing movement. For all their fanaticism we were amused to note that these CND people were capable of making jokes about their preoccupation ('Pass the Caesium-90, please!' I heard one bearded fellow say when he wanted sugar for his tea). It was here, on a winter's afternoon, that Kate's lover, as he now revealed himself, arranged to meet me. Kenneth, who was married, was a well-known journalist, a man I liked and admired, an honourable man whose behaviour and code of morals I knew to be very different from our own. He told me how things were, and said: 'I will ask you a question. If you answer "yes", this affair will go no further. Do you love Kate?' I thought for a time, peering at the CND workers chatting about their plan of campaign, their leaflets, their demonstrations; at the cakes and sandwiches in the smeared glass cabinet; at the card hanging on the door which said 'closed', which for those outside, of course, meant 'open'. Then I said, 'No'. Would it have made any difference if I had said 'Yes'? Considering Kate's wilful and determined character, considering that all her impulses of life, although I did not fully realise it then, and all her wild energies (even the FitzGibbons admitted they were enough, if harnessed, to supply a large town with electrical power), were already diverted into a new course, I do not think so. I had answered 'No.' '. . . Like the base Indian, threw a pearl away,' he murmured, 'richer than all his tribe'. Stiffly I acknowledged the possible aptness of the quotation, but repeated 'No'. When I had left him I began to wonder whether this was a true answer, as I have wondered ever since from time to time, though less and less often, but without coming to any definite conclusion for all my delving into our beginnings.

2
A Kind of Idyll

I shall try to write down everything I can remember about that
early time. In the year 1953 I was working for the BBC in
Manchester, writing scripts for programmes on all kinds of
'regional' subjects, from the history of the Duchy of Lancaster
to the centenary of the Manchester Ship Canal; and at the end
of my posting, as though in desperation, on medical subjects
which enabled me, later on, to pose at dinner parties as an oto-
rhino-laryngologist until at last I met a genuine one. At that
time Kate and I, at the beginning of our marriage, used to
spend weekends and any other days we could at my mother's
cottage at Amswick, a tiny hamlet in one of the smaller Yorkshire Dales.

There we had scarcely any company but ourselves and our
year-old daughter. My mother was then seventy-four according
to her own account – she had, I think, already got into the habit
old people have of adding a few years to their ages and, when
questioned, declared she had lost her birth certificate. She had
moved there from my elder brother's farm in the Lake District,
finding she got on no better with her daughter-in-law after my
father died, and possibly worse. Her cottage at Amswick was
quite roomy but fairly primitive, though there were one or two
pieces of anomalous furniture she had salvaged from the wreck
of what she thought of, more and more, as days of wealth and
grandeur, becoming richer and grander with every day that
passed. There was a fine chest-of-drawers, corner-cupboards,
some pieces of Dresden china, a historic barometer which my

paternal grandfather must have tapped daily in the sombre hallway of his mansion, Oaklea, in the Manningham district of Bradford, hard by the gates of Lister Park. There were two round German plates of the same provenance, always said to be of incalculable value, hanging on the wall of the sitting-room, and an expensive folding card table with chromium rings at the corners in which to hold glasses.

We had no glasses to put in them. There was nothing but tea to drink, but on wet evenings we used the card table to play 'Solo' whist. My father had had a passion for cards and in the days of his prosperity, when we lived in Harrogate, he often played bridge with the few friends he had. My mother, though willing, was so bad at the game that she induced almost apoplectic rages in my father. So, increasingly, they must have compromised with 'Solo', a simpler game which rated much lower on the social scale and was generally associated with commercial travellers or small businessmen who played it on trains on the way to work ('Why don't you join our Solo School on the 8.35?').

But even this humble relation of bridge, at which my mother's more sophisticated in-laws had been skilled, taking every opportunity it afforded of humiliating her, was now a link with the great days of the past. I am fond of cards myself, as of all games which, as closed systems with inflexible rules, are an excellent refuge from reality. So it was no hardship for me to play these nightly games of Solo after tea (it was still Yorkshire tea at six or seven o'clock in those days) with my mother, with Kate, for whom it must have been a novel experience, engendering some of the various fancies we shared, and with a widow in the village who was always called by the single name 'Berner', a name whose origin was never explained. When I asked my mother about it, she either repeated the question or seemed not to understand why anybody should ask it.

Berner was a sad-faced but quite animated woman of about fifty with a submerged, unused intelligence. She was the only person in the village whom my mother would allow into her house. Why this was so I cannot say. Berner, like my mother herself, spoke with a fairly strong West Riding accent and was in no way socially superior to the other village people, whether Mr Metcalfe the farmer or Mrs Askew, another widow, or Joe Bates, the elderly retired shopkeeper who spoke so slowly that it was possible to leave the room for a minute or so and be back in time to hear the end of a sentence.

Yet as my mother's idea of her past became grander, so her neighbours became more and more unworthy; she would even say of the rich man who had bought the largest house in the village but visited it only occasionally, 'I've heard his father used to work in your grandfather's mill'. In this way the neighbours, who liked my mother and perhaps felt sorry for her, for she was likeable and amiable enough beneath her stereotyped Yorkshire rudeness, were excluded by her obstinate clinging to delusions of grandeur. So it was that we found ourselves some evenings, always the four of us, at the card table under the hanging 'Aladdin' oil-lamp whose mantle periodically went black because of the draught and had to be adjusted until it burned clear again. There was no electricity in the dale then (it must have been one of the last places in England without it) and when a year or two later the 'electric' arrived my mother said she did not want it. They installed it in spite of her grumbles and, perhaps to annoy her, put the switches in awkward, even inaccessible places. This made her grumble anew: 'I can't abide waste in any shape or form,' she said in one of her stock phrases, unfailingly used in certain contexts; others were 'scrupulously clean'; 'hermetically sealed' and 'I have a rooted objection' to whatever it was.

My father had been a pathological gambler, and this, according to my mother, had been one of the main causes of our descent in the world. Yet she remained perversely true to his memory by insisting (not that anybody opposed her) that we always played for money however small the stakes, using my father's old poker-chips. These were well-worn cowry shells kept in a bag which had, I think, been made by 'Aunt', my mother's unmarried younger sister, who had been what was called 'simple' – that is, on the verge of half-wittedness – and played the part of a domestic slave. The bag was very badly made, lopsided and with a patch underneath where the stitches had gone wrong, the subject of frequent and unvarying comment ('she never could learn to sew').

When the shells had been counted and divided up between the players, the game proceeded. It went on for several hours with interruptions caused by shouting outside and thunderous knocks at the door, disturbing yet entirely predictable, for there were no shops in the village or anywhere near it and every evening of the week a different tradesman arrived in his van from Cassington, the nearest town. On Mondays it was the 'bread man', on Tuesdays the 'meat man', on Wednesdays the 'fish man', on Thursdays the 'vegetable man', and on Fridays 'Fred Williamson'. Faced with ironmongery and hardware my mother had run out of categories.

The card-playing scene – with its shuffling and dealing, its long silences ending with cries of exultation or despair when some player succeeded or failed in his bid at 'Solo', 'Abundance' or, most exciting of all, 'Misère', where the bidder can win only by losing all the tricks – would have made an excellent genre painting in the style of Karl Spitzweg, and had I been able to

34

paint or to persuade any painters I knew to paint it, I would certainly have done so. What would it have been called? Simply 'The Card Players'? Or there might have been a whole series, suitable, but for the fact that I would have preferred dark colours, purple and brown (in thick impasto), for hanging on the walls of some ideal saloon bar: 'Cardplayers Interrupted by the Fish Man', 'Cardplayers Interrupted by the Meat Man', 'Cardplayers Interrupted by Fred Williamson' and so on.

By the end of the game there were no sensational wins or losses, for the stakes were small. One evening Berner won 4s 2d, bringing a suspicious look, instantly suppressed, to my mother's face; and on another evening Kate, by an amazing run of luck with the cards and what was agreed to be superlative play ('What is he laughing at?' my mother asked. 'Ee, I don't know what your father would have said') won two 'Abundances' in successive hands and scooped the board for 6s 9d. There were none of the dramatic scenes of my father's time when sums which grew ever more vast in memory changed hands at a continually accelerated speed as in a fast-motion cinema film. But as we settled down to tea and biscuits between Berner's departure and bedtime we all felt agreeably satisfied. Kate and I lit our candles in those cheap round enamelled tin holders once manufactured in hundreds of millions (where have they all got to now?), and went upstairs to bed, where we always lay naked. Hearing my mother stirring in the next room, we tried to muffle our noises of pleasure and amusement. Entwined, we slept soundly.

On evenings when the weather was fine, we used to go down to the one flat field in the valley bottom; it was long and narrow, and by the riverside, where in some places the clear water ran swiftly over rocks, in other places slowly in deep ale-brown pools under the boughs of ash and sycamore. There, using a flat piece of wood about the size of a cricket bat but thinner, and a tennis ball, which we stored, when not in use, in a crevice in the dry stone wall which bounded the field, we played a game we had invented. I called it, in my affected way, the Minoan Ball Game, not because it resembled any game played in Minoan times but partly because everything had to have a fancy name and partly because Kate was not unlike a Minoan woman bullfighter to look at. The game was a combination of French cricket and rounders and tended to become more complicated with new rules as time went on; we took turns to bat and scored by innings, which sometimes accumulated such high scores that a game might have to be held over until the next evening.

It was there, on the smooth greensward where we ran about, pitching, hitting or catching as though our lives depended on it, that Kate showed her true Atalanta-nature. She liked the story and the comparison, and who would not? She was not graceful in the ordinary way, in fact she had in those days a clumsy, almost staggering gait acquired through having tried to minimise her height – as a young growing girl she had thought herself too tall – by a kind of half-stoop which held a certain pathos for me who knew, or thought I knew, its origin.

But when we were playing the ball game all this disappeared in her unselfconscious swiftness and skill. It was a delight to watch her and a delight to play. What I lacked in speed I made up for in tactics, bowling with varied spin on the ball or placing it in difficult positions; so we were evenly matched; often it was twilight, with a few stars beginning to glimmer, before we stopped play and took the homeward path. We always paused at the bridge over the river to peer down into the clear water and look for trout darting between the stones. Our northern streams were new to her; I liked to show her these things which had been familiar to me for so long. I showed her the obvious summer stars I knew: Vega, Deneb, Altair, Arcturus. She was very quick and intelligent. Because she had left school at the earliest possible age, out of rebelliousness and a wish to get out into the world, she 'had a mind uncorrupted by knowledge'; but it was receptive and retentive and rapidly filling up with what she thought worth knowing.

The village people knew of the game we played by the riverside and passers-by occasionally stopped to lean over the wall by the road high above our field to watch us for a moment in a puzzled way. But although they may have tapped their foreheads in private, they made no comment. Nor did my mother, though when we prolonged the game almost until dark she was always waiting anxiously at the front door, as though we were errant children. Had some wandering psychologist seen us, making his way on foot through the Yorkshire Dales in the hope of finding patients (he would have had to be a very optimistic or very crazy psychologist: another subject for a genre painting in the manner of Spitzweg, 'The Wandering Psychologist', perhaps) – had some such person seen us, he might have directed us peremptorily, even banging our heads together, to games more suitable for a newly-married couple on a summer evening, when even in this austere limestone country the scent of the earth was heavy and the leaves and tall grasses rustled seductively as the light slowly faded into embracing darkness.

Behind her cottage my mother had a small, narrow garden which sloped steeply up the hill and was overhung by the great rocks of the lowest of the limestone scars which rose in series out of the dale up to the moorland and rough sheep-runs of the 'tops'. She had some fine rose bushes, another vestige of her greater days, which she tended and defended against pests – particularly slugs – with the Yorkshire ferocity that was a dormant part of her nature. Here, on a seat among the winding paths, we used to sit on fine days, talking of this and that and playing with the baby, who took her first steps and said her first words about this time. I used to amuse her by bouncing a ball on the sloping lichened stone roof of the outhouse and catching it; one morning early Kate and my mother surprised me as I dipped my finger in the dew which collected copiously in the folds of the alchemilla, an ugly, aggressive plant which has this sole redeeming quality of collecting dew, and feeding it to the child's lips. The two women laughed at this foolishness. Perhaps I was thinking of Edward Thomas's poem in which he finds his child sniffing the bitter herb, Old Man, which grows by his doorway and wonders if she will remember it; I may have wondered if Jane would remember her grandmother's garden.

Like my mother, we had scarcely anything to do with our neighbours, though for different reasons. Our friends were nearly all in London and but for occasional visits we might easily have forgotten about them altogether during our remote life in the North. We occasionally passed the time of day with an odd middle-aged couple, Louis and Winifred Hotchkiss, who had settled down together in a bungalow on the outskirts of Amswick and made a living mainly by running a small nursery garden. Winifred had worked at the BBC in Manchester, as I was then doing, but had given up 'all for love' by running off with Louis, a man of aggressively working-class mining stock whom she had met on one of her broadcasting assignments (he had written a 'working-class' novel and was a local literary celebrity). She was a middle-class woman and a Cambridge graduate and, what was more, *they were not married*, at least at that time, so they were not popular in the neighbourhood. Unknown but suspected hands were said to have thrown bricks through their windows. They did not become any more popular by being declared socialists (Winifred must have been one of

few 'Hampstead thinkers' in the Yorkshire Dales at that time
– though she was without the essential quality of having a lot
of money). My mother contented herself with saying in a special
tone of voice: 'Silly woman! Just imagine, at *her* age!' But
nobody was particularly interested in imagining anything about
a pair who seemed happy enough with themselves.

We spent a good deal of time on the other bank of the river,
opposite our Minoan Ball Ground, at a place where a small
spring welled out, forming a tiny tributary among the rocks
which by means of dams and other engineering devices could
be made into a miniature valley with an imaginary city for the
entertainment both of the baby and ourselves. Kate was as fond
of makebelieve as I was, or maybe even fonder. One of her
favourite games was 'the resistance game', played at night
among rocky fields which took the place of the French Maquis.
It was all part of what I called her 'infamous war on reality'; it
was characteristic of her that far from being offended by the
phrase she thought it an excellent joke.

We made long expeditions on foot across the hills to places
like Malham Cove, then quite unfrequented (now, like so many
places in the neighbourhood, a weekend traffic jam). Once,
leaving the baby in my mother's keeping, we went on foot, then
by bus and train, all the way to Appleby, where we stayed in
the Tufton Arms, scene of so many stirring events in the days
when I lived with my first wife Pepi and our son Nicholas a
few miles away at Hoff, last seen on the summer day in 1942
when I left to join my regiment in Northumberland en route to
India.

The outer world had changed. But in Westmorland little
had changed. The Tufton Arms had grown smarter and more
comfortable, the daguerreotypes of the Crimean War on the
walls of the dining-room, about which Constantine and I had

39

fantasised, replaced by china plates with pictures of wild flowers; there were tractors in the fields and many more cars on the roads; and the house where I had lived and enjoyed my colloquies with the rats had been equipped with electricity and sanitation and turned into a comfortable 'holiday cottage'. The old outdoor privy, in which I used to sit and look through the open door across the orchard and the fields to the distant Pennines beyond the River Eden, still stood, unused. There was nobody about. Half ashamed of my sentimentality, I passed water in this hallowed place.

Kate seemed to take this rather morbid revisiting of the past without demur; she had the present. But looking at these once familiar scenes again I had an uneasy feeling that the past was still there and still sounding through the years between and interpenetrating the present: the voice of Hitler seemed to rant through our ancient wireless set in the stone-flagged kitchen; a bicycle wheel whirred; a spade stood upright in the garden plot; young Constantine, impulsively self-exiled from Oxford, came loping up the lane to meet the girl friend I so greatly coveted for myself; in the nearby beech wood ancient boughs scraped and squeaked an ungainly half-forgotten tune; and then a high-flying German reconnaissance plane, prime symbol of everything that had vanished beyond any possible recall, droned overhead and for a moment imposed its now harmless ghost of fear. The sense of the numinous I had felt in those days had almost completely disappeared. But even being there induced an hallucinatory state. 'I think I've got a poem on,' I said to Kate. It was a phrase we had taken from a young would-be poet, in fact a public relations man, whom we had met in London, and we now used it as a familiar in-joke. 'I think I've got a poem on,' I said, 'but you can have it if you like.'

*

Sometimes we would go on the bus to Skipton, the nearest market town, still a simple place unexploited by tourism and not yet described in a thousand coloured brochures as 'the Gateway to the Yorkshire Dales National Park'. But it did have a gateway, the entrance to its ancient castle, where a stern, sergeant-major type of guide kept parties of visitors in strict order, thunderously rebuking Kate, who had strayed off by herself to peer up a forbidden stairway. We used to go to a somewhat forlorn little pub by the canal, now demolished, to play darts in a little square room with an old framed photograph on the wall. It was turning brown and showed a group of elderly men, mostly bearded, standing outside the pub with pints of beer in their hands; it was dated July 1911. The photograph took my fancy as a representation of human felicity. I asked the landlord if he would sell it; I was a collector of old photographs, I explained unconvincingly. He shook his head, his face instantly clouded with suspicion. 'Nay, it were me father's,' he said after a long pause for thought. But he obviously suspected that I 'knew something' about this photograph: either it was of great value in itself or it concealed in its mounting some document – a missing will, perhaps – which would make its owner a millionaire several times over. Next time we visited the pub, the photograph had gone.

This life, almost totally separated from others, a mild case of *folie à deux*, could not go on for ever. One day in late summer, when I was having a long recess from Manchester, we made an excursion by bus and on foot to what I called the 'Great Wilderness', the wild country at the head of Wharfedale – now invaded by visitors in hordes and disfigured by pseudo-forests of conifers – then a lonely region inhabited mainly by sheep and curlews. There, in an isolated farmhouse, clinging to the side of the fell and approached only by a rough track, lived a

family Kate thought might make an interesting item for the
radio about life in lonely places. She was anxious to help earn
our living; and like all young women in what would now be
called 'the media' she had an absurd and touchingly serious
attitude to journalism.

We lost our way and struggling through bog and rough pas-
ture to the farmhouse, got only a doubtful welcome in this
tumbledown place where only the poorest and most desperate
of Dales farmers would even then have thought of living. But
Kate, unlike myself, was very good at getting on with almost
any kind of people. She praised the sullen children playing
among the sheepdogs and chickens on the stone-flagged floor;
asked the farmer and his wife some lively questions, and took
some flattering notes while I stared out of the doorway at the
grey-green fell across the valley and the great slowly-moving
clouds in the August sky.

We took our leave and, setting out on the right path, walked
slowly down the hill to a place I had known since childhood,
where the infant River Wharfe slid over limestone floors or fell
with a delicious murmuring sound, over strangely hollowed
rocks into deep pools. We sat together on the warm grassy bank
beside one of these pools and I gave myself up to one of
my favourite occupations: contemplating the sun-flecked water
through half-closed eyes and listening to its eternal quiet laughter until I passed into a trance-like state which, once achieved,
I would have liked to prolong for ever.

The minutes passed. 'It's time to go,' Kate said. It was not
that she was unaware of the delight of being in such a place
and of feeling lost in it. She was simply the more active one. I
stopped plucking blades of grass in a self-hypnotising manner
and got to my feet. 'I suppose it is.' Unwillingly, in what must
have been a maddening way, I followed her and we walked off

down the winding road to where human habitation began. In the first village we came to we drank some beer in the pub while we waited for the bus to take us to the end of the road which led to Amswick. But as soon as we had caught the bus we realised it would take us further down the valley to Haltonbridge, the place where on that very day, I remembered, they were holding the local agricultural show, the greatest day of the year in those parts.

It was early evening when we got there and the show was almost over. The sheep and cattle pens were already being dismantled, the winning animals, adorned with red, blue and yellow rosettes were already being hustled along with the losers into their trucks with much shouting and barking of dogs. The stalls were taken down, the hurdles stacked; the bookmakers who had taken bets on the fell-race up the crag and the trotting-races on the level showground between the hills and the river were packing up their stands and patting their bulging satchels; what remained of the cheap crockery, brassware and toys, prizes for the shooting gallery, coconut shy and boot-throwing competitions, were packed away; cars and coaches, with frenzied hooting, were already making for the narrow exits between the drystone walls, directed by policemen and helpers with ritual gestures. The declining sun shone on red, sweaty faces, on old and young; and from the departing crowd rose a collective noise of Yorkshire voices which I, never at a loss for the apt quotation, called 'the still, sad music of humanity,' scarcely acknowledging that my own more subdued voice was part of it.

It was a scene very familiar to me. My father, in his 'sheep-farming' days, would have enjoyed it, not only because he was at heart gregarious, but because it would have given him a chance to indulge, even in a small way, his passion for gambling. My mother never went near such places. She disdained the

43

crowd and maintained of its individual members that 'you never know where they've been'. My elder brother Geoffrey, who had died in the polio epidemic six years before, would have shunned it on principle, guarding his chosen solitude, though he might have been ready to show selected sheep there for the credit of his flock. I enjoyed such a scene as this all the more because of my family's disapproval. As for Kate, she enjoyed it because of its novelty for her; and because of her innate capacity for enjoyment. There could have been no greater contrast to the quiet solitude where we had spent the day.

There was a strong movement towards the open door of the King's Head, a long whitewashed building conspicuous in this very small hamlet built in the shadow of a huge limestone crag. We were both very fond of drinking. Constantine had said once, in his observant way, that Kate regarded pubs – which I imagine her devout Catholic family, however eccentric in some ways, seldom entered – as almost mystical symbols of liberty. We had met in a pub, the Stag's Head in Hallam Street, one of the statutory BBC pubs; it was on Kate's first visit to Amswick, in this very pub, that we had formally decided to get married, and had drunk in it several times since. It was very typical of the region in those days, before pubs all over England became uniformly gentrified and began to sell 'bar snacks' or, as vulgar signs announced, 'pub grub', or as even more vulgar signs later invited in the days of 'yobbos' and 'lager louts', 'Come in and Get Stuffed'.

It had a plain exterior and inside, flagged floors, simple furniture, two bars – one large and open, one smaller and cosier (this was the bar where we plighted our much-delayed troth) – and a few pictures on the distempered walls, caricatures of long-dead jockeys or local notabilities, and a big coloured lithograph, 'Friday', one of my favourites, in which a plump monastery cook displays a huge carp on a noble dish and the assembled *monsignori* raise their glasses in fine-ringed hands.

Yet it was no ordinary pub. It had a reputation for hard drinking and was notable for rapid changes of landlord. A previous incumbent, infamous in the neighbourhood, was said to have been almost continuously drunk. On Saturday nights, it was said, he was so drunk by closing-time that he was incapable of serving drinks or taking the money; so the regulars shut him in a cupboard and took over the bar themselves, drinking until the early hours of the morning and, being honest men, leaving a lump sum on the bar for him to count when he came round, provided he was capable of counting. The present landlord, an amiable man of about forty, was called Jacques Lebrun, but although his French name was often commented on in a wondering or jocular way, there seemed to be nothing French about him. Known as 'Jack', he spoke in a West Riding accent.

The only remotely French thing about him, and that only according to the popular myth of 'Frenchness', was his equally Yorkshire wife Cynthia, a small, well-made woman about ten years younger than himself, who exuded a powerful sexual attraction, all the more noticeable for her quiet demeanour. 'Hot stuff' was the general verdict on this slumbering volcano, and among her numerous admirers were some who either were, or earnestly hoped to be, something more than admirers. One of the farmers in the dale, Mr John Capstick, and a local garage man, Mr Tom Lambert, were deadly rivals for her favours; but unfortunately for them she was said to have a regular lover, a lorry-driver from Colne in Lancashire, whose vehicle was quite often observed standing for long periods outside the pub at times when it was closed to the public.

It may have been marital troubles which made the landlord

drink as much as almost any of his customers. Though he did not come anywhere near the level of his legendary predecessor he often complained of a morning hangover, jocularly saying, when offered a drink, that only a gin and Harpic or even a strychnine and soda would do him any good. In his later days, it was said, he drank more and more; tottering downstairs in the mornings, he could only bring himself to his senses by getting his wife, her sexual allure irrelevant in the circumstances, to fill up a glass with neat gin, place it on the bar and help him to lower his mouth upon it. Such alcoholic legends had a strong appeal for Kate and myself; Kate, for whom drinking, as Constantine had observed, had something of an ethical quality, was apt to judge people according to whether they drank or not and regarded those who did not as in some sense morally inferior.

On our previous visits to this place, usually in the early evening, we had found few customers and those quietly drinking and exchanging remarks on matters of local interest, with an occasional mention of politics, derived from the newspaper or the wireless. Because these people were not subject to saturation of information and entertainment by television, as their successors are, their opinions, though they may have been equally absurd or distorted, were at least their own. If it was nonsense, it was their own personal nonsense, not uniform nonsense pumped into their minds from a central source. Nor were they inhibited by fear and induced guilt about 'racism', 'sexism', or any of the other fraudulent bogeys which afflict us now. They would have laughed all such things to scorn, and they would have been right. It was a time when most of the international news was about troublesome denizens of the Middle East like Mossadeq, Neguib and Nasser. The only impression they had of Mossadeq may well have come from a newspaper photograph of him taken after his fall, showing him lying on a truckle bed, wearing striped pyjamas and crying bitterly. They could not understand how it had come about that our government, the government of a great nation which was supposed to have 'won the war' – and few at that time would have questioned that we had won it – was obliged to take such ludicrous and exotic foreigners seriously, or even take any notice of them at all.

On previous visits we had exchanged only a few polite words with the other customers. Some of them may have known that I had been at 'Oxford College' and an officer in the war and now worked with the BBC; they may have known that the young woman I was with was my second wife. They may have known the most amazing things about us, most of them partly or wholly untrue. We did not enquire, but sat in the small cosy bar by a tall window, with hens clucking outside and a view of old, stone-built barns across the yard, talking about whatever came into our heads, and were content. Had Constantine and Theodora suddenly appeared they would immediately have set about converting the pub into a distant fief of their dominions in Hertfordshire; but they would have found these stolid Yorkshire people, with their tradition of independence (an attitude summed up in the phrases 'I'll bow the knee to no man' and 'I'm as good as you are, whoever you are – and better') more difficult to convert to admiring subservience than the country people of the South, with their traditions of deference. Obstinacy, bloody-mindedness and even downright rudeness as well as the hatred of 'side', all well-established qualities of these West Riding people, elaborated in many a fearsome anecdote, are easily explained. There have never been great estates in the district – or very few – and those at the top have not been landed proprietors but industrial magnates who have risen from among people very like themselves.

The pub we entered that summer evening was very different from the place as we had known it. It was crowded with shouting drinkers from the show, some local but many from distant parts, sheep farmers from other dales, chance comers from Bradford, Keighley or Skipton, a few holidaymakers. Jack the landlord and the demure but dangerous Cynthia, with the help of a couple of young girls who had been taken on as temporary helpers, were frenziedly pulling pints, opening bottles and slamming glasses into optics as they tried to cope with the rush of orders. We entered unnoticed and made our way through the crowd with difficulty. Once served, we began to make for our customary corner by the window in the smaller bar. But in the press of people we collided with a merry-faced balding man a few years older than myself. Unlike most of the customers, he was drinking not beer but gin and tonic and had evidently had quite a few of them already. 'I know who you are,' he shouted in a friendly way. 'I've seen you walking by the river, aye, and playing catch, and I've seen you playing there with your baby. My name's Joe Tunnicliffe and I'm a terrible fellow!'

This was corroborated by several others who explained that he was 'noan so bad, really'. We soon found that this was so. Rapidly buying a round of drinks in which he included us, he confirmed what we had half-realised already from my mother's distinctly unfavourable remarks: that he lived in Keighley where he had a leather factory, and also owned the large white-painted wooden bungalow surrounded by shrubs and trees which lay on the other side of the river from the field where we played the Minoan Ball Game. He had a wife and three children, the eldest, a daughter, not that much older than Kate; but now he had been to the show and was on the loose.

Our new friend obviously had much more money than anyone else in the pub and was determined not only to enjoy himself but to ensure as far as possible that everybody else did so too. His sheer energy and *joie de vivre* were most attractive, and would have been so even if we and everybody else had not been getting rapidly into the kind of drunken state which inspires pure good-humour and pleasure. Yet we realised even then that Joe Tunnicliffe was more than a chance-met drinking acquaintance; that although we seemed to have nothing much in common (except, in Kate's case, difference of sex), he was going to be a friend. Later we found there were unexpected things about him, such as a love of music. Inheritor of a prosperous family firm, he had originally wanted to become a 'cellist, until the duties of business and an early marriage to the daughter of an even richer mill-owning family expelled such matters from his mind, though not entirely. All human faces in repose fall into lines of sadness; his, for all his habitual laughter and good humour, more strikingly so than most.

His father had sent him to a minor public school in the South of England. It was somehow typical that through a misunderstanding he had arrived at the wrong school and spent a whole term there before the mistake was realised. Like many West Riding businessmen of the time he was bilingual: in the ordinary way he spoke what is technically called 'improved West Riding', though without the sickeningly over-refined diphthongs and other phonetic prodigies of the womenfolk; but when he was in his factory with his workers he spoke with the broad accent without which they would not have respected him; and that was how he was speaking now with the even broader-spoken drinkers in the King's Head.

'Nah then, Mr Tunnicliffe, ista making a night of it?' one of these asked him in an accent which showed him to be native to the Dales, speaking a true North-Western dialect rather than the dialect of the West Riding which, though it would have been tactless to tell that to its speakers, is more exactly called North Midland. Not that anybody but myself was particularly interested in the matter. What did George Borrow do when people in pubs objected, as they must sometimes have done, to his interrogating them about the way they spoke? It does not bear thinking about.

'Aye,' replied Mr Tunnicliffe, 'we don't get a show every day of the year, or such a fine day for it, or such good company.' And he ordered drinks all round again. We were moving from one bar to the other and back again by this time and so observed that Mrs Lebrun had moved to the customers' side of the bigger bar and was receiving burning glances both from Mr Lambert and from Mr Capstick, one on each side of her, while she herself looked remarkably cool and composed. The Siren of Haltonbridge, as we came to call her, was quite used to such situations and knew exactly how to deal with them.

'Where have you been all my life?' said Mr Tunnicliffe to Kate, the first of a whole series of such stock gallantries, but delivered in a highly individual way which made them seem amusing even though I was now beginning to feel a twinge of jealousy. It was therefore something of a relief when Kate acquired another admirer, a rough-looking but amiable man who turned out to be a sheep-farmer from Swaledale, one of whose ewes had won first prize in its own class. 'Tha looks just like my best prize yow,' he said. 'Don't be offended,' said Mr Tunnicliffe. 'It's the greatest compliment he could pay you, isn't it, Dick?' 'It is that,' said the Swaledale man, 'and if tha comes to Swardale, tha'll be queen o't' whole flock.' His compliment, for it was certainly meant for one, was not so far-fetched as it might have seemed. Our old friend René Cutforth, a man with great associative powers, had compared Kate, with her long neck and strangely oblique 'Hunnish' eyes like his

50

own, to a llama. Seeing Kate the centre of attention and Mrs Lebrun temporarily relieved of her admirers, I tried to engage her in conversation. But I had scarcely begun my halting approaches when, after a mock tattoo on the main door of the pub it opened, revealing to my surprise that night had fallen.

A large, shambling man stood on the threshold, pulling off motor-cycling gloves from huge red hands, while behind him, below a flight of shallow steps, a motor-cycle and sidecar stood in the road. A general shout of laughter went up. 'It's t' policeman from Amswick!' bawled Mr Metcalfe. 'Has't come to put us all under arrest and convey us to thy dungeons?' he asked sarcastically. PC Albert Marsden, whom I now recognised from having seen him riding his machine about the roads in a diffident way and once making a terrible hash of directing traffic in Cassington, advanced into the room with a rather foolish smile on his big, lugubrious face and said in a hesitant tone: 'I know you folks have an extension till eleven o'clock, seeing as it's Show Day, but it's a quarter to twelve now, and if the Sergeant gets to know about this . . . ' He looked positively terrified. But his feeble expostulations were lost in a general shout of laughter. 'Nay, Albert,' said Mr Metcalfe, 'tha's blotted thi copybook wi't Sergeant often enough by now. I reckon he'll let thi alone this time. Come on, have a drink thisen.' With a great show of reluctance the policeman accepted a pint of beer and having swallowed that with immense speed and expertise, accepted another offered by Mr Tunnicliffe. Within a short time he was merely one among the crowd of drinkers, babbling away like the rest, though I noticed that from time to time a shade of alarm passed over his face.

PC Marsden, Joe Tunnicliffe told me, was a sad case. He was the son of a police superintendent from a town on the Lancashire border, a man of iron determination and stern devotion to duty. Albert 'had never wanted to be a policeman'. But his father had settled it in his mind that his son should join the force and if possible rise to a rank as high as his own or even higher. He died a disappointed man. Albert's heart was not in the job and although he did his best, telling himself it was 'a sacred trust', his repeatedly proven incapacity had ensured that he never rose above the rank of constable, finding himself in his late forties responsible for law and order in a place where there was seldom any crime more serious than riding a bicycle without a rear reflector. He was known to live in continual terror of his immediate superior, Sergeant Hoskins at Cassington six miles away, who was always threatening to put in an appearance in his fief and was 'particularly hot on drinking after hours'. It was believed that Marsden had an arrangement with sympathisers in Cassington living near the police-station, who had undertaken to warn him by telephone or by passing the word along whenever the Sergeant seemed to be heading in his direction. This accounted for his underlying terror now, even though he had drunk several pints of beer and had moved on to whisky. He had had no warning yet, but knew it might come at any moment.

Meanwhile he settled down to enjoy himself as best he could. 'You're a bonny lass,' he told Kate gallantly, gaining confidence for a moment. Then his face fell; I almost thought I saw tears in his eyes as a thought struck him. 'Do you know,' he said very slowly, 'I've had two wives myself and neither of them has been bonny.' This sad admission only served to produce more heartless laughter at his expense. 'What's Mrs Marsden doing tonight then?' somebody asked. 'Is it washday again tomorrow?' I remembered seeing a grim-faced, middle-aged woman of homely appearance pegging out washing outside the police house at Amswick. I also remembered Berner telling us, to my mother's outward disgust but secret amusement, that the policeman was said to wet his bed regularly and that his sheets were often to be seen on the washing-line, an object of derision to the villagers and an occasion for smacking any children who commented on them. The moral of all this seemed to be: don't have an overbearing police superintendent for a father; or if you do, run away to sea or join a circus as soon as possible. But the spirit of young Albert Marsden had been broken too early for that.

The arrival of the policeman seemed to have moved these rustic revels on to a new level of intensity. Mr Metcalfe had crossed to the publican's side of the bar and was trying to embrace Cynthia, who, as a sort of insurance, had her free hand tightly gripped by another admirer, Mr Baxter, who remained on his own proper side of the bar and seemed reasonably satisfied with this lesser share of her favours. As he was showing a tendency to slide to the floor, he may not have realised the true state of affairs. Mr Tunnicliffe was growing more and more gallant in his attentions to Kate, alternating these with beating time on a table as he tried to lead the singing of 'Ilkla Moor Baht 'At', 'Down at the Hole in the Wall' and other patriotic airs. Indefatigable, he suddenly pointed to a row of bottles on a high, remote shelf. 'Let's try some of those!' he shouted to the landlord. 'Nay,' said Jack, 'we haven't had any of those down for a good ten years. No call for them, you see.' I now saw, by screwing up my eyes, for my vision was becoming blurred, that the bottles had a thick coating of dust; it was just possible to read some of the labels: Danziger Goldwasser, a kind of schnapps with gold flecks in it, Parfait d'Amour, a sickly pink liquid, baleful Blue Curacão and many other exotics. Where on earth had they come from, and what were they doing here?

'Have you got any of Mr Weston's Good Wine?' I asked the landlord. But this feeble, painfully literary joke, which I instantly regretted though half hoping Kate had heard it, was lost in a concerted roar of 'Get 'em all down!' and 'Drinks on the house!'. The landlord was clearly unwilling to oblige: did he fear the breaking of some ancient taboo which could only lead to misfortune? The matter was soon out of his hands. Somebody, possibly Mr Baxter, fetched a pair of steps, positioned it against the wall behind the bar and requested the landlord to mount. While he hesitated, his wife, perhaps taking the opportunity of escaping from Mr Metcalfe's embrace, climbed up the steps, displaying her slim form to great advantage for all to observe, and began handing down the bottles with graceful gestures, releasing clouds of dust which made everybody splutter and adding to the general confusion. The landlord, evidently resigned to whatever appalling consequences might follow, began to pour out a selection of exotic drinks for anyone who wanted them. He evidently felt they could not be poured into ordinary everyday receptacles; instead he produced from a shelf below the bar various strangely-shaped glasses: flat ones for champagne; tall ones for white wine; small squat glasses of ruby colour; a big narrow purple glass marked 'A Present from Redcar'; a calibrated medical glass; and even a frosted glass marked in wedge-shaped patterns which resembled cuneiform writing.

Had this been presented to him or a previous landlord by some eccentric assyriologist who had stayed for a fishing holiday in the pub in what I vaguely thought of as 'the old days'? Anything seemed possible. And now, with this injection of fantasy into a scene which though ribald and uninhibited, still clove to the realities of life in the Yorkshire Dales, all was altered. The smoke-filled air hummed and twanged; faces like those which appear in hypnagogic dreams, bunched like fists or folded like old gloves, advanced and receded or vanished altogether into shelves, walls or tall curtains. I stepped forward, trying to feel my way towards Cynthia through a curtain or tapestry which seemed to be made of multi-coloured pliable stained glass, but found I had stumbled over the body of the landlord, who lay on his back with his legs half under a chair, still holding level a miraculously full glass of purple liquid. From behind the bar came sounds of animal pleasure, but even if I had had my ordinary wits about me I could not have told who was making them.

Suddenly I blundered into the policeman, who was peering this way and that with a look of panic on his large, foolish face. 'Quick, let me out!' he shouted through the din. 'Sergeant's on his way! I know he is!' He stumbled to the door and opened it, and I heard his heavy boots clumping down the steps, and shortly after that the sound of his motor-cycle starting up and receding into the distance. 'So he's got away,' I thought, expecting, with some alarm, the appearance of the sergeant, unknown to me but evidently an austere disciplinarian: would he, I wondered, call an abrupt halt to the revels and charge everybody with offences against the licensing laws? Or would he, for all his devotion to duty, find himself instantly absorbed into the crowd, singing, dancing and shouting quite as idiotically as the rest of us?

The door opened slowly. But it was the policeman's face which peered sheepishly round it. 'Me motor-bike combination's in the ditch,' he mumbled so indistinctly that it was hard to understand him. 'And' – he was nearly in tears again – 'I've lost me teeth.' A great shout of laughter went up at this new misfortune. But a couple of men, including, I think, the sheepfarmer from Swaledale, who was perhaps beginning to sober up a bit, went out to help him get his machine out of the ditch and on the road. They came back grinning. 'He's on his way. Just. But we couldn't find his teeth.' This struck me as irresistibly funny. The feeling of unreality, apparently induced by the exotic drinks, slowly evaporated. Instead a feeling of almost unearthly happiness seemed to flood this very ordinary room.

I opened the door, and found to my surprise a bright summer early morning; the sun was already shining gloriously on the hay meadows, the woods, the limestone scars ascending to the distant moors. I took Kate by the hand as we trooped out into the open air. With the rest we spent some time looking for the policeman's teeth but could not find them. With a politeness which was almost distinguished, and perhaps found only in men who have been engaged in a night of serious drinking, Mr Tunnicliffe drove us in his car, a powerful Jaguar, to the end of our lane and we parted, undertaking to meet again soon.

Clutching each other, we took the familiar stony path through the high meadow which led over the bridge past the field of the Minoan Ball Game towards my mother's cottage. Half way along the path I thought I saw something gleaming in the grass. Could it be a bright button mushroom? Or one of the country's small, exquisite snail-shells, some pink, some palest blue, some white like the pearl the base Indian threw away? Or the policeman's teeth? I bent to look again but now I could see nothing; and as I straightened up, by mischance I brought my elbow into Kate's face with enough force to bruise her cheek-bone. She cried out as I put my lips against it, then moved away. As we walked on, our separated shadows were long in the summer grass.

3
Unsteady Progress

As time went on, the 'Peter Simple' column began to gain a certain reputation, even notoriety. Its reactionary, 'eccentric' and independent opinions – in which my own Luddite tendencies and fervent hatred of scientific progress became more and more prominent – appealed not only to readers of the *Daily Telegraph*, then strongly identified with the Tory party, but to a wider public. There were, of course, people I met at parties who, when I told them what I did, said witheringly, 'I'm afraid I don't read the *Daily Telegraph*,' which, of course, settled the matter. It did not help when I said that as far as I was concerned I was still working for the *Morning Post*, the real true-blue Conservative paper which had been absorbed by the *Telegraph* as long ago as 1936. Even in its later days, when the *Telegraph* was no longer a Conservative paper in the proper sense of the word, and in its supply of scientific nonsense, low-grade entertainment and news of the world of 'showbiz', particularly television, became scarcely distinguishable from any other paper, there were people who regarded it as reactionary and looked askance at anyone connected with it.

There were, of course, people who disliked the column for its anti-socialist opinions, including some of my late colleagues (or, in a sense, continuing colleagues) in the BBC. 'It is pouring poison into the ear of England,' said one of them. But when, at the end of 1957, a paperback anthology of the first two years of the column was published by the *Daily Telegraph*, it received some surprisingly good notices even in quarters which might be expected to be hostile, such as *Tribune*, the old left-wing weekly full of the sort of stuff we were lampooning. Its critic wrote of our work: 'bigoted, violent, well-written . . . shrewd digs at pompous personalities and choice parodies of our more inflated culture-hounds'. Looking back at our quiet-toned, civilised 'satire' of that time (I suppose we must use this word, so lamentably devalued) from our *fin-de-siècle*, when writers compete for attention by outpourings of the most desperate obscenity and demented scatology, I am most pleased by the word 'violent'. We could not have been really violent in the *Telegraph* even if we had wanted to be, which I dare say we did. The whole tone of the paper, as of any 'serious' paper of that time, forbade it. Sir Colin Coote would have sternly suppressed any such tendencies.

This was the time before the trial of *Lady Chatterley* released 'four letter words' into the press. The spread of these once forbidden words was a gradual process; in fact they are not to be found in the *Telegraph* to this day, and when, many years later, Peregrine Worsthorne used the word 'fuck' in a BBC television broadcast, Michael Berry (or Lord Hartwell as he had then become, after taking a life peerage) sent for him and rebuked him in the following terms: 'You have disgraced your profession, your newspaper and yourself,' and forebade him to broadcast for six months on pain of dismissal.

We may have been violent and outspoken by the standards of the time but how the times have changed! They were beginning to change then, with the advent of 'satirists' like Lenny Bruce and Mort Sahl in America, followed by their imitators here; all, though glorying in their supposed 'revolutionary' ardour and unconventional attitudes, were, in fact, devoted to the most banal and modish opinions of the 'left-wing package deal', often attacking harmless targets like the Royal Family or the jam-making ladies of the WVS. Such fashionable money-making 'satirists' became suitable subjects for my own satire as they would have been for Juvenal; but, unlike Juvenal, I was handicapped by not being able to match them in obscenity.

So when Kenneth Tynan, the drama critic and celebrity, famous for having used the word 'fuck' on the wireless long before Worsthorne's unfortunate experience, praised Mort Sahl of New York for his 'nonconformist satire', and complained of the lack of similar 'liberal nihilist' entertainment in London night-clubs (this decadent drivel was then on its way, so he need not have troubled), I could only write:

> To call night-club liberal nihilists 'nonconformist' is nothing but a perversion of language. Nobody could possibly be more conforming than they are. They conform exactly to the fashionable desperation of their audience, its smart hatred of civilisation . . . that is why, far from being mocked and driven into the wilderness, they have grown rich and popular and fat with long-playing records. The role of Mort Sahl at Belshazzar's Feast, in that most expensive of Babylonian night-clubs, would have been to make liberal nihilist jokes about the writing on the wall, to the huge delight of his sophisticated audience.

I could operate only within the constraints of my newspaper; those who came later, such as the writers in *Private Eye*, were able to attack such people in their own language, a freedom I sometimes envied.

Naturally the column, with its then unfashionable opinions (some of them are unfashionable still) came in for a certain amount of abuse. For example when Colin, I think it was, pointed out, reasonably enough, that the white South Africans had a perfect right to call themselves Africans (or Afrikaner), he came in for sharp attack from the journalist Bernard Levin, in whatever column he was writing at the time: he referred to 'Peter Simple' as 'still hobbling after Beachcomber's rear light'. This was fairly wounding but on the wrong tack. I thought, and think, Beachcomber funny at his best (though not in some of his 'funny' names such as 'Cocklecarrot' which I find painfully unfunny). But if my early writing in the 'Peter Simple' column was influenced by any other column it was Myles na Gopaleen's column in the *Irish Times*, which is in an altogether higher category, the work of one of the greatest modern comic writers. Sadly, his column ceased around the time when 'Peter Simple' was coming into his own, and Myles na Gopaleen (alias Flann O'Brien, real name Brian O'Nolan) fell into decline, illness and, in 1966, death.

I had first come across Myles na Gopaleen when, demobilised in April 1946, I lived briefly with my first wife in Dublin. His column, by far the funniest newspaper column in history, was a great solace in what were difficult times. Because of my interest in Irish matters (part of my immersion in 'Celtic studies') and knowledge of them I was in a better position than most English people to enjoy his more recondite linguistic jokes and allusions. I never met him while I was in Dublin, though I might well have done since I met, if only briefly in various bars, associates and drinking companions of his such as Patrick Kavanagh and Anthony Cronin. But perhaps it is as well I never did meet my literary hero; he is said to have been 'difficult'. He had every reason to be. In his lifetime he was scarcely known outside Ireland and it was only after his death and the publication of his novel *The Third Policeman*, written twenty-five years before, immediately after his other masterpiece *At-*

Swim-Two-Birds, that he came into his own in England and the world.

As well as the new friends and acquaintances we were making in the world of Fleet Street – the Welches, the Worsthornes, Henry Fairlie, Paul Johnson and many others – we still had our other circles of friends from the BBC and in Hampstead, some separate, some intersecting. The FitzGibbons still held court at Sacomb's Ash, still gave their splendid weekend parties. But their marriage was beginning to show signs of breaking up. It was not that they threw more or heavier objects at each other; if anything, these performances seemed to become more rare, or it may have been that I was not so often around to observe them.

The countryside around their house was also changing. Considering how near it was to London, it had always seemed surprisingly rural, with real country people in it who still talked about their own country affairs as their forebears had done. It was not surprising to find, in a pub Constantine and I discovered just over the Essex border, a genuine example of folk art: a glass case containing four stuffed ferrets playing cards. The landlord, a deaf man with a beautiful white dog which he called, with great pride, 'my Pyrean mountain dog', could not explain the provenance of this artefact; he had 'always had it', and when we offered to buy it he looked every bit as cunning and dubious as the landlord in Skipton with his photograph of Happiness.

Now all this was changing. Hedges and trees began to disappear from this corner of Hertfordshire, between the little rivers Stort and Ash which, as Mr Rix (the landlord of the FitzGibbons' local pub) often said, the Romans had left alone as they drove their roads north and west across Britain, so that its inhabitants to this day were a race apart. They weren't, of course; they were quintessentially English; but the idea that they were different was part of the peculiar charm of the place.

Now this was rapidly vanishing. Big fields were opened up: between them the winding lanes where I had bicycled so intensively a few years before in search of a cottage for Kate and Jane were laid bare between hedge-banks brutally stripped of vegetation by the new machines, losing their beguiling secrecy. Soon the very pub where Constantine and Theodora had ruled, imposing their ideas, often strangely modified, of life on Mr Rix so strongly that at one time he was found in the bar studying the maxims of Rochefoucauld – this splendid pub, with its brown-painted, beer-stained walls and kitchen always full of washing or baking, began to change. Mr Rix himself – whose forward daughter had 'got into trouble', resolved by marriage, but to an unsuitable urban-minded youth who owned a washboard, a primitive 'rock' musical instrument of the period – began to work part-time at the malt-works at Sawbridgeworth, returning on alternate evenings to tell of the new world which was coming into existence.

Soon he left altogether to run a pub nearer London. A new breed of customer from the outer suburbs began to invade the pub, ill-mannered and vulgar, forcing the locals into corners; not easily impressed by exotic visitors or conversation about books or foreign places but self-assertive and even hostile. Very soon a juke-box was installed, impeding if not actually superseding our old in-jokes and the public reading of Constantine's short stories. Even croquet on the lawn at Sacomb's Ash – that leisurely, supremely civilised game where you could carry your drink round with you as you played – began to lose credibility.

In the spring of 1958 the three-year lease of our pleasant maisonette in Downshire Hill ran out, and when I consulted our landlady Mrs Uhlman – wife of Fred the painter and writer, herself a Croft of Croft Castle in Herefordshire, one of the oldest families in England – about this, she told me with perfect politeness that she was not going to renew it because she had promised to let the place to a friend of hers, a psychiatrist called Dr Marie Yehuda. This was not altogether surprising. Neither our political views nor our manner of life was acceptable to the Uhlmans. They might have put up with the views, as did many people – for example, Margaret Gardiner, a rich, left-wing lady who lived in Downshire Hill and who, hearing of Kate's troubles before we married from her protegé Harry Craig, a soft-spoken Irishman, BBC scriptwriter and alleged relation of Theodora FitzGibbon, had offered to adopt her. It was not clear whether she meant to adopt the coming baby as well. In any case nothing came of the project. But we became quite good friends with Margaret, one of those people who 'knew everybody', including David Thomson, now married to a beautiful though somewhat enigmatic girl, Martina Mayne, in whom I had once taken a feeble interest. She was one of the great number of girls – Riette, Ann, Muriel, Glenys, Frances (two), Denise, Vera, Jenny, Molly and so on – who make up a roll-call of lost apparitions extending over my whole lifetime, occasionally appearing in odd trains of thought, or even in dreams, to haunt me with regret. I suppose it is the same with most men, and all think themselves uniquely stupid for not having taken all these girls to bed.

The Uhlmans could have put up with our opinions, vile though they must have thought them. What they could not put up with was our fondness for drink, drunken companions and noisy parties, let alone our charades and dramatic performances, which included set-pieces like 'the French Revolution', 'the Russo-Japanese War' or 'the Battle of the Somme', which had more than once brought Fred Uhlman out in his pyjamas in the middle of the night to dance with rage on the pavement below our windows, and caused the lady novelist who lived opposite to threaten us with the police. The police station, as it happened, was only a few doors away at the junction of Downshire Hill and Haverstock Hill; an added irony was that when my son Nicholas, who was about to proceed on a scholarship from Skipton Grammar School to Christ's College, Cambridge, visited us, he worked part-time in the police station canteen, amusing us with his close observation of police behaviour within the station, including a 'love triangle' between two constables and the canteen manageress.

The loss of our home, for, however temporary, a home we must have thought it, was a severe blow. We had two months to find another place in which to live and no means of buying one at a time when rented accommodation was becoming scarce. It fell to Kate, being the more energetic of the two, to deal with this crisis (and, of course, I was fully occupied with my work on the *Telegraph* four days a week). First she found a rather derelict, ivy-grown house near Edwards Square in Kensington which, though it had evidently been badly shaken by bombing during the War, was still standing up with the aid of a few iron braces. I was not at all keen on this house, but Kate for a time set her heart on it and once, when I demurred in a nearby pub where we had gone to discuss the matter, kicked me hard and painfully on the ankle because of my negative attitude. Negative I habitually was, but in this case I was right; I luckily got the support of 'Tommie' Rowell, a middle-aged friend I had met when she was a director of Wingate the publishers; she was one of Jane's godmothers and had always been most generous to us, allowing us to stay in her house when she was away on our visits to London from Manchester and overlooking, like the

64

good Catholic she was, our destruction of beds and other articles of furniture. It was she who now saved us by pointing out
that the house Kate favoured was liable to collapse at any
moment.

The day of our departure from Downshire Hill arrived and
we had nowhere to go. So now began a curious period of
nomadism, made more curious by the fact that I had to go to
Fleet Street to work at my respectable job and produce daily
offerings of humorous fantasy which, though Sir Colin Coote
remained sceptical, found more and more favour with the
respectable readers of the *Telegraph*. There were people who
declared that the column was the first thing they turned to in
the paper, and even a few who said it was the only thing they
read in it.

Letters would arrive: 'Dear Peter Simple – you have the gift
of expressing what I think but have no words to express. You
are an oasis of sanity in a mad world; more power to your
elbow'. I would read these encouraging remarks in the intervals
of wondering where I was going to spend the night. Fortunately
it was summer and the weather mainly fine. The enterprising
Kate had also hit on a means of mobility and of conveying our
meagre belongings from one temporary home to the next. 'We
must buy a car,' she said. 'I can't drive it,' I said, recalling my
notorious inability when in the Army to bring any vehicle to a
standstill within several yards of the point desired and my
desperate escapes from death on the roads due to my not having
the knack of doing several things at the same time, such as
changing gear while operating the steering-wheel and looking
out for other traffic – a thing absolutely essential to any driver.

Kate assured me she could drive, as indeed she could, so
she persuaded me to see Mr H. J. C. Stevens, the secretary of
the *Telegraph*, the man who had charge of the money, and ask

65

for a loan of £500 to help us set up house. Stevens was a large, rubicund, sardonic man with the reputation of being a bully and a habit of laughing loudly and flinging himself back in his chair as though what was said to him was too killingly funny for words. This was what he did when I made my request. But after a statutory show of insulting scepticism and reluctance he granted it all the same.

I had never before had so much money in my possession at one time. Nor had it occurred to me that I was a person who would ever own a motor-car. However, Kate had set her heart on a small plum-coloured Singer convertible which she had found for sale at a garage in Hampstead just before our expulsion, price £300. It was on this that we spent the greater part of Mr Stevens's bounty. Kate collected it without delay and housed it in the convenient garage which was part of the modishly modern ('split level') house of the artist David Gentleman, a friend and neighbour of David Thomson who lived near Regent's Park Canal. I cannot remember whether Kate had made friends directly with David Gentleman and his kindly, jolly first wife or through David Thomson. It is immaterial. She never had the slightest difficulty in getting people to do things for her, which was just as well for me and Jane in our circumstances at the time.

David Gentleman's house was our first place of refuge during that summer of nomadism, and we lived in it for a whole week while the Gentlemans were away on holiday, making occasional forays in the new car to contact other people who might prove suitable hosts 'until we got settled'. There were so many of them that I cannot distinguish them all. For a time we moved between several addresses in Hampstead; one, Lion House, I remember because of the stone lion at the doorway, which made a strong impression on Jane.

But after a time this wandering life began to have a worrying effect on her. Now four years old and still of enchanting beauty and intelligence, she was attending the private Catholic school in Hampstead where she had started her schooling during the last year of our life in nearby Downshire Hill; now, of course, she had to be driven there in the mornings, from wherever we had taken up temporary abode, and collected in the afternoons. As is not uncommon among girls of her age, she had invented a phantom companion or *alter ego* called Janice (a name Kate particularly deplored, but her attempts to change it to 'Lucy' or 'Caroline' had no effect). Jane would often tell us that Janice had thought or said such and such; Janice often showed considerable shrewdness in assessing our curious way of life. Soon Janice went further, maintaining that Kate and I were not really Jane's parents at all; her real father, to my chagrin, was a full colonel in the American Air Force, over here on temporary duty while his squadron remained in America. This story, which became further elaborated, persisted throughout that summer, fading out of Jane's mind when things became more settled. If they had not become so, what might have been the effect on her?

This was a question we might have put to a new friend we had made a short time before, now one of those who gave us intermittent refuge. This was the psychiatrist Dr Desmond O'Neill. We had originally met him at the house of Denis Barnes – already a high-grade and rising Civil Servant, who eventually retired with a knighthood as Permanent Secretary to the Board of Trade – and his agreeable, amusing novelist wife, who wrote under her maiden name of P. B. Abercrombie and whose broadcast talks I had produced for the BBC.

Desmond O'Neill lived in a tall house with a long narrow back-garden in Cavendish Avenue in St John's Wood. He was a Protestant Ulsterman 'from the Black North', as he put it, and carried thereby a 'VHL' or 'very heavy load' of guilt – an expression he told me was used jokingly by his psychiatric colleagues, who were, of course, all to some extent afflicted in the same way. A tall, slender man of about my own age, Desmond revealed a good deal of inner tension by his slightly anguished expression and by the excessive smallness and tightness of the knot of his tie. He had one distinction unusual in psychiatrists – while serving in the RAMC in the War, he had won a Military Cross. He was noticeably disinclined to talk about it.

At that time he was winning a reputation for his researches into psychosomatic medicine, which was only then beginning to be taken seriously, as doctors started to realise the absurdity, which should have been long obvious, of making a distinction between body and mind. He was a consultant at the nearby Hospital of St Elizabeth and St John ('Betty and Jack's') and showed me several fascinating research papers he had written on subjects about which very little – that is to say, nothing – was then known, or probably still is: one was on Sneezing and the other on Itching, both recondite forms of pleasure. As for sneezing, who has not found himself, at moments of emotional failure, sneezing uncontrollably perhaps as many as twenty or thirty times? As for itching, why is the Devil sometimes called 'Old Scratch'? Such were the apparently commonplace but in fact mysterious questions with which this remarkable man was concerned when I first met him.

Although Desmond was always formally dressed, with a sober tie and well-polished shoes, and had a most respectable appearance, his medical colleagues thought him eccentric and even 'Bohemian' – a word still used even in those days when the onset of democracy was beginning to give everybody the 'human right', as it would come to be called later, to behave in a Bohemian way. This tendency, which reached its apogee in the next decade with the phenomena of mass 'hippiedom' and 'flower power', was annoying for those who had always conducted their lives on such principles, or lack of principles. Certainly Desmond had unconventional friends and gave excellent parties in the large basement room we called 'the ballroom' below his consulting-room. He even joined in the charades which Kate, when tipsy, would suddenly set in motion, pretending to take pot-shots at him with an imaginary gun from behind a sofa in the Wild West saloon which his house had suddenly become.

He was a widower whose wife had been killed in a motor accident some years before; he had two adolescent children. He also had in his household a young woman he introduced as his ward and also his patient. She was depressed, withdrawn, enigmatic and reputedly rich. She showed neither pleasure nor irritation at the appearance in the house of my nomadic family. The garden was a good place for Jane to play and the room we had at the top of the house was a good place to write. One of the articles I wrote there was on the building of the first motorway, the M1. The piece had been commissioned by the eccentric Donald McLachlan, who later became the first editor of the Berrys' new venture, *The Sunday Telegraph*. Driven by Michael ffolkes, who was to illustrate the article, in his big brown Bentley of which he was inordinately fond, to Newport Pagnell, the operational base of the motorway, we stayed in an hotel there and spent a day inspecting the work: the new road, cutting a great swathe through the woods and pastures of Northamptonshire for a mere twenty miles or so, was the first small precursor of the great network which now covers large parts of the country with concrete. But I found it sufficiently horrifying to write a

somewhat Luddite article about it. McLachlan, who thought I
was a 'funny man' in his serious world of journalism, did not
object to my questioning the necessity for progress; it was a
time when this kind of crankiness could still be taken as merely
amusing.

Our new car, now that Kate had triumphantly shown she
could drive it, was a great success. It was a small, old-fashioned
machine which later, when we visited France in it, drew loud
laughter from the mechanics of le Mans. In wet weather we
had to put up its hood, which was in several parts, assembling
them for maximum speed in a series of drill movements which
I devised on the analogy of the drill I had so much enjoyed in
the army. The car, I was aware, was useful for Kate when she
wanted to meet her lover; I did not greatly resent not being
able to use it for similar purposes myself. I thought of taking
driving lessons but when I remembered my former hopelessness
at a skill I believed I was incapable of acquiring, I did not
persevere. As Kate grew more confident we drove further and
further afield. There was still great enjoyment in motoring in
those days when there were comparatively few cars on the still
unstraightened roads and it took two days to reach my mother's
house in Yorkshire.

That summer we even reached Scotland, spending a week
with the Tunnicliffes, who had become great friends and drinking companions, at Gatehouse of Fleet, their favourite place in
Galloway, then beautiful, wild, open country, a paradise so
changed and ruined by intensive conifer-planting later on that
I cannot bear to go there any more. On another expedition we
stayed with René Cutforth and his wife Marguerite, who had a
cottage not far from Aberystwyth. On the way there we spent
a weekend at the hotel built into the ruins of the Priory at
Llanthony in the valley of the Honddu. I had last been there

twenty years before on my wanderings through Wales with Pepi, my first wife. The place was unchanged, except that the road through the valley had been metalled. We slept in a four-poster bed, perhaps the very same one I had slept in on my previous visit. We were the only guests and had breakfast at the very same polished table, brought by a uniformed maid who had to be summoned by a brightly-polished brass bell worked by a pulley.

Kate was as delighted as I was by this splendid archaism, as well as by the beauty of the country round about. We walked to Cwmyoy, lower down the valley, and looked at the little church, all askew on the hillside and said to have been knocked sideways hundreds of years before, when the vicar, entering the church one summer afternoon, found the Devil sitting on the altar and managed to eject him only after a fierce struggle. According to an even better legend, the landslide of the hill on which the church stood had taken place at the moment of the Crucifixion. We looked round the little, grass-grown churchyard, full of leaning tombstones of slate with fine-lettered, eighteenth-century memorial verses. One of them described the soul of some Jones, Williams or Davies as a bride, asleep and waiting for the Day of Judgement:

> 'Until she hear the Bridegroom say:
> Awake, my dear, and come away.'

The discovery of such a place, at a time (one of many times) when Kate declared, of course untruly, that she had given up her lover for good, brought us closer together. Then it was solitary and unvisited; now the whole world has been there and the Tourist Board is extracting from it every penny of extractable revenue. There are notice-boards, signposts, 'interpretive information facilities'. Nobody is permitted to find out anything for himself any more. I am glad to have been there before this happened. It is a privilege which we will not have again for hundreds of years, if ever.

We drove up the valley from Llanthony by the road, then a stony track, which my first wife and I had covered on foot, and reached the summit of the Bwlch yr Efengyl, the Gospel Pass, where we stopped to gaze over the Wye Valley far into the recesses of mid-Wales, where the horrible plantations of conifers were beginning to cover the hills and drive the hill-farmers from their farms in exchange for money. As a known Welsh nationalist, I did not speak of 'English imperialism' and a deliberate policy of extirpating the Welsh language and culture as I might have done. Kate would have been decidedly unsympathetic.

As the Cutforth's cottage was not big enough to accommodate all of us, they had arranged for us to stay at the pub in the village, where René, with his great gifts for entertainment, was already well-known. We spent most of the weekend in serious drinking. René had elaborated a mythical saga of his strange upbringing in Swadlincote, in the Derbyshire coalfield, even maintaining that he had spent his earliest years entombed in a mound or slag-heap constructed by his mother. This man had great literary talent which he had not really exploited in book form (except for one excellent book about his experiences in the Korean War as a correspondent for the BBC and another book of eccentric sketches of his experiences in Nigeria, which involved a good deal of African magic); instead he had put his gifts into story-telling, mostly in pubs, so that his fame will perish with the last of those who knew him. Does this matter in the long run? Did he not do better than I, with my persistent dream of literary fame and corresponding inability to live? René, a larger-than-life character if ever there was one, lived his life to the full. He was himself.

With multiple diversions the weekend passed agreeably enough. As with many Welsh villages in those days, and for all I know even now, the inhabitants were divided into two opposing factions: those who never went to the pub and were often militant teetotalers; and those who spent all their free time in the pub on weekdays, and on Sundays (this was one of the 'six-days-only' parts of Wales) in the local Liberal Club, whose main purpose was to provide a place for drinking. The moral power of the teetotalers, mostly supported by the women, was enough to terrify the drinkers into a certain furtiveness. One man who habitually took home a basket of bottles from the pub took the precaution of covering them with a layer of cereal or soap powder packets when carrying it home through the village, for fear the garage-man, who belonged to the abstaining faction, might refuse to repair his car.

The police station was opposite the pub and so zealous was the policeman that he spent almost the whole of his Sundays standing in his porch watching the pub door to check whether anybody was going in or coming out. People like ourselves who were staying in the pub were allowed to buy drinks, so some of the more fanatical drinkers used to go into the pub on Sundays carrying small suitcases and posing as guests. The policeman regularly staged a one-man raid on the pub, insisting on the suitcases being opened and spluttering with rage when he found toothbrushes, sponges and pyjamas neatly packed inside. All this, though it was a great joke, did not make him exactly popular in the neighbourhood; some months later, René told me the policeman was walking on the seashore, perhaps hoping to intercept a cargo of contraband liquor, when he was mysteriously run over by a tractor and went to hospital with an injured leg. When he came out he decided to give up the unequal struggle and got himself posted elsewhere. He would have made a nicely contrasting successor to the policeman at Amswick.

We resumed our nomadic life in London. We had already arranged to take over the agreeable house of William ('Bill') and Ruth Sansom in St John's Wood. This was a cut above our average bivouac. I am not sure how we (or more likely, Kate) had got to know the Sansoms; perhaps through the Worsthornes, who 'knew everybody' in well-to-do social and literary circles. Sansom was then quite well-known as a novelist and short story- and travel-writer, and it was while they were on a fortnight's trip somewhere abroad that their house was available.

As befitted a successful writer it was very civilised, with great numbers of books and *objets d'art*, including one of those pictures which when looked at from one angle showed a child playing with a puppy, and from another a skull. I spent a good deal of my leisure-time trying out these effects. One of the conditions of our stay was to look after the Sansoms' two cats, Edward and Arthur, who occupied a capacious cubicle of their own next to the kitchen, with a separate entrance by cat-door to the garden. These cats were of opposed temperament, Edward being arrogant and bullying, Arthur meek and subservient. Kate, who had some fascist instincts, favoured Edward's right to dominate. I, who had the same instincts, only more so, felt I had to compensate for Kate's preference, at any rate where animals were concerned, by favouring the weaker Arthur and seeing that he got his fair share of food and milk. Later on, when some critic accused 'Peter Simple' of being a 'well-known protector of the powerful', referring no doubt to white South Africa, I remembered Edward and Arthur. Was it so certain even then, that the white South Africans were really 'the powerful'? They were only standing up for themselves, after all, with the whole world ganged up against them.

We had several acquaintances in St John's Wood. In the next street, with a house and a garden much like the Sansoms', lived R. D. ('Reggie') Smith, the marxist *bonhomme* of the BBC who had first brought Kate into its ambit by way of the Stag's Head in Hallam Street, and his wife, the novelist Olivia Manning. Olivia, though perhaps more sincere, was less unfailingly agreeable than Reggie, whose character as 'friend of all the world' is precisely captured in her novels. She even wrote a book of stories in which he figured with no more disguise than a change of name. I sometimes wondered whether he objected to being thus displayed to the public; but if he did, he showed no sign of it, which itself was very much in character. Theirs seemed a remarkably ill-assorted marriage, with no perceptible sexual tie. This may have been one reason why Olivia was inclined to be acerbic, even waspish in manner.

My fellow Yorkshireman Rayner Heppenstall, author of *The Blaze of Noon* and other novels, and a critic and producer for the Third Programme, said of Olivia in his modified West Riding accent, 'Now there's my idea of a really plain woman'. It is true that Olivia was no beauty (her impersonation by an attractive young actress in a television version of her 'Balkan Trilogy' years later made me smile faintly); but Rayner's remark may have been due as much to literary rivalry as sexual conoisseurship. Most writers are jealous of other writers; but Rayner carried this to extremes. He was jealous of the alliterative Ulster poet 'Bertie' Rodgers, who also worked for the BBC and as well as being a writer was irresistible to women, which Rayner, much as he would have wished to be, was not. Once, when 'Bertie' was holding forth at a party to a rapt female audience,

75

Rayner suddenly snatched up a small bunch of grapes and threw it at him, but without noticeable effect.

Rayner seemed to resent even my own meagre literary efforts. Finding to his surprise in the course of some research that a short story of mine had been published in the first issue of Connolly's *Horizon* ten years before, he made a point of telling me: 'It won't do, you know'. I did not mind this; he was right; the story was a mere pastiche of T. F. Powys. Indeed I did not mind Rayner at all, but liked him both as a person and a writer. Has he, like so many writers of that time ('Bertie' Rodgers is an outstanding example) sunk without trace? I hope not; I think his autobiographical novel about his absurd experiences as a psychiatric case in the army, *The Lesser Infortune*, a better book than the equally autobiographical but more pretentious and showy war novels of Olivia Manning, with their stock fictional characters and situations.

At this time Reggie and Olivia were much plagued by the *enfant terrible* of the BBC Features Department, Peter Duval Smith, a man of reprehensible and irregular life who was even more irresistible to women than Rodgers or anyone else I have ever come across. Like us, though without a young child to restrict his movements, he had no fixed abode and would often park himself on friends or acquaintances for the night. Reggie must have brought him home drunk one night to St John's Wood (for all Olivia's habitual cry of remonstrance – 'Oh Reggie!'), and left him to sleep it off on the sofa in their drawing-room, relying on him to make a quiet getaway in the morning. But a couple of weeks later Olivia, while entertaining some respectable literary friends, was aware, as they also must have been, of a particularly unpleasant smell. Later, when they had gone, she traced it to a valuable teapot on a shelf, which

Peter, unable to find his way to the lavatory, had used as a night-vessel.

Another friend in St John's Wood, though we never stayed with him, was the composer Humphrey Searle, an abstracted though friendly man whose dodecaphonic music was utterly unintelligible to me. Meeting me in the local pub, he asked me back to his flat, then, thrusting a drink into one of my hands and a sheaf of music into the other, he began to play his one-act opera *Diary of a Madman*, after Gogol, on the piano, supplying the vocal parts himself. I cannot read music (it presents something of the same difficulty to me as driving a car), but as he rumbled and tinkled, droned and screamed away, apparently at random, I dutifully turned the pages, watching him furtively in the effort to judge how far he had got. He reached the final rumble and scream when I was still only three-quarters of the way through the score. 'What do you think of it?' he asked. 'Splendid,' I replied, as I hastily turned over the remaining pages and glared at the final bars (did the thing have bars anyhow?) in as appreciative a way as I could manage. Did he notice my intense embarrassment? If so, he gave no sign of it. Perhaps he thought, not without reason, that I was always like that.

With such diversions (and all this time, of course, I was putting in four days a week at the *Telegraph* and receiving frequent letters telling me how much readers depended on my courageous commonsense and rocklike sanity) the summer passed and we were still without a permanent home. We had now used some of our temporary bivouacs several times over and the supply of suitable or willing hosts was beginning to run out. One of the last of our camping-sites was an elegant flat in one of the Regent's Park terraces belonging to my old sweetheart Laura, who was now, not surprisingly, separated from her film-producer husband and awaiting divorce so that he could marry a younger woman, this time a genuine rather than a fun-Communist.

Laura, who was now forty-five, my own age, had lost some of that patrician prettiness I had once found so irresistible that even her careless manner of dressing and her chain-smoking had been fascinatingly attractive to me. But although I no longer had any wish to go to bed with her, once the summit of my felicity, I was still fond of her – the feeling which never leaves such relationships. She had always got on well with Kate; if they had nothing else in common they had irrationality and a fondness of drink. She must have been lonely anyhow, and so quite glad to offer us temporary refuge. However, she was in a sad state altogether; indeed she was suffering a kind of nervous breakdown, which meant that she spent much of her time in bed and soon began to find our comings and goings irritating. Before long she and Kate had a blazing row, probably arising from some domestic detail of washing or cooking, and we were homeless again.

We had now quite run out of hosts and were reduced to putting up at a small private hotel in St John's Avenue on the slopes of Hampstead Hill. This was the last of our camp-sites. We contrived at this time to find a suitable unfurnished flat in Putney, a part of London quite strange to us and, though less agreeable than Hampstead, not completely unacceptable. We went on staying at the private hotel while waiting to move into the flat and it was in some ways the most bizarre of all our temporary homes during this summer of nomadism.

It was bizarre because of its intense banality. There was a resident population of commercial travellers (or sales representatives as they would now be called) who spent most of their spare time watching the primitive black-and-white television of this early period when the advance of the world's scourge was only starting and conversations overheard on buses on my journeys to Fleet Street were only just beginning to be dominated by discussions of the previous evening's programmes. The banality of the hotel soon became frightening. It has occasionally supplied material for some of my most highly specialised nightmares, in which boredom is a major element and even dominates the 'feeling tone'. I believe such dreams are very rare; and I am glad of it.

Our new flat, which we moved into as autumn was coming on, occupied the first floor of a large pre-1914 villa in Chartfield Avenue, one of a number of middle-class streets in the district west of Putney Hill, between Upper Richmond Road and a council estate which had been built on the site of one of the big houses on the edge of Putney Common. Some of its attractions – cedar trees and even a small lake – had been spared, so that this council estate had quite a pleasant air about it, and although its working-class inhabitants had nothing in common with the inhabitants of our bourgeois streets they seemed to be 'respectable' people who showed no tendency to stray outside their own limits.

Our house, which had a long communal garden at the back, was divided into three flats. The ground floor was occupied, when we first moved in, by a pleasant couple, the Prings. Mr Pring was a Clerk in the House of Commons; a subordinate of Kenneth Bradshaw, a friend of the Worsthornes who eventually became Chief Clerk and retired with the statutory knighthood. The flat above ours was occupied by the Smarts, who had a baby and several large dogs. We did not have a great deal to do with the families in the other flats; I do not think, however, that they were greatly bothered by our own noisy and tempestuous life; our frequent quarrels and drinking sessions. The

79

house, which was not unlike a small version of Duchy Grange, my mother's long-lost paradise in Harrogate, was solidly built and our flat quite roomy and comfortable in a disorganised way, especially after we had furnished it with some of the furniture from Downshire Hill which Mrs Uhlman, who had a certain inherited sense of *noblesse oblige*, had let us have for a nominal sum.

We borrowed some additional furniture from my old friends Ernst and Eithne Kaiser (née Wilkins, ingeniously gaelicised by her as Nic Liamóg) who had become, since I had last seen them just after the war, the world's greatest authorities on the Austrian novelist Robert Musil, whose works they translated and commented on for the rest of their lives. They had furniture to lend because they were leaving England to take up an appointment connected with Musil Studies in Rome. In spite of my esteem for Eithne, and, when I got to know him, Ernst, I could never manage to read the works of Musil; still less the works of Heimito von Doderer (in spite of his wonderful name), another monumental Austrian novelist on whom the Kaisers were authorities, though not the world's greatest. Kate did not care for Eithne, whom she thought somewhat affected and even 'twee', but she was glad of the furniture. However, she resented it in her robust way when the Kaisers made a detailed inventory of their possessions with a view to reclaiming them if they ever returned to England. She thought this showed a mean-spirited attitude.

The Kaisers, who lived in Belsize Park, not far from the house where 'Zed' gave his dreaded wine-and-cheese parties, had a number of high-powered intellectual friends. Among them was Elias Canetti, the renowned author of *Auto da Fé* and *Crowds and Power*, both of which I had read with a certain jealous admiration, the second with some difficulty, since I find it difficult to think in a systematic or even rational way at all. After a party at the Kaisers' one evening, I found myself having a drink with Canetti at the huge, cavernous pub in Swiss Cottage. I can't remember what we talked about, if anything. He may well have dismissed me as irredeemably stupid and frivolous; for my part, though probably drunk, I was alarmed by the powerful aura of cerebration which seemed to surround this short, square, dark, Sephardic person. We parted after a short while; such a meeting was typical of my fugitive and trivial experiences of the great and famous, people I feared all the more because of my never entirely suppressed aspiration to join them in their fame and greatness.

When we were both undergraduates at Oxford in 1936, Eithne, who was then a promising poet, had been very encouraging about my novel *Sheldrake*, which I had been writing with immense, not to say unheard of application in the vacation before my last term, when I should have been working for my final examinations. This preoccupation had been one of the reasons (the others being conceit and boredom) for my failure to get even the humblest pass and for my leaving Oxford without a degree. I did not care about this at the time, believing that I would immediately get *Sheldrake* published and become rich and famous, or at any rate famous. This did not happen and the book remained unpublished.

I had been desperately carrying the typescript about with me ever since, even taking a copy of it to India during the War. But I had virtually ceased to hope it would ever be published, especially since Anthony Gibbs and Charles Fry of Allan Wingate, the publishers for whom I had done ghost work, had, after some hesitation, turned it down.

So it was about this time that I was able to present Eithne with a nominal triumph which pleased her almost as much as it did me. The firm of Wingate had got into some sort of difficulties and had been taken over by one of the partners, Anthony Blond, a rich Jew of exotic personality and literary tastes more sophisticated than those of Gibbs and Fry, the latter a debauched and unhappy homosexual whom I discovered later on, after his suicide, in the pages of James Lees-Milne's enjoyable books on his work for the National Trust. The author describes him as 'the worst man in the world' and 'a positive Satan'; it was humiliating to find that of all the hundreds of variegated and often very distinguished people Lees-Milne mentions, Fry was the only one I had ever met myself.

After taking over, Blond set up his own firm, at first called Blond-Wingate and afterwards simply Blond, and the first book he ever published was my long-despaired-of novel, though in a somewhat shortened form. He was, I thought, rather mean in giving me an advance of only £75 ('might have run to a hundred') but I was so pleased to get the book published at all that I did not really mind. When it came out it got rather dismissive reviews, with one exception – Kenneth Young, a colleague on the *Telegraph* (he was assistant literary editor under 'Zed'), wrote fiction reviews on the side for the *Yorkshire Post*.

I was gratified to find that this true friend and fellow-Yorkshireman had given my book a 'rave review' in his weekly selection, singling it out as a work of genius and one of the most remarkable first novels published since the war. This was more than friendship and our common Yorkshire origin called for. The book, a fantasy about Bradford, hardly more fantastic than a what has subsequently happened to the place, has some originality but is, as I now see, over-influenced both by Kafka and by what might be called the conventional surrealism of the Thirties. But I was grateful to Kenneth Young, a bearded man with a mysterious background who had certainly been in war-time intelligence and may have retained some connections with it afterwards. 'Scratch me and I'll scratch you,' as the great Colonel Sibthorp used to say. But alas, I never had a chance to repay Kenneth's kindness. Not long afterwards, to everyone's surprise and to Sir Colin's open disapproval, he became editor of the *Yorkshire Post*. He kept the chair only a short time, vacating it in circumstances which I never understood and which, perhaps, nobody was meant to understand.

He took up a mysterious job as 'political adviser to the Beaverbrook Press', whose nature and purpose it was difficult to fathom, like much in this puzzling man's career. Twice he asked me, for no discernible reason, to dinner at the Beefsteak Club. On the first occasion he was called away for half an hour during dinner, leaving me staring, with a wild surmise, at the only other person present at the single large dining-table, Sir Henry d'Avigdor-Goldsmid, a prominent member of the English–Jewish establishment. On the other occasion I was just about to leave for the Beefsteak Club when I got a message saying that Kenneth had had a severe stroke. He never regained his faculties, but lingered, speechless, for several years until he died.

While he was editor of the *Yorkshire Post* he had done Kate and myself another service by arranging a meeting with his friend and fellow-Yorkshireman John Braine, who had just become famous with his novel *Room at the Top*. By a coincidence I had read the book in typescript but pronounced it 'promising but unpublishable as it stands' – perhaps my outstanding achievement as a publisher's reader, but one I did not mention to Kenneth or the author. At the time Braine was living with his wife and family at Bingley, a small town in Airedale between Shipley, my own birthplace, and Keighley, home of the Tunnicliffes. We were staying with my mother at Amswick, so we arranged to drive to Skipton and meet Braine at the Hole in the Wall in the market-place.

He arrived there after driving the short distance from Bingley in his brand-new 'mini'. As he had only just learned to drive (part of the price of his new fame and success) he regarded this as quite an achievement, which it undoubtedly was. We took to him at once, helped by a mutual fondness, which soon became obvious, for serious drinking. There was something both impressive and endearing about his unaffected delight in his success. He patted a magnificent new pigskin briefcase as he took off a new ginger-coloured tweed overcoat as fine as my own black Crombie, which I had bought after leaving the BBC as a pledge of my new life. 'Do you know what I've got in this briefcase?' he asked in his unimpaired West Riding accent. 'I'll tell you. My library books!'

There was a poignant symbolism here. Before his sudden elevation to best-selling novelist he had for many years been a humble librarian. It was not long before a man in the bar, who had been watching us intently in a judicial, Yorkshire way for some time, got to his feet and came over. 'I know you,' he said. 'I've seen you on television. Aren't you John Braine?' It was beautiful to see the author's innocent pleasure in this public recognition of his fame, so beautiful and even moving that it never occurred to me to feel the slightest jealousy. Soon we were beginning to find a pleasurable warmth stealing over us, and it went on stealing over us so insidiously that we suddenly realised with surprise that it was half-past two and closing-time.

This did not worry Braine unduly. 'We'll go to the Black Horse,' he said. 'I know the landlord – and he knows me.' The Black Horse was just closing when we arrived. 'Good afternoon, Mr Braine,' said the landlord, with a surprised glance at us and an enhanced respect for people he had thought from our previous visits as of no particular account. 'Go up with your friends to the upstairs room. There's nobody'll disturb you there and you can drink as long as you like.' We stood drinking round the billiard table, talking animatedly of this and that. We were still drinking and talking when the pub re-opened at half-past five. Braine, still clutching his briefcase, began to show signs of uneasiness. We staggered through the market-place and down to the railway station, where he had left his car.

He looked at it with alarm. 'Let's have one more drink,' he said. 'All right, just one.' We shambled into the bar of the Station Hotel, a gloomy establishment with horsehair-stuffed seats and photographs of railway engines on the wall. A couple of commercial travellers were drinking Scotch and chatting to a hawk-nosed barmaid. Less interested in literature than the habitués of the Hole in the Wall and the Black Horse, they gave no sign of recognition. But Braine had had enough for one day. The problem was: how was he to get home? None too sure of driving at the best of times, as he admitted, he was obviously incapable of driving now. In the end we put him in a taxi and, extracting his address with difficulty, despatched him back to Bingley. It was a good thing Kate had a strong head, or she would not have got us home ourselves. We found my mother in an agitated state. 'There's been a Mrs Braine on the telephone, asking what you've done with her husband. Ee, I don't know what you'll get up to next.'

We became good friends with John who, though he could sometimes be boring in a ponderous Yorkshire way, was always endearing. I ran into him from time to time at literary parties after he moved with his family from Bingley into a mock-Georgian house at Woking, a daft southern place if ever there was one; moving away from the leftist orthodoxy which had caused him to join CND at their 'sit-ins' in Trafalgar Square, he became a man of ultra-right views and therefore a great supporter of 'Peter Simple', sometimes sending me encouraging fan letters if I had written something which particularly pleased him. He varied between bouts of heavy drinking and total abstinence when, glass of orange juice in hand, he would lecture me half humourously on the evils of drink.

Sadly, he never repeated the success of *Room at the Top* and the film of it which was made soon afterwards, but declined gradually through less successful books and television films about his repulsive hero, Joe Lampton, until in the end he left his home and family in Woking to live with a late-found love in one room in Hampstead, where he died untimely and almost forgotten. Much earlier, after he had been to America, he found himself in conversation with a progressive bishop and praised that country highly. 'Well,' said the bishop, 'I suppose it's all right if you're not black.' 'I'm not black, you silly bugger,' Braine replied. I have always thought this the perfect 'existential' answer to all such remarks. Ever a hater of cant and conformity and a champion of freedom, Braine, when the campaign of terror against smoking was at its height, put special stickers on his envelopes: 'Smoking is Good for You; Smoke More.' He was a man of exceptionally sound instincts, convinced that if the Government told you not to do something you should make a point of doing it.

Kate, quite sensibly, had not been impressed either by the publication of *Sheldrake* or by Kenneth Young's review of it. But a second anthology of the column appeared at the end of 1958, further enhancing its reputation. Colin began to think of spreading its wings and with the approval of the editor, who was coming to accept it as a permanent feature of the paper with a certain regular following (though it is possible that even after it had become really famous many readers of the *Telegraph* were unaware of its existence, tucked away as it was at the bottom of an inner page), arranged several expeditions out of London. First we two, along with Michael ffolkes, went to Geneva for a week, nominally because some international conference or other, possibly about disarmament, was being held there. I wondered whether it had anything to do with the ghost of the League of Nations, which was certainly still hanging about. Michael ffolkes, who was fond of good living, had been looking forward to staying at a first-class hotel like the Beau Rivage (which, I remembered, had been one of my father's favourites in the Twenties, when my elder brother and sister had been at 'finishing school' in Switzerland, one of the absurd anomalies which were to distort and haunt their lives). But, just as if we had been in the army, a 'shambles' had been made of arrangements for our accommodation and we ended up in a 'self-catering flat'. There, in the mornings, we wrote our respective items and Michael drew his drawings, and in the afternoons we either saw the sights of the place or got drunk after a late, prolonged lunch.

Colin, always fond of argumentation, felt himself at a loss among companions less accustomed or inclined to it. Rather than not have an argument at all, he would provoke me by making some obviously absurd statement such as: 'Switzerland, per capita, is the poorest country in Europe'. We spent one whole afternoon arguing about this, then went out to drink at a bar. Colin, still arguing, became so drunk that he suddenly rolled off his chair onto the floor, his possessions, notecase, money, keys, passport, spilling all round him in the manner of a drunken sailor on shore leave. We had to take him back to our flat, undress him and put him to bed, still feebly maintaining the dire poverty of the Swiss.

Our next expedition was to a more mundane destination: Manchester. Here Michael ffolkes's predilections were better catered for; we stayed in the Midland Hotel, then the most expensive in the city, and made visits to the stupendous Gothic Town Hall with its wonderful frescoes (like 'the Danish Invasion of Manchester' and 'Dalton Discovering Marsh Gas') or the Free Trade Hall or Didsbury and Withington, calling up memories of my BBC days: the mild rule of Brian Cave-Brown-Cave, the sensitive Controller of the North Region and a member of one of the oldest families in England; the formation of a Marxist cell by the folk-singer Ewan MacColl; days among the derelict leadmines of Derbyshire with John Mort, the great barmaster of the Leadminer's Court; Professor Max Newman the mathematician, with his fondness for marmalade pudding and Enochian logic and his formidable wife who, as I learned long afterwards to my amazement, had not, at the time we lodged with them, been his wife at all. Why, being in Manchester again after only five years, did I not look up old friends and acquaintances? Had Kate, a friendly soul, been with us she would certainly have wanted to do so. But it never occurred to me. I had passed into another world which had no more connection with the BBC than either world had with the army or with my time at Oxford. All were separate spheres of my life and I must have felt instinctively that it would be inadvisable, even dangerous, to mingle them.

Our last expedition was to Dublin. We travelled by the night train to Holyhead, thence by boat to Dun Laoghaire (or Kingstown, as Colin, who did not share my 'Celtic' predilections, insisted on calling it). We had a nasty shock at the outset, for travel by air to Ireland had already superseded travel by train and boat for all except the poorer travellers. Though we travelled, of course, first-class as befitted substantial journalists, we found there was only one first-class compartment, indeed only a section of one, and that rather squalid and neglected, and part of the guard's van. When I had last travelled on this line, the year after the war, on my flight from my first wife in Dublin, there had been an excellent first-class service with meals adequate enough at a time of rationing. Now there was only a fry-up and an offer to make up a game of cards with the guard.

Michael was better pleased when we reached Dublin and put up at the Shelbourne Hotel, everything which an hotel should be. Here Colin was almost on home ground; we were met by his old friend from Peterhouse, Dr Desmond Williams, now Professor of Modern History at the National University of Ireland, a well-known character of mythological dimensions, of whose charm, unreliability and wit a thousand anecdotes were told. Although lame from a bone disease and running to fat, Desmond was almost as irresistible to young women as his compatriot 'Bertie' Rodgers. He also had Rodgers's ability to be in two places at once; in fact he often improved on this by not being in any definite place at all, particularly if he had arranged to meet someone in a definite place or had invited someone to lunch there. Many of the most amusing stories about him were based on this peculiarity of his. He was also addicted to absurd flattery: I had hardly met him before he told me that some Cabinet Minister or famous writer had just told him how much he admired my work. I treated this, even before I had heard of his reputation, with a certain reserve.

Desmond had a German wife (he had been in the Control Commission in Germany and had married her, I believe, to give her British or Irish nationality) but had never lived with her. His present companion was a fierce South African woman doctor, Sheila Murphy, former wife of the Irish poet Richard Murphy and a woman of some means with a sad little eight-year-old daughter. She and Desmond lived in her expensive but squalid house in a superior part of Dublin. Their lives, which involved a good deal of drinking, were haphazard. She was good-looking but surprisingly dirty and ill-dressed and appealed to me more than she did to Michael ffolkes, whose taste in women was somewhat conventional.

Under Desmond's tutelage we met a great many people in Dublin, but for all I can remember I may have been drunk all the time – no uncommon thing on a visit to the Republic. I wrote a sketch about Conor Cruise O'Brien, who, himself decidedly drunk, walked out of a dinner party, offended by my reference to the *Táin Bó Cuailgne*, an epic poem he evidently thought no Englishman ought to have heard of. We met the solicitor and novelist Terence de Vere White in the Kildare Street Club, a man with an Irish voice of almost painfully exquisite refinement who asked us to his house, where his wife was quite amazingly rude, telling Michael ffolkes that he 'knew nothing' and asking her husband what he meant by bringing home low companions from the Dublin gutter.

One comparatively sober afternoon we saw a special performance of the film *Mise Eire* which George Morrison (or Seoirse Mac Giollamhaire) had made for Gael Linn, the Irish language publishing company. This presented the history of Ireland from pre-Norman times up to the 'War of Independence' by means of designs, and for the later period, photographs and clips from old films with a commentary in Irish. The music was by the composer Seán O Riada, a man of genius who might have been recognised as one of the greatest composers of this century if he had not lived in Ireland and died untimely of what is sometimes called the national malady, drink. For the film score he had used some of the finest Irish folk-songs (and there are no folk-songs finer) notably *Róisin Dubh* ('Little Dark Rose') in orchestral settings of great skill and beauty to produce an over-whelming effect.

By the end I was in floods of tears. It was enough to bring anybody to his feet, shouting support for the cause of Irish nationalism, that most tragic and hopelessly lost of all lost causes, lost when the Irish language was lost more than two hundred years ago. One generally overlooked reason why Ireland, unified or not, can never be a nation is that when all the 'unhistorical nations' of Europe, the Czechs, Slovaks, Finns and so on, were asserting their nationality, only Ireland, though gaining nominal independence, lost her language beyond hope of revival. The latest heirs of that lost cause, the Provisional IRA, must know this in their hearts. Perhaps that is one neglected reason for their desperate savagery. When they are assembling their bombs or planning operations, do they use the Irish language? Are they not obliged, for their own sake, to use the language of the English enemy? It is the ultimate irony.

I came back to England with O Riada's music ringing in my head. That night Kate and I made love as we had not made love for a long time, and for the rest of that week spent successive nights of delicious love-making. It was an interlude I cannot explain. I don't think it ever happened again.

The FitzGibbons' ménage at Sacomb's Ash had for some time now shown unmistakable signs of breaking up. There seemed to be a correlation between this process and the change which was coming over the neighbourhood, a cloud of uneasiness and decline: its magic – at its best it had been that – was disappearing. Constantine's own behaviour was becoming more and more desperate. He had always been a heavy drinker; now he drank more and more, and his round face beneath a prematurely bald skull – Theodora said he 'looked like a mad Dutch baby' –

began to lose what had been its habitually amiable and friendly expression. He had a nervous trick of swinging his right arm in an arc of a circle; this gesture now began to express anger and aggression. On returning drunk from the pub at night he more than once took off his clothes outside the door, piled them into a heap and tried to set fire to them – a thing much easier in intention than execution.

I saw little of him at this time, but learned of the final collapse of his marriage from his neighbour Elizabeth Foster-Melliar. It seems he had arranged to abscond – where I cannot say – with the wife of another neighbour. Perhaps he only imagined, in his drunken confusion, that he had made this arrangement. But the woman changed her mind – supposing she had had a mind to abscond at all – at the last moment and failed to keep the assignation. Constantine therefore went home with his packed bag to face what may have been one of the most remarkable of all the FitzGibbons' scenes of controlled violence. Or it may be that with things getting really serious the throwing of food, drink, plates and bottles was inadequate to express their feelings. There had always been an element of fun and affection as well as theatrical contrivance in these displays.

It was not long before Theodora made a far more effective counter-move by herself absconding in fact. She went to Ireland, which she had always claimed was her native country (she had been, she used to say, the daughter of an Irish peer, guarded in her nursery by six gigantic Irish wolfhounds). An old admirer, George Morrison (who made the wonderful film *Mise Eire*), was waiting to give her refuge and after the divorce had gone through they married. For a time Constantine stayed on in his house, either alone or consoled by one woman or another. But he was a man of great resilience; it was not long before he found another wife, Marion, a dark, rather mysterious person who, though she lacked Theodora's gift for fantasy and amusing rudeness, and probably her outstanding gift for cookery, no doubt had other qualities I did not discover.

It was not long, either, before Constantine, whose ability to go on writing books even under the most adverse circumstances I admired and envied, wrote a novel about a coming Communist takeover of England, *When the Kissing Had to Stop*, which was serialised in a newspaper and even televised, making him well-known for the first time, and put him really in the money. His reaction was characteristic. He sold Sacomb's Ash and bought, with a typical illusion of grandeur, an immense, rambling, dilapidated house in Dorset called Thornhill. He and his new wife had not nearly enough furniture to furnish it, nor enough money to keep it up. This did not prevent him from giving a wedding party in the empty, echoing house, the last of his memorable parties I ever attended, full of improbable people from the top of his league tables, such as the novelist Sibylle Bedford, Noel Annan the thinker and Constantine's vast, rumbling uncle, Sir Philip Antrobus of Avebury Manor in Wiltshire, whose family had once owned Stonehenge and who, whatever else he was, seemed every inch a baronet to me – I had, at that time, met very few baronets.

Rapidly 'outsoaring the shadow of our night', as I told Kate in a self-pitying moment, though remaining just as friendly as before, he soon sold Thornhill and moved to a somewhat smaller but much more beautiful house not many miles away, Waterstone Manor near Puddletown, famous for appearing in Hardy's *Far from the Madding Crowd*. Here I stayed once or twice (Kate, I think, never, for she had by this time incurred Constantine's permanent displeasure, partly by her serious infidelity to me, and had dropped out of the league tables altogether). There was still not enough furniture to fill this large house, but there were many of the right appurtenances, such as a sideboard in the breakfast-room with dishes on a hot plate – bacon, eggs, mushrooms, kidneys, kedgeree and so on – from which guests helped themselves in approved country-house fashion.

There was a terrace, there were fine lawns and stately trees, even a dower-house where Constantine's formidable American mother was, I think, meant to live in her old age, though I doubt she ever did. For me there was a particular bonus: a mysterious avenue leading from the garden to a prospect of distant blue downs; I had only to walk along it a short way to feel that clouding of the mind, that sense of the numinous I had known in childhood and youth but thought lost or only faintly recovered. Constantine showed me this avenue with great pride; he also knew what kind of feelings it was likely to arouse in me, even though he may not have shared them himself. It was as if he were giving me a special treat, as indeed he was.

Here in this beautiful place Constantine lived for several years, writing with his usual diligence though never repeating the success of *When the Kissing Had to Stop*, and entertaining in his usual generous, if unpredictable, way, until that marriage too broke down in acrimony after producing his first child, a son, Francis, and his dark lady departed, leaving him alone again.

It was not long, of course, before he found another wife. I am not sure whether this was his third marriage or his fourth. There had been rumours of a very brief marriage when he was at Oxford, to a beautiful Burmese girl, Margaret Ay Maung; but this, if it ever took place, was soon obscured. His latest wife seemed to me by far the best of them. Marjorie was a very attractive and amiable young American, formerly married to a millionaire and presumably well provided with alimony. With her he left Waterstone and England for good and settled in Ireland, at first in west Cork, where there was a considerable English colony attracted, as Constantine himself must have been to some extent, by the Republic's remission of income tax to all residents who could show themselves to be 'creative artists' by having published a book or musical work or held an exhibition. He soon tired of these people and moved to Dublin where he had a house in the superior suburb of Killiney, an establishment of some splendour, I was told; mainly through apathy, I never visited him there.

Very soon, he took Irish nationality (his father had been Irish-American) and with it Irish nationalist opinions which gave rise to several books on Irish history such as *Out of the Lion's Paw*, an account of the last Irish struggle for independence. Apart from his writing and his family (Marjorie produced a daughter, Oonagh) he devoted himself to two ambitions: to become a Senator of Ireland and to establish his claim to the Earldom of Clare, extinct since 1864. Considering that the first and best-known Earl of Clare, John FitzGibbon, had been the most prominent Irish supporter of the Union of 1801 and was accordingly one of the greatest of all Irish historical villains in nationalist eyes, this seemed an odd ambition indeed.

He succeeded in neither ambition. But he was, I think and hope, reasonably happy with this best and comeliest of his wives. He certainly ought to have been. But he was a conspicuously 'difficult' man to live with. He told me, on one of his visits to London, that he had been doing his best to wreck his marriage to Marjorie, 'just as I always do'. If so, he did not succeed. But I have no doubt he was angered and frustrated by the decline of his reputation as a writer and, it may be, by his unacceptability in Dublin literary circles as well as English ones. In his later years, heavy drinking passed into dipsomania. He wrote a book about this, confident, he told me, that it would re-establish his literary reputation and be a bestseller. This did not happen.

Toward the end of his life his misfortunes multiplied. He had an operation for double cataract, which left him with 'tunnel vision' – he could see only straight ahead with the aid of immensely powerful spectacles. Claudie, whose mind was inclined to dwell on such things and who disliked him anyhow, told me she believed he had had a colostomy, one of the ultimate medical horrors. However that may be, it is certainly a fact that on my very last meeting with my old friend, only a few months before his death in February 1983, he seemed to be partly paralysed. Yet he faced all this 'with immense courage and cheerfulness', a cliché which in his case was no more than the truth. In the pub where we met he drank several pints of beer and talked excitedly of a book he was writing about Charlemagne. As I put him in the taxi which was to take him to the airport for the plane to Dublin, he smiled just as he had smiled in the Fitzroy Tavern where I first met him in 1937, a precocious young man of seventeen just back from a sort of Grand Tour of Europe and full of ideas for writing.

It was curious and also sad that I, whose unwritten books he had offered to write for me in Sacomb's Ash days since I seemed utterly incapable of writing any for myself, slowly attained, even though pseudonymously, a greater literary reputation (of a sort) than he, whose writing career had started off with such a bang. But for him I might possibly never have written anything at all, but have remained, a fading hanger-on, on the margins of the BBC, gradually declining into alcoholic hopelessness – if, that is, I could have found enough money for the alcohol. It was he who, in my wandering life after Oxford, showed me the possibility of better things by encouraging what some people might have called snobbery but others discrimination.

It was he who had brought me into the circle of Much Hadham, the Welches, Worsthornes, Moores and Foster-Melliars by which I eventually secured, on the *Telegraph*, the first regular job I ever had in my life. And he had been, in spite of all the nonsense of social league tables, a warm friend. We shared, up to the end, a whole domain of jokes and associations which were renewable whenever we met: the days before the war which my first wife and I had spent in Chelsea, rapidly moving from one bed-sitter or half-furnished flat to another, one rented from the 'married' homosexual pair, Potter and Baxter, whose screaming rows with each other and with Quentin Crisp, a flamboyant homosexual who later became famous, were promising material for fiction; summer days in Westmorland at the beginning of the war; the statutory pub crawl of the nine pubs in Appleby, in one of which, the Golden Ball, Constantine had only just escaped being arrested as a spy because, though dressed in the uniform of a bandsman in the Irish Guards, he had been heard speaking German; odd meetings during the earlier part of the war, when I had spent a weekend at Grosvenor House with my rich Yorkshire girlfriend and we had got drunk with him at a night club, the long-lost Coconut Grove; parties at Sacomb's Ash when we 'went on' to a curious, dilapidated country club called Gilston Hall and sometimes stayed the night to resume drinking at dawn: alcohol, though not the only bond between us, certainly suffused our relationship with its kindly influence, making possible a friendship between two people as disparate as could well be.

A weekend I spent at Waterstone in the Sixties before his final departure for Ireland – the last occasion I saw him for more than a few hours at a time – was typically bizarre. I knew his second wife had left him, and as far as I knew he was not yet in the way of acquiring a third. What I was not prepared for was to find George and Theodora, by this time Mr and Mrs Morrison, installed as a sort of butler and housekeeper and running his house with commendable efficiency. He had sent for them from Ireland in his imperious way and there they were just as if nothing had ever happened between them. Theodora had always been a magnificent cook (she was now making a name for herself as a cookery writer, author of a series of books illustrated by George's fine old photographs of peasants and fisherman – *A Taste of Ireland*, *A Taste of Scotland*, *A Taste of Yorkshire* and, for all I knew, *A Taste of the Back of Me Hand* – and was in her element in the Waterstone kitchen, turning out splendid feasts as in the old days.

I was glad to find she was still as free as ever with her insulting witticisms ('I've taken an instant dislike to you,' she would say to someone like myself whom she had known for years, or 'Look, his little face is all puckered up with disappoint- ment'). George, a large, quietly-spoken leprechaun, asserted his place in the world in a whisper which contrasted with Theodora's shout. But there was no mistaking their good opinion of themselves, which went with a certain puzzlement at my own self-depreciating attitude ('But then,' Theodora said, 'you always were peculiar'). And so, after a pleasant weekend of serious drinking in the old style, I left them to play their peculiar charade.

As positive and eager to extend the bounds of our lives as I was negative and inclined to shrink from new enterprises, Kate decided to make new, sensational use of our curious little car. We would go to the South of France in it. So, in the autumn of 1959, through one of her innumerable friends and contacts (she was now quite successful with her journalist's work, and for a time had a well-paid job writing for a mysterious body called the Wool Secretariat, pattern of all the proliferating organisations set up to publicise and promote anything you can think of) Kate arranged to rent for a whole month a small house in the forest near Vence, only a few miles from the Riviera. With misgivings on my part we set off from Putney in the little car, the back part of which was so crammed with luggage that Jane, then nearing her seventh birthday, had to fit into a little nest in one corner.

As often with Kate's enterprises, my misgivings soon vanished and gave way to what most people would have described as pleasure when we boarded the car ferry at Dover and savoured the delights of 'going abroad', not yet a thing which almost everybody in England did. The democratic horrors of mass tourism were still ahead. It was ten years since I had last been to France. Then it had been my BBC girl friend Anne who had organised our holiday in a château on the Tarn. Now, under a different tutelage and with a beloved young daughter to enjoy unfamiliar sights, sounds and smells and wonder at the foreign people, thus providing vicarious wonder for myself, all was changed. In 1948, what was more, Anne and I had had to subsist for a whole fortnight in France on the travel allowance the Labour government allowed us, £25 each; now, with the Conservative dispensation, the travel allowance, if it existed at all in practice, was much more generous; besides, I was now rich, or if not rich, had a great deal more money than I could ever have expected.

We loaded our car onto the train at Calais and reaching Lyon in the early morning, drove steadily south and down the Rhône, through the brightly-coloured country by way of nougat-infested Montelimar (fascinating only for Jane; I suggested buying a twenty-ton block of the stuff but was persuaded to reduce it to reasonable proportions). We spent the night at Les Baux in a pleasant enough inn, excited by all the signs that we had reached the true South – the sound of massed cicadas, the smell of pine resin and lavender. Next morning I was astounded by the strange mirage-like Alpilles, which I had never heard of before and had not even noticed on the map. Entrusted with the map-reading, one of my few practical skills, I deceived Kate by choosing, instead of the obvious main road, a lesser one which took us through the inland hills, with their beautiful forests, ruined villages on hill-tops and small towns where nothing much had changed for centuries. So by the time we had taken on necessary supplies, further restricting Jane's nest-space and overloading the car, and were nearing our destination, it was late evening. We lost our way, descending a steep, rugged track in the gathering darkness, then, saved by a skilled piece of reversing by Kate, who was getting more confident in her driving every minute, came upon our little house, buried in trees and in a labyrinth of tracks, almost by accident.

The house, amid olive trees and pines, was in a place near enough to the coast to be occupied by many similar though widely separated houses belonging to French or Belgian bourgeois, largely retired, and a few foreigners, none English. The cleaning woman, supplied by the owner, was a monopod. This fascinated Jane, who may have acquired from this experience her later fascination with cripples, physical cripples at first, later mental. There was also a beautiful tabby cat named Baudouin after the King of the Belgians, whom Jane grew fond of, inventing a chant she sang when Kate crossed her: 'Beautiful Baudouin, Horrid Mummy'. I seldom crossed her myself ('you spoil that child,' Kate would have said if she had been addicted to talking in such familiar clichés).

The holiday started badly on the first morning when we went to Cagnes by the sea, the scene of Cyril Connolly's book *The*

Rock Pool, whose hero, Naylor, has such a disquieting resemblance to myself that I have always wondered on whom, apart
from the author, he could have been based. This must have
been the time when the Riviera was beginning to turn into a
squalid inferno (the strange villas of the rich still remaining
here and there, with rocky steps leading down to private
beaches, gallantly defended against the hordes of the too-many,
to serve as a reminder of the paradise it must have been). The
beach of Cagnes was not only smelly and bleak under a grey
autumnal sky but almost deserted. It was a horrible let-down.
Careless of Jane, for whom it was perhaps enough to be by the
sea and in a foreign land, we quarrelled fiercely.

The holiday was not like that all the time. There were more
agreeable beaches; there were cafés where we sat drinking and
watching passers-by; there were expeditions to Vence (already
famous for terrible amateur and professional painters, tourists'
knick-knack shops and false potteries), Grasse, Miramar and
Vallauris (famous for Picasso); and one day we even set out for
Italy, a country where neither Kate nor myself had ever been.
I had absurd plans to reach Liguria and even Tuscany, unwilling
to accept that the distances were too great for such megalo-
maniac ideas; in the end we got no further than the unpleasing
coastal resort of Diano Marina, spending the night in an inferior
hotel where we were kept sleepless by our first experience of
the amiable noisiness of Italians. Next morning, on a beach
occupied almost entirely by fat Germans, there was another
treat for Jane: an artificial leg lying ownerless on the sand, a
striking symbol, but of what? ('I've got a poem on,' we both
said simultaneously, united for a moment.)

We turned back towards France under grey, thunderous,
menacing skies; through San Remo where, hot and fly-
tormented, we ate a disgusting lunch, looking disgustedly at the

dull Alpine foothills, bristly with scrub and disfigured by dried-up ravines. But next day, the 16th of September, was Jane's seventh birthday; asked what she wanted for a treat, she chose the beach of Juan-les-Pins, with its expensive beach-huts and umbrellas, delicious iced drinks and the occasional bit of swimming, of which she was already inordinately fond.

Now we had only two days left. Next day the postman brought a shock for Kate from England: a letter from her Kenneth, telling her that his wife had discovered their affair (it was amazing that she had not discovered it long before; there is a proverbial but true saying: 'the wife is always the last to know') and consequently it was all over. Kate set her considerable jaw: 'Oh no, it isn't,' I could almost hear her saying (and there, of course, she was right). As was her habit, she made no secret of her private life to people in general, least of all to me, and was soon telling me all her troubles. Was this openness, even boastfulness a part of her persistent wish to flout her family's Catholic conformity; or was it part of her persistent need to reassure herself that she was lovable and loved?

We set off on the long journey to Lyons and home in a mood on her part, half despairing, half determined; on mine, passive, no longer caring greatly one way or the other. We simply gave ourselves up to the pleasure of the journey. We spent the night at an hotel in Avignon after duly inspecting the papal palace. Its restaurant was fascinating to all of us in different ways. At the next table was an elderly French couple who gave an amazing exhibition of greed, putting on protective clothing when they ate shellfish, then laying it aside as they got down to business with enormous helpings of *coq au vin*. I had always annoyed Kate with my seemingly perverse but in fact genuine dislike of French cooking ('perfectly good food ruined with ridiculous sauces') but here was an exhibition of gourmandism which even she, with her claim to sophisticated taste, could laugh at with me.

These people even talked about food as they ate it. 'What do you do,' said the man, 'if you wake up hungry in the night?' 'I always keep a chocolate cake under the bed.' The man considered this. 'Moi,' he said at last, 'je prefère un Port Salut.' We could hardly contain ourselves, and failed to notice that Jane was amusing herself and propagating anglophobia by blowing into the long narrow paper containers of bread fingers and propelling them to great distances across the room. Next day we caught the car-conveying train at Lyons and reached Calais in the early morning. It was a beautiful, golden autumnal day, the sea like glass, and glass of a very high quality, as we crossed the Channel back to England and our various troubles; we reached Putney on an afternoon so calm and warm in golden light that I imagined I could hear cicadas in the gardens beside the leafy suburban roads.

4
Evenings in Fleet Street

With the success of the column and our growing prospects we began to acquire, in our Putney villa, some of the appurtenances of middle-class life. We bought a new, or rather second-hand, car to replace the comical little machine which had given such good service, a smart-looking green Hillman Minx convertible, a popular model at the time. We also began to have *au pair* girls to look after Jane when either or both of us were away and to take her to and from her new school, the Virgo Fidelis Convent School in Kensington (Kate, a lapsed Catholic, was anxious that Jane should have a Catholic education, though this, whatever it may have done for her moral welfare, and it probably did a lot, meant that she suffered disadvantages in an academic sense). The first *au pair* girl we had was a large, dark, fierce and overpowering German with lesbian tendencies. She did not stay long and was replaced by Gabriela, a plump Italian girl of amazing amiability and simplicity who was quite happy to put up with unlimited teasing and practical jokes.

In the summer of 1960 we took Jane to Ireland. We stayed at the Glenbeigh Hotel on the Ring of Kerry, recommended by some friend of Kate's, an extremely jolly establishment and a credit to the efforts of Terence Sheehy of Bórd Fáilte Eireann, then beginning to attract tourists, both English and foreign, to a country which, outside Dublin, had had few good hotels. The more convivial guests, that is to say most of them, gathered in the bar every night for drinking, singing and other entertainments. A Dublin barrister, Dermot Kinlan, was famous for a recitation in which he reproduced in succession the accents of the four provinces of Ireland, ending with that of Ulster, whose harsh back-vowels and grimly menacing tones caused much amusement. Who would have thought, at a time when peace seemed to have settled on Ireland for good and nobody seemed to take old hatreds seriously any more, that twenty years later those tones would be no matter for merriment?

One evening we went to the celebrated Puck Fair at Killorglin, where a goat is hoisted to a high platform but no longer sacrificed as it must once have been. Satisfactorily, the electric lighting in the town failed that night; we peered into a rough and primitive bar and saw by flickering candlelight a crowd of dark wild faces which had not changed in essence from those a traveller might have seen a hundred, even two hundred years before. All this delighted me; the Tourist Board was probably beginning to think about the touristic possibilities of this picturesque Fair of Killorglin, but then it still belonged, without self-consciousness or artiness, to the Irish farmers and tinkers as it had for untold centuries. We must have seen it in its last days before it was swallowed up by the 'modern world' and transformed into a show, an entertainment for everybody to gaze at on the television screen, with a neat commentary, perhaps, and a discussion by 'experts' in which its ancient symbolism would be analysed at a simple-minded, even moronic level, enough to justify its being described by people who should know better as a 'serious programme'.

In old age I have 'gone off' the Irish, and even begun to doubt whether there are any people, apart from the aboriginal Gaelic-speakers of the west, who can really be called Irish at all. In my youth, and even up to the time of this holiday in Ireland, I was as fervent a believer in the myth of Irish nationalism as any of those English people, such as Arnold Bax the composer or Cecil Day Lewis the writer, who upheld the romantic cause of what might have been called 'England's little playground in the west'. I even tried to learn the Irish language, which is far more difficult than Welsh, but although I occasionally pretended to understand it, I retained little from my studies. Rolleston's *Myths and Legends of the Celtic Race*, particularly the Irish part of it, was a powerful influence on my childhood, and to this day I can reasonably claim to know much more about the background, mythical and historical, of Ireland's troubles than the majority of English or for that matter 'Irish' people – which is not saying much.

It was the blatant failure of the Irish nationalists to create a nation; the fiasco of the language movement (de Valera was right when he said 'without our language we are only half a nation'); the headlong surrender of the Irish in the Republic to the 'modern world' I abhorred so much, typified by their setting up a television service (I had advised them in the column to set up a jamming station instead, preferably one powerful enough to do England a good turn by making it impossible to receive television programmes there either): these were the things, fatal to my reactionary hopes, that cured me of any Irish addiction and left me weary and cynical about that country which seems, in spite of the outburst of violence in the North, to be growing more like England (and the worst things in England) every day. As Hitler in a more serious context said of the Germans, I have felt like saying, 'My Irish have failed me'.

We had only just got back to England when Colin (who for some time had seemed to have something on his mind) announced that he was leaving the column and that if I wanted to take it over it was mine. He was ten years younger than I and took his career as a journalist more seriously. He felt, rightly, that the column was a dead end. It could not help him to achieve what he wanted, which was, of course, to be an editor, preferably, I suppose of, the *Daily* or, failing that, the *Sunday Telegraph*. Meanwhile, he proposed to revert to what he had been before the column started, a leader writer.

I felt a certain amount of panic, for although I had got used to writing the fantastic, whimsical or 'satirical' parts of the column, I doubted whether I could manage the political side. However, it would mean more money; and I would become the 'head of a department', responsible only to the editor. Of course I agreed, after an uneasy interview with Sir Colin Coote. He was anxious that I should have an assistant. This I did not want, mainly because I preferred to be in charge of something which was entirely my own. So without actually refusing to have an assistant I left the matter in abeyance, and in fact never had one. Not long after I took over, a candidate presented himself. He was young Auberon Waugh, then working on the *Telegraph*'s Peterborough column but maintaining that nothing he had ever written had ever appeared in it. He would probably have done very well – perhaps too well; my unconscious reason for refusing his offer, which he made with great charm and politeness, may well have been a fear, typical of me, that with his superior social connections and greater confidence in himself he might soon have taken over the column altogether.

I did have a regular contributor who could write the column when I was on holiday. This was Colm Brogan, a famous journalist in his day, who had written eloquent pamphlets against the post-war Labour government but had since fallen into comparative obscurity. He was a Glaswegian, a Catholic and a vehement 'reactionary', a man to love and admire but one who was often described as 'his own worst enemy'. He was handicapped both by his bibulous appearance – a fiery red face on a small but wiry and energetic body – and by his Glasgow

accent, which made him difficult to understand in person until
you got on to the right wavelength, and on the telephone completely unintelligible. But he was a witty and forceful writer who
in those early days was a great help to me.

The column had, of course, started as the work of several
hands, including my own, and this it continued to be, though
less and less so (I never wrote less than four-fifths of it myself
from 1960 up to the mid-Seventies, and after that I wrote all
of it). One fairly constant early contributor was Charles Herring,
a big, lumbering, very shy man who lived in Birmingham and
sent in a weekly supply of material in which amusing ideas were
apt to be embedded in overmuch verbiage but, when edited,
were often useful. Later on, an established humorist, Michael
Green, author of popular books about sport (*The Art of Coarse
Rugby* and so on), wrote occasional items. It was he who invented
'Squire Haggard', the wicked landlord of eighteenth-century
Stretchford, extracts from whose journal, said to be edited by
my fictitious all-purpose literary hack, Julian Birdbath, appeared
regularly in the column over a period of ten years and were
sometimes singled out for particular praise by readers, causing
me some slight mortification.

They were, in fact, very clever and funny pastiche, different
in their broader, coarser humour from the rest of the column.
Green, a sardonic man whose character I found difficult to
fathom, was, unlike Herring, a professional writer and after a
while secured legal copyright in the character of the wicked
squire. It was when he began to claim rights in other columnar
characters I had already invented, on the grounds that he had
written items about them, and to intimate that I was getting the
credit for his work, that we fell out. I pointed out, reasonably
enough, that the column was pseudonymous, that I had never
claimed copyright in my own inventions and often got no credit

for them myself – many people, never having heard of me, believed the column was written by A. P. Herbert, Lady Pamela Berry, Randolph Churchill or all of them at once. But, muttering that it was 'all very well for people who got a regular salary of seven thousand a year', he seemed unconvinced, went his own way and I saw him no more.

Soon after I took over the column, Claudie Worsthorne gave up her job as columnar secretary, not because she was unwilling to work for me (in fact she returned in 1969 and was secretary from then onwards) but because of her domestic and social duties. As her successor she introduced Annabel Dilke, a granddaughter of the notorious Sir Charles Dilke, a stunningly beautiful girl about twenty years old, amiable and intelligent (she later wrote novels and married Georgi Markov, the Bulgarian exile who was murdered by a poisoned umbrella). I was somewhat taken aback by this apparition. But she seemed quiet and anxious to please, and though we never became really great friends we got on together well enough. It might be thought that I would find it distracting to sit at my desk every day opposite a strikingly attractive girl of upper-class background. But very beautiful upper-class girls never appealed to me, perhaps from a deep-seated feeling that I was not good enough for them. If Annabel had had some defect in her beauty, such as my favourite 'goofy teeth' or had been of an inferior class or no class, like myself, things might have been much more awkward, not to say impossible. But as it was she never gave me a single moment's uneasiness. People like Michael ffolkes, who was habitually gallant to all attractive girls, sometimes commented on this, but I noticed that they never 'got to first base' with Annabel either.

Thus I toiled on, with a narrow scrape very soon after I took over the column, when the deputy editor, John Applebey, suggested a radical change in its function: I was to travel about England, writing it from various different places. Applebey, who had taken over from the eccentric Donald McLachlan, was a serious-minded man, unmarried, a teetotaller, non-smoker and devout Anglican. There was no nonsense about him, which made his suggestion – presented almost in the form of an order – even more alarming to me: I instinctively objected to change of any kind and thought that on the whole things were very well as they were. Perry Worsthorne, whose mother, Lady Norman, was associated with Applebey's sister in some charitable work, had once called at the Applebeys' semi-detached house in Wimbledon. Accustomed to the halls of the mighty, he reeled away incredulous. 'Do you know, they live – I can hardly believe it – they live in – in' – he was at a loss for a comparison ' – a postman's house!'

This suggestion by Applebey threw me into dread and confusion, with nightmares that lasted a whole weekend. I was delivered by astounding news. Applebey, who was about forty and looked extremely healthy, had suddenly died of a heart attack. Was I responsible? Was I the possessor of supernatural powers, evil powers at that? It was not the first time something of this kind had happened, I remembered. At my Harrogate prep school a games-crazed tyrant among the masters who, I believed, would make my life a misery, had suddenly died of a heart attack soon after my arrival. But I cannot say that either coincidence – what else could it have been? – worried me for long.

A minor event was my dispossession from the office which Colin and I had jointly occupied; the authorities now thought this was unduly large for me alone. It was proposed that Reg Steed, a leader-writer, should share it. In vain I made representations to the editor: my work, I said, was not routine but had a 'creative' element. I therefore needed solitude and quiet. I can imagine what he thought of this; but he rejected my plea politely and Reg Steed was installed. I had no objection to Steed, indeed liked him very much. But I looked for another home and soon found one in an obscure corner at the back of the third floor.

It was a small room, formerly occupied by three music critics, and had a door at the back of it marked 'Fire Escape', for the very good reason that it led to one. So it was with this notice at my back in this uncarpeted room with a restricted view of a courtyard that I sat at my desk, weaving my curious fancies, for the next fifteen years, until moved, greatly against my will, to superior, standardised, carpeted accommodation on the fifth floor under a scheme of reorganisation. There was something about my tiny room, which had just enough space for my desk, Annabel's desk, a table, a cupboard, a bookcase and a large old-fashioned hatstand, which appealed to me strongly. What did not appeal to me was a disaster which occurred when Annabel innocently put the greater part of my books in an outsize waste-paper basket, ready for removal. The night-time cleaners, taking it for rubbish, sent the whole lot for burning. So perished, among other treasures, my rare copy of Marsden's translation (with notes) of *The Protocols of the Elders of Zion*. Did it cry out, I wondered, after the manner of the Old Orange Flute burned by the Papists, 'Perish Judah!'? I did not reproach Annabel. Perhaps she had done me a good turn.

There was certainly no lack of material in the world for me to write about. This was the time when all the main themes which were to occupy the column for the rest of its existence first appeared; the time when the quagmire foundations were laid of the tottering England we now inhabit.

The column as I began to develop it became more and more

'controversial' and a byword for 'right-wing' opinions, that is, the opinions which most people in England held before the 'great semantic shift' by which the Left gradually took over the Centre and what had been the Centre became known first as the Right, then as the Extreme Right and finally the 'backwoodsmen' and even the Fascists. This meant that I got a good deal of correspondence, both for and against, both congratulatory and abusive, both, since on the whole intelligent people do not write to the papers, largely based on false premises.

The only threat of actual physical violence I ever had was from a member of the National Front. I had written, apropos of the arrival of Ugandan Indians fleeing from Idi Amin, that there must be plenty of these Indians I would rather have in England than some of the people who were here already. 'Traitor!' wrote this patriot. 'We counted you on our side and you have let us down. If I wasn't too busy I would come round and punch you on the nose.' Another time a sausage-shaped, flexible parcel arrived. 'Don't open it,' said Claudie. 'I know it 'ees sheet.'

Another time a small irregularly-shaped parcel arrived; it proved to contain two crossed straws, a pebble and a small empty bottle smelling faintly of urine, probably horse's. It was a genuine African 'bad juju'. But the parcel was marked 'Insufficiently secured and repackaged in the Post Office'. In some London post office, I suppose, an innocent clerk had opened it, received the full blast of the magic spell and dropped dead on the spot.

To balance these hostile manifestations there was an equal or greater number of favourable ones, equally mistaken. Many *Telegraph* readers became tremendous fans of the column mainly because, particularly in the 'lead' or 'serious' first item, it could be taken to support their most dearly-held prejudices. I had one letter from a reader who applauded my views about Ireland and 'the blacks'; as far as he was concerned, he wrote, they were all the same and he could not distinguish between them. This was an interesting survival of an English prejudice which must have been quite common among uneducated people in the first half of the last century. I got plenty of letters commending my support for hanging and flogging, neither of which I had ever written about, let alone recommended. Such people held a complete set of opinions corresponding to the 'left-wing package deal' and equally immovable by any argument. I preferred them to the Left, however, because, being simple-minded English people, they were at least instinctively on their own side, unlike the bigots of the Left, with their imbecile assumption that their own country must always be in the wrong.

I came across another kind of misconception among some of my middle- and upper-class readers. They thought I must personally resemble the aristocratic, Blimp-moustached figure, with his deerstalker, gold hunter and glass of port which Michael ffolkes had drawn as the writer of the column and which, of course, I had self-mockingly fostered myself. These people, who sometimes invited me to luncheon or even dinner parties, were taken aback to find that I was not like this at all, and far from being a brilliant conversationalist I was usually tongue-tied, or, if my tongue was loosened by drink, tended to rant away about subjects they knew and cared nothing about, such as the Welsh mutation system or the methods by which a new incarnation of the Dalai Lama was identified. Besides, I knew none of the rich, famous or well-connected people they talked about, so that embarrassment made me more uncommunicative than ever and ensured that I was never asked again.

Such people might just as well have lived on another planet; afterwards I thought of these occasions as affording a glimpse of some unattainable paradise. A rich and cultivated Jewish property developer, who had given up property developing, I think, because he had been among the first to make a great deal of money in this way and was not interested in making any more, took it into his head to ask me to lunch at his house in Hill Street, in Mayfair. The marble-floored entrance-hall, the Portuguese manservant who took my coat, the drawing-room with its original Zoffanys – boring paintings in my opinion but very valuable, I suppose – on the walls, the bibelots of jade or Roman gold on ormolu tables, the magnate's tall, blonde and beautiful young Italian wife with her stunningly elegant clothes and stunningly elegant jewellery: all these things made my head swim, the more so from the fortifying drinks I had taken before-hand and the powerful additives this excellent host was now supplying.

The company at the table in the elegant dining-room reinforced this dreamlike impression: a young English Marquis and an older Earl with perfect, easy manners; a woman older and less beautiful than my hostess, but equally elegant; a famous journalist whom, to my host's surprise, I had never met before; a retired soldier famous for his wartime exploits and for peacetime activities which made him a prime object of suspicion to the Left . . . what was I to say to these people or they to me?

They could not understand that everybody was not as rich as themselves. 'When you fly to Australia,' said my neighbour the war hero, 'have you ever thought of travelling via Samarkand? It makes a change. I found it most interesting to stop overnight and have a look at the place.' 'I don't suppose it's very romantic any more,' I said, evading the original question. 'Well, no, it isn't,' he said, looking at me suspiciously.

I did not even know how to take my leave. At last, stammering and bemused by this glimpse of fairyland, I staggered out into the grey world and back to my desk as though waking from a dream. It took me hours, even days, to recover; for quite a long time I had a fading sense of lost opportunity. But what in fact, hopelessly unequipped as I was by nature, by training or by experience, could I have done to secure even a foothold in such circles? I have never ceased to marvel at people, obviously no better equipped than I, who have contrived to do so. What is their secret? A firm self-confidence? An ability to overcome the shyness which springs from acute selfconsciousness? I gradually learned, after a few experiences of this sort – and I always accepted these invitations in the never quite extinguished hope of doing better – to resign myself to personal obscurity. It was galling to be at the same time pseudonymously famous.

Another class of readers, and among the most numerous and tireless correspondents, were the cranks and adherents of 'conspiracy theories', who as time went on found plenty of material in my column to encourage them to think I would be sympathetic. To some extent I was. It is not difficult to believe that the world is shaped by secret influences which move it ineluctably in a certain direction; how else to account for what has happened in two world wars and all that has flowed from them: the destruction of Europe, the end of the British Empire, the predominance of the United States, the establishment of the State of Israel and its key role in the world; the power of credit or imaginary money especially condemned by some of my conspiracy-theorists, who owed a lot to the Social Credit theories of Major Douglas which, though unintelligible, had attracted me so much before the war?

Some of my correspondents were straightforward believers in the Jewish World Conspiracy. An obvious objection was that, if this conspiracy was, as they maintained, all-powerful (it secretly controlled both the United States and the Soviet Union and even Hitler had been in its service) as well as being hidden not merely from the masses but from most of the world's statesmen, what hope was there of resisting it? They did not seem at all clear on this point themselves. Other correspondents at least had an answer: to them the world was in Satan's hands and awaiting the Apocalypse, when Satan would be cast down and God would triumph in the Second Coming, and all would be transformed in a new Heaven and a new Earth. But this scheme of things was also pre-ordained; and if the principle of Good was going to triumph in the end over the principle of Evil whatever anyone did, why should anyone do anything?

In the course of time I amassed a vast collection of 'conspiracy literature' sent in by readers, much of it of American origin (there is even a 'Conspiracist Publishing Company' somewhere in the States, with a copious catalogue). But I contrived to avoid meeting the conspiracy-theorists; one of Annabel's main duties was to ensure that they got no nearer than the other end of the telephone. Only once, and much later in my time at the *Telegraph*, did I actually meet one of these people, and he was obviously untypical. He rang up one day when I was without Annabel to discourage telephone-callers, and in a pleasant public school voice explained that he was obliged for certain reasons to use an assumed name; but would I do him the great favour of lunching with him at a certain restaurant in London where we could be sure of having a quiet conversation?

It was a restaurant I had heard of, an unfashionable but expensive one; I accepted. My host turned out to be a youngish man, well-dressed and with excellent manners. His opening remark was, 'Before we go any further, I must tell you that I think your column is a work of genius'. I could hardly fail to be predisposed in this man's favour; and we did in fact have a most enjoyable luncheon, helped by two bottles of delicious

Sancerre, almost all drunk by me. As I got more and more pleasantly drunk, he gave me his views of the world. Some of them were already familiar from correspondents who certainly did not patronise this kind of restaurant, or wear gold cufflinks or bear, as it turned out this friendly and agreeable man did, an aristocratic name. But now I heard them laid before me with quiet certitude; and the more outrageous they were to generally accepted opinion the more quietly certain he seemed to be of their unarguable truth. Of course the American astronauts had never reached the moon; it was a transparent confidence trick intended to deceive the people and divert their attention from what was really happening in the world. Hadn't I noticed in the television film that the simulation of the supposed moon-landing was far more convincing than the 'real thing'? If I had looked carefully in one corner of the screen I would have noticed that the identical boulder shown as being on the moon could also be seen in the Arizona Desert. All this seemed extremely persuasive.

My host asked me, when the conversation (or monologue) turned from the supposed moon-landing to other things, what I thought of Pope John Paul II. I said, as most people would have said, that I thought him a remarkable man who promised to have great influence for good and might even reverse the destruction of the Roman Catholic Church. He laughed, though without patronage or unkindness: 'My dear fellow, my dear Michael' – we had got on first name terms by then – 'how can you be so easily deceived? We live in a world in which everything is turned upside down. What is generally thought good is bound to be evil, however cleverly it is disguised. No, the mere fact that the Pope is universally praised proves that he is an agent of the Devil.'

I did not try to argue. What would have been the use? And

the easy hospitality, as well as the charm of this strange person-age made him most persuasive. What was I to make of him? Was he himself an agent of the Devil? He ended by telling me that I must enter the Catholic Church without delay. I explained that I had no faith. 'Go and see Father So-and-So' – he named a priest in South London – 'and mention my name'. I said I would think it over. I did nothing about this. Some weeks later I had a letter from my strange host. It ended: 'I fear you are determined to fry in Hell ever more. Yours, with very best wishes . . . '

Another kind of misconception may have arisen from what hostile critics might have called an occasional 'high camp' element in the column. A high-ranking naval officer professed to be a great fan and even sent in some suggestions and ideas, some of them quite good ones. Meeting him for a drink I found a gentlemanly person of unmistakably homosexual tempera-ment, discreetly and skilfully made up, who after some amusing conversation invited me to spend a weekend at Plymouth on the ship he commanded. I was non-committal. Later he asked me to a party in a flat in Battersea; it was in one of those mansion flats along the south side of the Park where I was later to live myself, though in a humbler block (this one had a lift and central heating). It was a good party of decidedly upper-class people; the waiters were young naval stewards, all notice-ably good-looking and wearing white gloves. One of the guests was the current Chief Scout. He told me of a disastrous jam-boree held in incessant rain on a Scottish island; 'but the worst thing was, do you see, they had sent the wrong kind of claret'. But I had taken Kate along to this party and although she was a great success I heard no more from my host the naval officer.

Another invitation came from a rich middle-aged Parsee (a tautology; in my experience all Parsees are rich) who was living at one of the big hotels in Park Lane. He asked me to come and sign a copy of my latest anthology. Flattered, I was even more flattered to find that he wanted me to sign copies of all the previous anthologies as well; he had had them beautifully bound in dark green leather by a bookbinder in Lisbon 'where I lived until this ghastly revolution . . . ' – it was 1974 – ' . . . made things so disagreeable that I simply had to leave. So now I'm camping out here with some of my furniture. I'll move on somewhere else in due course. I suppose I'll die alone in some hotel like this one.' he said, and I had a vision of the sad death of a rich, lonely homosexual. 'Where would you think of moving if you were me?'

Here again I had come across the inability of the rich to acknowledge that there are any other kinds of people, though my shabby mackintosh folded on a chair should have suggested there might be. I murmured non-committedly. 'I thought of Lausanne,' he said, 'dear, dear, little Lausanne. But no, it is not what it was. Istanbul, perhaps. I've always loved it. I once bought a kitten there from a brute who was going to throw it into the Bosphorus. And do you know, when I got home I found it was dumb! How I loved that kitten!' He looked at me with mournful eyes. 'Did you ever think of living in Persia?' I asked desperately. I had noticed that he used a Mongol–Persian version of what must originally have been a distastefully Indianised Parsee name. 'Oh, no, never!' he exclaimed in horror. 'You see, the Shah's courtiers are so terribly *common*.'

The conversation languished. 'What school did you go to?' he asked. I told him, but it was clear that the Bradford Grammar School meant nothing to him whatever. 'I was put down for Eton,' he told me. 'But I was too delicate.' He smiled delicately. 'So I had tutors. My mother was a Wardha.' I nodded acknowledgement of this fantastically rich Parsee ship-owning family.

'I always loved dear Queen Mary,' he said, the ghastly common-
ness of the Shah's courtiers evidently still on his mind. 'Didn't
you?' Later I wrote him a note of thanks, but got no reply.

There was yet another class of correspondent, probably
representing a much larger number of *Telegraph* readers. These
were the people who thought my column was simply part of the
news, or at least was meant to be taken literally. I had only to
mention a book by Henry Miller, *The Naked Afternoon Tea*, to
get a letter from a reader complaining that she could not get it
at any bookshop (it was said to be published by 'the Lavender
Press', and I got another letter from a real Lavender Press,
pointing out angrily that they had never published any such
title). I had only to write about the sole Tibetan monastery still
remaining in South London to get readers complaining that in
spite of following my directions they had been unable to find
it, and what did I mean by misleading people? I wrote a 'Lingu-
aphone' advertisement, 'Learn Etruscan the Way He Did',
offering gramophone records, with a drawing of an Etruscan
warrior by ffolkes; I got so many requests for the records that
I had to write another item saying the Etruscan records were
sold out, but we still had stocks of Old Prussian, Aztec and
Pictish. And sure enough, several requests for these came in.

Colin Welch, who in due course rose from chief leader-
writer to deputy editor before leaving the *Telegraph*, had been
right when he said the column was a dead end. But it was a
dead end which suited me. I was not, except in a formal sense,
a journalist and had no ambitions to rise in that profession. As
I had never been a reporter, my knowledge of its technicalities
was nil and I surprised the printers on the 'stone' by wondering
at their skill in reading upside down and in reverse when we
dealt with the beautiful lead galleys of my column in their
wooden frames. Oddly enough, I got on quite well with these

blue-dungaree'd printers, Jim or Fred or Frank, with their absolute self-confidence and assurance. No wonder they were like that; in those days the printers ruled the newspaper; they had only to stop work and bring the presses to a standstill to face their employers with enormous, daily mounting losses. No wonder the employers always gave in; they had no alternative, and it was quite forbearing of the Father of the Chapel, a suitably huge and complacent man who regarded journalists with kindly contempt, not to call a strike every other week. As it was, the printers must have been among the most highly paid of all English workers.

They were also the most truly conservative people in England, resistant to all change and operating a strictly hereditary, hierarchical system which made it impossible for anybody to enter their trade unless he had a father or other close relative who had already been in it. I used to maintain that all the printers were descended from Caxton's apprentices. Certainly the names on the duty rosters were splendidly and transcendentally English: Bates, Charlton, Breakspear, Muggeridge, Mudd. It would have been no more impossible for a dog to become a printer on this or any other national newspaper than for an Indian or a Negro or indeed any foreigner. As for a woman printer, they would have thought you were daft if you had suggested it; and you would have been. All this delighted my reactionary soul.

I was not, of course, socially acceptable to the printers myself, though tolerated as a harmless freak. In my leisure hours in Fleet Street I did not drink with the printers in the Kings and Keys. They kept to themselves, and in the early days, before it was tarted up with flock wallpaper, electric mock candle-holders and an elaborate wooden ceiling with gilded emblems of crowns and keys, it had a separate bar, a small cubicle near the doorway which non-printers entered at their peril.

One of the few who occasionally tried to do so, with mildly violent results, was Philip Weston, a senior leader-writer with masochistic tendencies and remarkable drinking habits. He was to be found every evening in the Kings and Keys or in the alternative *Telegraph* pub, the Falstaff, on the opposite side of the street. So was a regular group of senior *Telegraph* journalists, including myself, though I was not as regular in my attendance as some, occasionally drinking in other places, such as the celebrated wine-bar El Vino, though this I found uncongenial because it was patronised by the famous – or sometimes not drinking at all, or even just going home.

It was a well-known fact in those days, though most of the *Telegraph* readers would have been shocked and incredulous if they had known it, that some of the hardest drinkers and most eccentric, even disreputable, characters in Fleet Street were members of the staff of what was to them one of the most respectable newspapers. Whereas many journalists on the low, tabloid papers, who daily dealt in smut and scandal (remarkably harmless and innocent though it was, compared with what was to come) regularly caught trains, after finishing their work, to places like Oxshott or Esher, where their wives met them at the station and drove them home, the *Telegraph* journalists remained in the pub for hours, some of them getting so drunk that by closing time they were in a state bordering on mania.

Of these Philip Weston was by far the most remarkable. A tall, distinguished-looking man of about the same age as myself, in his late forties when I first met him, well-dressed and always carrying a furled umbrella, he was, when sober, charming, intelligent, reasonable and amusing. It was impossible not to like him. But he had another quite different side. I used to maintain that if various data – quantity of whisky drunk, food (if any) taken, temperature, barometric pressure, wind force and direction and so on – were fed into a computer, it would be possible to forecast the exact moment when he would 'go critical'. He was one of those drinkers who become drunk, or at least change their mood, in the middle of a sentence, switching unnervingly and without warning from rational amiability to raging fury.

His speciality, for which he became notorious, even famous, was outrageously insulting rudeness. For this he was specially qualified by an instinct for spotting the weak point in the person he had chosen to insult and then concentrating on that, so that his remarks, however fantastic and exaggerated, always seemed to contain a proportion of truth, however minute, which could be worrying for the victim. He was a novelist, perhaps even a poet, *manqué*, and this, I think, may have been one source of his latent anger. His brother Robert was a painter, once quite well-known, of the *avant garde* variety and was even ruder than Philip, though without his artistry. Awarded a prize for painting in some provincial competition, he was photographed aiming a kick at his own winning 'abstract' picture, rightly observing, 'If they give good money for rubbish like that, they must be out of their bloody minds' and loudly demanding his cheque for £1,000 forthwith, so that he could get the first train back to London. He was also perhaps the only man who ever reduced Kate to speechlessness, instantly shouting when she tried to order drinks in a pub, 'Shut up you! Can't stand bossy women!'

But this was feeble stuff compared with his brother Philip's performances. He had developed a special voice, between a croak and a snarl, which made him sound like a demented bird of prey as, having 'gone critical', he selected a victim among the people in the bar and set about him.

He was particularly insistent on the niceties of behaviour in pubs, which may seem paradoxical but was not. He believed in a strict code which would have involved the exclusion of certain people from 'his' pub altogether. So when the editor – not Sir Colin, who had almost certainly never been in a pub in his life, but his successor Maurice Green, a more easy-going person – appeared in the pub one evening, perhaps to pursue some point in a leader, Weston, who had just 'gone critical', was extremely angry. 'Get out!' he croaked. 'This is no place for you! Get back to your gentleman's club where you belong!' This probably deserved the sack. But Green, who knew about Weston's act, wisely took no notice at all and Weston had to seek another victim.

One member of the staff whom Weston thought had no right to enter the pub was Perry Worsthorne, partly because of his upper-class status and partly because he had become deputy editor of the *Sunday Telegraph*. One evening he came in and, with an unconscious infringement of Weston's sense of what was fitting, said to the barmaid, 'Oh, get me a Scotch, would you?' Weston's furious croak was heard at once: 'Get me a Scotch, would you?' he mimicked hideously. 'If you don't know how to behave in pubs, don't go into them! Now get out and don't let me find you in here again!' A few weeks later Perry disobeyed this order and, as Claudie, who was with him, told me later: 'Weston was like a madman' – she pronounced the word with the accent on the second syllable. 'He came crouching forward and I 'ad to place myself between them!'

But this was not the last encounter. One evening, when Weston found Perry, who was for some reason in an over-wrought and nervous state, seated at the bar with Claudie, he at once began a high-flown tirade which ensured total silence. 'You're a phoney!' he croaked. 'You're a hollow man! You're a tinsel king, on a cardboard throne!' He went on like this for some time. Big tears had begun to roll down Perry's cheeks, but this phenomenon, watched in fascination by the whole company, did not deter Weston in the least. 'Look!' he cried in glee. 'Look, I've made him blub, I've made him blub!' Perry could take no more. But as he left, Weston looked round with glowing eyes. 'I made him blub! I made him blub! Now who shall I make blub next?'

He had a regular sparring partner, an assistant editor, Martin Jameson, a fierce-looking, red-haired man, professionally a strict disciplinarian and much feared by his subordinates. Jameson was able to give as good as he got, but of course he could not match Weston in style or imaginative power. One day I came into the pub to find a strange battle in progress. The two men were standing side by side at the bar, both obviously very angry. Weston had just poured salt in Jameson's gin and tonic. Jameson had countered by putting pepper in Weston's whisky. 'Pass the mustard!' shouted Weston. 'Bring me the biggest sausage in the place!' Such scenes as these, which seemed to take both these successful journalists and esteemed employees of Lord Hartwell back to their schooldays, were nothing out of the ordinary.

Weston's performances, of which I can give only a faint, inadequate impression, became quite famous. He would sit on a barstool convenient to the door, eyeing each new arrival as he or she came in and estimating his or her fitness to be insulted. He did not spare women; and the unmistakable element of masochism in his nature was shown when he insulted a hefty blonde reporter, who instantly fetched him such a clout with her handbag that he fell headlong to the ground. Next moment he was up again, laughing as though in triumph. He made a particular point of trying to get knocked down by printers, but only once succeeded even in getting one of them to trip him up. I have seldom seen him look so pleased with himself.

The Master Insulter, though obviously proud of his gifts, was overtly modest about them; when sober and in what might be called a normal state of mind he was capable of discussing his achievements as though they belonged to another person altogether; it was as though he wondered at an inspiration that might have come from another world. His consumption of whisky was stupendous. Once he told me that when he consulted a doctor about some ailment or other, the man asked whether he drank at all. 'Yes,' said Weston, 'a certain amount, I suppose.' The doctor hemmed for a bit, then said: 'Well, if I were you, I'd try cutting out that second glass of sherry before dinner.' Minutes after Weston had amiably shared this joke with me, he had 'gone critical' and was roaring abuse.

He became a legend. There was talk of sending him on a world tour, so that he could insult people of all nations in the interests of world peace. It was said that psychiatrists were sending some of their patients to the Kings and Keys to be insulted, believing it had therapeutic value. But he received a check to his all-conquering career one evening when he was performing at the Falstaff across the road. This he occasionally did, as it was said, 'by special request', though the landlord there, a stolid Englishman, eyed him less favourably than the Irish landlord of the King and Keys who appreciated the wild poetry and eloquent flights of fancy of the man. A party of elderly American women, Daughters of the Revolution with blue-rinsed hair and the earnest mien of cultural tourists, entered. 'Pardon me, sir,' said their leader, addressing Weston, who was waiting expectantly for a victim. 'Pardon me, is this your Doctor Johnson's house?' Weston, brandishing his umbrella, rose to his feet. 'I *am* Doctor Johnson,' he croaked maniacally. 'Now fuck off!' The ladies fell back in confusion, turned and fled.

'Right, Mr Weston,' said the landlord. 'That's enough. You have gone too far for once. Please take your custom elsewhere. You are barred.' Smiling in triumph, Weston crossed the road to the Kings and Keys, where he found me talking to Sheila Murphy, Desmond Williams's companion, over from Dublin on a visit. 'Who's this?' shouted Weston. 'I know all about you, whoever you are. You've got a purple bottom!' Whether Sheila actually had a purple bottom I have no idea; but such was the force of Weston's personality that it seemed perfectly possible, even likely, that she had.

The landlord of the Falstaff's ban on Weston did him no good. Next time the brewer's man called he noticed from the records that the consumption of whisky at the pub had sharply declined. 'We had to bar one of our best customers,' the landlord explained. 'Well, get him back at once!' ordered the brewer's man. But Weston, who claimed he had never been so insulted in his life, refused to patronise the pub any more. Soon afterwards it went out of business, but not before Jameson and myself, visiting the place for a quick drink, had had a curious experience. Instead of serving us, the landlord took a thick photograph album from a shelf and consulted it carefully. 'I thought so,' he said. 'I'm afraid I can't serve you gentlemen.' 'Why on earth not?' 'You've been seen in the company of that Mr Weston, and I've made a rule not to serve him or any friends of his.' Such was the terror of the man that he could even impose guilt by association.

As time went on, Weston passed his peak. His inventiveness declined. He began to content himself with shouting 'Poofter!' or 'Superficial!' or 'Homosexual South African policeman!' – this to my friend and columnar contributor Charles Herring who, needless to say, was none of these things, yet somehow *looked* as though he might be any or all of them. Weston still had one or two minor triumphs. One evening he accused a Salvation Army man who was selling the *War Cry* of being a rapist wanted by the police in three counties. But the strange thing was that this frenzied behaviour in drink, abhorrent though it seems, had nothing evil about it but was curiously innocent. Most people enjoyed it as pure entertainment, even when they were the victims. I certainly did myself, but I noticed that any attempt to encourage Weston to go into his act produced a perverse refusal to do so. He was an artist in insult and would perform only in his own good time. Nobody who heard him perform when he was at his best will ever forget it.

This sustained act of Weston's was not, of course, an isolated phenomenon; it was the centrepiece of a drunken 'Theatre of the Absurd' which was played out nightly over a considerable part of my time at the *Telegraph* and (not to be pompous) anticipated in some ways the 'alternative comedy' acts which became fashionable in the Eighties, though these made much more use of obscene language and sexual and scatological material. Weston had certainly missed his vocation, as he must have realised. But there were other actors besides him. Jameson, a stern disciplinarian in the office, was almost as heavy a drinker as Weston and occasionally contributed a solo comedy act. At one time he had a part share in a racehorse. This was the cause of a lot of derision and teasing, particularly when it was entered for the Derby. But in the event it ran surprisingly well, finishing fifth or sixth, and thereafter had several wins and places until it unfortunately broke a leg. This was a bitter blow to Jameson. That evening in the pub he became spectacularly drunk, for once upstaging Weston, and ended up lying on the floor with his arms round a big well-mannered woolly dog belonging to the landlord, crying 'this is my *Cavalry*,' as though the spirit of James Joyce had descended.

There were other stock characters too, such as Stephen Daneff, the witty, polyglot Communist Affairs Correspondent, since his boyhood an exile from Bulgaria, where his grandfather had been prime minister. He had a great deal of out-of-the-way knowledge which matched my own, and we would sometimes find ourselves, when agreeably drunk, discussing the Bulgarian Exarchate or the history of the Bukovina in the midst of a roar of raving voices, among which Weston could be heard shouting: 'Look at them! Poofters! I know what they do when the pub closes! They've got a room in Soho they go to! Haven't you? Haven't you?' In fact Stephen, who became a great friend, would sometimes take me back to his highly civilised house in Chelsea, where we sobered up at supper with his highly civilised, long-suffering, agreeably sphinx-like and very pretty wife, a dark-haired member of the Welsh squirearchy who owned a country house on the outskirts of Welshpool. After supper we would listen to Bruckner or Wagner on the record-player and in the small hours I walked out into the night and got a taxi back to Putney.

Other supporting players appeared from time to time: Ronnie Payne, a large, friendly, bearded Yorkshireman given to elaborate charades and rôle-playing and with something enigmatic about him which may have been due to his being an expert on espionage and Middle Eastern terrorism; Ron Hall, the archetypal journalist, another Yorkshireman, a man of great goodness and generosity of character, a militant atheist whom I offended by telling him he had a naturally Christian soul; and besides these there was a large supporting cast of journalists, any one of whom might suddenly acquire a non-speaking part and attain negative stardom by being singled out by Weston as the victim of the evening.

Although the Theatre of the Absurd dominated the pub in the evenings and also for occasional matinées, there was one group which was outside its domination, and because of its moral authority was largely immune from Weston's histrionic insults. I had the impression that the landlord would not have tolerated any attack on it, though he was generally indulgent to Weston's antics, perhaps because he knew they were good for business. But his forbearance was not entirely for this reason.

Mark O'Donnell was no ordinary landlord (we called him 'the greatest publican of the twentieth century'). A handsome and intelligent Irishman whose brother (he occasionally appeared at the pub with a good deal of ceremony) was a member of the Dáil, he had seen something of the world, spoke French fluently and obviously enjoyed Weston's performances as much as anybody, as he watched sardonically from his own side of the bar. An altogether more sophisticated man than the old landlord Seán Macnamara, he yet had certain gifts in common with him. It was noticeable that if by ill chance some stranger who did not know the conventions of the place was so grossly insulted by Weston that he put up his fists and threw a punch at him, it was not Weston but his victim whom the landlord asked to leave and, if he seemed unwilling, came round the bar and threw him out into the street in a practised manner one could not help admiring, however unjust his action may have seemed.

The group which O'Donnell quietly watched over and protected was that which gathered round one of the most distinguished journalists in Fleet Street, T. E. Utley, always known as 'Peter'. He had been totally blind since the age of eight, but had surmounted this and other difficulties – he was, I think, an orphan – in what can only be called a heroic manner. He was now a leader writer on the *Telegraph* and an authority on two subjects, the politics of Ulster and the Church of England, particularly in matters of 'faith and morals'. Should a leader be required on either of these subjects, it was Utley who wrote it, and as he was one of the few journalists on the *Telegraph*, or for that matter any other paper, who could write English in an elegant and lucid style, his leaders and other writings were always worth reading.

He was a slight man of middle height, carelessly dressed and usually with a good deal of dandruff on his shoulders, fallen from hair worn rather long and curling up over his collar from the pressure of the black ribbon which held in place the eye-shade over the crater of his damaged eye; his other eye, equally sightless, was of a disturbing milky blue. Perhaps to compensate for his blindness he had a very loud, vibrant voice which sounded overbearing and exaggeratedly 'upper-class', causing ffolkes, who was as conscious of class distinction as I was, but did not mind who knew it, to take an unjustified dislike to him. Utley described himself as idle, but was in fact a man of great energy both for work and social life. He was said to be one of the most rapid readers of braille in England, but needed an efficient secretary to read the morning papers aloud to him and do any research he required.

As for his secretaries, he seemed able to command the services of an unlimited supply of young girls. These were invariably personable and in some cases extremely attractive, so that jealous fellow-journalists sometimes wondered whether he could really be blind at all. But he always claimed, when asked for the secret, that he could tell by a woman's voice whether she was attractive or not; and he may have supplemented the clues he got by ear with easily-acquired tactile data. He could often be seen sitting in a certain corner of the pub, especially at lunchtime, in the middle of a circle of attractive girls, including his present secretary as well as some of his past or future ones. If any other member of the *Telegraph* staff required a temporary secretary he could usually offer a choice of two or three. I came to think of him as the T. E. Utley Secretarial Agency. There he sat with his circle in the Kings and Keys, imperturbable, booming wisdom, with something legendary and noble about him as he reached with a blind man's vagueness for his glass of whisky and soda, or waveringly held out his cigarette for a light, chain-smoking and dropping long tubes of ash anywhere but in the ashtray.

The circle he presided over was not, of course, confined to girls; other members of the staff such as Colin Welch, Nicholas Bagnall, a learned, likeable, sometimes irascible man with a game leg, later literary editor of the *Sunday Telegraph*, and many others also joined it. And Utley could sometimes be seen in earnest private conversation with people who could be recognised by some instinct as Ulster politicians or others concerned with the affairs of the province. In spite of his blindness, Utley was extraordinarily good at getting about by himself. He often visited Ulster even at the height of the Troubles. He was, I think, totally fearless, nor was his courage the less admirable because, so it was said, the Provisional IRA themselves had declared they would not assassinate a blind man, even though he was, with Enoch Powell, by far the most intelligent and persuasive of all exponents of the Unionist cause.

No wonder Donald McLachlan, when appointed first editor of the *Sunday Telegraph* thought of offering Utley the job of television critic! But he's blind,' they pointed out. 'I can't see that's any objection', Maclachlan said. 'It will help to give him a balanced view'.

His admirable wife, by whom he had three children, was of Anglo–Irish descent, the former Brigid Morrah, whose brother Dermot was occasionally employed by the *Telegraph* to supply heraldic information to the 'Peterborough' column I was so often accused, not without reason, of parodying in my own. Dermot Morrah, an elderly man with a loud, harsh, plangent voice, worked in the College of Heralds and sometimes appeared in the *Telegraph* office in full regalia, wearing a tabard with the Royal Arms and, for all I knew, carrying a silver trumpet. I was going up in the lift with him once when he was thus glorified; a negro workman who got in at an intermediate floor was so amazed at this apparition that his jaw dropped and I thought he was going to fall to his knees. Instead, he shuffled out, gibbering with wonder, at the next floor.

The Theatre of the Absurd occasionally changed its venue, usually to a strange establishment, long demolished, at the corner of Fleet Street and Chancery Lane, called 'Peel's Hotel: Founded 1347' (can this be right?). It was immediately opposite El Vino's and sometimes the overflow from that famous place, which closed at eight in the evening, would spread across the road and coalesce with elements of the Theatre of the Absurd. The bar at Peel's had a large pipe running diagonally across it from floor to ceiling and there were many packing cases and barrels standing untidily about; it resembled part of the lower deck of a ship, very satisfactory to people like myself who were fond of illusions of departure, though here I had to supply the vibration of the ship's engines from my own imaginative resources. The landlord and his family were Italian and as Stephen Daneff, who knew Italian, discovered, were still strong supporters of Mussolini; he claimed he had seen the aunt, Zia Maria, giving the fascist salute and had established the name of their Alsatian dog by a process of elimination: when he said 'Duce' softly, it rolled over and waved its paws in the air.

Here, one memorable evening, there was a gala performance, with several journalistic notabilities from El Vino's such as the witty and melancholy Philip Hope-Wallace, instantly greeted by Weston with harsh cries of 'Poofter!' and 'Jew!', the latter term certainly inappropriate. Peter Duval Smith also appeared, as well as the critic John Raymond, sometimes called 'Raymond Revuebooks' because of his habit of carrying round piles of books he was reviewing and leaving them in unexpected places, a man of irascible temper, with Weston's own peculiarity of passing from sober affability to furious drunken rage in mid-sentence. There was a man with a blocklike wooden-looking head who claimed to be the inventor of fish fingers. He also claimed he could sing a song about any kind of fish you cared to mention. But after 'herring' and 'haddock' had been disposed of, his rendering of 'a swordfish song', no doubt a *tour de force*, was lost in the general uproar. The evening ended when the landlord closed the bar and threatened to call the police. The shouting mob spilled out, some elements drifting down the street to the Kings and Keys, to resume the performance.

Such was the Fleet Street Theatre of the Absurd, famous in its day, deserving to be remembered for ever in the annals of serious drinking. A lifelong serious drinker myself, I was both participant and observer and, being a cautious drunkard as well as a cautious amorist, got blind drunk almost as seldom as I fell blindly in love. It was good to know, as I toiled away upstairs in the *Telegraph* building, that this resource and catalyst was always or almost always at hand when I needed it. Immersion in this anarchic riot undoubtedly helped me to construct, in my column, dreams of ideal beauty and hierarchical order.

So, perhaps, did my personal or private life, so much at

variance with the steady respectability of the *Telegraph* that Constantine called it a 'horror comic'. In the background was Kate's commitment to a lifelong love affair (the crisis at the end of our French holiday had long passed away and so had many subsequent ones); my own uneasy complaisance, once initial jealousy had faded, alleviated by occasional rather meaningless affairs of my own; and my determination, which Kate, for all her vagaries, undoubtedly shared, to bring up Jane as well and decently as possible. Jane was my reason for not leaving Kate; or so I told myself and others assumed; yet I had, after all, left my first wife and child, though they were perfectly blameless, without qualm or hesitation; so it is reasonable to infer that I still had enough attachment to Kate to find living under the same roof with her not absolutely intolerable.

Nor was it; she was still what is repulsively called a 'fun person' and for me a valuable link with other people, sometimes a purveyor of friends I might not have made for myself. For all her egotism, her innumerable deceits and broken promises, for all our ferocious rows, for all her 'infamous war on reality' she was (to use another repulsive term) 'on the side of life'; more than that, I sometimes felt she had heroic stature. I admired her ferocious clinging to the man she loved without hope of marriage; and although I had reached the point of being merely amused at reports which reached me of their stormy relationship – Michael ffolkes told me he had seen them in a restaurant and witnessed a really outstanding bout of food throwing ('When the Food Began to Fly') – I sympathised and perhaps even envied it a little. The time came when Kenneth, desperate at his predicament, would come to me and ask my advice. What was he to do? What was I to say? Of course I could not help him; I did not even feel the sense of ironical triumph which the circumstances seemed to dictate; only sadness, impatience and a certain guilt. The only upshot of such meetings was that we both became extremely drunk.

This manner of life was to last another three years, but it was ten years before I left Putney and twelve before our divorce and my own re-marriage. Thus the 'horror comic' went on for a very long time, but though often comic it was not always horrible. In 1961 and 1962 we spent several holidays in Cornwall. I had never been there before and was intrigued to find the Celtic past still underlying the holiday present. Besides, it was the first time I had ever had a seaside holiday. After an unfortunate experience with a flea at St Anne's on the Lancashire coast when I was three, my mother, I was told, had banned seaside holidays and thereafter we always went to the Yorkshire Dales. It was a new experience for me to be able to watch the sea for hours on end, a new method of auto-hypnosis and a new source of pantheistic feeling. As an old man who lived by the sea once told me: 'You never get sick and tired of it'. Nearing fifty, I played at sandcastles for the first time in my life.

It was about this time that we acquired the last and best of our au pair girls, Dixie von Pilati, whose family *schloss* in Austria lay among forests on the Czech border, almost within sight of the Iron Curtain. She was a pretty girl in her early twenties, but of neurotic temperament, which was not surprising considering the circumstances of her upbringing during the war and afterwards, with a father taken prisoner at Stalingrad and returning home crippled and soon to die. It took me some time to realise that Dixie, who was not, of course, without English admirers, had taken a fancy to me. But although one day when we were alone I made my customary opening gambit, 'What a funny girl you are,' we were interrupted and the opportunity never occurred again.

It was in the early summer of 1962, when we were on holiday at an *auberge* on the banks of the Dordogne, not far from the little town of Martel, that Kate told me she was pregnant, and not by me. This did not make much of an impression on me at the time except as one more ingredient in the 'horror comic'. We were sharing our holiday with the military historian Correlli Barnett and his wife Ruth, friends I had for once made for myself and afterwards introduced to Kate. A lively, amusing and intelligent man, 'Bill' Barnett shared my reactionary views, though later on he became well-known for his thesis declaring that the decline of England had been due to the cultural ideals of Matthew Arnold, 'the public school ethos' and the neglect of science and technology, a view abhorrent to me. Neither he nor Ruth shared our fondness for drinking and staying in expensive hotels. So there was a certain amount of latent friction on the journey by car to and from the Dordogne, when the Barnetts' preference for economy threatened to interfere with our enjoyment of good living. There was no open quarrel, but it is a well-known fact that the surest way for two married couples to ruin their friendship is to spend a holiday together.

Back in England I began to digest Kate's news. I went so far as to consult my old army friend Stuart Daniel, now a barrister, whose acquaintance we had taken up again, often visiting him and his wife in a delightful little house they had in Hampstead. He referred me to a divorce lawyer with a reputation for aggressive methods. I did not care for this brisk, matter-of-fact Jew, who told me brusquely to leave Kate at once and then come and see him again. That was probably why I did not do so. A more sympathetic lawyer would have made a better impression and might even have induced me to take action which would have changed my whole life.

As it was, I did nothing. Passive and lacking in initiative as always, or almost always, I let things be. In my column, I noticed, I had written, without realising its meaning at the time, an item in my parodic 'Nature Diary' about a preposterous bird, the dotterel, which could never make up its mind whether to migrate or not. There was a strong subjective element in my writing. Why did my sad, defeated man of letters, Julian Bird-bath, who lived at the bottom of a disused leadmine in Derby-shire, constantly dream of going to 'glittering' literary parties?

That autumn was the time of the celebrated 'Cuba missile crisis', when for a week the 'nuclear holocaust' – which had haunted everybody's dreams for so long and brought the legions of CND walking each Easter to Aldermaston, to sit down in Trafalgar Square and generally try to put other people's nerves on edge as well as their own – seemed near fulfilment. Kennedy and Khrushchev, both equally preposterous in their contrasting ways, gobbled on the television set we now, to my disgust, possessed like everybody else; sinister warships slid across the grey Atlantic waters. Most people looked apprehensive, some looked frightened. Our two old friends from Mick's Café, Peggy Duff and Pat Arrowsmith, the stalwarts of CND, actually fled to Western Ireland. This struck me as very amusing. Should they not have been at their posts, waiting with righteous indig-nation to the end, to be vaporised and turned to shadows by the horror they had warned us against for so long?

For myself, I was not in the least bit afraid. I knew with absolute certainty that the time was not yet, and would not come for another thirty years. Was this certainty due to my reading of the apocalyptic literature which so many kindly read-ers sent me? Whatever the reason, I felt calm as few people in London must have felt, apart from the Jehovah's Witnesses. Normally cowardly by nature and a confirmed worrier, I saw with satisfaction how much I was surprising friends and acquaintances by my reassuring words. Kate obviously wondered whether I had taken leave of my senses. But I think I helped her (she was, after all, seven months pregnant) to keep calm as we carried on with our normal life. In fact it was not quite normal. For some reason I never discovered I had been put on the complimentary list of the Sadler's Wells Opera and two tickets arrived for every production. So almost every night we went to the opera, a thing I never did before, or have done since, finding it difficult, with my part-West Riding soul, to accept, any more than my mother could, the obviously 'dotty' conventions of this musical form. Afterwards we had champagne suppers and even went dancing. In the mornings I smoked cigars, greatly enjoying this 'role-playing' as a man-about-town.

The Tunnicliffes had invited us to spend a weekend with them at the Metropole Hotel in Brighton – the same hotel, then an apparent paradise of luxury, where I had stayed with my parents in the golden autumn of 1922 – savouring for the first time the mysterious smell of the sea, coveting the cream cakes in the lounge of the hotel and watching on the pier-cinema a newsreel of the burning of Smyrna by the Turks. Now the sea was grey and sad, and the hotel had fallen into decay – that ancient glory gone forever. As the tension mounted we walked by the sea, drank a great deal, ate lavishly, visited a casino where rouged and extravagantly-dressed old women with terrible greenish faces, who looked as if they had been exhumed, sat staring at the cloth with eyes gleaming dully like paste jewels.

From time to time I had to reassure my companions when they spoke of trying to enjoy our last hours on earth: 'Please do not worry. Nothing is going to happen.' It was my finest hour except for the even finer hour on Sunday evening, after a day when the smell of fear was everywhere, as the news came through: Kennedy and Khrushchev had come to an agreement.

The crisis which for me had never been was over. 'How did you know?' asked Joe Tunnicliffe with gratifying wonder and respect. 'Oh, I just did, that's all,' I said. But I could not resist the temptation of telling him that I had to go up to our room for a moment to transmit a message. The old jokes, as everybody knows, are still the best.

That winter Dixie suddenly decided to leave us. She gave no reason but Kate, I noticed, showed signs of unusual discomfiture. Not long afterwards I had a letter from Dixie, telling me how she had gradually become disgusted with 'what was going on', how much she sympathised with me and how she strongly advised me to protect Jane by sending her away to school as soon as possible. I did not reply to this opening; much as I liked Dixie, I did not think she was a girl with whom I ought to get involved; so she became one of my long list of might-have-beens. Years later she came to London in the company of her protector, a rich Munich businessman, and on her suggestion we met briefly for drinks at Claridges where they were staying. It was an awkward meeting. Dixie had changed, grown more worldly and cynical; her friend was intensely German in the worst sense of the word, with most of the bad qualities of that race and few of the good. We had little to say, and I took my leave awkwardly, realising, not for the first or last time, what a mistake it is to meet old friends or acquaintances after a long interval: they have always become different people as I have become a different person.

At Christmas, which unusually we did not spend with my mother in her gradually degenerating cottage at Amswick, Kate went into hospital at Royston in Hertfordshire and on 27th December her baby was born, a girl she called Victoria. It was intensely cold – a blizzard had been raging and the country was under deep snow. I stayed by myself in Putney; Jane, now ten years old, had gone to stay with the Foster-Melliars at their cottage in Allen's Green near Sacomb's Ash, which was now occupied by strangers. Meeting Jane at Sawbridgeworth Station, Andrew Foster-Melliar found it was impossible to reach their cottage because of deep snowdrifts. He and Jane had to spend the night at the pub where the FitzGibbons had once ruled. For Jane, it was an adventure she never forgot; the snow, the silence, the unaccustomed supper they ate in the pub by candlelight because the electricity had failed. If she should ever write a book herself I think this adventure will figure in it.

It was about this time that I learned that the Granada Television programme '*What the Papers Say*' had voted me 'Columnist of the Year'.

5
A Nasty Turn

Ever since I had had an attack of the horrors in a lonely house in the Berkshire woods ten years before, I had been subject to intermittent feelings of uneasiness and dread. They were now getting more frequent and more intense. During a visit with Kate to the valley of the Loire, I had a particularly nasty attack when confronted with the Château of Chambord. I have always disliked French château architecture, and the low, open landscape of the Loire, with a wide river running between pebbly, sandy shores, often dividing into separate channels, then reuniting, does not appeal to me. Looking at Chambord – the monstrous size of the thing, the unreal feel to it – like painted scenery – I felt a powerful dread, an overwhelming desire to escape. At the restaurant which faced this alarming building I rushed into the lavatory and swallowed with difficulty one of the small white phenobarbitone tablets which my doctor had given me. This somewhat reduced my terror; but I still felt I must get away from Chambord and the Loire as soon as possible. Grumbling slightly, though she understood something of what I was feeling from her own experience, Kate drove us northwards to Normandy; this brought immediate relief.

What was the meaning of this experience? Why should Chambord, a show-place visited by hundreds of thousands of people every year with evident pleasure, have set off in me this feeling of intolerable dread, this glimpse of the Void from which our ordinary daily lives are so thinly separated? In fact it was not Chambord which was to blame. As an experiment, I visited the place with my third wife many years later. There was the monstrous building just as before, the restaurant, the crowd of visitors. As architecture, I found it just as unpleasing as ever. But now it was just a French château I did not like. There was no fear; I could even laugh at the fear as I tried to describe my experience to a woman who, having a mind free of phantoms, had never known it. Had Kate been the cause of the fear? By no means; the cause was neither in her nor in the château; nor in the park, the fields, the trees, the empty sky; it was in myself.

As the year 1963 went on, I had a deepening feeling of depression and more frequent recourse to the doctor's pills. My ability to write was not impaired; indeed my inventive powers had never been better since I started work on the column, sometimes producing complex and elaborate fantasies which made ffolkes, when I read some effusion over the telephone for him to illustrate, exclaim in alarmed appreciation, 'You're going mad!' This should have been a warning. But I was on a path from which there was no straying. And after all, wasn't I 'Columnist of the Year'? Perhaps because of this award, I was approached by a publisher to produce an anthology of the column, using material which had appeared since the last anthology in 1958.

Dr Donald Johnson was no ordinary publisher. He was a medical doctor who had been a GP in the North and then, entering politics, had become Conservative MP for Carlisle. He was a tall, shambling, ill-dressed man, then about sixty, with traits of eccentricity which I found endearing. He had founded a small 'family' publishing firm, but up to that time seemed to have published very little apart from a satire on Parliament which he had written himself, a booklet on the menace of Chinese opium imports into England and a book of Conservative essays by T. E. Utley, the blind *Telegraph* leader writer. Dr

Johnson lived with his second wife, formerly a nurse and in her own way almost as eccentric as he was, in a villa in the south London suburb of Sutton, which also served as his publishing headquarters. He had another office in Stanhope Mews off Cromwell Road. It was approached by a steep staircase where there was a powerful smell of fish from a neighbouring smoked haddock and kipper store.

If the approach to his office was unusual, the office itself was even more so. It was one of the most untidy rooms I have ever seen. Piles of books and papers lay everywhere, under layers of dust. There was no room at the desk to write. A half-eaten sandwich on a plate was balanced on the telephone. Perhaps deceived by the smell on the staircase, I thought I caught a glimpse of a kipper on a shelf of books. In this strange den Dr Johnson transacted his business with me. I was obliged, of course, to get Sir Colin Coote's permission for the publication. This meant that I had to bring Dr Johnson to see Sir Colin in his office. It was evidently not the first time they had met. If he wished to be ungracious Sir Colin was not lacking in the talent to be so; his face expressed sardonic suspicion, as much as to say, 'Well, Johnson, if you want to take this on, that's your funeral'. The interview over, we shambled awkwardly out. I invited Dr Johnson for a drink at the Kings and Keys next door. He drank a half pint of beer, listening uneasily to the background noise through which the snarling voice of Philip Weston could be distinctly heard. It was early in the evening and he had not yet 'gone critical' – by the time I had seen Dr Johnson out and taken leave of him, he had. 'Poofter!' croaked Weston. 'I suppose that's your new protector!'

The work of choosing about three hundred items from the previous five years' output for the anthology, was considerable. But it was welcome at that time; routine work, the counting of words, the compiling of lists, is always soothing, a great ally in the struggle – no, not the struggle, because if you regard it as a struggle it is already lost – in the avoidance of *angst*. So when I was not writing the column itself I spent a great deal of my time on this task, paying as little attention as possible to Kate, the new baby and the mother's help who came in daily. At this time Kate was carrying on with her freelance journalism. At the beginning of spring she had a commission from some magazine to write a series of articles on hotels in different parts of the South of England which catered especially for children. So off we all went for long weekends, Kate, myself, Jane and the tiny baby in her carry-cot, to stay at these various places.

These trips seemed to bring on attacks of dread within a deepening cloud of depression. I had powerful feelings of unreality at an hotel at Sandbanks, a suburb of Bournemouth, a town I had not seen since my first marriage at its register office on the day the Spanish Civil War broke out; I peered into the Void at an hotel at Battle in Sussex, as the rain poured down on the field of Hastings; and dread was hovering about as we drove through Norfolk on our way to an hotel at Cromer when an event occurred which put a temporary stop to those excursions and to my fears as well.

We had stopped for a cup of tea near Wymondham and then were making towards Norwich when, as we approached a minor road on our left, a dark green van came towards us, hesitated and then turned across our path. I saw that a collision was unavoidable, braced myself, cried out a warning, and then came a jolting, jarring, glass-shattering crash. My injuries were small: a cut on my forehead where I hit the windscreen and a triangular tear in my left knee, bleeding a bit and spoiling a new pair of check trousers, where I had hit the edge of the glove compartment. Kate was knocked unconscious. In a few seconds, she came to; in the back seat, Jane was shocked but unharmed; while the baby had been jerked right out of her carry-cot and had landed on a pile of baby-food tins on the floor. As is the way of babies, she was the only one of us who seemed entirely composed.

We staggered out into the road, dazed and cursing. The van driver, a middle-aged teacher-like man who confessed he was in the wrong and, what was more, was a drama organiser for the county council, was apologising and dabbing at a gash on his head. He helped us to separate the locked vehicles and push them on to the verge. The side of his van was bashed in and so was the nearside wing of our car. Someone telephoned the police and soon a police car arrived and took us all to the police station in Wymondham ('Could you please be careful not to bleed over the new upholstery?' a policeman said nastily as we went along). After some time an ambulance took us all to Norwich General Hospital, where my leg was stitched and bandaged and we were all examined. A kindly nurse hung the baby upside down to demonstrate her amazing indestructibility.

The Barnetts, who by chance lived in a village a few miles from Norwich, gave us beds for the night. When we woke up, we found ourselves bruised all over and almost unable to move. But as it happened the Barnetts had a friend and neighbour, Calvin Wells, a retired doctor who devoted himself to research on palaeonosology, the study of diseases of past times as revealed by the examination of bones; in this unusual branch of learning he was a distinguished expert. More to the immediate purpose, he was an expert in getting insurance companies to pay damages to people involved in motor accidents (he had recently got Ruth Barnett £250 for being run into from behind). As I had never been involved in a motor accident before this form of alleviation had not occurred to me. But good Dr Wells arranged everything. 'Get you at least a thousand pounds for this,' he chuckled as he took us in his car to Norwich to be x-rayed. Our car was a 'write-off'. Supplied with a new one by the garage which collected it, and still somewhat bemused, we drove off back to London.

I was away from work for a fortnight. Whether or not the accident had really worsened my mental state (Dr Wells's cheerful, matter-of-fact contention that it had was a help to us later on, to collect the £1000 he promised) I cannot say. In theory, it might have had the opposite effect, the physical pain jerking me out of my melancholia. But whatever the reason, things got worse. I had just reached my fiftieth birthday, a notoriously bad time, when the futility of life becomes apparent and the possibility of change for the better recedes. Many factors contributed to my gathering depression, my ever-deepening sense of unreality. It came to a head at the beginning of July just before we were due to go to Brittany for a fortnight's holiday. I had been invited to spend a weekend at Waterstone with Constantine and his dark, shadowy second (or third) wife. As it happened, Kate, Jane and a woman friend had arranged to go camping that weekend at Long Burton in Dorset, not very far from Waterstone, and were to drop me off on the way.

Our connection with that part of Dorset went back a long way. We had stayed several times at a pub in Buckland Newton which Kate had discovered during some journalistic assignment. It was a great pub for serious drinking. The landlord, a Dorset man who verged on dipsomania, was often at odds with his wife, who was from Lancashire and had pretensions to refinement, including an 'improved' accent of great phonetic interest. She was anxious, since custom was not brisk, to bring in more trade by selling ice-cream to weekend visitors. This the landlord resisted; he felt, rightly, that to sell ice-cream was an affront to his manhood. This was a man out of an older, still rural England. In his youth he had been a carter, visiting places as distant as Salisbury Plain, the memory of which he described most movingly: miles of rolling downland which had never known the plough, let alone the war machines of the army, when Stonehenge was still a solitary wonder and the neolithic barrows were undisturbed. This unlettered man knew what poetry was. He knew the poems of William Barnes, Hardy's friend, well, and could repeat some of them by heart. He was the wreck of the strong man he had once been and the phantom of the poet he might have been. In his cups he raged against the ignoble present. It was no wonder he wanted nothing to do with ice-cream. But his wife prevailed, and soon the cheap plastic symbol of the ice-cream future sat above his doorway. He did not long survive it, but died as he swore he would. Nor did his widow long remain at the pub where we had drunk and talked so pleasantly into the small hours. She sank into a state of melancholia and was soon a sedated inmate of Charminster Mental Hospital. Thomas Hardy might have made something of their sad story.

He could have made nothing of my weekend at Waterstone. I have a faint recollection of struggling against a feeling of unreality which grew ever more powerful and irresistible. We went, I think, to several parties at rather grand houses in the neighbourhood. Crichel Down may have been one; Cranborne another (the name of Pitt-Rivers surfaces through dense fog). On the Sunday we certainly lunched with the engraver Reynolds Stone and his family at their house at Litton Cheney and afterwards walked in their water-garden. Did they notice my increasing anguish, my efforts to keep it under control? Or did they think I was always silent and found it hard to understand what people were saying to me, let alone reply? We returned to

Waterstone, where Kate, though barred from entering the house, was to pick me up in the car that evening. I took a long time to pack my things, finding some relief in this routine activity. It was a fine July evening as we drove east towards London. I had had a good deal to drink, but with no more than an anaesthetising effect; one kind of non-feeling seemed to be superimposed upon another. At Salisbury, where we stopped for supper, I had more drink. I became garrulous, revelling in fantasy, piling on more and more absurdities ('you were in really good form'). At home in Putney I fell into bed, dog-tired, and slept.

But I woke early in the blank, ominous summer morning. The full horror had come upon me: a deadly sense of non-existence; pervading terror; coldness of the extremities and the genitals; convulsive trembling. It was like the affliction I had suffered ten years before, but worse. Trying to recall that experience as 'a queer turn', as I had facetiously named it in an attempt, hitherto successful, to defuse the horror, I told myself: it will pass. But now this hitherto useful formula was not working. I had sunk beneath the level of words into pure unfeeling. It was Monday, a working day. But I was obviously incapable of work, indeed of any activity. Kate sent for the doctor. He gave me a sedative, then arranged for me to go as a voluntary patient into a mental hospital he recommended, Halliwick Hospital at Southgate in North London. So all day long I waited while people came and went, until the time came for Kate to drive me there. I checked in, was shown to my bed and given an injection which put me into a dreamless sleep for thirty-six hours. I woke and for a few seconds had an overpowering feeling of relief and happiness until the leaden burden of nonentity came and weighed down on me once more. I had become a mental patient, and for all I knew, was doomed to be one for the rest of my life.

Halliwick was no ordinary mental hospital, though it had the standard appearance of one, with its long range of grey stone Victorian buildings and its tall tower set amid a dull garden of shrubberies and pebbled paths. It had a wing for 'serious' cases, some violent, but the part of it I had been assigned to was devoted to cases of 'mild clinical depression'. Although it belonged to the National Health Service and was free, it had a high proportion of middle-class patients, many of them from places like Hampstead. I found out later that the writer Maurice Richardson, an occasional member of the FitzGibbon circle, had been an inmate for a time, suffering from a mild attack of mania; so had my old friend, coeval and former colleague at the BBC, David Thomson, who was to suffer from schizo-phrenia for the rest of his life.

He had been on a trip to Tanganyika, as it was then called, in connection with some BBC programme, when he was suddenly seized with violent, highly-coloured delusions and was flown home to England and Halliwick. He had quite enjoyed his stay there, he told me, when we exchanged reminiscences later. As therapy he was given large sheets of paper and some bright colours to paint with; he began painting huge figures of naked women amid tropical vegetation and became so absorbed in this work that he used up all the hospital's supply of paper and for that reason, if for no other, was reluctantly discharged. Other people from similar backgrounds as Richardson, Thomson and myself had been inmates, I believe, of this 'sick bay of Hampstead'; later I suggested having a special Halliwick tie designed, but nothing came of it. And in the course of time, no doubt, the privileged status of the place was done away with and it became a National Health hospital like any other.

I was heavily dosed with coloured pills and no longer felt the acute horror which had brought me there. But I still felt that everything about me was unreal and some things, like my shaving-brush, were tinged with evil. I had a room to myself but fed, when I had any appetite, which was seldom, in the communal dining-hall, a bleak, institutional room with separate tables in whose hinges lurked an uneasy feeling. I was sent to a psychiatrist for interview. He was a young Scotsman who made no particular impression on me, nor I, perhaps on him, for he referred me to a senior consultant, Dr Silver, a stocky, powerful-looking Jew who made a strong and very unpleasant impression. He was clearly interested in my case and may even have known of my profession; if so he gave no hint of it.

I was told to report for occupational therapy. This consisted of basket-weaving. I was so superlatively bad at this, producing after much effort a tangled mass of straw, that the instructor made it clear that he regarded me as hopeless and wished me elsewhere. Unlike David Thomson, I was given no paper, paint or other therapeutic material, but was left very much to my own devices. I walked the pebbled paths under the menacing summer sky with its slowly moving clouds and felt the presence of the Void. Applying my own therapy, I sat on my bed and tried to write some sonnets, choosing for the sake of difficulty the strict Italian form. I completed several, metrically correct but probably without any other merit. I do not know what became of them.

In the afternoons I went to the large patients' lounge, comfortably furnished with armchairs but with a noticeable absence of books (in any case Kate and Michael ffolkes, who also visited me, had brought me books which I tried to read, but finding them meaningless, desisted). In the lounge I got talking (this was a good thing) to a sad woman of my own age from Hampstead, called Wendy Porter. She lived alone and had fallen into a mild depression after the death of her dog, whom she had loved in a way I could not understand until, late in life, I kept dogs myself. With her I played innumerable games of Scrabble and exchanged symptoms, gaining some slight momentary relief.

So the days passed. I was allowed out in the morning after breakfast to buy newspapers and cigarettes. It never occurred to me that as a voluntary patient I could simply decamp; I had no will to do anything so positive. I read the *Daily Telegraph*, in which my holiday relief, Colm Brogan, was writing the column; it meant nothing to me whatsoever. I had several interviews with Dr Silver, and at each one he seemed to become more hostile. I began to implore Kate, when she visited me, to get me out of the place. Dr Silver, I gathered, was strongly against the idea. He believed 'I would benefit from further treatment'. Since, apart from great quantities of pills, I was not having any treatment, I have no idea what he meant.

After ten days this living death came to an end. My deliverer was Desmond O'Neill, whom Kate had called upon to help. Dr Silver put up a good deal of resistance; but as a psychiatrist himself, and a distinguished one, Desmond was in a position to overrule him and secure my release by undertaking to treat me himself. What he proposed was that I should undergo a course of electro-convulsive treatment in his own house in St John's Wood, one of our refuges during our nomadic period and scene of many enjoyable parties. I agreed. I was not much in favour of having an electric current passed through my head in order to shift and jumble up the pattern of depression which had seized on my brain circuits. This is, roughly, the theoretical basis of this kind of treatment; I have heard young doctors refer to it crudely as 'a bash of the box' or 'plugging 'em into the mains'. But anything seemed better than the state I was in. 'The most important thing,' said Desmond, 'is to get you back to work as soon as possible.' In this he was undoubtedly right, and for this I am everlastingly grateful to him.

What followed jumbled up not only my depression but also my subsequent memory of everything to do with that period of my life. To compensate somewhat for the loss of the Breton holiday, Kate had rented a cottage at Ash, a village near Sandwich in Kent. I see myself, between the electro-convulsive sessions, standing in the untidy cottage garden with Jane, and Victoria in her pram; sitting in the car on the way between Kent and London; visiting some Kentish village pub where I was allowed to drink only one half pint of beer; looking out over a calm sea at Sandwich; meeting the Phillimores for a vague dinner at an hotel at Winchelsea, where we had driven over circuitous roads; or, back in London, being led out of Desmond's house in the afternoon, with a blinding headache, to nearby Lords to watch a few overs in the sun. Kent had always been the part of England I knew least, being in the opposite corner of the country from mine, in the extreme south-eastern and most civilised corner of England; because of the unpleasant associations it collected at that time it is still the part of England I know least and the part I have never wanted to know better. Now that it is cut up and destroyed for the sake of the Channel Tunnel, the epitome of everything I detest, it is doubly lost to me.

Of the electro-convulsive sessions I remember little, except lying down on the couch while Desmond and his assistant arranged the apparatus; the prick of the anaesthetic needle; oblivion and waking, for a time unable to tell who I was or to recognise my surroundings. Kate told me (she may of course have invented this) that once I came to and asked her who she

was, and when she told me, said, 'You can't be. You are beautiful'. I felt that the treatment, apart from the headaches, was
doing me good; at least it was making me feel different, even
making me feel as much alive as I was then capable of feeling.
So, after I had been away for five weeks, Desmond advised that
I should return to work. On a morning in mid-August I took
the train from Canterbury to London and sat down at my desk
again. The first column I produced with a brain which had
been electrically deprived of its previous pattern of thought was
not a distinguished one. I had also been deprived of the pattern
of thought which produced the column. Perhaps it would have
been better for me if it had never returned, so that I might have
got some more sensible work to do. But gradually it did return
after an uneasy period when, Annabel told me later, she had
grave fears for me.

It was necessary for me to find out what had been happening
in the outer world while I had been 'under the weather' – a
very apt description of my state of mind during those five weeks
of my absence before that dismal feeling began to retreat or I
to move out of its influence; the matter could be put either way.
A great deal had been happening, as I soon discovered. The
Profumo Affair had exploded while I was in hospital: the War
Minister, convicted of lying when he told the House of Commons that he had had no 'improper association' with the
delicious call girl Christine Keeler, had resigned, and the reper-
cussions of the matter were still sounding away in the courts;
such characters as Mandy Rice-Davies, Dr Stephen Ward,
'Lucky' Gordon and Christine herself filled the newspapers and
were continually talked about.

These matters in fact offered little for my column. I was
more affected by the death of Louis MacNeice, though I cannot
say exactly why. I had not known him well, and though I had

once or twice got drunk in his company I had always been wary of his dark horse-face with its slightly sneering expression and threat of a possible nasty bite, and of the black notebook which he would often take from his pocket to write down a phrase or line. Unlike 'Bertie' Rogers, whose alliterative poems seem to have gone permanently out of fashion and even sunk without trace, MacNeice will live. His wonderful poem on the fire-blitz on London, 'Brother Fire', would alone be enough to ensure it. So it was sad to hear of his death. This happened, I was told, when he got soaked to the skin while on a BBC assignment in a cave and developed pneumonia. He was taken to the Middlesex Hospital where his request for a bottle of whisky was rejected. He was accustomed to heavy drinking and this foolish piece of hospital routine probably cost him his life.

Gradually, as I recovered, I picked up the threads of my working life. Seeking guidance, I looked at the columns I had been writing before what Constantine, in his American style, called my 'crack-up'. The very last one, suggestive of mounting hysteria, contained a piece in which I found myself, while 'working on a research project on alcoholism in a Fleet Street bar', suddenly producing 'Tibetan-type thought-forms' of the columnar characters:

General Nidgett peering forcefully through his glinting spectacles, Shri Swami Ron J. Bhattacharya, Ted Bloke and Eric Lard, 'Redshank' the nature writer, babbling of badgers and of dotterels' nests among the watercress, Mrs Dutt-Pauker and even Mrs Dutt-Pauker's late husband with his snowy locks, Stalinist pipe and blood-red knitted woollen scarf of Revolution. So real were they, these forms, so far beyond even Tibetan psychic skill, that they could react on each other, I found, without my interposition. Soon Lard and

'Redshank' come to blows and Nidgett, ever susceptible to feminine charm, began absently stroking Mrs Dutt-Pauker's *Daily Worker* Bazaar Roumanian raffia-work handbag, as he talked on, stimulatingly, of service, initiative and leadership. Bemused by the din, I let my attention wander for a moment – the production of thought-forms is extremely tiring – and when I looked again the whole lot had vanished. Only a vague diminishing murmur of voices seemed to come now from the lamplit streets, now from the clouds.

There was a certain poetic imagination at work there, I thought – as well as an unmistakable unease – and now it was my task to recover it and even, if possible, turn my unpleasant experiences to the service of the column. It was perhaps at this time that I began to think of the column not merely as something which provided me with a living, but as something to which I was going to devote the rest of my working life. Or was it that the column itself, exacting this daily labour which sometimes seemed a burden not to be borne but sometimes gave me pleasure in creation, had become a monster, making me its slave? In my old age, when it already seems forgotten, superseded by more violent, obscene and outspoken writings, I have come to dislike it and to lament – God help me! – that this is all I have to show for a lifetime's work. It is far removed indeed from my youthful dreams of becoming rich and famous. I have succeeded in neither.

Slowly I recovered, not without setbacks. Desmond had laid down a 'regime' of pills I was to take – some green and white, some red – respectively 'uppers' and 'downers' as they came to be called later on when taking drugs became more and more common among people like myself who were being driven mad by the egotism laying waste themselves and the technological

progress laying waste the world. Which was worse? Obviously
the former. What is a 'nervous breakdown' but an extreme form
of self-regard and therefore deadly sin?

While I was taking these pills, Desmond told me, I should
not drink alcohol. For a time I followed this advice quite strictly,
avoiding the pub and even taking a masochistic pleasure in
passing the door on my way to the bus-stop, receiving a momentary blast of enticing noise as my former drinking companions
shouted their heads off within. I took a solitary lunch, preceded
by one glass of campari and soda – a bitter drink I disliked then
and have disliked for its associations ever since – in an Italian
restaurant, long defunct, at the lower end of Fleet Street. I
never asked Annabel to accompany me, either at that time or
later. I felt instinctively that although I liked this beautiful,
amiable and intelligent girl we had nothing much to say to each
other. She must have got only an impression of austerity and
gloom radiating from the other end of the little room we shared
four days a week for eight years.

On the fifth working day of the week, Friday (there was no
column on Saturdays) I went to the BBC to attend to the part-
time job I had cunningly retained of reading short stories; I was
still treated by the BBC administrative machine as a member
of the staff, with the normal four weeks holiday a year and
regular increments in my salary, which at its highest reached
£12 a week. During my prolonged absence, which I counted
as an official holiday, a huge pile of these short stories had
accumulated; this had been noted by some busybody, and my
friend James Langham, the producer of 'Morning Story', had
had some explaining to do. He had managed to pacify his
immediate superior in the Talks Department (everybody in the
BBC had an immediate superior, a thing which delighted my
hierarchy-loving soul), but, as he told me, I was under suspicion

of not being sufficiently conscientious about my work; mental illness was not regarded as a valid excuse unless officially certified.

Some months later, when James retired, another member of the Department, a very conscientious woman who succeeded him and who had had her eye on my job ever since suspicion fell on me, managed by a series of elementary intrigues to annex it to her own. The day came when I was summoned to the office of a high-grade administrative official in the lofty heights of 'B.H.'. There was a re-run, to me most satisfactorily ironical, of the interview I had had with one of these 'greymen' seven years before. It was not the same 'greyman', but he used much the same words: 'reorganisation of the Department ... rationalisation ... necessity of retrenchment ... sorry that the time has come for a parting of the ways ... very grateful for the services you have rendered ... ' I looked at the 'greyman' as he spoke his piece, and a feeling of genuine pleasure and amusement came over me such as I had not felt for months.

For a moment I thought of making a scene: bursting into tears, going on my knees, kissing his well-polished black shoes, begging him to think of my wife and five small children, now threatened with starvation and beggary. But I was no Peter Duval Smith, and did no such thing. Instead I got up, looked out of the window and said 'What a wonderful view you have from here'. Perhaps this was more effective than tears. He certainly looked nonplussed as I took my leave, smiling hideously to myself as I descended in the lift, already composing a request to the *Telegraph* to increase my salary as I passed through the heavy bronze doors of 'B.H.' into the street.

Thereafter, except for one occasion in the Eighties when I was interviewed about my autobiography for a radio programme – how changed was the studio, crammed with elaborate, incomprehensible machinery, technicians and girl assistants, whereas in my time the producer would have been alone except for one engineer – I never passed through those doors again, except sometimes late at night when Kate and I and some companions would 'go on' after an evening of heavy drinking to the BBC's underground all-night canteen. We were never challenged when we entered this delightful place, where the 'buck rabbit and chips' was legendary and the kindly manageress, a Welsh-speaker, could sometimes be persuaded to sing 'Bugeilio 'r Gwenith Gwyn', my favourite Welsh folk-song.

We also used the services of the BBC duty officer, who lived in a room to the left of the central lifts and was said to be able to give the answer to any enquiry. Once in the small hours we telephoned to ask him to supply a missing line in the song 'Home on the Range'. He did so without hesitation. How heartrending is the decline of the BBC into barbarism since those days! Its marble foyer – where once a special subsection of pious women had the duty of arranging flowers in enormous chaste white urns beneath Eric Gill's bas-relief with its noble Latin inscription – is now disfigured by a platform where an official presides over security, while posturing rock-stars with fantastic hair-dos and strange, barbaric leather costumes impatiently await a degenerate breed of obsequious producers. And cracks are appearing in the walls.

Desmond had told me that attacks of depression often came in series, and I was aware during the next few months how precarious, though gradually strengthening, was the balance of my mind and how near I often was to falling once again into the pit. We had arranged a boarding school for Jane, who was now eleven; it may be that if I had been in a normal state I might have been against the idea of sending her away from home so young. But I remembered Dixie's advice and made no objection.

A Catholic school in Dorset, Leweston Manor, a few miles from Sherborne, had been recommended. Run by a teaching order of Belgian nuns, with the redoubtable Mother Eleanor as head, it was a former country house in a large and beautiful park surrounded by woods, not far from Kate's former camp-site at Long Burton.

Jane's first departure for school from Waterloo Station was the model for such repeated leavetakings, with floods of tears on both sides. Worst still was the first weekend when we were allowed to take Jane out on Saturday afternoon. It was raining heavily, of course, so the only place to go was the cinema at Yeovil, where we saw a terrible epic film, *El Cid*, and then took Jane to a tea-shop in Sherborne before returning her, with more harrowing scenes, to school. It was the first of such experiences, which gradually grew more bearable as time went on and she progressed at the school, marked out by Mother Eleanor as a potential head girl until she became not just normally rebellious but excessively so, thus missing that eminence. Mother Eleanor, a shrewd woman, had realised that all was not well between Kate and me. She soon began to show a marked preference for me. I am easily frightened by nuns, particularly strong-minded ones, and soon began to behave towards her in a sycophantic, Uriah Heap-like manner which Jane noted with derision; this naturally made me exaggerate it to the point of caricature.

It was not long before I began to disregard Desmond's recommendation about not drinking alcohol. Soon I was taking his pills and alcohol as well. This did not seem to have bad effects at first; in fact it seemed to improve my ability to write the column. But it did make my behaviour more erratic. For a time I was convinced I was in love with Liz Hogg. This was not particularly surprising; I had always thought her delightful, both for herself and for her knowledge of 'Celtic' matters. However, my pursuit of her, such as it was, cannot have been very convincing. When drunk, I would drop in on her at the Hoggs' house in Woodlands Road in Barnes, a pleasant shambles of children and musical instruments, liable to be invaded by various neighbours we called collectively 'the Woodland Folk'. Among them was the elderly and eccentric retired Admiral Sir Caspar John, son of Augustus John, and his even more eccentric wife, who when he was Chief of Naval Staff must have been a continual source of worry at official functions.

Sir Caspar himself, a handsome, majestic man, had fallen into a state of melancholy in his declining years and was liable to appear in the Hoggs' house declaring in a deep and sombre voice, 'I am the Mayor of Casterbridge,' while Lady John, a small, lively, sparrow-like person, jigged about and tried to persuade everybody to dance. Other people who belonged to 'the Woodland Folk' were Christopher Wordsworth, a critic whom we had come across earlier on, among the English settlers on Clough Williams-Ellis's estate in North Wales, and Basil Davidson, a marxist and almost single-handed inventor of the history of Black Africa, which he peddled so persistently that many people actually came to believe in it.

My courtship of Liz Hogg virtually ended, though we remained friends, when the Hoggs asked me to spend New Year's Eve with them. I got very drunk in the Kings and Keys and arrived in Woodlands Road long after midnight when they had long given me up and only let me in, reluctantly, after I had thrown several snowballs at the window. My courtship of Martin Jameson's wife, for whom I suddenly took a violent fancy in the same pub, having known her for several years without showing any interest whatever, was even briefer. My courtship of a young and attractive Scots girl, Morag MacMunn

– whom I had met in some Fleet Street pub with an acquaintance of Stephen Daneff whom we had nicknamed 'Gimli the Dwarf' (it was the time of the great vogue of Tolkien's *Lord of the Rings*, which I was reading in bed, a chapter a night, giving myself stupendous, partly drug-induced dreams) – was more protracted.

Morag was a friend of the dying poet Brian Higgins, a protégé of the wild-living George Barker; both were thoroughly disreputable. Things between Morag, who was about twenty years old, and myself became difficult when she declared a passion for me which soon eclipsed mine for her. Very drunk, I took her to a party given by some respectable friend of the Worsthornes, probably Kenneth Bradshaw, Clerk at the House of Commons. We were not well received, so retired and went to bed in her very unrespectable room somewhere in Bayswater. I crawled out into the street in the early morning, wandered about in the fog and at last got a taxi to Putney. But for all that I was at my desk in the *Telegraph* by noon that morning settling down to write the column for the day.

Such unseemly goings on could not be sustained. I arranged (or Kate arranged, I dare say) a week's interlude when I took the column to Rome, Kate accompanying me to help write the copy, with ffolkes to do the drawings. We stayed (courtesy of the *Telegraph*, of course) at an excellent hotel, the Inghilterra, and visited the sights; the Colosseum, Keats' death chamber, the Café Greco; the English tea-house below the Spanish Steps, the gardens at Tivoli, Hadrian's Villa.

It was the time of the crucial Vatican Council, though I don't think any of us, Catholic or not – and ffolkes was a 'militant atheist' of an unthinking kind, which many people would be if they were honest with themselves, and could not understand why anyone should give any religion a second thought – had any idea how crucial it was. What I witnessed in St Peter's was a scene of almost unbearable splendour: the Swiss Guards marshalling us, together with the faithful and unfaithful of all nations, to watch the white-robed Pope, triple-crowned, borne along in his golden chair past the black barley-sugar *baldacchino*, while the cardinals of the whole world – white, brown, yellow and black – applauded, like a theatre audience, with cries of 'Viva il Papa! Viva!' Organs and choirs thundered; censers swung, releasing clouds of incense; my head swam; facile tears streamed down my cheeks. 'I'm getting out of here,' muttered the indignant ffolkes. And in fact he and Kate almost had to drag me out of this quasi-religious orgy into the Sistine Chapel for some more sober art appreciation (I was surprised by the smallness and brownness of the celebrated ceiling).

I found it difficult to adapt the column to writing about a foreign country, far from the safety of my desk, and the administrative arrangements, which I had to look after as well, were formidable. I never attempted such an enterprise again. This was a pity, for the *Telegraph* would gladly have been the means by which I could have visited any place I chose. So in the end I got nothing much out of it except a living and a little doubtful pseudonymous fame.

After we had spent the four columnar days in Rome, we flew bumpily over the Appenines to Venice, where we put up at the most expensive hotel I have ever stayed in, the Daniele. It was full of Americans, the cheapest drink cost about £4 and the air-conditioning, a thing I have always hated, ensured that I got scarcely any sleep at night. Venice in October, misty, dark and slimy in its maze of canals and alleyways, dangerously lowered my spirits, such as they were. Only later did it occur to me that the sinister unreality of the place was at least partly due to what ought to have been a prime attraction: the absence of motor traffic. Venice, in the state I was in, was not for me. I have never been back there, or felt the least inclination to risk a better state of mind by another visit, or try the test I passed on my second visit to Chambord. On being told, as I have often been, that I must surely love Venice as all civilised people and partisans of beauty love it, I have to keep silent or, with a groan of anguish, explain my sad predicament.

Back in London, Sir Colin asked me in his sardonic way if 'I had enjoyed my holiday', which was how, perhaps rightly, he regarded it. I had not enjoyed it, if only because the concept of enjoyment was not at that time part of my confused universe. Under Desmond's watchful eye, I had many narrow escapes from total relapse. Feeling in particularly low spirits one winter morning, and oppressed by the lurking hell of unreality, I went to see him for a consultation. I found him sitting in his consulting room, a big transparent plastic box of many-coloured pills beside him which would have delighted children. 'As it happens,' he said, 'I've just had a new anti-depressant drug sent in from America. It has to be injected. Would you like to try it?' I hesitated. 'I'm going to try it myself,' he said. I could hardly refuse. So he injected us both, and within a few seconds we were laughing together in a powerful state of euphoria and exchanging childhood reminiscences. I have no idea what the drug was, but the subsequent let-down was formidable. It was some help to learn that it had been as bad for him as it had for me.

The child Victoria, who naturally became known as 'Vicki', was now in her second year, and I began to grow fond of her. She was an engaging, lively and mischievous child, pronounced 'wick' (or lively) by my mother, who liked to come out with Yorkshire-dialect words, when we took her to Amswick in the spring of 1964. There, in the sitting-room with its fragments of

Dresden china and other relics of the splendours of Harrogate, looking out across the dale to the limestone scars, Vicki learned to take her first steps, as Jane had done ten years before in that very same room. My mother seldom approved of girl-children. She did not approve of women in general, always maintaining that in matters of courtship and marriage it was women who 'chased' men and that if any of them caught me, as occasionally happened, I 'must have encouraged her'.

With these prejudices it was quite surprising that she took to Vicki as she did. It was an accolade indeed; when we took Vicki over to see Emma, my brother's widow, settled ever since his death in her native Swaledale, she pronounced the child an 'elf' or 'changeling' and for once my mother did not condemn this fancy talk with her customary 'silly woman!' Did they realise that Vicki was indeed a changeling? And was this for them, as it may have been for me, part of the child's unusual charm? Even her extreme naughtiness, only intermittently checked by Kate, a loving but careless mother, and scarcely at all by me, was irresistibly attractive. When, later on, we began to take her with us on visits to Jane, she got herself barred for life from all the tea-shops in Sherborne; in a tea-shop in Cerne Abbas, the place of the giant, she unravelled all the rolls of lavatory-paper in the washroom, so that paper came cascading down the stairs and out into the street. We thought this most amusing, and so did she, thereby spurred on to even greater feats of disruption.

It was in April, a bad month for the depressed, that I came nearer to falling once again into the pit. To struggle with this black woe of non-feeling was merely to add terror to it. One evening, while Weston and Jameson were performing in the Kings and Keys, I felt such despair – how could I go through all this again? – that Kate unwillingly hurried me to Desmond's house. He kept us waiting, as psychiatrists necessarily do, a very long time, while glasses of white wine – he was a very understanding doctor – appeared regularly for our refreshment. In his consulting room he listened, then advised another course of electro-convulsive therapy. He arranged a first instalment for the very next evening.

There was no reason, he said, why I should not carry on with my normal life and work – indeed he strongly recommended it. Only I was to eat nothing in the meantime, and drink only a little water, while taking my customary pills. I obeyed his instructions and next morning sat down at my desk, perhaps staring at Annabel more portentously than usual. I tried to write about whatever came to mind at that time – immigration, 'Mods and Rocker' riots, aggressive trade-unionists, who can say? – but could get down no more than a few disjointed sentences. Suddenly a miracle occurred – a paradoxical idea! I wrote it down; the cloud lifted from my mind, and when at lunchtime Kate came in to see how I was getting on in preparation for my ordeal I told her I felt better. 'Good,' she said in her masterful way. 'Ring up Desmond and tell him you don't need the treatment, and come out and have a drink!' So that is what I did.

It was about this time that Sir Colin Coote retired from the editorship, resplendent in years and honour. There was a farewell luncheon at the Savoy Hotel, the first of many such luncheons I attended in the days when the *Telegraph* was generous with its money – even 'Zed', the Literary Editor, got a luncheon at the Savoy when he retired, and L. Marsland Gander, the aged radio (and, I suppose, television) critic, got a hilariously comical one at which recordings of early radio stars like Wilfred Pickles and Henry Hall were played between the speeches. Sir Colin was succeeded by Maurice Green, an economist from *The Times*, a very different sort of person who, though fairly suspicious of my column and apt to worry more than the robust Coote about possibly libellous material, was amiable and cordial and even, unlike his predecessor, occasionally relieved our evening sessions by laughing at things I had written or complimenting me on being in good form. In fact the ten or eleven years of his editorship did find the column (which he always quaintly called my 'notes') at its zenith, if it ever had one.

However, it was not long before he complained that he could not get on with Colm Brogan, who looked after the column when I was on holiday. Green could not understand a word Brogan said in his admittedly ferocious Glasgow accent; whatever he might actually be saying, Green complained, he always sounded as if he was swearing, and it was beginning to get on his nerves. I explained that Brogan was really one of the kindest of men and could not help it if, when Green asked, for instance, what the time was, he seemed to be making ferocious threats. It was no good. Brogan, who badly needed the money, had to go.

His departure was no credit to me; I felt remorse because I had not defended him as strongly as I might, and for all his phonetic and facial ferocity, he was not good at defending himself, or at any rate at looking after his own interests. He was one of the most lovable and honest men I have ever known. He was also capable, when he forgot to be irascible and was mollified by alcohol, of being extremely entertaining and amusing. I sometimes visited the gloomy flat in Bloomsbury, where dark brown was the predominant if not the only colour, in which he lived with his wife and daughter Mary, who worked on the *Telegraph*'s women's page. She cooked terrible brown meals of Irish stew and offered Guinness and Irish whiskey. Colm would play alternate records of Irish 'rebel' and Orange songs, delighting equally, as I did myself, both in 'The Battle of Aughrim', that wonderful dirgelike song of defeat, and 'The Old Orange Flute', that wonderful, rollicking song of preposterous bigotry. He used to say that he was the only man in the world who was both an Orangeman and a Sinn Féiner. A universal nationalist, I had much the same attitude to the 'Irish problem'; but as a Scots–Irish Catholic he was more directly concerned.

Towards the end of his life the most undeserved misfortune fell on this truly good man. He became a modern Job. First he fell ill with an ulcer, requiring a serious operation; then his wife, who with her cheerfulness and patience had been his faithful support and safeguard, fell ill with cancer and died within a few months. This was both shocking and amazing. I had always assumed, as some doctors believe, that only unhappy, introverted and selfish people die of cancer. Mrs Brogan was the very reverse of this: happy, at least to outward view, extrovert and unselfish. After her death, Colm soon became ill again, undergoing another operation, and although his daughter looked after him as unselfishly if not as cheerfully as his wife had done, she could not replace her. He was reduced to shuffling about, with rueful anger, by means of a walking frame until he died. He never lost his faith.

Colm was succeeded as holiday relief by Anthony Lejeune, a clever man of suitably reactionary views not leavened, like mine, by a certain tendency to self-mockery which, however despicable, was necessary to put them across in an acceptable way. Lejeune was also a tremendous snob and extremely knowledgeable about gentlemen's clubs and the habits and diction ('U and non-U') of the upper class.

His attitude to me was rather patronising, and after a year or two I became tired of this and of his somewhat wooden and uncharitable attitudes. An inaccuracy in an item which demanded a correction when I returned from holiday gave me the opportunity of dispensing with a deputy altogether. Henceforth when I was away, the columnar space was filled with other material, usually short articles, and apart from occasional contributions from Colm Brogan, Charles Herring and Michael Green – and even those gradually fell away for different reasons – I wrote the column by myself.

The anthology had had some success; Dr Johnson published a new edition, with some supplementary matter, and proposed to bring out a second anthology in 1965. He even gave a party in the upper room of a pub in Sutton. It was a joint party; the other publication to be celebrated was a book of poems by an elderly Australian woman who had probably paid for publication herself and may have been a relation of Dr Johnson's by marriage. Michael ffolkes, who, apart from the host, was the only person I knew at the party, was impressed by the extreme dimness of the arrangements. There was nothing to drink except beer and British sherry and nothing to eat except potato crisps and peanuts. There was a general air of bewilderment. What was it all for? As we came out into the rain ffolkes said it was probably the worst party he had ever attended.

I was inclined to agree; but the very hopelessness and obscurity of this parody of a 'glittering' publisher's party appealed to the masochistic side of my nature, a certain instinct for self-abasement inherited from my father, so strongly that I was almost hysterical with amusement as we made our escape from Sutton and fell into some brightly-lighted restaurant in the West End. I thought of the worst party in English literature: Giles Winterbourne's party in Hardy's *Woodlanders*. But apart from underlining my failure to become rich and famous, this party in Sutton had done me no harm; it had not, for instance, like poor Giles's debâcle, lowered me in the eyes of the woman I loved.

It was in the summer of 1964 that I found a woman who for the first time in my life offered the promise of a strong, steady mutual love and at once began to alleviate, if she did not entirely remove, my neurotic fears. Susan was thirteen years younger than myself, a painter, partly Swedish and in all ways appealing. She was a devout Catholic, and it was another ten years before we married. Before that, Jane had graduated at Bristol University and I thought myself free of the duty (though by a typical wish to have my cake and eat it, not entirely free of the inclination) to go on living at Putney. Even when, in 1965, Kate had had another baby, not, of course, by me, I did not leave. The 'horror comic' continued, and Constantine was able to quote the familiar saying about history repeating itself, the second time as farce. In fact, because of my new attachment and frequent absences, there was less horror, less verbal abuse; fewer plates were smashed and fewer handbags or briefcases flung from the windows of taxis in motion. Kate and I visited Jane at Leweston just like respectable parents (were we, in fact, less respectable, had the truth been known, than many of the other parents?). We went on foreign holidays together. In that same year, 1964, we spent a fortnight in the Minho. Jane, who was now in her twelfth year and very beautiful, innocently captivated a susceptible young Portuguese.

For the voyage back to England we took a boat from Vigo, in Spain, to Southampton. It had brought a cargo of negroes from the West Indies, part of the flood of alien people who were invading and part-colonising England, transforming it in ways which nobody, certainly nobody among the easy-going mass of the indigenous population, could possibly anticipate. We ourselves, of course, had no idea at that time of what the appearance of these people was going to mean; we looked at them with surprise as they came up on deck from the lower depths of the ship, some hesitant, some compensating for their own bewilderment by an overbearing attitude. We looked at them and thought no more of it. If we – the indigenous population – had taken thought then, could we have prevented the tragic consequences? Was this fatal loss of our racial homogeneity due to human error on the part of our rulers, to their stupidity – or to a deliberate conspiracy against England, the one country in Europe spared for centuries from invasion, occupation or revolution, the one country, therefore, whose destruction must be brought about if the final ruin of European civilisation were to be assured?

Signs of such a conspiracy were all around us: the importation from the vilest gutters of America of degenerate sub-musical rubbish, of drug addiction, pornography, aggressive feminism, aggressive homosexuality. Even worse in principle was the inversion of values by which the 'media' welcomed these evils as signs of human liberation, collectively called 'the permissive society'. Perhaps there was no conspiracy and no need for one; perhaps the people of England were unconsciously conspiring against themselves. Perhaps Satan, the spirit of evil, was loose in the world, as some of my readers believed. Perhaps, as I explained in an ironical 'note', I objected to these things only because I was getting old, jealous of young people and out of touch. But I do not think so.

At any rate there was plenty of material for my column, evils which I could either rail against or satirise, or sometimes both; this way of treating them often produced the most satisfying results. And while I railed against the 'permissive society', I was living, as I always had, what the famous crusader against that society, Mrs Whitehouse, would have regarded as a 'permissive' life. There was no hypocrisy in this: I was not promiscuous, I did not listen to rock music or take drugs or enjoy pornography.

I led two separate lives: one based on Putney, with Kate and her family; one with my friend and companion with whom, whenever possible, I travelled about England and Wales, exploring the vanishing countryside – and twenty-five years ago there was still a lot that had not vanished.

At midsummer we stayed at a delightful hotel in Savernake Forest and walked in its still enchanted glades; in autumn we travelled in Northumberland or in North Wales or in the limestone dales of Derbyshire; in March we once saw genuine mad March hares leaping and boxing on the Wiltshire Downs.

As for my life in Putney, it was good to see the children growing up and revive, vicariously, my own lost sense of wonder; it was good to visit Jane at Leweston and observe her progress in the intervals of toadying to Mother Eleanor. It was good to visit my mother in Yorkshire and to get drunk, as Kate and I often did, with the Tunnicliffes, either in their capacious bungalow, hidden in trees above the now forgotten Minoan Ball Ground, or in various pubs and hotels in that part of Yorkshire. They lived what John Braine thought of as 'life at the top' but with an element of raffishness and high spirits which made it irresistibly attractive. When their second daughter, Patricia or 'Trish', married the young scion of another West Riding industrial dynasty, they gave a splendid party with vast marquees and red carpets in the garden of their big house in Wharfedale; we went on drinking until the small hours, to Jane's alarm, though we were able to allay her anxiety when she telephoned from Amswick for news.

The pleasure of those days is best summed up in a shared fantasy we had of buying a mysterious, derelict mansion called Oughtershaw Hall, in Langstrothdale, not far from the sources of the Wharfe. This house was a piece of romantic Victorian mediaevalism, originally built by the Woodd family, friends of

Ruskin; it was buried in shrubberies; its furthest walk over-looked a gloomy waterfall which in winter must have permeated the lives of all who lived there with its ceaseless boom.

Of course our fantasy of living there came to nothing. In later years, when this period of our lives was long over, I often passed that way, to find the house just as mysterious and more decayed, with signs of occupation by squatters or wandering people. But 'Oughtershaw Hall' has remained a symbol of the unattainable, a Yorkshire version of Alain Fournier's lost domain.

There was a reverse side to all this: boredom, inertia, occasional attacks of *angst*, though never of great severity or long duration, which made certain places where these inexplicable afflictions broke the surface of my mind into places I have always subsequently avoided. Orford in Suffolk was one place where I suffered one of these 'queer turns' lightly attributed to 'bad vibes', while ascending the castle tower on a day of dismal rain. Deep breathing, together with one of Desmond's green and white pills and a large gin-and-tonic, brought relief.

Simple loneliness could also be an affliction when, as some-times happened, both sides of my life failed and I was left to myself. A low point of middle life: I was returning from Fleet Street to Putney on a dismal autumn evening when there was nobody at home. As though by a masochistic instinct I entered the most depressing pub in Putney High Street, ordered a bottle of beer and a portion of pure cardboard pork pie and sat down at a small table, swimming with liquid and covered with the abandoned plates of previous eaters. As I began this miserable repast with Gissing-like lassitude a rough-looking young labourer sat down at the table opposite me. We did not speak, but I discerned in him an additional, satisfying element of boredom and menace.

There was a kind of perverted pleasure in this humiliating situation; even a mystical sense of freedom, hard to explain, but analogous to an experience I had years later on a wild road in the mountains of Galicia when returning from a pilgrimage by car I made with my third wife to Santiago de Compostela. We had lost the way – it was still blissfully possible to lose the way in those days, as innumerable pilgrims must have done before us, before the tourist signs appeared for the tidy regulation and direction of travellers – and quarrelled over my reading of the map. Losing all patience, she drove away, leaving me sitting on a large granite boulder by the wayside in this totally deserted place.

My anger left me; and what came over me was an overpowering sense of freedom. It was not freedom from my wife; there was 'nothing personal in it'; I still loved her. It was the 'absolute' freedom to go anywhere I pleased. I had my passport and enough money for my immediate needs; I could as soon walk away in one direction as another: return to England, my job and responsibilities; take a ship from Vigo or Coruña to the ends of the earth; or remain in Spain, find a small town and settle there to await whatever might come. I did none of these things; the moment of illumination passed; my wife, her temper recovered, drove slowly back, and we resumed our journey in silence. I did not try to explain what had happened to me until long afterwards, and even then I am not sure she understood. But any life must contain such inexplicable moments of illumination in which it seems all may be changed for ever. Perhaps, like so much else in life, the ecstasy of physical love included, they are anticipations of death.

6

Some Reactionary Causes

Bringing to an end what he called 'thirteen years of Tory misrule', Harold Wilson won the General Election in the autumn of 1964. The election-night party which Lady Pamela Berry and her husband (later to become a life peer under the name of Lord Hartwell, converting her into Lady Hartwell) gave at the Savoy Hotel was a much less triumphant affair than the previous election parties I had attended; as the results flashed up on the big screen and the coming Labour victory became unmistakeable, the champagne-swilling guests showed signs of unease, which naturally made them swill champagne at an even greater speed.

Dr Johnson decided to call his new anthology 'Peter Simple in Opposition'. This was misleading because I was always in opposition, scarcely more so when there was a Labour Government than a Conservative. I am quite incapable of understanding 'the economy', 'the trade gap', 'the balance of payments' and so on, which everyone on the *Telegraph* said would be more seriously mishandled by the Labour Party; indeed, I have never been able to understand what 'the economy' is, and when I asked people like Colin Welch, who evidently did, for enlightenment I came away none the wiser. They could not answer my fundamental question: how did money originate, and if, as appeared to be the case, the world economy was ruled by a system of manipulation of imaginary money by credit, who ultimately controlled the system? It may be that these questions led us on to quaking ground. They were fully explained by

Major Douglas, inventor of Social Credit and patron of my friends the Greenshirts; but unfortunately I could not understand his explanation either.

In everything which really interested me and which I thought I *could* understand, there seemed little to choose between Labour and the Tories: neither seemed concerned with the moral degeneration of England; neither seemed concerned with the flood of unassimilable alien immigrants who were altering the character of entire cities to the dismay and anger of the indigenous population, which were eventually suppressed by law and by the monstrous growth of the Race Relations Industry (a term I invented about this time); neither seemed concerned by the infiltration of every government department and every sizeable institution by people who, whether they were Communists or not, had no loyalty to the State and in many cases were actually working to overthrow it.

Dr Johnson, unlike myself, was a party politician and naturally regarded the advent of the Labour Government in 1964 as an unmitigated calamity. However, he was (it was one of his many admirable qualities) a man independently-minded to the point of eccentricity. During what he rightly thought were humbugging goings-on in the Commons and behind the scenes which accompanied the Profumo Affair and the advent of Sir Alec Douglas-Home as Prime Minister, he had frequently declined the whip and during an important debate openly declared he was going to play golf instead of attending. This annoyed his constituency association as much as it delighted me, and he was forced to resign his seat as MP for Carlisle. At the consequent by-election he stood as an Independent Conservative and lost, but succeeded in splitting the vote and letting in the Labour candidate. Henceforth his name was mud in the Conservative

Central Office, and although I think he tried, he never managed to get nominated as a candidate again.

The later history of this lovable man was even more curious. He and his wife bought an hotel at Woodstock in Oxfordshire, but soon contrived to alienate the staff. One morning they all concertedly walked out on him. Later he maintained that they had been taking cannabis and, more serious, had introduced cannabis or other 'substances' into his and his wife's food, and they found themselves acting so strangely that they were both certified insane by (he believed) corrupt doctors and committed to a mental hospital. They were released after a short time; but the case caused quite a sensation. Years later, when I happened to be having a drink in this hotel, I noticed on the wall a crude comic drawing showing Dr and Mrs Johnson staring aghast as a procession of their staff made their way out of the door and into the street.

It may have been a mark of Dr Johnson's eccentricity that he went on publishing anthologies of my column at intervals until the last one appeared in 1973; henceforth they were published by the *Telegraph* publications department. Johnson Publications had only meagre sales arrangements and no money for advertising, so the books' sales were small; but at least they looked like books; the *Telegraph*'s productions, cheap-looking affairs printed on grey paper and with the appearance, as one friendly reviewer, Dick West, complained, of 'samizdat publications', did not. But perhaps it was right that these books, which purveyed unfashionable opinions and got away with them because they were supposed to be funny, should have a clandestine air about them.

It was in 1965 that I was presented with a cause after my own heart: the declaration of UDI by the Rhodesians after prolonged negotiation with our own Government had driven them into a corner, giving them no other option. I wrote a 'note' entitled 'Compelled Romantics' which explains why I became such an enthusiastic supporter of this most unfashionable cause. The Rhodesians, I explained,

> can hardly be called a romantic people. Yet their cause must surely appeal irresistibly to those like myself who instinctively support the weaker side . . . Here is a group of British people like ourselves – only more so, since they represent a simple, rather suburban attitude to life which is vanishing in our own country – with almost the whole world against them.
>
> They face the fanatical power of black nationalism; tongue-tied themselves, they face the supremely vocal, embattled Left-wing moralisers of the world, the daily propaganda which seeks to persuade us that their mild paternal rule is one of the most vicious tyrannies the world has ever seen. These simple farmers, shopkeepers, tennis-players and devotees of afternoon tea are trapped in a situation – a truly heroic role – which does not suit them and which they are only just beginning dimly to understand. The most unromantic of people, they may soon acquire the romantic dignity of all those who, though their cause seems lost to start with, resolve to stand and fight.

So unfashionable was the Rhodesian cause that my colleague Kenneth Rose, an excellent writer but somewhat given to snobbery, told me incredulously: 'You really oughtn't to support these people, Michael. They're – well, terribly common, you know. None of them has ever read a book.' I was aware of this, but did not see how it justified people recommending their black subjects to cut their throats. Among 'Hampstead thinkers', of course, there was a large element of snobbery in their fanatical loathing of the white Rhodesians. In my column, Mrs Dutt-Pauker condemned them for talking about 'afternoon tea' and 'serviettes' and saying 'pardon?' If they had read books and possessed a symphony orchestra and an opera house, the tone might have been different. This snobbish attitude was to surface again in the loathing of English intellectuals or would-be intellectuals for the white South Africans and Ulster Protestants and is a minor reason why I have always been on their side.

The Rhodesians in London, whom I met after the declaration of UDI and who often asked me to their wonderfully boring parties at Rhodesia House, were not entirely happy about their new friend. One middle-aged lady with an outsize flowery hat actually said: 'Mr Wharton, I sometimes think you must be a repressed intellectual,' clearly a term of serious reproach. But I went on supporting them through the fifteen years of their amazing and heroic struggle against terrorism and organised mendacity, whose final act I witnessed at first hand when I went to Rhodesia to write about the fraudulent election of 1980, when Mrs Thatcher's Conservative Government was forced, probably if not certainly against her own inclination, by its American overlords to betray them.

The end of white-ruled Rhodesia (it had already been renamed 'Zimbabwe-Rhodesia' in an absurd attempt to placate the international bawling for racial equality and 'a commitment to black majority rule' which temporarily elevated the pathetic Bishop Abel Muzorewa) was both tragic and farcical. 'Fair and free elections' had been promised under the auspices of Lord Soames, created 'Governor of Southern Rhodesia' for the purpose, and the two rival black terrorist groups, led by Robert Mugabe and Joshua Nkomo, had agreed to participate in these, mainly because the former, the more astute politician of the two, had been privately assured he would win. The fairness and freeness of the elections was supposed to be ensured by the presence of British observers at points where the black terrorists, who for years had been raiding the country with growing ferocity and with increasing quantities of weaponry supplied by the Communist empires, were required to assemble and give up their arms. Many but by no means all did so. The observers were supposed to prevent intimidation of the voters. Intimidation took place on an enormous scale, but when the Rhodesian officials reported this to Soames, he ignored their complaints.

It must have been odd to be a Rhodesian at that time, vaguely realising that power in your own country, the country which had been wholly created by white people and ruled by white people with at least as much justice as most countries in the world, was being mysteriously and furtively taken away from you without your being able to do anything about it. There was, to be sure, talk of a military coup. I asked General Walls, the very intelligent and efficient Commander-in-Chief of the Rhodesian Army, if he had considered this. He smiled at my romantic notion and said, perhaps implying that he had, that it could not succeed. The fate of Rhodesia had been decided, he said, when the South Africans withdrew their support; his forces could have gone on fighting indefinitely so long as the southern frontier remained open for supplies. Without that, Rhodesia could not hold out for long. There is a myth, one of those Left-wing myths like the myth of the innocence of Alger Hiss, that the 'war' in Rhodesia ended in the defeat of the white Rhodesians by the black 'Freedom Fighters'. This is not true; the Rhodesian army was never defeated in the field and the black terrorists never occupied or even entered any urban centre. The myth has now, of course, become accepted as historical fact.

The *Telegraph*'s correspondents in Salisbury (such people are admirably capable of looking after themselves) were based at Meikle's Hotel, an excellent, well-run hotel of the old-fashioned kind, and there I stayed while I carried out the week's programme they had arranged for me. There were times when I felt as I had felt on my journeys round India forty years before; but then I had been in uniform and subject, however tenuously, to army rules and regulations. Here in Rhodesia I was one of a horde of visitors: journalists, politicians, observers from all kinds of bodies from the League of Proportional Representation to the Association for the Advancement of Human Rights. Among all these people I must have been one of the very few who had any sympathy at all with the white Rhodesians as they saw their country being filched from them in the name of various hollow abstractions. Every evening officials of Lord Soames's secretariat gave press conferences at which they spouted soothing disinformation, and every evening the press turned up in great numbers to absorb it; when questions were invited they all came from journalists who were plainly dissatisfied because the Rhodesians were not being punished enough for the crime of existing.

I went to see a farm about thirty miles from Salisbury where a white farmer whose ancestors had been in Rhodesia for two generations ruled over a domain larger than many landed estates in England. There were portraits of his forebears on the walls of his large, cool bungalow; unlike most Rhodesians he had bookcases too; among the books I saw some of my own, and was sorry that I could not live up to the image of the writer he cherished. However, he and his wife (his sons were away, serving in the army) made the best of it. They led me to their paradisical garden, with lawns, beds of enormous flowers and trees decked with red and purple flowering creepers. From the shade, to complete the picture, emerged two fine yellow labradors, looking at the stranger with mild, sad eyes. What more could anybody want? And who would not fight for such a place?

This farmer, who grew mainly maize and tobacco and also had herds of cattle, showed me over his well-tended lands, defended, as all such places were, by a perimeter of electrified wire, its current now cut off for the truce. There was a simple hospital, and a school for his black workers' children. It was a Sunday, so the school was empty, and I could glance at the neatly-ranged desks, the neat exercise books with sums or spelling corrected. A group of small black girls in their Sunday best, white-socked and pigtailed, watched me curiously from a distance. In the workers' village, with its neat, one-storeyed houses, a witch-doctor did a statutory dance as we drank horrible but reputedly very intoxicating Shona beer. And all seemed prosperous, happy and contented under the iron heel of the colonialist oppressor who at that very moment, in the pages of the British press, was lashing out with his whip at his miserable starving slaves and setting his dogs on them.

Another day I went with a *Telegraph* correspondent to a press conference given by Mugabe himself, in the grounds of a capacious villa which had been put at his disposal for the election. We were made to take off our shoes for inspection before we could approach him; his men had evidently heard of the possibility of concealing sharp knives or other weapons in the toe-caps of European shoes. Then we sat in a crowd round a table where the great man presided. He made a short speech in a quiet voice about his confidence of victory, then answered questions. Many of the questioners seemed to be Canadians. They were intensely respectful. Among themselves they always referred to Mugabe as 'Bob', but when one Canadian girl, who got as near to him as possible so that she could gaze yearningly into his face, actually addressed him in this way there was a shocked silence and subsequent rebuke.

This formidable Jesuit-educated Marxist who was soon to be Prime Minister and thereafter president of the new state of 'Zimbabwe', named after mysterious ruins in the south of the country which were considered of great importance because they were the only stone buildings in Africa attributed to black builders (the current joke among the less devout was that they were polling-booths for some prehistoric 'fair and free' elections) – Mugabe, though shiny black, did not have pronounced negroid features; he had a reptilian, even saurian look, a hint of Nilotic origin. He was obviously very intelligent; what he thought of his white adorers, whose powerful combined delusions, compounded of a perverse hatred of their own kind and a genuine sympathy for those they thought oppressed, would soon bring him to power, it was impossible to say.

I retired thoughtfully to my hotel; later that evening I had dinner with my colleagues and watched a curious scene. There was a resident pianist at Meikle's, an old white man called Jack Dent, a general favourite, who must have played his piano for innumerable Rhodesians, both in the days of peace and in the days when they came on leave from the war in the bush, where they had built up a formidable spirit of cameraderie as only men who are consciously defending their own can do; now he was playing the last notes of the old order in Rhodesia. At a table not far from ours sat Lord Soames and his party of ladies and gentlemen from Government House. A large dinner consumed, he rose with his partner, all paunch and jowls, and danced to the tunes, loaded with sweet nostalgia, of wartime England: 'These Foolish Things', 'Don't Fence Me In', 'Begin the Beguine', 'You Must Remember This'. At the time we had not thought that war, with our illusory victory, was being fought to reduce our country to a cypher, to destroy our Empire and hand over the Crown Colony of Rhodesia to a gang of educated, power-seeking savages. Ponderously danced this fat, smiling politician; he danced the end of what, for all its faults (and it had fewer than most) was a country decent and just and well-managed enough; with jowls and belly quivering he danced deceit and calculated surrender of the better to the worse; the triumph of all that was false and silly in distant England. I watched him dance; and a powerful feeling of disgust welled up inside me.

I was still swallowing it down as I flew back to England (a seemingly interminable journey of thirty-six hours, owing to compound failure of air-flights, an overnight stay in Johannesburg, a long doze jammed in a narrow seat relieved by whisky and the sight of dawn creeping up the south-western edge of Crete); and next day as I wrote rapidly, and in great excitement, in my room at the *Telegraph*, an elaborate dithyramb, which somehow fell into the four movements of a symphony, for inclusion in the last columnar space that week; soon I heard the news that Mugabe had won the elections 'in a doddle', as Ian Smith himself had predicted in his irremediably 'common' parlance.

Smith was now out for good, to the concerted cheering of all the liberal thinkers of the world. No more would Janet his wife open garden fêtes for the denizens of the Rhodesian suburban paradise; no more would Desmond Lardner-Burke, a highly respectable solicitor and 'rebel' minister for internal affairs, described in the British press as 'the Himmler of Rhodesia', sign terrorists' death-warrants; no more would Rhodesia's citizen army parade with home-made weapons, or the 'crack' Selons Scouts on their swift grey horses (hated as few bodies of men had been hated since the Waffen SS, with whom they were constantly compared in the *Observer*) remorselessly pursue the terrorists in the mountains and forests; no more would Smith himself, asked by the band at some exaggeratedly old-fashioned English function if they could play his favourite tune, unhesitatingly choose an anthem of the ruefully unpretentious: 'Side by Side':

> Ain't got a barrel o' money, may look ragged and funny,
> But we're marching along, singing this song:
> Side by side.

If he had chosen something by Mozart or better still, Schoenberg, would the *Observer* have forgiven him, and Rhodesia survived?

Back in 1965, the year of UDI, Rhodesia had involved my column in its first and only libel action (though in the early days the newspaper had to pay Lady Chatterjee, widow of a Parsee lawyer, damages of £100 when I used the title 'Lady Chatterjee's Lover' for a fictitious book – but even so she was good-humoured about it). While the uproar about Rhodesia was going on in the United Nations, and that fraudulent body was discussing what measures could be taken to bring the Rhodesians to heel, a left-wing Labour MP, Lena Jeger (afterwards Lady Jeger, a life peeress) said in the House of Commons that she 'saw no objection to the presence in Rhodesia of troops of the Red Army wearing the blue berets of the United Nations'. For this I described her as 'an unconscious fifth columnist', and she immediately sued. The *Telegraph* decided to defend the case and a long drawn-out legal process began. I prepared a statement defending my remarks, describing the record of the

Red Army and its atrocities in Eastern Europe at the end of the War – which are, even now I suppose, largely unknown to people in England – and explaining the mentality of people like Mrs Jeger, who even twenty years after the war still had a vestigial admiration for Stalin and 'our gallant allies' which no revelations of the truth about them would ever entirely dispel. It was reasonable, I wrote, to describe such people as 'unconscious fifth columnists' on behalf of the Soviet Union, then our potential enemy.

Legal processes, I was now to realise, take a very long time. It was three years before a date was fixed for the hearing at the Law Courts: 21 August 1968. Our dispositions were made: I had discussed everything with the *Telegraph*'s admirable solicitor, Richard Sykes, a man so huge that I thought of him as Quinbus Flestrin, Gulliver's 'man mountain'; I was keyed up for my appearance and cross-examination, a considerable ordeal for one who has always disliked public appearances. Then, barely a week before the hearing was due, Mrs Jeger, without any explanation, suddenly dropped the case.

On 21 August, the Red Army, with contingents of the Warsaw Pact forces, invaded Czechoslovakia and ended the 'Prague Spring' of the unfortunate Mr Dubcek. I was relieved in a way, but also disappointed: in the circumstances we could hardly have failed to win. But what were we to make of Mrs Jeger's withdrawal?

That year, 1968, was the year of the Paris students' uprising, celebrated by Paul Johnson, in his romantic Leftist phase, in lyrical articles in the *New Statesman*. 'A spectre is haunting Europe – the spectre of student power', he wrote, fatuously parodying the opening words of the Communist Manifesto. There was plenty of mileage for the column here: it was only too easy to comment that the spectre which was really haunting

Europe was 'the same spectre which had haunted Europe for fifty years – the spectre of the Red Army'.

There was plenty of mileage, too, in the students' demonstrations and sit-ins in the London School of Economics; in the demonstrations in Park Lane, where a small mob tried to build a barricade – so inefficiently that it took only one policeman to remove it – and then, in its frustration, tried to invade the Bunny Club and the Hilton Hotel and set them on fire. A good example of the misunderstandings I often met was when a 'right-wing extremist', Lady Birdwood, told me how horrified she was at this behaviour; I said it was a pity they didn't succeed, thus adding puzzlement to her horror. A great demonstration against the Vietnam War in Grosvenor Square that autumn was followed by a huge procession through London which took in Fleet Street and passed the *Telegraph* building, where, to my delight, the modish horde raised banners with slogans against the 'Fascist Peter Simple'.

It was the heyday of the weird American activist Ralph Schoenman, secretary to the aged Bertrand Russell and, it was thought, organiser in his name of such ludicrous stunts as the trial for war crimes of President Johnson *in absentia*. I had a fantasy, which may have contained some truth, that Schoenman was holding Russell a prisoner in his house at Penrhyndeudraeth in North Wales, where Schoenman acted as 'works manager' of his 'peace factory'; I devised a plan for rescuing Russell by means of a parachute drop and hiding him in a place of safety in the columnar territory. Schoenman greatly resented these fancies and telephoned me several times, ordering me not to write anything about him in future without discussing it with him first. But it was not long before this most bizarre of Sixties 'fun-revolutionaries' became the subject of scandal and dropped out of public view.

While these stirring public events were going on, Kate and I, with her growing family, were having trouble in 'Chartfield', as our Putney house, swelling in fancy to a large country estate, was commonly called. The agreeable dog-loving family which had been living above us moved to the outer suburbs, while almost at the same time the Prings, the quiet and respectable middle-class couple below us, moved to the country. The Prings were succeeded by a strange married pair of disparate age and valetudinarian disposition; the top flat was occupied by a gang of stage-Australian students whose most senior member, distinguished by his coffin-shaped, rat-trap face and nasal whine, was known to the others, evidently as a mark of respect, as 'Mr S.' He was the quietest member of the gang, but that was not saying much; they often spent their nights playing a kind of Rugby with what sounded like a tin can, booming and roaring overhead so that it seemed our ceilings would come down.

We were going through a strangely cosy domestic phase at that time, sometimes retiring to bed in friendly chastity with mugs of hot chocolate or, if we had colds, hot whisky and lemon, and even reading the novels of Elizabeth Taylor aloud to each other, so the rowdy antics of the Australians were very trying. Complaints brought some alleviation; but they soon relapsed and reverted to their normal behaviour. There was poetic justice in the situation; we were now on the receiving end of the punishment we had meted out to the Uhlmans in Downshire Hill ten years before. But I do not think this irony occurred to us. Our torment ended when the Australians went too far; one evening two of them were leaning out of their window, as was their custom, and scanning the street, when Mr S. approached. 'How are yer, big prick?' one of them roared. This led to general complaints from the neighbours and threats to call the police. Perhaps realising they were not wanted, the

Australians left soon afterwards. 'Are yer glad we're going?' said Mr S., when I met them in a group in the street. I smiled but made no answer, every inch a po-faced, whingeing pom.

It was about this time that Annabel, who had been sitting opposite me in my little room for over eight years, patiently typing my column, repelling madmen on the telephone and enduring my gloomy countenance, decided to leave. She had published a novel which I could not read, though that was no reflection on her literary talent, and was going through a difficult phase in her private life, or so I judged, and wanted a change. She had been ill with glandular fever earlier that year, and had been absent from the column for three months. For a temporary replacement I naturally applied to the Utley Secretarial Agency, which supplied a delightful blonde – an attractive and intelligent girl called Jenny Dale. She was of 'genuine working-class origin', a fact reflected in what I at first thought of, in my instinctively self-defensive way, as 'pretty but blunt, plebeian features'.

Her father was a lifelong Communist; Jenny had the statutory left-wing views of the time, but she had won a scholarship which had taken her to a famous girls' public school and given her a small, rapid, breathless, upper-class way of speaking which was at variance with everything else about her. She had nice grey eyes, wore the mini-skirt, à la mode at the time, which suited her slight figure, and she had good teeth, though they were without any tendency to my preferred 'goofiness'. This was perhaps just as well, for I found her very attractive and, incorrigible, often repined at the difference in age between fifty-four and twenty-seven. She was deaf in one ear, perhaps as a result of a blow in childhood, for, as she related in a very well-written, clearly autobiographical novel she published many years afterwards, she had had a tough, motherless childhood at the mercy of a sadistic grandmother. I could never remember which was her deaf ear, but was often near to going up to her and shouting into it: 'I love you'. But I might well have chosen the wrong (or right), good ear; and what would have happened then?

When Annabel announced that she was leaving, I would have liked to secure Jenny as my permanent secretary. But she was not available, because she had got a highly-paid job with a monstrous American-Jewish bestselling novelist whose private life was disordered to the point where he had actually been accused, falsely for all I knew, of murdering his wife. So the Utley Secretarial Agency supplied another girl, a friend of Jenny who had graduated with her in English at Keele University.

She was a pleasant girl but no substitute for Jenny; nor did she seem to know much English. I was amazed to find that she had never heard either of Mrs Gamp or Mrs Grundy; when I used the word 'quisling' in the column, she asked me what it meant. In my explanation I said it was unfair to the Norwegian leader Vidkun Quisling that his name had become a synonym for traitor, and if she did not know it there might be a chance that it would drop out of common parlance. This probably did not endear me to her; nor did my rebuke, which I could not repress, when she said she thought Brigadier ('Skipper') Thompson, the admirable and dauntless Defence Correspondent of the *Telegraph*, 'inherently funny'. My mutterings about 'making fun of them that guard you while you sleep' must have seemed Blimpish as well as incomprehensible.

She left next year and with some misgivings I gave the job to Claudie Worsthorne, who thus resumed it after an absence of nine years. Our relations were difficult at times; older and more sophisticated than Annabel, and moreover, wife of Peregrine and frequenter of 'glittering' social circles to which I had no entry, she was disinclined to take the role of secretary seriously. Her English spelling was sometimes erratic; but another reason for my frequent impatience with her was a typically base one: my resentment at her superior social arrangements, at first conducted on the telephone until my obvious annoyance – or even direct veto – caused her to spend a lot of time in neighbouring vacant rooms so as to carry them on undisturbed. I then had to answer the telephone myself, sometimes finding to my chagrin that the caller wanted to invite Claudie to a party and would be awfully grateful if I would give her the message.

There was a certain element of masochistic pleasure mingled with my rage, which when I had been drinking at lunchtime sometimes discharged itself in violent scenes in which I would curse Claudie and ineffectually try to sack her. This behaviour, as well as being noted with amusement by our neighbours along the corridor, put me firmly in the wrong. As far as Claudie herself was concerned, of course, I was always in the wrong by definition; no woman, in a disagreement with a man (or, for all I know, another woman) will ever admit she is in the wrong. When her friends asked her why she put up with my ineffectual bullying, she would say in her amusing French accent, 'Poor boy, 'e cannot 'elp it' or, more charitably, 'I stay because I enjoy watching 'is creative mind at work'. She was herself 'creative' in her own way, writing such long letters in French and English that I called her 'the last of the world's letter writers'. One day, I hope, these letters of hers will be published.

As time went on we established a *modus vivendi* and grew, I think, to like as well as hate each other, the liking on my part at least gradually supplanting the hate. There was much to like about Claudie: her liveliness; her vivid gossip which sometimes seemed extravagantly malicious but was not – it was gossip for gossip's sake, an art form; her courage – she had faced danger fearlessly both in war and peace; her gift for mimicry – she could take off other members of the staff without any pretence of phonetic accuracy but presenting, by means of their physical foibles, an amazingly accurate impression of their characters. Her imitation of myself was particularly good, even better than my own; it usually consisted of speaking inaudibly into a telephone. Enjoyable, too, were her 'Claudieisms', part genuine, part contrived, as when she said of some dupe, 'So you see, 'e 'as swallowed the 'ole trick, bell, hook and stinker'. Or did I improve on that one?

In the late Sixties I began to see more of my son Nicholas, who had taken a Ph.D. at Leeds University and was doing post-graduate work there before taking a post as lecturer in philosophy at Reading. His first marriage, to the high-born Dinah Livingstone-Learmonth, a leftist poetess, who bore him two children, Tom and Zoë, had predictably collapsed. He was now in search of a second wife, presenting me with one or two candidates who, though agreeable enough, did not seem suitable. Elated by the triumph of Jewish arms in the Six-Day War and no doubt for other reasons, he had reverted to his and my original name of Nathan and although hardly more than one-eighth Jewish by blood, declared: 'I look Jewish, so I might as well *be* Jewish,' – an argument scarcely worthy of a philosopher. I was not in favour of this, though I did not, as I was at first inclined, 'cut him off with a shilling' but became reconciled to what I thought perverse eccentricity.

When he declared he was in love with a half-Jewish girl and intended to marry her, I strongly advised him against thus reinforcing the Jewish element in his prospective offspring. I met the girl, Alex; she was delightful, attractive and intelligent as well as good-natured, a fine linguist and pianist. Alas! But not, no thanks to me, alas in the event. They married and had two sons, Max and Isaac, both amiable and highly intelligent, the younger inheriting her musical talent. What is more, they have, as far as I can judge, one of the few marriages I have ever come across which seem to be genuinely happy.

Towards the end of 1968 I was idly looking through a copy of *Country Life*, one of the publications supplied to me by the bounty of the *Telegraph*, when I suddenly came across an article, illustrated by photographs, which almost brought me out of my chair and to my feet. It was about a 'threat to the Eden Valley' and described a scheme which for sheer horror I could not have invented in a nightmare. In my time at Hoff, in Westmorland, where I had lived before the War and during the first year of it, we could see, out of our front, eastward-facing windows across the valley, a wonderful prospect: the line of the North Pennines from Merton Pike and High Cup Nick in the south to Crossfell in the north. There, below the line of the hills, an entrepreneur was now planning to construct what would today be called a 'leisure park' covering acres of beautiful country centred on the woods of Flakebridge, once part of Lord Hothfield's Appleby Castle estate, but already sold off by his eccentric heir. There was to be an hotel, a casino, a marina or glorified boating lake, nature trails, a night-club, shops and all conceivable delights for the too-many. Merton Pike itself, one of the conical outliers of the main Pennine range, was to be turned into an artificial ski-run with a chairlift. Several sheep farms would be incorporated, with large sums of money offered to the farmers in compensation.

The article said that local people and national bodies like the Council for the Preservation of Rural England (it had not yet changed Preservation to the more defensive Protection) were organising protests against this plan; local opinion was divided, some councillors believing that the project 'would provide work in an area of high unemployment' (a standard parrot-cry in such cases); the Vicar of Appleby was said to be in favour, perhaps believing that the project would 'inject new life into the area' (another standard parrot-cry); Appleby shopkeepers were also said to be in favour for reasons of their own; whilst the Conservative MP for Westmorland, Mr Jopling, was non-committal.

I cared nothing for all this. If I have ever dreamed of an earthly paradise it is of the Valley of the Eden, suitably glorified, that I have dreamed. Now the landscape I had looked at daily through changing seasons with unchanging delight was in danger of defilement, indeed destruction for ever. In a state of excitement and anger I sat down to write what I felt in a 'note' of about four hundred words and put it at the head of next day's column. Within a week I had a strange, rambling letter, written in a firm, spiky hand on yellow lined foolscap paper, from a Mrs Ruth Rose who lived at Keisley House, in the very middle of the projected outrage. She told me how glad she and her husband, Major Rose, would be of any help in repelling it; she also invited me to stay at Keisley, adding, by a sure instinct, that they could not only offer me home-brewed ale but that there were half a dozen bottles of whisky, collected by a grateful public, awaiting me, stored in a grandfather clock.

Who could resist such an invitation? I accepted, but before I could make any further move, Ruth Rose herself appeared in London, on a mission to gather support from anybody she could think of. One evening, waiting for me in the 'Lodge', was a woman in her forties with wiry black hair and a lined, humorous face which had once been very good-looking and was still attractive. She was eccentrically dressed in makeshift clothes, the most remarkable part of which was an army-issue khaki pullover. She had an individual way of laughing, deep, loud but melodious. She was one of those beings who are completely themselves, without selfconsciousness, and always the same whatever class of people they are talking to. We became friends and allies at once, and would have done so, I think, even if we had not had in common the urgent cause of repelling this attack on my paradise and her home.

We went into the pub and drank a great deal of Guinness as we discussed what might be done and what influential people (she seemed to think I was one) might be enlisted in support. She told me that her husband, Jimmy Rose, had just retired from the army, that she herself was an army wife who had lived with him in many postings in the distant lands of our receding Empire – Borneo, Malaya, Burma and lastly Arabia, where he had fought in Aden and the Yemen. They had returned to Keisley, the only home they had, only a few months before. It had originally been a shooting-lodge and then a place to stay in the holidays, belonging to her father, Dr Boddy, a well-to-do physician in Middlesbrough. It was a wonderful place, she said, apart from being their home. It must be saved. I fervently agreed. She was staying that night with friends somewhere in south London and returning to the North next day. She was in an even more frenetic state than usual, she explained, because her car had just been run into from behind by a madman. But she would give me a lift wherever I wanted to go.

I could not see any evidence of damage to her car, a solid old Jaguar, the only sort of car I could imagine this delightfully forthright, vigorous and eccentric woman driving. We had a confused and hilarious meal at an Indian restaurant in Putney; I noticed that although she drank a good deal she ate hardly anything, explaining this by the fact that her false teeth did not fit. She demonstrated this. We parted after I had promised to pay a visit to Keisley 'for a top-level conference' the very next weekend. I could get a train from King's Cross. She would meet it in her car at Darlington.

I thought about the Valley of the Eden, and about this remarkable woman who lived in it, a good deal during the next week. In the Kings and Keys one evening I ran into John Chisholm, the *Telegraph*'s architectural correspondent, and told him about the threat to Keisley, with some vague idea that he might be able to help. This was only about the second time I had met this man who was to become a close friend. He was from Lancashire, Wigan-born, and spoke with the attractive accent of the area. He was a strongly-built man with a pale though healthy-looking face and the general appearance of a Baltic stevedore.

He tended to wear bright blue shirts, drawing mechanical shouts of 'Poofter!' from Weston. I soon found, on closer acquaintance, that although he claimed never to have read a book he was both intelligent and witty and that his cast of mind was not unlike my own. He was intensely musical. He was married, though uneasily, to a formidable half-Jewess from Manchester, Judith, and lived in Hampstead. When I told him about the trouble which was agitating me he undertook to do what he could to help. I arranged for him to come to Keisley; he could not come with me in the first place, he said, but promised to get there as soon as he could manage later in the weekend.

So on a dark night at the beginning of December, I found Ruth waiting for me at Darlington station with what seemed a perfectly intact Jaguar, though the story of how it had been damaged tended to recur, part of a whole saga of inter-twining stories, mainly drawn from army life, which if related by anybody else would have been boring. But I did not find this saga boring when it came from Ruth, at least not then; I was caught in a spell in which my old love for the numinous countryside of Westmorland, now powerfully revived, and my love for this curious woman seemed to be combined. She drove fast and expertly westward through Barnard Castle, where we stopped for a while by mutual consent to drink Guinness, and her loud, melodious laugh astounded the regulars in the bar; then by the Roman road across wild Stainmore into the Eden Valley. It was typical of her that nearing Keisley she took a wrong turning, leading us to open moorland where the road turned to a stony track. When we reached Keisley we had long been expected.

A flagged path leading to a strong square whitewashed house overshadowed by sycamore trees whose branches dripped big droplets on our heads; tall lighted windows with frames painted, in the Westmorland fashion, dark green; dogs barking at the door; and a great noise of people within. Major Rose, Jimmy as everyone called him, came to meet us and led us into a big, long room with log fires burning at each end. Bookcases crammed with books covered two walls up to the ceiling; Persian rugs and other trophies hung on other walls; there were sofas, armchairs, and camel saddles covered with sheepskins which served as footstools. The Major was a big, strongly-built man of about fifty, with a military moustache and a military bearing; he stood among his guests like some ancient chieftain in his hall, laughing, talking, dispensing hospitality.

The guests were of all kinds and conditions: one or two sheep-farmers and their wives and sons from neighbouring farms; another retired soldier, Brigadier Heelis from Milburn, one of a string of villages under the Pennines; Dr Delap, the doctor from Appleby; Mr Bunney, the architect from Kendal, who lived at Hwith, near Ravenstonedale, not far from Uldale, the farm where my dead elder brother had presided over his strange ménage. And all these people, in their different ways, were determined to repel the invasion by a citified fun-fair of what still remained in those days an entirely rural place, with rural thoughts and rural ways of living. I had a sense of glory and privilege because such people as these thought me a person with enough influence to help them.

The Major put an extremely large glass of whisky into my hand. 'Hope you'll stay with us as long as you like,' he said in a deep voice without accent. 'I can offer you some rough shooting. No fishing at present. A bit of rabbiting with ferrets with Tom Dargue here – hey Tom?' he gestured at a man, about his own age, with an oaken squareness and strength. I demurred feebly, explaining quite truly that as I got older I got less and less inclined to kill creatures of any kind. Not surprisingly, he looked a bit disappointed at this. 'You'll be a strange sort of guest,' he said, and for a moment I was afraid I had got myself, as with the Rhodesians and the hangers and floggers, into a misunderstanding.

But I need not have worried; we became great friends, all the more so, perhaps, for having little in common except a fondness for drinking and card-playing, a love of the country and of history and a humorous, curious turn of mind. Isn't that enough for any friendship? Beneath his military exterior and bluff manners, Jimmy had a lively, imaginative, unconventional nature. He was also, as I found, a man of infinite generosity and patience. I came in time not only to love and admire him but almost to revere him.

Some of the guests began to leave. But there must have been a dozen at the long table in the dining-room next door. Jimmy himself, who was an accomplished cook, had prepared a huge and magnificent curry. Everything in this house seemed to be on an heroic scale – the host, the guests, the food and drink, the good old Westmorland voices talking of sheep, country pursuits, neighbours' disputes, the vileness of councillors and all officials. Within was the chieftain's mead-hall; outside the lighted house a thick, starless, soundless night.

The guests had all left and my host, after giving us both several more drinks, went off to bed, taking with him his two big yellow labrador dogs, Leo, the noble-looking male, and Ready, the softer bitch (short for Ready About, a name acquired on some aquatic adventure). Ruth declared she was going to have one last drink, and so was I. So there we sat into the small hours by the log fire, this woman of extraordinary energy telling me her life history: how she had been coming to this house ever since she was a child, and had come to love it more than any other place on earth; how her three brothers had all been killed in the War, flying in the RAF; how her mad, boring sister had married a man who was a bore but not even mad; how she had taken a degree in biology at St Andrew's; how she had been a despatch-rider in the Blitz and later joined the Wrens; how she had married Jimmy, probably the only man in the British Army who had been, in the course of his career, both a sergeant-major and a major; how he had fought in the North African Desert, been captured by the Germans and escaped; how he had served in the Far East, where, when it was possible, she had served with him; how she had taught English to Malayans and later to Arabs in Aden; how she had lost her baby at five months and was now childless; how they had come back to Keisley to live, and how it was now threatened.

At four o'clock I staggered to bed and woke the next morning to find that the Major, this man of iron, was planning to drive up the track beside the ravine of High Cup Nick in his Land

Rover, with a neighbour, a former comrade in the army with the strange name of Derek Import. For what purpose I never discovered. Would I like to come? I was exhausted and had a considerable hangover. But after my failure with the country sports I felt I had to accept his suggestion as a chance of rehabilitating myself. Was it a test of my character? I never discovered, though I suspect it may have been. In the event I passed, though only just. After driving in the Land Rover up the stony, deeply trenched, pot-holed and in places almost vertical track, wrenched this way and that, we got out and began to walk, well above the cloud-line, across the moor towards the upper end of the famous geological prodigy, High Cup Nick.

As I did my best not to fall behind in my heavy black Crombie overcoat, Jimmy, who during the summer months, I learned, worked as a warden of a nature reserve at Ravenglass on the coast of Cumberland, pointed out a buzzard, a peregrine falcon and other notable birds. I asked if there were any dotterel, rare birds I had introduced as comic creatures in parodic nature notes in my column. He gave me a keen look and said there was a nest of dotterel at the top of Crossfell and he would be delighted to take me there. As Crossfell, the highest hill in the Pennines, was about ten miles away and at least a thousand feet higher than our present position, I declined.

Back at Keisley, we found Ruth busy organising the Resistance, as I was beginning to think of it. She had got over Mr Howard of Greystoke, an important landowner in Cumberland, to discuss matters; since he had had to cope single-handedly with, and repel, a similar project led by the same entrepreneur not long before, though on a smaller scale, he was most sympathetic and helpful. So, in their different way, were the local farmers we canvassed later that day. Many of them could expect large sums in return for the use of their land; some, whose land would be bought if the scheme went through, could expect to become rich, enabling them to retire and live in Morecambe for the rest of their lives (these were the days when the newly affluent were not yet buying properties on the Costa del Sol). Their angry rejection of these prospects was heartening to hear. So was the reaction of some of the younger farmers who gathered at Keisley in the evening.

It was the time when Welsh Nationalists were blowing up pipelines as a protest against 'England's theft of Welsh water'. These young Westmorland men spoke, not altogether jokingly, of blowing up the fun-fair installations if they ever got built. 'If t'Welsh can do it, we can do it – and better,' said one. My own pleasure at this remark warned me against giving way to fantasy. I would have to be entirely serious about this campaign if I were to help. And yet both Welsh Nationalists and Westmorland farmers were in rebellion equally against the 'modern world' and the newly-emerging attitudes which measured everything in terms of money, the quantifying cost accountancy which both political parties stood for. Labour Ministers were already telling small farmers like these that they were fools to work their guts out as their forebears had done when they could make more money and have an easier life by 'diversifying' into the bed-and-breakfast trade and selling ice-cream and souvenirs to tourists.

Later on Conservative Ministers were to tell them the same thing more persuasively and seductively, and with greater success. It is not easy for a poor man to stand against the times. Twenty years later the odds against the small farmers and their 'way of life' – a term which had become disgusting because it was favoured and constantly used by the very people who were doing their best to destroy it: the executives of the hideous 'tourist industry' – were to become overwhelming. Yet these small farmers, in so far as they still survive, are almost the last truly independent-minded people remaining in this country. What sort of a country will England be when there are no such people left in it? It was reflections like these, as well as my desire to preserve a place I loved and stop this beautiful part of England from being changed into something other and worse, which drove me to devote so much time and energy to this campaign.

All that afternoon Keisley was at cloud level and it was impossible to see more than a hundred yards or so from the front windows which looked across the valley. But towards nightfall the cloud lifted and I could see beyond Appleby and Hoff to the hills which concealed the small tributaries of the Eden – Lyvennet, Leven and Lowther – to the Lake District hills in the west and in the south the Howgill Fells and Wild Boar Fell where I had wandered idly and usually alone during my vacations at Uldale. I was looking out from the place I had looked at daily during my life with my first wife and child in our cottage at Hoff before the War. This was a strange sensation, as if the self of today stared at the self of thirty years before, and that lost self stared back.

Next day we were to meet John Chisholm off the London train at Oxenholme Junction, on the Kendal road from Appleby. But first I was to go to Appleby Castle at the invitation of the present proprietor, who was a reader of the *Telegraph* and, Ruth implausibly maintained, an admirer of my column. I had always wanted to visit the Castle, indeed I had always had the ambition of owning it. It was a real castle, with its main gate at the top of Boroughgate, the main street of Appleby, balancing, in a paradigm of Church and State, the parish church of St Lawrence at the bottom. In my time at Hoff, Lord Hothfield had lived there with his estates still intact, including the now endangered pheasant-woods at Flakebridge; he was a figure of legend:

tall, stately and as well as being lord of the castle, he was the perpetual Mayor of Appleby itself, towering, as was only right, over the puny councillors at the mayoral procession during the annual assizes. Now many of these councillors were in favour of the Flakebridge Horror; Lord Hothfield was dead and his eccentric son had sold the estate and, it was said, converted to Islam, and perhaps worse, worked as a casual labourer.

The present proprietor was a Mr Coney (it was odd how these rabbit names kept cropping up – there was Mr Bunney the architect, and two of the local farmers were called Warren and Burrows). He was a large, affable man, with a leg in plaster from having lately fallen down the stairs; he had made a lot of money from the West African trade and had been captain of Southport Golf Club, a distinction which did not impress me as much as it evidently should have done. Placing in my hand a very large gin-and-tonic which he took from a trolley that a white-gloved servant had wheeled into the enormous drawing-room, he himself took one of the same dimensions and showed me round his tapestried halls, bidding me look out of the windows at the swimming-pool he had lately installed in the courtyard and then, turning to the interior, at the elaborate new electric lift which brought up food from the vast underground kitchens to the vast mahogany and crystal-infested dining-room. He led the way back to the drawing-room, handing me another even larger gin-and-tonic and taking one himself.

This fulfilment of my old dream was not turning out quite as I had expected. Perhaps sensing my slight disappointment, he asked if I would like to have a look at the tower, the old Norman keep, by far the oldest remaining part of the house. He handed me a huge, ancient iron key and another large gin-and-tonic, not forgetting to take one himself. With difficulty I unlocked the door of the tower, which stood at some distance from the eighteenth-century range where we had been, and, balancing my drink as best I could, made the perilous ascent of the dilapidated staircase, emerging at the top to look out over broken battlements towards the little ancient town in whose pubs I had sat drinking beer so many years before, playing dominoes with anonymous men or meditating alone on time and chance.

In my altered circumstances I meditated on them again, and with good reason, before making the even more perilous descent. The large gin-and-tonic Mr Coney handed me in exchange for the key and my empty glass was just what I needed. Ruth, who had been about some business in the town, was already chatting away to him in her enviably easy way and was also holding a large gin and tonic. I had the impression that both she and Mr Coney had had at least one of these each while I was up the tower.

Taking leave of Mr Coney, whose hand was already moving towards the trolley, we drove out of Appleby on the road I knew so well, past the New Inn at Hoff, scene of so many pleasant evenings thirty years before (it would have been foolish to stop there, even though it did not seem greatly altered from those days); past the end of the lane which led to our old cottage, still rough, stony and apparently unchanged (I resisted another foolish impulse) and through the woods to the limestone-flagged uplands already beginning to be plundered for the rockeries of Surrey. Ruth had an alarming way of driving rather too fast in the middle of the road, talking incessantly and sometimes with only one hand, or none, on the wheel. When I asked her why she did this she said it was because it was easier to see traffic coming in the opposite direction if you drove in the middle of the road.

We reached Oxenholme Junction a few minutes before John

Chisholm's train was due. So we had more drinks in the neighbouring pub, emerging to find the train had already come and
gone. We peered this way and that and eventually saw his blue-
shirted figure, wearing a formal suit and carrying an architect's
portfolio, walking in the wrong direction and looking remarkably
out of place in the grey Westmorland village street. He and Ruth
immediately got on well. Although the pub was just closing, she
persuaded the bewildered landlord to give us more drinks by
saying we were two VIPs who had just got off the train from
London.

We were to call on Mr Bunney the architect at the house
which he had built himself, Hwith, in wild country near Ravenstonedale. It was difficult to find, and my whistled inquiries for
Hwith had Ruth in fits of laughter. We were still laughing,
since I for one was decidedly drunk, when we found the quiet,
serious Mr Bunney in his house and persuaded him to write a
statement for the public enquiry. He was just as angry about
the Flakebridge project as we were (he was very active in what
would now be called conservation and as a Friend of the Lake
District) and took very little persuading; I borrowed his typewriter and typed his statement on the spot. He also said he
would write a letter to *The Times*.

It was dark when we reached Keisley. Brigadier Heelis had
arrived with others for drinks in this house of plenty. John, who
had an instinct for outrage, caused a sensation by saying he was
a pacifist and had been a conscientious objector during the
period of National Service. Jimmy playfully threatened to expel
him from the house. The Brigadier put him on several charges:
(1) being improperly dressed; (2) speaking to Ruth with a cigarette in his mouth; (3) dumb insolence; (4) ordinary insolence.
To my embarrassment, Ruth said I had held the rank of
lieutenant-colonel during the War. I admitted this, but

explained to the Brigadier that I had not been a 'proper lieutenant-colonel', but only on the General Staff. This caused a good deal of amusement, as the Brigadier himself had reached that rank only as a staff officer.

More guests arrived: Brian Doe, an Arabic scholar at Cambridge and an authority on the archaeology of South Arabia, who had served with Jimmy in Aden; Tom Dargue the man of oak and his son Edwin the shepherd, a younger version of himself; the Harker brothers and their wives, sheep-farmers from Merton, famous for their silver cup-winning Swaledale tups, and other farmers who had 'heafs', that is, grazing rights for certain numbers of sheep, on the common land where the projected ski-run would be. Another evening of serious drinking was under way. Tom Dargue offered to show John, a fairly hefty man much younger than himself, the art of wrestling, Cumberland and Westmorland style. This involves the two antagonists putting their arms round each other and staying like that for a very long time until one of them gets a minute momentary advantage in posture. But it was no more than thirty seconds before John was on the carpet. Later he challenged one of the Harker wives, a bold, good-looking blonde woman of thirty, to a fall. He was on the carpet in twenty seconds, amid wild rustic cheering. But Ruth, who had, unexpectedly, a marked puritanical streak, was also a delightful snob and easily offended by what she believed to be breaches of protocol, later rebuked him for this.

I left for London next day, leaving John, already a firm friend of the house, behind to do further work for the cause. I was in a state of great excitement; I had fallen in love with Keisley and everybody and everything in it and about it. I wrote another 'note' about this threatened paradise. When John returned that week, he made this 'threat to the environment', as it would now be called, the subject of his weekly article. A correspondence was starting about it in *The Times*, and the *Telegraph* itself printed a letter from Mr Bunney. In the Kings and Keys John and I began to converse in the accent of Westmorland – I from what I remembered of this way of talking from my previous life there, he from an astonishing facility for picking up English accents, even this unusual and rather difficult one. This private joke, for once, baffled Weston, and after a few shouts of 'Poofters!', and 'If you want to talk in that stupid Welsh accent, go somewhere else!' he gave up.

As in all such cases, the people in the Appleby neighbourhood who were in favour of the scheme argued that it was what the local people wanted and that it was opposed only by a handful of the 'selfish middle class'. Appleby was technically in a 'depressed area' of 'high unemployment'. I had seldom been in an area which seemed less depressed. It was, however, necessary to counter these misleading arguments.

Ruth suggested that Tom Dargue, Edward Harker and two or three others whose land was threatened should write a short letter to *The Times*, submitting it to me before sending it there. They duly produced one. It was movingly written but in the sort of unnatural, 'educated' style they thought suitable for such a letter. But when I had finished with it, it was in simple, direct language and really sounded like the voice of down-to-earth, honest Englishmen. I have seldom been so pleased with anything I have written as the letter from the sheep-farmers of the North Pennines which duly appeared in *The Times*. I had given them better words than their own and expressed their real thoughts as they could not express them for themselves.

I felt, in a strange way, that what I was defending in them was what I was defending in the Rhodesians – their admirable determination to stand up for what they had got against those who wanted, for whatever reason, whether profit or abstract theories of equality, to take it from them. Add to that the new friends this cause had brought me – not only Ruth and Jimmy Rose, but also John Chisholm, that talented, funny, lively yet melancholy man – and the glimpse of an enchanted life in Keisley – and it was no wonder I was lifted for a time out of my customary miasma of boredom into a euphoric state, like being in love. The *Telegraph* people, however, began to grumble about 'the Westmorland lobby' which was filling the paper; John was ticked off and told that his job was to write about architecture, not scenery or the lives of reactionary sheep farmers.

The public enquiry called by the Ministry of Works, as it then was ('the environment' had only just been invented as fancy jargon for what I preferred to call 'the Creation', and there was no Ministry yet in charge of it) was duly held in Appleby. I could not attend myself, as I was occupied with my column, and in any case could hardly have given evidence to the effect that I just wanted to stop a beautiful part of England which I was particularly fond of from being destroyed. But Ruth and several farmers and outside experts spoke against the scheme. According to John, Ruth made a particularly good impression on the inspector from the Ministry. So now all we could do was wait for the Minister's decision. We had good hopes of Greenwood, one of the more civilised Labour Ministers.

But there was some danger that the scheme would go through on the grounds that the site was not part of the Lake District National Park. Had it been, of course, there would have been no question of allowing such a development. Yet the fate of the Lake District has not been less tragic because of its favoured status. It has escaped serious disfigurement but suffered intensive planning which has not saved it from being overwhelmed with visitors and has imposed the additional blight of tasteful schemes of 'interpretative' and 'educational facilities', turning it into a 'museum of scenery'. It is no longer a place which anyone who knew it before this fate overtook it would wish to visit. But at least it has done a service to the Eden Valley by attracting hordes of people who might otherwise have turned their attention to the less spectacular scenery next door. The 'tourist industry', now supplemented by the 'heritage industry', is perpetually seeking new places to exploit. The Eden Valley is now in greater danger than ever.

During the period of waiting, John Chisholm and I made several visits to Keisley. There was an excellent train which left St Pancras at about eight o'clock in the morning and proceeded slowly through the Midlands to the North by way of Sheffield, Nottingham, Leeds and Settle to arrive at Appleby at about three o'clock in the afternoon. This meant that we could start having breakfast in the restaurant car as soon as the train left St Pancras and go on having breakfast until it merged into lunch, so that we were pleasantly drunk by the time we arrived. Or we would vary this by taking the Glasgow train from Euston, enjoying a similar session, with different scenery, until we arrived at Penrith in the afternoon, when Ruth would meet us in her still mysteriously functioning Jaguar.

These journeys were often very entertaining, offering insight into the workings of the higher échelons of British Rail. On one such journey we noticed that, as we approached Preston, the stewards were getting themselves into an unusual state of readiness, dusting down a certain table, obsessively arranging and rearranging the cutlery and side-plates and even placing a statutory vase of railway flowers on it. At Preston they welcomed aboard, with many a nod, wink and antic gesture, a cheerful, rubicund man who looked as if he had already lunched well but was not averse to having a second luncheon. Relieving him of his briefcase and furled umbrella, the head steward ushered him to his seat, unfolded his napkin, placed before him a large glass of brandy and ginger ale (or 'B.G.A.') and took his order. He got through the soup satisfactorily but when the entrée was placed before him his head fell forward onto it and he remained there, breathing heavily and producing rather beautiful fluted patterns in the mashed potatoes. 'It's the district manager,' the steward explained. 'Is he always like this?' 'Yes, sir, always. We'll have a job getting him out at Glasgow, I can tell you.'

Kate was inclined to be scornful about my infatuation with Keisley and its inhabitants. She had met Ruth on one of her visits to London but was not entertained by her tales of lost teeth and damaged Jaguars. Nor had Ruth's visit to the Kings and Keys been a great success. As she insisted on wearing her khaki pullover and other military memorabilia, Stephen Daneff maintained she was a thought-form I had projected (was there some truth in this?) while Weston, I could see, was trying hard to think of some way of insulting her. He eventually gave up in disgust and retired to the far end of the bar, from which his croaking roar could be heard for the rest of the evening. But Ruth made a good impression on the only genuine old soldier present, Mac the commissionaire, a man of great charm who habitually got so drunk that in winter he often spent the night wrapped round one of the boilers in the basement below the rolling presses.

In the spring, after Jimmy had left Keisley for his nature reserve on the Cumberland coast, I persuaded Kate to visit Keisley and bring her two children, Vicki, now aged six, and Kit, aged three. John Chisholm, his wife Judith and their two children, both boys and a bit older than Kate's, were also there. I have never stayed at Keisley without enjoying it. Kate, however, soon decided, and said, that it was 'not her scene'. She had come up against a woman who liked to be the centre of attention just as much as she did, and although there were no disagreeable episodes, we were continually on the verge of one.

The children all slept in an improvised dormitory in a big room over the old stable, where Vicki, who had a good deal of her mother's leadership qualities (sometimes called 'bossiness') soon established her domination. On the first morning she dared Kit to release the two beautiful, fierce white ferrets which lived in a cage under the dormitory, and only one of them was recaptured. Some of the guinea-fowl were reported missing. Ruth had arranged for the girls from the nearby farm along the fellside to bring some ponies for the children to ride, but Vicki, already a promising horsewoman, was disappointed with hers, a mild beast with a tendency to go to sleep standing up in a corner of the paddock, unresponsive to her wild shouts. John did his best to help by mounting another pony and immediately sliding off under its belly.

Ruth, who for all her unconventionality held to strict rules of behaviour as an army wife, did not like Kate's bad language, fairly usual among our acquaintance in London, and liked Vicki's language, which was almost as bad, even less. As for Kit, he was only just beginning to develop his talent for objurgation. After a few days at Keisley Kate cut her visit short and left with the two children, driving stylishly away in her new white convertible. When I got back to London, I found she had jaundice and so was in low spirits, angry, too, that she would be confined to the house for several weeks. It was the beginning of the end of our curious ménage and of the 'horror comic'.

One day news came from Keisley that the Minister had turned down the Flakebridge plan. Keisley was saved; John and

I, after an evening of inebriation in the Kings and Keys under Weston's scornful eye and with some sarcastic comment from the *Telegraph*'s features editor ('Can we really hope for the winding up of the Appleby Lobby?') went to stay at the beloved place, now liberated from the threat of destruction. We all agreed that for once we must be grateful that we had a Labour Government and a civilised minister in charge of planning. There is not much doubt that a so-called 'Conservative' Government, keen on profit, the tourist industry and thrusting, dynamic businessmen, would have been more likely to approve the plan. There is not much doubt, either, that this odious project will be put forward again, this time, perhaps, by a more dynamic and thrusting entrepreneur with more money behind him; and who can say what will happen then?

Meanwhile Keisley was saved. We could look out every day over the unsullied woods and fields rolling down to the Eden, with the lost country round Hoff beyond it, rising to the distant fells and the long line of High Street on the far side of Haweswater. For me this is the finest panorama in England. I would not like to count up the number of hours – it would probably run into weeks – I have sat on fine days on the narrow flagged terrace in front of Keisley employed mainly in looking at this vista, either alone or with John, Ruth and other friends. I have sat there through all seasons, even with snow on the ground and muffled in my good black Crombie greatcoat, watching the changing light, the flight of birds, noting the occasional car on the lane beyond the paddock which Jimmy called 'the Keisley motorway', and sinking into a mystic trance to which the abundant drink available at all times may have contributed something but not all. If anything is imprinted on my memory, perhaps to present itself at the moment of death – or even afterwards – it must be this well-beloved scene.

In the summer, when Ruth joined Jimmy on his nature reserve for short periods, I sometimes visited them there, finding a whole new body of myth which insistently demanded to be turned into fiction. Some of it found its way by the back door into my column. I made copious notes, too, and wrote innumerable beginnings of 'the novel' I had been trying to write for most of my life, seldom reaching more than one or two thousand words before running into the sand. During the six months he worked as warden of the reserve, Jimmy lived in a well-designed caravan, large enough for us to fit into for a prolonged session of serious drinking during rainy weather. He must have been alone there for weeks on end. But he was one of those men who can cope perfectly well with solitude. As for the hardship of a cramped life with monotonous meals he cooked in a caravan which in windy weather rocked like a ship at sea, what was that for a man who had seen service in desert and jungle and, escaping from a prison camp, had killed German guards with his own hands? He had the run of the sand-dunes, with their vipers, natterjack toads and rare butterflies; he had the great flocks of migratory birds to observe and, as part of his duties, to report on for the distant bureaucracy of the National Conservation Council or some such body; and he had the wide sweep of sand by the sea-shore to walk along, from which in clear weather the Isle of Man could be seen, a seemingly enchanted island where, perhaps wisely, I have never yet set foot.

Spring at Keisley; summer; autumn; New Year, when once we were snowbound for several days – an experience which, if there is plenty of time, food and drink and good company, everyone should have at least once in a lifetime: so many sequences of days run together. At the end of August we always went to Dufton, the nearest village, for the annual Show –

jocularly known as 'the Royal Fellside' – where for several years Jimmy was, as the saying goes, a popular President. There were sheep-dog trials, groups of sheep and cattle in their pens – John and I had a plan to buy a noble Swaledale tup with curved horns and keep it in Fleet Street – and numerous tents for the vegetable and flower competitions as well as the arts of cookery ('best three ginger biscuits', 'best group of carrots') and for writing, drawing and photography. A magnificent photograph taken by John, which showed the view from Keisley through a pint glass of Jimmy's home brew, magically suffused with the golden light of autumn, was never exhibited; it would certainly have won first prize as one of the great photographs of all time.

And in this place, that broad field between the Pennines and the lower valley, there was not a single thing which was not wholly of Westmorland and England. It was the quintessence of what I wrote for, though well aware I wrote in vain. All this which had endured so long and was now for the time being reprieved, was yet condemned to death. It was some consolation to know that the megalopolitan horror which would succeed it – within a few years it was beginning to creep unmistakably in – was itself, like everything on earth, under sentence of death.

Through all those years Ruth had gradually grown more and more eccentric. Eccentric she had been when I first met her, but eccentric in a lively and attractive way. Now it was as though her hold on life began to fail. She had put all her vital force, which must have been immense when she was young, into the task of saving Keisley; now, that task accomplished, it seemed to drain away. She drank more; became repetitive in her conversation; became vague and unreliable. She had always been unpunctual; now she began to carry unpunctuality to the point of lunacy. One summer evening, when Jimmy was away on his reserve, Mr Bunney, the architect of Hwith, who had done such good work for the great campaign, invited Ruth, John and myself, as well as Major Doe the Arabist, who was also staying at Keisley, to a dinner-party at his house. Owing to several long telephone conversations, her inability to find the right clothes, some necessary preliminary drinks and various other reasons, Ruth, who was to drive us in her Jaguar, was ready to leave only at about the time we were expected to arrive. Since the journey would take about forty minutes, we were already late. We had not gone more than a few miles before we met some farmers on the road. Ruth felt she had to talk to them. She talked for about twenty minutes. A few miles further on the car ran out of petrol. So in the end we were more than two and a half hours late for Mr Bunney's dinner-party. He was not pleased.

Another time, in the winter, Ruth proposed that she drive John and myself over to Longsleddale to see the Lunesdale Hunt. She had promised to attend the meet. But what with one thing and another, it was one o'clock before we left Keisley. Our route lay near the Shap Wells Hotel, a place of which I had always been fond, partly because of its singular situation in a hollow below the Shap granite works, partly because of the oddity of finding what looked just like a railway hotel in such a remote place, and partly because during the war it had been the administrative centre of a German officers' prison camp whose Commandant had been billeted at our cottage at Hoff in the winter of 1940 while I was away doing my primary military training at Topsham Barracks, Exeter. I was unwise enough to tell Ruth all this and we had to stop there for a drink. We had several drinks; then Ruth took it into her head to ask for a glass of the mineral water which had been the reason for the attempt, which came to nothing, to establish a spa there. It was obvious that nobody had asked for this mineral water for a very long time, perhaps not within living memory. But Ruth had to have it, and after a long, rambling conversation about the history of the Spa, she got her glass of water, and plain ordinary water was what it probably was. Dusk was falling as we reached the head of Longsleddale; hounds had just killed and the hunt was over.

This sort of rambling behaviour was not to everybody's taste. Gradually Ruth's friends began to fall away. The big room at Keisley, which had made such a deep impression on me on my first visit, began to be empty of guests. And Ruth, though she talked as much as ever, seemed to be losing heart. She began to fall ill, though of no definable illness, and, more and more, to take to her bed, on which the two labrador dogs took to sleeping at all times, growing fat and heavy as she grew thin and pale. It was sad to see this woman, once so full of life and energy, take on the rôle of confirmed valetudinarian. When we took her food on a tray, she did not eat it, but left it for the dogs, who thus grew fatter than ever. She had the doctor from Appleby to see her. He prescribed some treatment, but Ruth, convinced it was the wrong treatment, told him and others that he did not know his business. Thus she lost another friend and, when she absurdly threatened to report him to the General Medical Council, gained an enemy. She sought more doctors, only to discard them. After a time, it seemed that all the doctors between Penrith and Kirkby Stephen had become characters in this valetudinarian saga. Ruth was able to see the humour in this, but that did not help her to bring it to a conclusion. She had lost the will to live, and there seemed to be nothing we could do to help her.

The neighbouring farmer's young wife, a perfect woman of a breed almost extinct, looked after Ruth's immediate needs.

But when Jimmy came over from his work on the reserve all the responsibility fell to him. Never had this great-hearted man seemed more admirable than now, when as well as running the day-to-day affairs of the house and maintaining good relations with his neighbours he became both cook and nurse to a wife whose slow, inexorable decline must have filled him with sorrow and gloom and sometimes with impatience. But I never heard him utter a single word of complaint. 'She's all I've got!' he would say ruefully, as he sawed logs, or carried coals or cooked one of his magnificent curries or took up books she asked for to her bedroom. I do not think she read many of them, not even Burton's *Anatomy of Melancholy*, which she asked me to get her. Sometimes, when I was there, she would come downstairs for a while and drink a terrible concoction of brandy and Cyprus sherry which must have gone ill with the multifarious pills she was taking on the prescriptions of several different doctors.

The coal-black hair she had inherited from her Welsh ancestors, including the genius and false bard Iolo Morgannwg (she hated the Welsh anyhow) turned grey; her cheeks hollowed and the bones of her finely-structured skull protruded. Death was unmistakably hovering. She suffered, Jimmy told me, a slight stroke which confined her permanently to bed. And then, one morning in December, twelve years almost to the day after my first visit to Keisley, I was in my room at the office when the telephone rang and Claudie answered it. I lifted my own telephone at once and knew from Jimmy's broken voice that it was over. Claudie looked at me enquiringly. She had often shown curiosity about my eccentric woman caller with the distinctive laugh. 'You won't be getting calls from Ruth Rose any more,' I said.

7
Blank Misgivings

It was time for me to leave Putney – or Chartfield, as we called our establishment, giving it, as part of that 'infamous war on reality' in which both Kate and I were such strenuous warriors, the status of a country estate, with all the longed-for splendours that went with it – the cedared lawns, terraces, walled gardens, avenues, lakes, a noble park and a home farm, with a staff of dozens of servants to run it from Venables the butler and Mrs Brewer the housekeeper – this one borrowed from Kate's own mythologised childhood home at Mountbeacon, near Bath – to the humblest groom or gardener's boy. I had a place to go to, a small flat high up in Prince of Wales Mansions, in Prince of Wales Drive in Battersea. There was no make-believe about this flat, though it overlooked Battersea Park which, from the front window, I could imagine was my own property. Prince of Wales Drive is one of those London streets, like certain streets in Chelsea, Oakley Street or Redcliffe Gardens, of which it is said that everybody has lived there at one period of his life and some people twice, 'once on the way up and once on the way down'.

It had taken me something like twelve years to prise myself away from Putney, and the actual leaving, which took place in September 1971, was not easy. Jane had left school and was studying at Bristol University, living at Bristol for part of her vacations and otherwise doing odd jobs. One of these summer jobs involved looking after an amazing collection of delinquent children from Glasgow at a gloomy, mock-Gothic Victorian castle in Galloway. It was managed by a strange tartan-clad dwarf and his tall wife, figures who were later to appear quite often in my dreams. Invited to visit them with Jane when I was in the neighbourhood, I suffered an affliction to which I am occasionally prone – uncertainty about my own identity and inability to think of anything to say or, when addressed, to answer. This may have been one among many of the painful experiences which later led Jane towards the study and practice of psycho-analysis.

I had nothing, in principle, to detain me in Putney except old habits, habitual inanition, a settled belief that any change must be for the worse, a residual attachment to Kate and a fondness for her children, particularly Vicki, who was now nine years old, a remarkably lively and attractive child, with a mind open to wonders of every kind, from the naming of the stars to the observation of butterflies: these were particularly plentiful that fine late summer, when I carefully released a magnificent peacock trapped in the nursery window. Vicki had the intense love of animals which a child of her age should have; she kept white rats in the cellar, to Kate's alarm, and once nursed a pigeon with a broken wing down there among the waste paper and bottles, releasing it when healed to almost certain death from a prowling cat or the wheels of some heedless motorist. But she had the right instinct not to grieve too much.

I had bought the essential furniture and household necessities for the flat. But it was a melancholy place in which to be alone, which out of necessity I often was, in the period before I could get a divorce and a dispensation from the Catholic Church to marry. The procedure for securing this was curious in the extreme. Since Kate was a Catholic by birth, however lapsed, the Church regarded my marriage to her as null and void because of my first marriage, dissolved in 1947; it was only this marriage that the Church was concerned with. To make *that* null and void it was necessary to show that it had not been a marriage at all, and since there was a child of the union, my son Nicholas, this could only be on the grounds that I had not been in a state of mind at the time which made me capable of marrying. In other words, I had to have been so irresponsible as to be barmy. I needed two witnesses who had known me at the time, as well as my first wife, to prove this to the satisfaction of the Church. I chose Con FitzGibbon, now living in Ireland, and Eithne Kaiser, formerly Wilkins, who with her husband Ernst had returned to England from Rome and was lecturing in German Literature at Reading University. On their arrival in England they had not unnaturally asked for the return of their borrowed furniture. This set off a truly comical set-piece explosion of moral indignation in Kate and a new source of masochistic feeling in me: I had to give back my desk to them. So all were satisfied.

Con and Eithne composed moving statements testifying to my disturbed state of mind in the late Thirties, and in due course, after I had been interviewed by several priests, the Church, on the authority of the Vatican itself, declared my first marriage dissolved, leaving me free to marry, if I wished, in a Catholic church. Surprised at this outcome, I asked the priest who had been dealing with the case, a pale, ill-looking man attached to Westminster Cathedral, whether all non-Catholic marriages like my own first marriage, where neither party had been a Catholic, were regarded as valid by the Church, and therefore a bar to any subsequent marriage. Yes, he said, they were. I could not resist asking what happened, say, if a Muslim who had divorced four wives wished to marry a Catholic girl. Did only his senior wife count? And would a Nazi pagan marriage, solemnised by the mingling of blood and leaping through a bale-fire, be regarded as legitimate? Wisely, he merely smiled a wan smile.

I had found a number of new friends in Fleet Street, notably the journalist and writer Dick West, a man of admirably reactionary opinions who liked to lead a wandering life in dangerous places like Vietnam and Central America; Christine Verity, a very amusing and intelligent blonde Yorkshire girl who because she had a Cambridge degree in Law was regarded with some awe by the ordinary run of semi-literate journalists; and Celia Haddon, a journalist, animal-lover and perfect woman who later married the fortunate Ronnie Payne; I spent a lot of weekends with these new friends and others at Ron Hall's electronic house in Hampstead, which I had named 'Klingsor's Magic Garden' because it had glass doors at the back, operated by a switch in a central keyboard and opening to reveal, beyond a terrace so narrow as to be two-dimensional, a mysterious, illusionary wilderness.

But Ron had no other resemblance to Klingsor. With his wife Ruth, a fine harpsichord-player who was also good at my own favourite Yorkshire charades ('She should never have had that clock, Edie' – 'No, and if you'd been half a man you'd have seen I had my rights' – 'He was hardly cold in his grave when Alice was in there, picking up whatever she could get', etc, etc), he gave a famous New Year Party every year at which all or most were welcome. So much so that even after Ruth had died untimely and he ceased to give the party, little groups of people used to turn up at his house on New Year's Eve and, finding no party, hang about incredulously. Perhaps they still do.

Apart from such diversions I led a life of routine boredom while in London, taking a masochistic pleasure in keeping to a strict timetable which favoured efficient work at the *Telegraph* office. Roused by my alarm-clock at 7.30 a.m., I sprang out of bed immediately, groaned a few times, took a bath and, deferring shaving, prepared an unvarying breakfast of fresh orange juice, cereal including bran, bacon and egg, toast and tea. I then shaved and dressed, walked down six flights of stairs to the street and then two hundred yards to the No. 137 bus stop in Queenstown Road; on this bus, often delayed, I travelled to Sloane Square, where I bought a copy of the *Telegraph* and took a No. 11 bus to Fleet Street, where I arrived by 11 o'clock. I found these very slow bus journeys conducive to composition, and on a good day would have large parts of the day's column already written round the edges of the paper even before I got to the office. The grotesque quarrels between passengers and conductor which often occurred during these journeys sometimes provided the germ of a 'note', as well as more writing time when, as might easily happen, they brought the bus to an indefinite standstill.

By half past two I would usually have almost all the column ready for Claudie's typing. I would then go to the Kings and Keys and drink two large brandies and ginger ale with my luncheon, invariably one thick corned beef sandwich without mustard. I seldom spoke to anybody during this performance, though various journalists, mostly very boring ones, occasionally came and stood beside me, talking of whatever interested them without seeming to require me to take much notice. Kate, perpetually active in her freelance work, occasionally dropped in, and we had more drinks in a friendly spirit, talking of old times and random fancies; sometimes we went on drinking at a neighbouring restaurant which Kate, in her enterprising way, seemed to have taken over so completely that some people believed she owned it. On these occasions I was apt to get back perilously late to the office. Claudie, who was highly intuitive, invariably guessed or rather knew the reason.

If I was not otherwise occupied in the evening I returned to Battersea by a different combination of buses, such as a No. 9 to Hyde Park Corner, then a No. 137 the rest of the way.

Sometimes, on my way home I would call at the launderette in Pimlico Road to collect the laundry I had left that morning. Here, as often as not, I found one or two odd socks missing. Then the kindly manageress would bring out the Great Bag of Socks, a collection, continually augmented, of all the odd socks which had turned up in the machines since time immemorial. Great was our satisfaction, even triumph, when we found a sock to match a bereft companion in my own day's wash. I grew quite fond of this homely ritual (another subject for Spitzweg). Once, when I called just as the shop was closing, I found the manageress playing Snap with her two small children, and was glad to take a hand. This might have been the start of an unusual friendship. It was my loss that it was not.

Back in the flat I scared away, in vain, the pigeons which infested the back balcony with their disgusting detritus. I took nothing more to drink except iced lime juice and water and set about preparing my evening meal. This invariably consisted of grilled fish fingers, normally five, mashed potatoes and frozen peas, followed by an apple. I ate rapidly, usually listening to music on my transistor or occasionally to science programmes edited by John Maddox, a friend of the Worsthornes, which because of their smug certitude I often found unintentionally amusing. I then washed up, read and went to bed by 11.30, sometimes reading in bed until the small hours without any noticeable effect on my ability to get up next morning and resume this almost unvarying routine.

If I have described this routine in what may seem insanely

boring detail it is in order to present the background to a state of melancholia which gradually came over me. It would be surprising if it had not. This mere sadness was not like my former 'breakdown'; there was little terror in it, or if there was it could be dispelled by the 'Tibetan' methods of deep breathing I had half-unwittingly learnt. There was no morning when I woke to find I could not go on. There was a dead feeling, just bearable and usually relieved by the company of friends. Yet I could not allow it to persist. I went to see my former deliverer, Desmond O'Neill, with whom I had lost touch. He had sold his house in St John's Wood, to one of the Beatles, I believe, and now lived and had his consulting room in a large house on the edge of Regent's Park which belonged to the uncle of his patient or ward, whom he had married. I found him sadly changed. He had himself suffered a severe 'breakdown' and was, I judged, on a 'régime' of drugs which meant that he was in a far worse state than I was. How bad it was I did not then realise. The man who had saved me from Dr Silver and his minions in dismal Halliwick and set me on the road, if not to full recovery, at least to a hopeful and sometimes reasonably contented life – this noble, talented and friendly man could not save himself. A few years after our last meeting he fell into such despair that he took his own life by hanging. How great must have been the self-hatred and anger in him that he, a doctor with recourse to so many ways of suicide, should have chosen this most brutal way! Peace to his memory; of him I can most sincerely say: Requiescat in Pace.

Though nobody could take his place, I found another admirable doctor, recommended by Claudie, who was not unacquainted with 'nerves' herself and therefore sympathetic to occasional 'queer turns' and other manifestations. Dr Raymond Rowntree, a tall, grave, yet humorous man whose consulting rooms were in Kinghtsbridge, himself knew, I think, what it is to peer into the Void, a necessary qualification for any doctor of mine. He prescribed various kinds of treatment which kept me going. But what really saved me, oddly, was a physical illness. Here I proved for the second time in my life the truth of Groddeck's theories. Georg Groddeck was a German psychiatrist who maintained mental pains could take physical form in some malady affecting an appropriate organ or part of the body – a thing universally acknowledged, of course, in common parlance. Thus 'pain in the neck' or fibrositis, indicates that the sufferer is carrying a burden of worry and indecision. In my first experience twenty years before, the symptoms of fibrositis had vanished immediately when I decided, after long hesitation, to marry Kate. Now, after I had divorced her and before my new marriage, a manner of life which I 'could not swallow' expressed itself in the form of a pharyngeal sac, brilliantly diagnosed on the spot by Dr Rowntree when I consulted him about an apparent swelling in the throat, assuming I had cancer.

This sac was a small pocket which had developed in the pharynx, causing food to lodge in it, with feelings of nausea and loss of appetite. An operation was indicated for this disgusting condition. Dr Rowntree sent me to Mr (later Sir) Douglas Ranger, a hearty, ebullient, confidence-inspiring New Zealander regarded as the best otorhinolaryngological surgeon in England. After he had explained matters, I asked him what would happen if I did not have the operation, a complicated one which had become feasible only quite recently with the general advance of surgery. 'Well,' he said in his reassuringly loud and cheerful voice, 'you could always stand on your head after meals and try to bring the stuff up – I mean down – that way'. Shortly afterwards, on this endearing man's advice, I entered King Edward VII's Hospital for Officers, a splendid establishment where, since I had reached the rank of lieutenant-colonel in the War, I automatically got a private room.

In any case this was a hospital where, by definition, only patients who were at least honorary members of the middle class were admitted. This was such blatant class discrimination that I occasionally wondered why the hospital had not been suppressed by egalitarian fanatics: as I went through the various stages of the operation from the bliss of the pre-operation shot in the buttocks to waking with a tube up my nose, another attached to the incision in my neck and another attached to my wrist for an intravenous drip – I am told I looked like a witch-doctor – I was thankful it had not. I was in the hospital for a fortnight and, once I had got over the pain in my throat enjoyed my stay there so much that I was rather sorry to leave, acquiring a dangerous taste for hospital life, or at any rate life in this particular hospital. I even liked the process ('nil per mouth') of being fed through the nose by the tube, which, ordinarily taped to my forehead, would be hooked behind my ear for a feed of soup. I asked a doctor if it would be possible to send whisky down; he said it would, but there were more efficient ways of inducing euphoria.

This operation, which as Mr Ranger told me in his amusing way, was 'tricky' and, as it involved by-passing all the main life passages of the body, carried some risk of death, did me a lot of good. So did my long-delayed marriage to my companion of ten years. We were married in the Catholic church in Cirencester and spent our honeymoon in the Budock Vean Hotel, near the Helford River in Cornwall. There was a most auspicious conjunction of Jupiter and Venus at the time; it was also the time of the much publicised predicted arrival of the Comet Kohoutek. But this, as we scanned the skies in vain, was a sad disappointment. And the year was not altogether happy.

Time had caught up with my mother at last. She had stayed in her cottage at Amswick until she was in her nineties, still evasive about her exact age and sometimes saying 'It's not right' or 'I don't *feel* old' and reminiscing as she had always done about the splendours of her early married life, which became more extravagant as her memory grew more confused. My elder sister Kathleen – who had come back to England from Rhodesia in the sixties after her divorce, to live in a cottage in a neighbouring village bequeathed by her mother-in-law (the formidable Alsatian dog-breeder) – did what she could to attend to our mother's needs but was apt to grow impatient at reminiscences of the mythical past. She had always preferred the company of her mother-in-law, whose passion for dogs she shared. As she got older herself she could no longer cope with Alsatians; so, by an interesting exchange of large and fierce for small and whimsical, took to breeding Pekingese instead.

The obvious solution to my mother's problems would have been for her to share her daughter's cottage. But this she steadfastly refused to do, clinging fiercely to an independence which she was less and less able to support. Her cottage grew ever more ramshackle and neglected; her remaining treasures went undusted; in heavy rain the spring in the hillside opened and flooded her back kitchen, swirling round the antique mangle and the mouldering flower-pots. My sister and I made some improvements and would probably have made more, but my mother, who had always had some of my own ingrained resistance to change, was obstinate, set in her ways and obstructive to all suggestions. 'It'll see my time out', she would say, and there she was right. A time came when for her own safety she could stay in the cottage no longer. So the heart-rending business of moving her began, at first to her daughter's cottage and then, after a little while, when that did not suit either of them, to an old people's home not far away.

It had been the mansion, built in mid-Victorian times, of a West Riding magnate: a big, solid, square-built house of stone set in a fine park where cattle grazed by an ornamental lake. From the terrace there was a pleasant view of woods and beyond them a group of small, conical hills, outliers of the Pennines. It would have looked, to a casual eye, like an ideal place in which to end one's days. But my mother, though she often said she was ready and even anxious to end her days, was really no more willing to do so than most if not all of humankind. She hated this place, asked repeatedly when she could go home and once, setting out to make her way there, for she remained surprisingly active, was apprehended at the lodge gates and led back uncomprehending to the only home she had.

Extreme old age seemed to come on her all at once, as though to make up for being so long delayed. Soon she was confined to bed, no longer able, even had she wished, to sit amongst the dismal group in the big, comfortably-furnished common room before the ever flickering but scarcely heeded television set. True to her old ways and lingering delusions, she shunned her fellow inmates, sometimes with a ferocious rudeness that used up some of what little energy remained. Did she repeat her old sayings: 'I can't abide waste in any shape or form' or 'I've got a rooted objection' to this, that and the other? In this way she may have puzzled and irritated those who looked after her. How could they know or care about whatever life she had lived or its strange vicissitudes before she came to this final place?

To be three-quarters deaf, with failing sight, disfigured by baldness and the growth of facial hair: this was the end of this being who had borne me and given me far more love than I ever gave her. I was at her bedside on a summer evening just before she died, to hold her small, arthritic hand and to observe, as I looked intently at her face in an effort to communicate – what? – a single tear start from her fast-blurring eye.

Soon we had a new editor at the *Telegraph*. He was William Deedes (later, as a life peer, Lord Deedes), a man of the same age as myself, but with little else in common. He was an affable, humorous man, always known as 'Bill', rightly popular with everybody and in some ways a contrast to Maurice Green, the outgoing editor. Green had been cautious in his columnar policy, inclined to worry about 'pressure groups' such as the 'family-planning' industry, whose financial and propaganda machinations I had been concerned to expose in several 'notes' under the general heading 'That Hideous Strength'. But in spite of his worries he never succeeded in inducing me to apologise to these repulsive people or to go further in placating them than allowing that some of them genuinely believed they were doing good in propagating 'the contraceptive mentality'. I believe this is one of the worst contemporary evils, substituting the techniques of the laboratory for the honest congress of the sexes. The most brutish copulation is preferable to the technology of Eros. Where Green had been cautious, Deedes was easy-going, even indulgent to my vagaries; indeed I sometimes thought he was inclined to pass things I had written which I myself feared might attract legal action; but they never did.

We spent a fortnight in Germany just after Deedes took over; Nicholas, who had now moved from Reading to the University of East Anglia at Norwich, was doing a six-month exchange with a lecturer from the University of Munich. So, taking Jane with us, we stayed in agreeable lodgings in the centre of Munich after crossing by sea to Ostend and then driving in my wife's blue mini-car, almost as crowded as Kate's Singer had been, by way of Trier, Heidelberg, Mannheim and Ulm. Jane was now working in London in a school for 'difficult' children; she had emerged self-cured from a period of mysterious malaise, involving homoeopathic medicine, an operation for appendicitis and even hypnotism, under the ministrations of various doctors, to buy her own flat in Battersea not far from mine and to find her first vocation in a difficult branch of education: child delinquency.

Once she had moved out of the shadows of the past, this remarkable girl, who had some of her mother's energy and determination directed into different channels, seemed to grow in moral stature every day. As an armchair psychologist I thought the origin of her troubles might have lain in the trauma of being fostered, in Redhill of all places, during the first twelve months of her life. I remembered how, after we removed her from her foster-mother because we had at last found a place to live, she seemed in a state of total shock, physically healthy but quite impassive, showing no reaction to her surroundings or to the people round her, not even to Kate and myself. It was only when her cot, bedding and other familiar objects were restored that an amazing change took place: from being a tiny zombie or, perhaps, contemplative Buddha, she suddenly turned into a living baby. Our relief was extreme; and so must hers have been.

Jane did not like Germany, but I did, though not unequivocally. It was the first time I had been in this country which still, thirty years after the War had ended, seemed under an evil spell. In their dealings with us foreigners the people were polite and correct but inhibited and ill at ease. I had a pervasive feeling that the territory of West Germany, contracted by the victors of the War, was not big enough for their bursting energies. It was late March, cold with persistent snow-flurries and occasional heavy falls; but the wintry landscape was disappointing. Where – amid the brand-new factories and the stage-scenery restorations of ancient cities and towns demolished during the last months of frenzied, vindictive bombing by the allied air-forces – was the fabulous landscape of the German forest I had come to see? The sense of something lacking and of something latent intrigued me. This was the country from which my paternal grandparents had come. I felt a tenuous link with it, difficult to grasp; even a perverse sympathy for the Third Reich which led me to dwell on its terrible and violent end and to speculate on the real rather than the assumed attitudes of its survivors.

I noted, at the entrance to the nave of the huge rebuilt cathedral of Ulm, a single red rosebud placed at the exact centre of the pavement. Was it secretly replaced from time to time, a war memorial more moving than any monumental statuary? Memorials to Hitler's forces hardly existed; those that did were hard to find. I found one in the centre of the untended square of grass in front of the derelict Alte Residenz in Munich. A rough slab of stone covered a small underground chamber where lay the bronze effigy of a dead or sleeping knight; on the walls were bas-reliefs of armies, with angels bearing crosses and the inscription 'Our fallen shall rise again'. There were one or two unkempt and furtive wreaths in memory of those who in the end had fought alone against the whole world with its weight of technological weaponry, and had fought against it for so long when all hope of victory was gone.

However vile the Nazis were (and who from Stauffenberg down doubted their vileness?) there can be no doubt of German heroism. With such forbidden thoughts in my mind I looked at this unpretentious war memorial, so carefully hidden away; soon a couple of urchins rushed into the underground chamber, whooping and scrambling over the recumbent warrior. This had a painful symbolism of its own. Nobody rebuked these children; they had probably been taught at school that Germany had no history between the rise of Hitler and his end. But this unprecedented voluntary self-censorship cannot endure forever. There are unmistakable signs that the Germans are breaking free from their guilt. Will it turn into pride? Who can predict the chances and changes of history? If there are any Germans (or any other people) in Europe a few hundred years from now is it utterly unfeasible that Hitler and his followers may have turned, by a strange twist of fate, into legendary heroes? Or will a World Government ensure that all legends are forbidden apart from its own, intolerably flat and boring as they will be?

We wandered around Munich; walked in the English Garden; saw the Isar rolling in wintry flood; visited the splendid art galleries in the only surviving buildings of the Nazis' preferred monumental style; saw the Nymphenburg and the silvery Amalienburg; travelled from the spotless railway-station, infested with dangerous-looking Turkish migrant workers, on a spotless, impeccably punctual train to Regensburg and the house of Kepler alongside the rushing Danube; drove over the Austrian border to Salzburg, where from the castle's battlements I looked towards Berchtesgaden and indulged in some more of my perverse and wicked thoughts; saw a relieved Jane off at the airport on her way back to England, then sank into a tea-room where on buying a newspaper I found it was the eightieth birthday of Ernst Jünger, the greatest living German writer, and a hero of mine: holder of Germany's highest military honour, the Knight's Grand Cross of the Iron Cross, in the First War, and in the Second, preserver of Laon Cathedral and its Merovingian manuscripts during the German advance in 1940; diarist of the Occupation and of the weird life of the *haute collaboration* in

Paris; naturalist; aesthete; scorner of the Nazis; author of at least one strange masterpiece, *On the Marble Cliffs*; protector of animals and of the weak; himself the epitome of the strong.

When the time came to leave Munich we set off northward to spend a few days in the Franconian Forest, which promised something of the Urforst of German legend. But here again I was disappointed; it was a small square of hilly woodland, heavily signposted with coloured markers for graded walks and interspersed with sour streams. We stayed at Muggendorf, a grim village inhabited by grim country people, not particularly friendly to the English (and why should they be?). One evening in our hotel there was a meeting of local farmers to discuss some matter or other, big, thick-set men whose fathers must have supported the Nazis fervently; from the next room the deep, harsh drone of their voices came intimidatingly. Before we left Germany, on the *autobahn* north of Ingolstadt (a small brand-new ancient town about the size of Skipton, on the Danube, where the restored buildings had a particularly unreal and uneasy feeling about them), we had a curious encounter. We had stopped in a forest lay-by to eat our lunch. I was sitting in the little car while my wife took some photographs when I became aware that a big old-fashioned Mercedes had drawn up behind us. Presently a huge man, about sixty, loomed over me. 'English?' he said unnecessarily, with an ogre-like smile. There was something ogreish and larger than life about him altogether. 'I go to England soon,' he said, 'England, Scotland, perhaps Ireland. I am going to look at your English gardens. I am a gardener.' I told him the names of a few famous English gardens. We talked desultorily. 'It must be funny in England now,' he said at last. Indeed it was. Harold Wilson was Prime Minister. 'It depends what you mean by funny', I said cautiously.

But he only smiled in his ogreish way and began to walk back towards his car.

Snow, which had been falling in intermittent flurries, began to fall steadily. The brown-black forest began to look as a German forest should. I noticed that on the radiator of the ogre's car were fixed two small metal letters, 'R.A.': Republica Argentina, notorious as the refuge of 'war criminals'. Was he a 'war criminal'? If so, would he be likely thus to advertise the fact? Was he really a gardener (he might, of course, be a fugitive Nazi leader as well)? Or was he a genuine German ogre, perhaps the Erl King himself? He faded away with the forest as we resumed our journey. I immediately began to regret it. I have regretted it ever since, certain that this encounter was one of the great lost opportunities of my life. It would have been easy to exchange addresses, ask him to look me up when he came to England in search of gardens. It is a strange paralysis of the will, an instinct for the negative which is at the root of such folly. Here, perhaps, was the secret of the German forest; it had been offered to me, as in the best fairy stories, by a chance encounter on the road; and I had rejected it. It would not, I knew, be offered a second time.

Back in England, I entered the third decade of my columnar service. Colin Welch, who had become deputy-editor of the *Telegraph*, resigned when he realised he was not going to achieve his ambition of becoming editor, and took up freelance work. Dr Johnson found he could no longer afford to publish two-yearly anthologies of my column; so the next two anthologies were published by the *Telegraph* itself. Soon Dr Johnson had a severe stroke which paralysed one side, and died not long afterwards. I had regular news from various sources, of Kate's love-affair, which had now continued for twenty years; after all that time, in my own newly-settled state, I began to take a benign attitude to what was clearly going to be one of the great love-stories of the twentieth century.

8
The End of Fleet Street

The years passed in my tiny office on the third floor; for four days a week, week after week, allowing for the six weeks' annual holiday and rare absences through illness, I sat at the same desk while Claudie sat at the same desk opposite me. Behind me was the door which led to the fire-escape, marked 'Fire Escape' in large red letters. It had a complicated locking system which in the case of fire might have caused trouble; the door was as difficult to close as it was to open, and sometimes in windy weather it would swing wide, leaving my back exposed to the elements and my papers blowing around the room. Our desks often tended, through the vibration of Claudie's vigorous typing, to move together, causing my own desk to vibrate with increasing force until I invariably said, in the muttering tone she imitated so well, 'I think we've got a bit of osmosis'. Apart from the desks with their trays and blotters, there was little furniture. There were two small tables, one holding a file of the *Telegraph*, the other a file of *The Times*. There was a dull green filing-cabinet with four drawers. One contained very little except the remains of Miss Thompson's filing system with its neat, pink cards, virtually abandoned when she left in 1957, a mouldering monument of efficiency which I kept for superstitious reasons; it was of no practical use whatever. Claudie's own filing system was simple: she put almost all correspondence into the waste-paper basket as soon as she had answered it, retaining in a green folder, for a few weeks only, such letters as she thought interesting or important, then putting most of these into the waste-paper basket in turn. In our early days I used sometimes to complain about this system; but after a time I became reconciled to it. After all, in its rough and ready way it did prevent the room from filling up entirely with waste-paper.

The two middle drawers of the filing cabinet were largely empty except for my 'personal files' and details of publications; the lowest and largest drawer contained a pair of Claudie's shoes, a carton of cigarettes and one or two other personal possessions such as unwanted Christmas presents of talcum powder or children's books. It also contained a bottle of vodka with only a teaspoonful of liquid in it, together with a small cheap drinking-glass, relics of some forgotten party. As with the column in general and everything that concerned it, there was a strong feeling of immemorial custom about this filing cabinet and its contents. If Claudie ever felt any inclination to clear it out, and I doubt if she did, she never acted upon it. We understood each other.

The only other notable piece of furniture in the room was a tall, antique hat-cum-umbrella stand, surmounted by antler-like extrusions and possessing for me an almost sacral character. There was a hanging bookcase on the wall on my left, opposite the window, containing a fine collection of books sent in by readers, almost all of them unreadable and carefully kept by me for that reason: some were volumes of execrable poems published at the authors' expense, but most were works of 'conspiracist' literature such as *Kissinger – KGB Agent*, *Commu-capitalism* and *Wall Street and the Rise of Hitler* – this an alarmingly persuasive book which suggested that Hitler had been, whether wittingly or not, a tool of international finance in its plans for world domination. It was certainly 'calculated to make you think', as the left-wing BBC programme-makers said of their own productions. But its weakness was that it explained everything too convincingly.

On the fourth side of the room, facing me, behind Claudie and next to the door, was a wide shallow steel cupboard with sliding doors, painted dark green. It contained a mass of stationery – boxes of typing paper, carbon paper, writing paper, plain or with the *Telegraph* heading, envelopes of various shapes and sizes, paper-clips and rubber bands, mingled with certain readers' letters and sometimes with magazines Claudie had secreted for her personal use, all in a state of indescribable confusion. It was difficult to slide the doors open; they often jammed on protruding boxes or other items; and when Claudie had to move her chair back into the narrow space between it and the cupboard after I had complained of 'osmosis' it was difficult to get at the cupboard at all. This was part of our system of office management. Irritating though it might seem, I regarded it as traditional, 'given', part of the eternal order of things. To alter it in the slightest would have brought my whole way of life to an end.

On the wall above the cupboard were two framed maps, one of Europe and one of Great Britain, the latter with its ancient counties intact and with proper pre-metric measurements; both were turning yellow. I would have liked a map of Europe as it was at the outbreak of war, or even a map of the Europe of Hitler's New Order. But that, as well as being hard to obtain, would have offended Claudie, a commendable French patriot, to such an extent that she might well have torn it down during my absence. I would have been too passive to restore it.

The decorative scheme of my room was suggestive not so much of the rich eccentricity and nostalgia I might have gone in for if I had followed my inclinations according to my public 'image' as of neglect and decay. It was the only room belonging to a senior journalist on the paper which had no carpet but retained its original brown linoleum. Offered a carpet by the kindly functionary who dealt with office furniture, I declined it. I obstinately retained my uncomfortable high-backed chair until, returning late from the Kings and Keys one night, I fell asleep in it, some time later plunging backwards and waking with a start to find a cleaning woman looking at me with disgust as I lay on the floor amid the chair's irreparable ruins. Though unwilling, I had to accept a modern cushioned swivel-chair instead. Believing 'all change was for the worse' – this was by way of being a columnar motto – I resisted change even in the most minute particulars. I felt a superstitious dread that if there were even the slightest change either in my surroundings or my routine I would be unable to continue my obsessive work on this column which by the early Eighties had reached a total of something like four million words.

Locked in this unvarying manner of life, I thought it must go on unvaryingly for ever, or until death or imbecility supervened. As with my life as an undergraduate at Oxford or my life in the army, I began to feel there was no life conceivable outside it; that the organisation which upheld it – the *Telegraph* with its unchanging ways of working, its hierarchy from the Proprietor and Editor-in-Chief, Lord Hartwell, downwards through the Editor, 'Bill' Deedes, the leader-writers, feature-writers, columnists, correspondents, sub-editors and reporters, and the printers on the 'stone' with their punctually thundering presses, their inviolable privileges and age-old customs and practices – I thought this whole self-contained world in which I had so unexpectedly found myself a special, personal, self-contained niche must also go on, unchanging and for ever. But now the first signs of possible change began to appear.

For some time there had been talk of 'the new technology',

a thing by definition quite as abhorrent to me as it was to the printers whose ancient way of life it threatened. Because of the special, personal nature of my job on the paper (it was simply to write about one thousand words a day on any subject I liked and, within obvious limits, in any way I liked) I had been free of the conferences, meetings and departmental discussion groups which had plagued and bored me so agonisingly at the BBC. Apart from making sure through the sub-editors that my writings were printed – I had gradually and insensibly phased out my evening meetings with the editor, probably to his relief as much as mine – I had no connection with the rest of the paper, making a running columnar joke out of my daily defence of the columnar territory. Then one day came a summons, signed by Lord Hartwell himself, for all 'heads of departments' to attend a meeting on 'the new technology'.

It was about the new electronic techniques which were going to revolutionise the production of the paper, substituting computerised word-processors for composing and printing machines and eventually enabling journalists to produce the paper themselves. We listened sceptically. The general view was that the present system would last out our time and that we need not worry about these fancy innovations. As for the printers, secure in their union power, their closed shops, their ability to bring the paper to a stop at a cost of millions of pounds a week whenever they chose, I doubt if they thought twice about these new notions. As it happened they had just been on strike for a few days, forcing the management to surrender. The printers stipulated, if I understood rightly, that they had no objection to new labour-saving machines being introduced so long as none of the existing labour-force were laid off.

It was said that new print-machinery *had* been introduced, but had simply been put under dust-sheets while the labour-force, recently augmented, used it as a table for their tea-mugs, to play cards on. My Luddite soul applauded. I was all for the printers and their shameless defiance of technological progress. Because of it, I liked to see these overalled figures leaning against the front of the *Telegraph* building in off-duty hours, surveying the world with conscious superiority as they had always done. There was a pretentious restaurant opposite the *Telegraph* where journalists and other such people took their meals. One evening a leader-writer who had eaten unwisely was carried out of it as an ambulance came screaming up the road. The lounging printers gave a rousing cheer. So might their brutish ancestors have cheered the writhings of some greedy burgher. They did not know their time was short, that in a few years this kind of life would disappear forever.

If I had been looking for signs I might easily have found them. A certain restlessness began to be apparent. There were continual repairs in the building. Scaffolding appeared for no clear reason; often I had to write my column under difficulties; the noise of hammering, shouting, the howling of pop singers on transistors as Irish faces stared through the windows. Even the 'Lodge' was changed: tasteless and intrusive partitions of plywood now marred the noble symmetry of its mahogany and marble. The cash-desk where I negotiated my preposterously small expense claims was moved from one place to another and back again. It seemed like trivial change for the sake of change, an aimless shifting from one foot to the other while waiting for the really important changes to begin. Lady Hartwell, Lady Pamela Berry as she had been, died. The Hartwells' son, Adrian Berry, became Science Correspondent, a friendly, boyish man and a total believer in conventional science; he may well have agreed with the Russian cosmonaut who blithely announced he had been into space and found no God or Heaven there,

convinced he had thus disposed of all such outmoded super-
stitions. Adrian did not resent my fictitious astronomer who, if
the universe did not fit his theories, rearranged it till it did.
Once, when I had this character give a sound kicking to a white
dwarf he had trapped in his observatory, Adrian told me: 'You
know, if he really did that he'd get the worst of it! It would be
solid diamond.'

Soon there was a new dispensation by which the whole *Telegraph* building, except for Lord Hartwell's own sacrosanct Fifth
Floor, was rearranged. Protesting, I had to leave my squalid
little room on the third floor and move to what was admittedly
a pleasant, civilised room, slightly larger too, on the fifth floor.
It had carpets and press-button telephones. But I kept our
furniture intact, including the sacred symbolic hat stand, and
as far as possible in the same relative positions. There was a
better view out of the window, west instead of north-west, along
Fleet Street to the Strand and the distant top of Nelson's
column. One November evening, as Claudie and I, our day's
routine finished, looked out of the window at sunset at a sky
leaden and overcast, we saw a *sign*. A narrow band of dying
light stole up from the western horizon, gradually suffusing the
dull grey cloud until the whole sky was a solemn elegiac purple.
It was a sky fit for an emperor's funeral, a thing never seen
before or since. There was even a paragraph about it in next
day's paper.

There were other, more mundane signs of change, breaches
in what had seemed the eternal order of things. Mark O'Donnell, the man we called 'the greatest publican of the twentieth
century', retired from the Kings and Keys, whether to take over
some other pub or to engage in the affairs of the great world I
cannot say. He was succeeded by Andrew O'Connor, an excellent landlord but a very different kind of Irishman. Where Mark

had been cheerful and confident, Andrew was melancholy and retiring. If, as occasionally happened, he allowed drinking after hours on the ground that the drinkers were his personal friends, as in a sense they were, he showed signs of nervousness and hesitation at the possible appearance of the police, whereas Mark would have handled them, if they had appeared, with masterful bonhomie.

Andrew combined a certain meanness with fits of almost painful generosity. One day, for instance, appearing to take pity on me for my unvarying diet of corned-beef sandwiches, he offered me a plate of his own Irish stew, muttering its praises in his rapid Kerry accent, and almost reducing me to tears. When he discovered I knew a certain amount of book Irish he became, not unnaturally, extremely suspicious. After all, the new round of Troubles was in full swing, and although the Provisional IRA had planted no bombs in Fleet Street, it was not unusual to find, on my way to work, streets barred by the emergency white tape of the police. I sometimes wondered why the Provisionals did not put a bomb in Lord Hartwell's dining-room on the occasion of the annual staff Christmas luncheon which all 'Heads of Departments', including myself, attended, listening through a haze of alcohol to the statutory speeches and eating the statutory meal of smoked salmon, turkey and plum pudding which, though always the same, seemed to decline subtly in quality through the years. The Provisionals could have made a clean sweep of the staff of the English newspaper they must have thought most hostile to them. Was our immunity due to Peter Utley? Or had they taken note of my own vestigial Irish nationalism? It had led me several times to object to the spelling of Cardinal O'Fiaich's name as 'O'Fee', on the grounds that as well as being incorrect, it was gratuitously discourteous not to spell his name in the way he spelled it himself.

For some reason I never discovered, Weston never forgave O'Donnell for leaving 'his' Kings and Keys and took an immediate dislike to his successor, who perhaps did not protect him with O'Donnell's open-handed injustice. Very soon he swore that he would not enter the pub again while Andrew remained landlord. And so the Theatre of the Absurd, which had given so much innocent amusement to thousands and become famous throughout Fleet Street and beyond, came to an end. In any case, its great days were gone; for some time Weston's genius for insult had been in decline; although he still performed, to diminishing acclaim, a few favourite set pieces, he seemed unable to add to his repertoire and his powers of improvisation were failing. Occasionally there was a reminder of the old fire as he obliged with a bravura performance. Once, in a rare flash of poetry, he denounced Stephen Daneff in a fine, florid passage: 'Daneff! You're superficial! Shallow! Swimming on the surface of life like a – like a water boatman!' and went on to extend this entomological simile in brilliant style, drawing much applause from all who heard him, particularly the victim.

But it was not long before Weston and his one-time sparring partner, Jameson, both of whom had reached the statutory age of 65, retired, Weston to his garden (it was one of the paradoxes of this extraordinary and very gifted man that in his other primary character of urbane and civilised person as opposed to raving lunatic he was a dedicated gardener) and Jameson to his bungalow and precarious boat on an island in the Thames. Both separately swore a vow that they would never again set foot in Fleet Street; and as far as I know they kept that vow. About the same time my friend Stephen, with whom I had enjoyed so many drunken conversations on historical matters, also retired, not for reasons of age but to enjoy a life of leisure, study and writing. He produced one excellent book on 'Foxy' Ferdinand of Bulgaria. I got very drunk with him on his retirement, unusually so for me; and after I had climbed the stairs at Prince of Wales Mansions and fallen into my flat I got up from the floor and immediately fell into the bath, but transversely, so that my legs dangled over the edge and, as I was wearing my good black overcoat of heavy Crombie cloth, I could not get out again for all my struggles. There I remained without hope of rescue, till the wintry light of morning glimmered through the panes. There was still no hope of rescue; I felt like a character in one of Kafka's humorous short stories; but as I grew sober my powers of muscular coordination returned and with a supreme effort and a dexterous twist I was free. Later that morning, when I reached the office with an appalling hangover, I found, as I knew I would, more than one letter congratulating me on being an oasis of sanity and commonsense in a world gone mad.

Would my readers have thought this manner of life disqualified me from having serious opinions about the madness of the world and from attacking, as I tried to do in my column both directly and by irony and fantasy, lying, dishonesty and humbug? Did they imagine I spent my time in grave discussion with my intellectual peers rather than drinking and talking nonsense in a rather low-grade pub? I was disqualified, as I have always been, from any place in what they would have thought of as respectable society by my ambiguous origins, by temperament and by lack of social graces. There had been a time when I resented this; but it had passed; I had long been reconciled to a life of obscurity.

I have always had an instinctive fear of people, a defensive attitude impressed upon me from my earliest years. It may have sprung from my mother's perpetual fear of being exposed as inferior to those whose society she had entered through an unequal, even preposterous marriage. For all my dreams of wealth and fame, perhaps as an inverse reflection of them, my conviction of necessary failure has never shifted for a moment. It is possible that if I had been able to overcome this feeling I might have achieved worldly success and mixed in more elevated company. But would there have been any point in getting drunk in the Garrick Club rather than in the Kings and Keys? And would I then have been able to write my column, which in some ways was a compensation through consoling fantasy for a somewhat meagre social life? Would I have been able to write anything at all if I had been at home in the halls of the mighty rather than retiring into a corner as I did on such rare occasions as I was admitted?

Since my third marriage I had had two distinct lives, one during the working week, when things went between the little room in Fleet Street and the flat in Prince of Wales Mansions as I have described, the other at weekends, which I spent in our cottage in the Chilterns, a pretty spot among beechwoods very suitable for dog-walking, mild gardening, doing nothing in particular and thinking about writing a novel, all of these activities except the last being very congenial to me. As for the flat, it was inevitable that it should grow more squalid through the years. The roof of my bedroom began to leak in the autumn of 1976 and in spite of the landlord's attempts to repair it was still leaking five years later. I took a certain amount of masochistic pleasure in the placing of bowls to catch the drips, sometimes waking in the night to lie in the darkness calculating the rate of stillicide on my luminous clock until warned that an overflow was imminent and emptying and adjustment of the bowls essen-

THE END OF FLEET STREET

tial. I knew none of the other flat-dwellers except by sight but was greatly helped by Mr Gates, the caretaker, a remarkable man of whom I grew very fond. Tall, gaunt and then about sixty years old, he was rather dirty, usually unshaven, and wore an assortment of cast-off clothes. He lived in a ground-floor flat in a distant part of the block, an Aladdin's cave of objects he had acquired from all manner of past tenants: broken armchairs, defunct wirelesses, fragments of crockery, mouldering clarinets and other musical instruments, treadles of sewing machines, hammers, rusting saws, parish-hall chairs, melted gramophone records.

In fine weather, or even in a slight drizzle, whatever the time of year, he spent a great deal of his time standing outside his front door on the pavement, 'keeping an eye of things, sir'. He was a great one for calling me 'sir', partly, perhaps, because he had discovered I once had had the rank of lieutenant-colonel, but also because of a genuine rapport and regard we had for each other. He sometimes hinted at a mysterious and important career in Army Intelligence for himself, once even implying, as I thought perhaps mistakenly, that he had spent most of the War in Spain, based in Gibraltar, though when I addressed him in my meagre Spanish he did not reply but spoke of the iniquity of the police, who made no attempt, he complained, to catch the burglars who infested the flats. These burglars, mostly juvenile West Indians in search of a little cash, had twice broken into my flat, but to my humiliation had found nothing worth taking except a gold Mao Tse-tung badge which my friend Richard West had given me on his return from Communist China. 'I saw them, sir', Mr Gates told me. 'I was after them, sir, but they can run like monkeys, and at my time of life, Dr Gollom says, I have to take it easy.'

I often met Mr Gates, as he stood keeping an eye on things,

on my way from my flat to the bus-stop and we always had a short but most enjoyable conversation. He had a fierce attachment to Prince of Wales Mansions, or 'Prince' as lesser people called it. He felt for it rather as an Oxford college porter would feel for his own college above all others. 'Prince' was only one of a series of mansion-blocks running the whole length of the south side of Battersea Park and beyond it to the west into Battersea proper. It was the oldest block but socially by no means the best; York and Overstrand, which had lifts and central heating, were regarded as socially superior and if, as I imagined, these colleges of my fancy, with their college-like staircases complete with nameboards on the ground floor, went in for rowing on the Thames, 'Prince' would most probably have finished up rather badly. But Mr Gates would have none of this. 'Look at our pavement, sir, clean as a whistle', he said when the dustmen's strike left the London pavements piled with stinking rubbish. 'And look at York, their pavement's a disgrace'. Modestly, he did not point out that this was due to his own hard work and defiance of Dr Gollom's orders. But he knew that I knew.

Mr Gates could not repair my leaking ceiling. But he was sympathetic, lending me a plastic baby's bath with a design of rabbits on it out of his treasury to cope with the widening area of stillicide. He was solicitous about the full and correct presence of my name on the board in the entrance-hall of my staircase. The names were made up of separate plastic letters which he got from the menu-board of the canteen at the local branch of the British Legion, where he was highly respected. Pointing out the imperfect state of some of the other names, which were mere approximations like 'A. S. Own' or alarming Maltese-like constructions like 'X. N. Pxemdezgasx', he lamented that some letters were 'in short supply though there are as many spare X's and Z's as you could wish for'.

So it was a much appreciated privilege and mark of esteem to find 'Lt Col M. B. Wharton' on the board, embarrassingly bogus though it may have seemed to those who saw only an old, mackintoshed figure shambling up the stairs. With all his vagaries, Mr Gates was a valued friend and solace in the stylised loneliness and squalor of my life in Battersea which my wife, who disliked the place, was understandably disinclined to share unless she had things to do in London. Jane, though she lived not far away in a house she had bought after moving out of her flat in Gambetta Street and gradually beautified with enterprise and good taste, was even more disinclined to visit me in 'Prince' for similar reasons. But as a psychologist, she understood my attitude: that unless I could live in a magnificent castle I did not much care about my surroundings so long as they were not actually verminous. My old armchair with the springs gone might be uncomfortable, but 'it made a statement'.

It was in the year 1985 that signs of change began to multiply in Fleet Street. 'The new technology', so long anticipated by some, such as Adrian Berry, with rapt excitement, by others, such as myself, with boredom and scepticism, by others again, particularly the printers, I suppose, with nameless dread, was actually beginning to appear. Were the printers, on the other hand, so armoured in complacency, so certain, through years of having their own way with the management, that they were invulnerable, that nothing untoward could possibly happen to them? There were sporadic strikes; for a time I could never be certain that my column would actually appear. Even more annoying, I sometimes had to complete it ahead of time or suffer other changes in the routine which was so important to me. Suddenly all the talk was of the malpractices of the printers, or, even worse, of the workers who made up the papers into bundles in the evening and until the early hours. These were largely casual workers and there were said to be hundreds of them or even thousands, drawing enormous wages for doing nothing merely by signing on. Many of them did not even exist, it was said, except by way of fictitious signatures like 'Mickey Mouse', 'Popeye' or 'Benito Mussolini', but someone drew their wages just the same.

The various malpractices of the printers and manual workers, together with all their hereditary privileges, were collectively known as 'Old Spanish Customs' and the new technological reformers were determined to abolish them. I don't know how soon it dawned on these workers that they were not merely going to be reformed, but done away with altogether as their beautiful presses and hot metal composing machines – all the ancient paraphernalia down on 'the stone' – gave way to electronic word-processors and other gadgets. It all happened very quickly. There was a period of confusion. I still went on writing my column by hand and Claudie still went on typing it and sending appropriate copies of it to the 'printers'. But soon the printers turned into something else and what happened to the column before it appeared in print next day became mysterious, inexplicable and very worrying. My concentration suffered, and something of the general unease began to communicate itself to Michael ffolkes.

He had always been a steady drinker rather than a drunk. Whenever I climbed the steep stairs which led to his studio and entered that room full of confused bric-à-brac and unexpected contrasts I would find him sipping away as he worked and happy to offer as much wine – often champagne – as anyone could want. Now he began to drink more. His second marriage to

Sophie, a small Scotswoman with pale red hair, of the type I have always found irresistible myself, had collapsed in furious quarrels and he took it badly. Sometimes, when he telephoned for orders at the customary time of 1.30, he would be incoherent, or declare he felt incapable of drawing anything; or he would fabricate absurd obstacles, maintaining grandly that he could not draw a council house or the interior of a bus because he had never been in either.

Sometimes I would lose patience and say: 'Oh, just draw anything! Draw a rhinoceros!' He was particularly fond of drawing animals and very good at it. 'I suppose nobody ever notices my drawings anyhow,' he would retort sullenly. He was in financial trouble too, partly from the cost of his impending divorce and second lot of alimony, partly from an investment he had made in the ghoulish world of fashion, inhabited by corrupt grotesques for whom he was an innocent. He went to see 'Bill' Deedes, the editor, about getting more money, but since he strolled into the office in his battered hat, wearing his artist's 'Bohemian' clothes, he made a bad impression on a man who was also eccentric in his way but, being of an ancient landowning family and holder of a Military Cross, with a different kind of eccentricity. ffolkes, this lovable man who had always been 'difficult', was becoming 'impossible'. Yet it was impossible not to love and forgive him.

I think of one absurd incident, one of the most absurd which ever took place even in the Kings and Keys, as a true sign of the impending collapse of the old order. One hot afternoon in late summer I was drinking 'BGA' and eating a corned-beef sandwich in the pub when a full-grown lioness stalked in. She was accompanied by several young men and women and a photographer. It was, I soon realised, some kind of advertising stunt. Yet it had an unmistakably mythological character. The lioness, who looked thirsty and unhappy, as well she might, was manoeuvred into the far corner of the L-shaped bar where Utley sometimes held court. He was there now with his female attendants, booming away, chain-smoking and oblivious of the animal, which came to a halt just behind him. Did the most comely of his handmaids rest an elegant white hand on the lioness's tawny head or shoulder, completing a picture which might have hung in the Victorian Royal Academy?

I do not know, because at that moment there was a commotion by the door and in came Hugh Westwood, an important member of the *Telegraph*'s management staff, then much preoccupied with 'labour relations'. A portly, youngish man with the air of a pompous waiter – somewhat like one of those cardboard, dinner-jacketed figures which used to be found outside cheap restaurants with 'Today's Special' written on the broad shirt-front – Westwood had probably never before been in this or any other pub in his life. But he had heard of this intrusion on *Telegraph* property and resolved to deal with it himself. 'Get that animal out of here at once!' he shouted. 'You know perfectly well it's against the rules!' What rules? He stalked out, as though unwilling to stay in the same room as a creature which, he may have thought, could not really exist and was therefore extremely undesirable.

But it was not easy to get the animal out. She flopped down at Utley's feet, evidently exhausted. One of his attendants got a bowl of water for her. She drank noisily and deeply and seemed grateful. Then Westwood returned, angrier than ever. 'If that animal is not out of here within five minutes I shall send for the police!' he roared, then stamped out again. A taxi was sent for; somehow the lion was ushered out, manoeuvred into the taxi, a lengthy process, and driven away. It was an incident which made a deep impression on all who beheld it; most of all on me. From that moment on rumours of doom began to proliferate.

For years now, Lord Hartwell had been warning us in his Christmas luncheon speech that times were hard and the papers, both *Daily* and *Sunday*, were losing money, and for years now we had been paying no attention. But that year, just before Christmas, when we should all have had our invitations, came the sudden announcement that *there was to be no Christmas luncheon.* Then we all knew the end was near. Never again would we sit, inwardly groaning, at the board; never again would our eyes stray to the framed historic pages on the walls in their quaint antique type – 'Mafeking Relieved', 'Kaiser Abdicates', 'Hitler Invades Russia' – or to the portraits of the founding fathers of the newspaper, the Burnham and Camrose dynasties, looking down on us so commandingly as we ate our less and less appealing food and talked, boring and bored, to neighbours who seemed to grow more unintelligible every year. Never again would I glimpse, through the tall windows, Lord Hartwell's magic garden which extended in my imagination over vaster and vaster distances and defied ever more outrageously the laws of spatial relations.

In the New Year we heard that Lord Hartwell's annual warning that his newspapers were losing money was only too disastrously true. Amid reports of recriminations, perhaps ill-founded and certainly confused as far as most of the staff were concerned, we heard that a Canadian millionaire, Conrad Black, had taken over control of the company, the only way, it seemed, in which the newspapers could be saved at all, and that hence-forth the Berry family would have only a minority interest. Lord Hartwell, not surprisingly, fell ill and went into hospital for an operation. Not long after he came out I had the dreaded experi-ence of descending several floors in the lift with him. The poor man was in agony, which added helpless sympathy to my dread but still did not enable me, to my guilty regret, to think of one single word to say to him.

More changes were on the way. 'Bill' Deedes who, being seventy-two, had been of retiring age anyhow, duly retired and was succeeded, to everyone's surprise, by Max Hastings, the illustrious war correspondent who had been the first man into Port Stanley at the end of the Falklands War. Previous editors had been in their early sixties when they took over. Max was only forty, an amiable, intelligent man with a lot of genuine charm; tall, lanky, black-haired, energetic and physically active, with long limbs he obviously found difficult to accommodate at his desk when they should have been striding over rough mountains, if not under shot and shell then at least with the sound of sporting guns not far away. I took to him at once, though I perhaps had even less in common with him than with previous editors. But he went out of his way to impress on me that the *Telegraph* was anxious to keep my services. As I was now nearly seventy-four, long past the age of retirement, I had been seriously considering it. So a comical period of negotiation began.

I had an offer from Charles Moore, the editor of the *Spectator*, to move my column from the rapidly changing *Telegraph* to the safety of his own weekly in Doughty Street. Moore was then a man of about thirty who to me seemed too good to be true. He was an Etonian of impeccable family, handsome, intelligent, amiable, sufficiently rich, with a handsome, intelligent wife and I imagine, though I never met them, children of equal excellence. So fortunate did this man seem to be that I feared for him; was he not tempting Fate to strike him down, or liable to be the subject of a 'Job-type' experiment? So far, I am glad to say, my fears for him have proved unfounded.

I was tempted to accept his offer. But my habitual prudence and self-doubt prevailed. Would the *Telegraph* allow me to transfer their property elsewhere? Was I capable of writing the column in unfamiliar conditions? I was beginning, after thirty years, to tire of it anyhow. So I dithered for months, no doubt infuriating Moore, though typically there was not the slightest modification of his habitual good manners as he several times gave me lunch 'to discuss matters' at the sort of expensive restaurants I would never have thought of going into myself, even though the *Telegraph* would have paid up without a murmur. Eventually caution prevailed. So that matter passed away, and with it my last chance of achieving notice under my own name. I remained at the *Telegraph* to the end, flattered by the blandishments of Max and his determination to retain my column as one part of the paper which would not change, though everything around it was changing moment by moment.

The 'new technology' was now triumphant, though the fierce battles which ensured the total defeat of the printers largely took place elsewhere. On the *Telegraph* they seemed to fade away insensibly as the old machines, with their reassuring rhythmic uproar, gave place to noiseless electronic flickering. Adrian Berry ran courses of instruction in word-processing for all journalists, with the exception of myself, as a known Luddite and relic of the past, and Peregrine Worsthorne, who declared after one lesson that he could not get the hang of the thing and was excused. In any case, in another quite sensational change among all the other changes, this flamboyant figure had now been appointed editor of the *Sunday Telegraph* in succession to the more sober John Thompson. Perry was a great success, and soon became the necessary 'fabulous monster' of the right which the left required. He appeared on television a great deal, often in discussion programmes where, needless to say, he was the only participant who did not subscribe to the 'left-wing package deal' and was therefore, for all his eloquence, at the required disadvantage.

Should I not have been filling this role myself, as a more thoroughgoing reactionary and, moreover, one not constrained by having a responsible position on a newspaper? Yes; but not only did I hate and despise television in itself, as the most evil and superfluous of all inventions, but my own experience of it had not been fortunate. Years before I had been interviewed on a late-night programme by Robert Kee, whom I had met occasionally in the FitzGibbon circle, though we hardly remembered each other. Urged on by my wife and others, I had agreed, most unwillingly, to submit to a fifty-minute programme of questioning, and as the time drew near for the advance filming one afternoon in an independent television studio in London I grew more and more nervous. As well as drinking a good deal of brandy in the company of John Chisholm, I took several pep pills left over from Desmond O'Neill's prescriptions, and when the time came for me to appear before the cameras and the television people had given me more brandy I was literally 'stoned out of my mind'. I was no longer nervous but was scarcely reacting to my surroundings at all.

So when poor Kee, a state-registered melancholiac like myself and suffering from a bad head-cold, asked me questions about my opinions on various subjects, such as the future of the world, I merely answered 'Yes, in a way' or 'I suppose so'. Although I did manage at the end to advise people to 'get on their knees and pray', the conversation was a 'goalless draw'. I am told by friends who saw the film broadcast that it was one of the funniest performances they had ever seen on television. As I stumbled out of the studio into the 'hospitality area' they gave me yet more to drink and in the end found it quite difficult to get rid of me. I was never asked to appear on television again. So yet another road to fame – today the greatest and most instantaneous of all – was closed to me.

Now the mania for change which had destroyed traditional printing methods and introduced the new electronic technology to Fleet Street was taking a further, terminal form – it was destroying Fleet Street itself. One by one the national newspapers – or rather, those who owned and controlled them – began to sell their premises for enormous sums and make their plans to move to cheaper sites and build new offices on them. The *Telegraph* newspapers, which had been the Berry family's chief personal possession but were now merely a part of Conrad Black's international financial empire, were constrained to move with the rest. New kinds of business executives, wearing identical suits and carrying identical document-cases, were to be seen moving in groups about the building; the soft noise of their incessant conferences could be heard coming from behind closed doors. They seemed to look at such aboriginals as myself, who still remained, with blank, unseeing eyes. Rumours of their decisions abounded: the paper was moving to Battersea; it was moving to Kensington; it was not moving anywhere.

But at last, after months of uncertainty, a decision was announced. It was moving to the Isle of Dogs, to a site in the former docks of the East End, where a new glass palace would be built to house it. The move would be complete by September 1987. So now I knew the date of my own retirement. In his kindly efforts to persuade me to move to the Isle of Dogs with the rest, Max put forward many pleasing fancies: I could be taken there each day in a gold-plated Rolls-Royce; each day a special launch could wait for me on the Thames at Battersea and convey me to the Isle of Dogs by water. But for once my mind was made up. Meanwhile Claudie and I continued to produce the column, sticking as far as possible to the old routine.

I was now the oldest journalist on the staff. All my coevals and many of my juniors had retired or taken 'early retirement', that is, been made redundant with some sort of handout. There were a lot of retirement ceremonies, usually painful, at which speeches and presentations were made. Utley left the *Telegraph* and took the post of Chief Obituarist on *The Times*, dying untimely two years afterwards. I spent solitary lunch intervals at the Kings and Keys. Sometimes, as I stood in a state of half-melancholy with my double 'BGA' and corned-beef sandwich, a new friend, the strange, diminutive genius Roy Kerridge, with his plastic bag and interest in many congenial matters from Celtic myths to what Borrow called 'the affairs of Egypt', would materialise beside me in the intervals of his wanderings around the country, drink his moderate 'light and lime' and, after a little conversation which must have baffled any eavesdroppers, set off on his wanderings again. Or the one-eyed Irish Republican journalist and left-wing borough councillor, Gerry Lawless, would pass rapidly behind me as I stood heedless at the bar, whispering to me messages of Irish import, sometimes, triumphantly, 'We're winning' and once, mysteriously, 'Arthur Scargill's mother was Irish'.

Most of my old friends were dead by now: Con FitzGibbon, René Cutforth, 'Jack' Dillon, Colm Brogan; David Thomson, who was getting long-deserved recognition for his books, notably *Woodbrook* and *The People of the Sea*, was growing frail and was soon to die. But Denis Hills, another friend from my Oxford days, would turn up looking worn, watchful but undefeated from a life as varied and adventurous as mine had been the reverse (he had been rescued once by James Callaghan from the dungeons of Idi Amin). One rainy evening, as I searched Fleet Street for a missing bus-stop I came across John Davenport, a ghost from the past if ever there was one, now penniless and spending sad last days at his mother's house in Worthing. Forgetting that he was barred for life from El Vino's, I bought him a drink there; dirty and unshaven as Davenport was, his flies gaping open and his high patrician voice shrunk to a papery whisper, the manager, usually so mercilessly vigilant, may not have had the heart to throw him out.

It was a consolation to visit Keisley now and then, though it was haunted by Ruth, over whose ashes in the garth Jimmy had planted a walnut tree. For a time he stayed on there; and thanks to him we could still spend sunny hours on the narrow terrace in front of his house, drinking and looking at that incomparable prospect. That last summer of 1987, with my wife and our two yellow labrador dogs, Rosie and Daisy, the latter Rosie's puppy by Jimmy's Leo, I carried out a long-planned undertaking: to climb from Outhgill in Mallerstang, near the ruins of Pendragon Castle, King Arthur's reputed birthplace, up the rocky, pathless slopes of High Seat to the source of the River Eden. I have always been fond of tracing the sources of rivers, whether in England, France or Spain; and of all rivers in the world I love the Eden the best.

Back in Fleet Street the last act was now played out. In the 'Lodge' the bronze memorial plaques from the two wars had been unscrewed and removed – where I cannot say. The space on the wall where test match scores had once been shown – part of a lost England and a lost *Daily Telegraph* – was now a mere patch of discoloration; the mahogany fittings at the reception desk where great ones had once loitered had been removed, and 'Inquiries', now few, had to be made at a peep-hole in one corner; the racks of newspapers remained, but it was months since they had been kept up to date. And from everywhere in

the great building came the sounds of departure. By mid-
August most of the staff had already left for the Isle of Dogs.
Soon Claudie and I were the only editorial staff still working
in the building, transmitting the column by a new-fangled fax
machine whose workings we did not understand to the sub-
editor far away in the new glass building in the East End. We
had become objects of suspicion. Sometimes, as I worked away
at my desk at an intricate paragraph, a face came round the
door: 'Still here?' We put a notice on the door: 'This room is
still a working area'.

The last day came, a mild, sad day of early autumn. We had
burned some of our archives, thrown away most, including Miss
Thompson's filing system and many files of old, mouldering
letters, in the great refuse bins provided for the purpose; most
of the books, too, including a great deal of 'conspiracy' literature, had to go; now the question was: what to do with the
furniture? Since none of it was suitable for the ultra-modern
open-plan offices of the new glass palace in the Isle of Dogs,
the whole building was full of unwanted objects: desks, tables,
bookcases, filing cabinets, anglepoise lamps, unwieldy cup-
boards full of paper.

A man I had never seen before, evidently a member of the
office furnishing department, had come into his own, as someone must in such moments of crisis, and assumed authority; he
had even devised a kind of uniform for himself, with an official-
looking peaked cap. It was he who restored order among the
dozens of people milling round to see what they could pick up,
some of them, perhaps, people who had walked in off the street
and had no connection with the *Telegraph*. But for this natural
leader of men there might have been scenes of looting and
pillage as in the sacking of a great city. He put a fair price on
everything and if there was any dispute as to how many desks

or chairs any one person could have, he dispensed justice, operating with his minions from a strange headquarters full of swivel chairs and rolled-up maps. He set guards on the doors and handed out chitties and receipts, making sure that the high-piled cars and pick-up trucks speeding from the building contained no loot that he had not himself approved.

Hysteria was mounting as we despatched the last column via the fax machine and prepared to leave the room where so many thousands of words had been written to be turned into ephemeral newsprint. Will any of them survive? At Claudie's suggestion, I took the bottle and glass from the bottom drawer of the filing cabinet and solemnly prepared to drink the meagre half-measure of vodka that remained. Then, as a confused uproar of voices and the crash of furniture mounted from below, I had a better thought, pouring it on the carpet as a libation to the departing tutelary gods. Was smoke rising from a final holocaust? Was that the crackle of statutory flames which came to our ears? No; but it should have been; likewise a pair of ravens should have winged across the tawdry street, and the noisome Fleet River should have risen to engulf this final scene. Where was Lord Hartwell, I wondered, with a rapid shift of scenario. Where was the once all-powerful master of this doomed domain? As we walked down the marble stairs for the last time, noting that with utter rightness all the lifts were out of order, I had a sudden vision of him, poignant and noble, striding up and down his battlemented garden where the grass grew rank among untended, weed-grown borders, on a Fifth Floor emptied of all its grandeur, lashing with his stick at the overblown, already mouldering flowers of Fleet Street's end.